Albert Nelson Marquis

Marquis' Hand-Book of Chicago

Albert Nelson Marquis

Marquis' Hand-Book of Chicago

ISBN/EAN: 9783337399177

Printed in Europe, USA, Canada, Australia, Japan

Cover: Foto ©Andreas Hilbeck / pixelio.de

More available books at **www.hansebooks.com**

MARQUIS'

HAND-BOOK ⊕ OF ⊕ CHICAGO

A COMPLETE

HISTORY, REFERENCE BOOK AND GUIDE
TO THE CITY.

Illustrated.

CHICAGO:

A. N. MARQUIS & CO., PUBLISHERS.

1887.

PREFACE.

In presenting the third annual edition of Marquis' Hand-Book of Chicago to the public the publishers desire to express their gratification at the favor with which the former editions have been received, and the general recognition accorded the book as a standard work upon the subjects embraced in its pages.

The original edition of the work was issued in October, 1884, and in the present edition such additions and changes have been made in the text as have been rendered important by lapse of time, and a few new illustrations have also been introduced.

The work continues to occupy a field peculiarly its own, carrying out the original design which, as stated in the preface to former editions, is to give a comprehensive view of the leading features of the great metropolis of the Northwest, bringing out into bold relief the social, business, religious, charitable, educational and other lines of its progress, through tersely drawn sketches of the most striking details of each, so grouped as to convey a clear and strong impression of the growth and condition of that element of Chicago life.

The aim has been to produce a book which would answer the questions of every class of inquirers, at home and abroad, and it is believed that the task has been at least measurably accomplished, and with as great a degree of accuracy as was attainable by the employment of every available means to that end. It has been the endeavor to secure the utmost economy of space consistent with fullness and accuracy, with such an arrangement of the matter as will afford the greatest facility for reference. Hence, so far as possible, subjects of a kindred nature have been collected under appropriate headings, and an index appended which the reader will find useful.

The book will be subjected to frequent and thorough revisions, and suggestions for improvement and information of changes and corrections are solicited, and should be addressed to A. N. Marquis & Co., Lakeside Building, Chicago.

January, 1887.

CONTENTS BY CHAPTERS.

CHICAGO.

AN HISTORICAL SKETCH.

SOME two hundred and eleven years ago, Louis Joliet and Father Jacques Marquette, who had journeyed from Canada in canoes to the Mississippi River, *via* the Wisconsin and Fox Rivers, returned to Lake Michigan—then known as Lac Des Illinois—by way of the Illinois. Desplaines and Chicago Rivers.* The last named rivers were till then unknown to the two explorers, who followed them by the advice of some friendly Indians, as a means of shortening the return route.

In time they came into a narrow stream which was probably then but little more than a slough. Paddling along its sluggish current, the keels of their canoes soon glided down the south branch of the Chicago River, through the site of the present city of Chicago, and into the clear waters of the lake.

So far as is known, this trip of Joliet and Marquette—one a holy man, in search of savage souls to be saved and locations for the establishment of missions, and the other an explorer in search of wealth—revealed to white men their first glimpse of the site of the great city.

*Mr. Albert D. Hager, the well known librarian of the Chicago Historical Society, who is jus'ly regarded as high authority, contends, in an able paper read before the Society, that this was not the route followed, and shows clearly that it might have been—but, as we weigh the evidence, not conclusively—that it was, by way of the Des Plaines, the "sag," Stony Brook, and the Calumet.

Evidently what they saw made no striking or abiding impression on them. There was nothing around this embouchure of a little muddy stream which led from the prairie into the lake, to indicate its magnificent future. If the travelers saw anything of importance, or which suggested the site of a populous city, they made no mention of it in their diary. They were weary with their long journey, and poor Marquette was oppressed with a premonition that he was close to the end of the journey of life. And so the first white men who ever saw the site of Chicago passed it without comment. Fancy the holy exaltation of the dying Marquette, could he have glanced forward two centuries!

SITE OF CHICAGO.

One may picture with some degree of fidelity the scene these two men looked upon, if they cared to lift their weary eyes and glance about them during the few moments that preceded their entry into the lake. Away back on the horizon a dead level of green, with not an interruption to break the monotony. The water on which they paddled was sluggish, turbid, inert, covered with a slimy green, and contained within banks that scarcely rose above its dead level. Back of the lake for leagues the adjacent country was a level morass from which rose stalwart reeds and brawny grasses, and over which prevailed an inundation that seemed limitless as to extent and eternal as to duration. Along the shores of the lake, to the right and left, interminable stretches of sand, now smooth as a floor, now blown into dunes, with here and there patches of gnarled timber, squat, unhealthy, and adding a feature of desolation, to the scene, instead of relieving the monotonous aspect of the waste. If the two travel-worn voyagers glanced at all over the surroundings, they must have felt that nature had here made an especial effort to construct a region to be avoided.

This was in August, 1673, and, considering the character of the location, it has been none too long since to afford time in which to transform that area of desolation into the marvelous city which now fills its place.

For more than a century the sand dunes shifted, the dwarfed vegetation died and was renewed, the marshy areas of sedge were undisturbed. Cincinnati, Cleveland, Detroit, St. Louis and other places were founded, and began their growth. There occurred the French and English wars in which Wolfe and Montcalm died and filled adjacent graves. There were British and Indian massacres, Pontiac, and other notables, and finally it was decided to build a fort on Lake Michigan for the protection of the country from Canadian and Indian incursions. The site at first selected was on the east side of the lake at St. Joseph, but for some reason the present site of Chicago* was chosen. And then began to exist, or to become visible, the protoplasm which in time would, by the processes of evolution, become the city of Chicago.

The river gave the name to the city. The stream was called Checaugou by the native Indians, and is said to have taken this designation from a mephitic animal peculiar to the locality, and whose odor may have been a foretaste of what the completed city was to experience in after years from the rendering establishments of " Bridgeport." There were Indians all about in those far-off days, when the lake winds sighed or roared among the sodden rushes, and Chicago slept in the womb of the future. There were first the Miamis and Mascoutins, and later the Pottawatomies and others, who made forays for scalps and plunder on adjacent tribes, and were in turn raided by their enemies, when they yielded such of their scalps, ponies, and other aboriginal assets as they could not retain.

For a time the region about the mouth of the Chicago River was in the possession of France. French priests visited it, and there are various legends, traditions and the like, which go to establish the fact

---

*Chicago is situated about the fork and mouth of the Chicago River, on the west shore of Lake Michigan, and near the head of that fine inland sea, in latitude 41° 52' north, and longitude 87° 35' west. The city comprises an area of 23,040 acres, which is divided into north, south and west divisions (commonly known as North Side, South Side and West Side) by the river and its branches.

that there were a half dozen or more white men who were "the first" to visit the locality. Marquette is the one who stands most prominently in this connection and, as the original white pioneer, will probably go down to posterity on the stream of history. This much, however, seems to be settled: In 1795 the Indian residents ceded to the United States an area of six miles square, on which, in 1803, Fort Dearborn was erected.

Back of this date, there is but little which does not belong to the age of myth, like the period of Romulus with reference to the future city of Rome. Back of all great cities there lies a period which is dim and mysterious, of which much is conjectured, asserted and denied, but little or nothing is known. Even Chicago, the newest and most enterprising of modern cities, has its mythical past into which enter few save the disputatious, and whose character, even if fully known, would confer no great benefit on posterity. It was, then, in 1803 that Chicago entered on her historical period. For over a century prior to this date, the French had more or less occupied the locality ; and when the time came for their removal, they must have felt as did the Moors of Grenada when expelled by the Spaniards after some eight hundred years of almost undisturbed ownership.

From 1779 to 1796, a period of seventeen years, one Baptiste Point DeSaible, a San Domingo negro, resided here as a trader among the Pottawatomie Indians. His cabin was situated on the north side of the main branch of the river, and near where it turns to the south. In 1796 he sold his landed possessions to LeMai, a French trader, and returned to Peoria, whence he had come, and soon afterward died.

July 4, 1803, marked an event in the history of the place that signalized the beginning of a new epoch. In those days the selection of a site for a frontier fort was generally made with an eye to the advantages of its location in respect to certain facilities and surroundings that constitute prime elements in the growth and prosperity of a city. This was the case with Chicago. The government having found the situation most favorable for its purpose, Capt. John Whistler, who was in command of a company of regular troops stationed at Detroit, was ordered to proceed to this point and construct a fort. Capt. Whistler came in a sailing vessel, accompanied by his wife and son George, and his eldest son, Lieut. William Whistler, and young bride, leaving Lieut. Jas. S. Swerrington to bring the soldiers around by land. The vessel arrived at the mouth of Chicago River on the day mentioned, and thus, on the anniversary of American independence, in

1803, began the story of a municipal growth that was destined to surpass that of any other city of the old and new worlds. Capt. Whistler commenced operations by the construction of Fort Dearborn, on the point of land extending between the lake and the south bank of Chicago River, the enclosure including a portion of Michigan Avenue as it now is. The fort consisted of two block houses, from which there led an underground passage to the river, for the purpose, probably, of securing an outlet to water in case of siege. The grounds occupied were quite spacious, being sufficient for a parade ground, and also to furnish a garden for the cultivation of vegetables. The entire space was enclosed by a strong palisade. Just outside of the palisade, on the west of the fort, was a log house used as a warehouse for the storage of goods intended for distribution among the Indians. The fort was garrisoned at this period by a force of sixty-two officers and privates. There were three pieces of artillery and the necessary amount of small arms. The site of the fort was very charming, being one of the highest points on the lake, and commanding an excellent view in every direction. There is a vague legend that this fort was not the first which occupied the spot, and that as far back as 1718 there had been a fort in the same locality. But this misty legend cannot be allowed to rob Fort Dearborn of the honor of having been the pioneer enterprise of the kind in this vicinity.

The first permanent white settler was John Kinzie, who came to Chicago in the spring of 1804, and who was the progenitor of the numerous and respectable family of that name that was so much identified with the early history of the Garden City. He was a silversmith by trade, but acted as Indian sub-agent, and Indian trader. He was a Canadian by birth, and died here in 1828, at the age of sixty-five years. He is regarded as one of the founders of the city, although it was many years after his death before it began to exhibit any indications of its surpassing future.

Mr. Kinzie became the owner of the cabin formerly occupied by the San Domingoan, DeSaible. He enlarged and improved it from time to time until he made it a comfortable home and a hospitable shelter to all who found its doors. The old "Kinzie House," as it is now familiarly called, was last occupied by Mark Noble who, with his family, lived in it as late as 1832. At that time, however, it was fast going to decay, and it shortly afterward became a thing of the past. It was the first family residence in Chicago.

There is a lively discussion as to who had the honor to be the first

white child born in Chicago. A daughter of John Kinzie, just mentioned, named Ellen Marion, was born in December, 1805. Some
children had been born in the fort, but as the military were not permanent residents, and perhaps a little out of deference to the sex, the
honor is generally conceded to Ellen Marion Kinzie.

There was but little change in or about Fort Dearborn for several
years. The visitors were chiefly Indians; the inhabitants were few
although fairly prosperous. In the summer of 1812, the entire population consisted of John Kinzie and family; a French laborer named
Oulimette; a Mr. Burns with wife and children; and some four miles
up the South Branch was a farmer named White, tenant of a land-
owner, named Lee, and three French laborers in White's employ.
Within the fort there resided Capt. Heald, Lieut. Helm and Sergt.
Holt, and their families. In addition to these there were some sixty-
four soldiers, of whom twelve were militia. All of the officers of the
year 1803 had been changed, Heald taking the place of Whistler;
Lieut. Helm held the second place; George Rohan was ensign and Van
Voorhis, surgeon.

And now there came into view on the horizon a cloud, at first "no
bigger than a man's hand," but which speedily became a hurricane of
most deadly force. War was declared by the United States against
Great Britain, and the Winnebagoes and Pottawatomies became hostile
to the whites. As early as April, 1812, the first-named tribe made a
stealthy raid against the settlement, and managed to kill and scalp
White, and one of the French laborers employed by him. The other
two escaped, made their way to the fort and gave the alarm ; but from
this time till August nothing serious occurred, beyond some small raids
made by the Indians for the purpose of stealing cattle, or in the hope
of securing the scalp of some unsuspicious laggard about the settlement.

An order came from Gen. Hull, at Detroit, for the garrison of Fort
Dearborn to move out and go to Fort Wayne, unless in a condition to
stand a siege. Capt. Heald is represented as a man who lacked decis-
ion of character, and hence did not comprehend the situation. It is
now conceded that had he moved at once after getting the order, or
even had he staid and made a determined defense, he would have escaped the calamity which soon after overtook him. He concluded to
evacuate the fort, against the advice of his subordinate officers, of Mr.
Kinzie, and of some friendly Indians; but in place of carrying out his
resolution at once, he determined to try and placate the Indians by
calling them together and dividing among them the stores which re-

WOLF POINT IN 1830. SEE PAGE 15

mained on hand, and which he could not carry with him. The meeting with the Pottawatomies was held on the 12th of August, and it was agreed that the stores should be divided among them, and that they should furnish an escort for the garrison to Fort Wayne, for which they were to receive a liberal reward.

The agreement to give the Indians arms, ammunition and whisky was so clearly disadvantageous and dangerous to the whites, and Mr. Kinzie protested so strongly against its being carried into effect, that Capt. Heald took advantage of the darkness of the night to break open the barrels of whisky and let the contents run into the river, and at the same time to throw the surplus ammunition and muskets into a well. This operation was witnessed by some prowling savages, who reported it to the others and thus aroused a deadly animosity against the whites. On the 15th, the evacuation of the fort was begun. On the day previous Capt. William Wells, with some fifteen Miamis, reached the fort from Fort Wayne, but it was concluded that it was useless to attempt to defend the place, even with this addition, as the Indians were too numerous and the means of opposition too limited. Mr. Kinzie had been warned that the Pottawatomies meant mischief, and that he must not accompany the troops overland, but must put his family on a boat and proceed across the lake where he could join the troops on the other side—provided the troops were allowed to proceed on their march.

Mr. Kinzie acted on this advice, and placed his wife and four younger children in the boat, in which there were also the nurse of the children, a clerk of Mr. Kinzie, two servants, the boatmen, and two Indians who were acting as their protectors. Mr. Kinzie was urged to join the party in the boat, but declined to do so, as he foresaw the storm,. and thought he might be of service in warding off some of its effects. The boat started, but had scarcely gotten under way when a messenger from the friendly Indians arrived and told them to remain where they were. They had reached the mouth of the river, and from this point saw much of the conflict which almost immediately followed. Mr. Kinzie and his oldest son accompanied the troops in their march from the fort, the former knowing that he would not be attacked, as the savages were friendly to him, and he hoped to be of some service to the others. The troops filed slowly out of the fort, the band ominously playing the Dead March. Capt. Wells led the way with his Miamis, and knowing that death was almost certain, he had blacked his face in accordance with the custom of the Indians among whom he had been reared.

The little column proceeded south along the shore of the lake, keeping on the sand. On the prairie higher up moved the escort of Indians, numbering some five hundred warriors. All went well until the column had reached a point on the shore of the lake near what is now the foot of Eighteenth Street. Just then Capt. Wells, who had been riding a little in advance with his Miamis, came furiously back, and announced that the Indians were about to attack them. A moment later the Indians commenced firing on the column from the sand hills along the edge of the prairie, and at once the troops formed in line and charged up the bank. At the first discharge, the Miamis fled without firing a shot. Capt. Wells alone disdained to fly, and was speedily shot, scalped, and his heart taken out with the savage idea that his captors might acquire some of his courage by devouring it. Mrs. Helm, the wife of Lieut. Helm, was one of the party marching from the fort, and her account of the massacre has become historical. The troops fought gallantly, forced their way through the Indians, and reached a little elevation on the prairie, where, finding the fighting useless, they sent an interpreter and negotiated a surrender on condition that their lives should be spared, and that they should be allowed to ransom themselves as soon as practicable.

The loss of the Indians is stated at about fifteen. The loss of the whites was large, about fifty in all. Of all that left the fort, there remained at the surrender twenty-five non-commissioned officers and privates, and eleven women and children. All the wounded prisoners were killed and mutilated. Among those killed were Surgeon Van Voorhis, Ensign Rohan and Capt. Wells. The wounded were Capt. Heald and his wife, and Lieut. and Mrs. Helm. The latter, however, managed to retain her senses and preserve for posterity the only reliable and connected account of the fight. She was a most gallant woman, the step-daughter of Mr. Kinzie, to whom she was indebted for examples of courage and gallantry that did her essential service. She was attacked by a young Indian who attempted to tomahawk her, but she avoided the blow aimed at her head, and received it on her shoulder. She was just then seized by a friendly Indian in disguise, who bore her to the lake, and, in pretending to attempt to drown her, he saved her life. Mrs. Heald was badly wounded by bullets, and was on the point of being scalped, when she was rescued by a friendly Indian on guard at the boat of the Kinzie party, her captor foregoing the pleasure of scalping her on condition of the immediate payment of a mule, and ten bottles of whisky at a later date. The latter portion of

the reward seems to have proved irresistible; the savage released her
and she was taken into the boat. Rohan, the ensign, fought to the
last and died courageously. Surgeon Van Voorhis was wounded, and
pitifully appealed to Mrs. Helm, who was near him, to do something
to save him. He died very unwillingly.

Mr. Kinzie and his family were cared for by the friendly Indians
who saved their lives, but Mr. K. underwent a long and shifting imprisonment at the hands of the British, and was at last released uncon-
ditionally. After his death in Chicago, January, 1828, he was first
interred on the shore of the lake near his residence. Later he was
reinterred in the burying ground near where the North Side water-
works now stand, and again in the cemetery formerly located in the
southern portion of what is now Lincoln Park. A few years ago his
post-mortem wanderings were terminated by his remains being transferred to Graceland Cemetery.

The Indians burned Fort Dearborn, and Chicago had undergone its
first great trial.

The same year the first territorial legislature of Illinois met, and it
is said of them, in "Western Annals," that "they did their work like
men devoted to business matters. Not a lawyer nor an attorney is found
on the list." Six years later the territory was organized into a state.
In 1829 the state, by authority of Congress, inaugurated operations for
the building of the Illinois & Michigan Canal, and soon after this the
real evolution of Chicago commenced. In 1831 the county of
Cook was organized, Chicago being made the county seat, and on Aug.
10, 1833, the town of Chicago came into being. The vote by which
the people decided to incorporate themselves was thirteen—twelve
for, and one against. There were twenty-eight votes cast at the election for town officers five days later. The first public building constructed after the town was established was a log jail, and the next was
an estray pen. T. J. V. Owen, George W. Dole, Madore B. Beaubien, John
Miller and E. S. Kimberly were the first trustees. They proceeded to
lay out the town of Chicago in modest dimensions, as follows : Beginning at the intersection of Jackson and Jefferson Streets, thence north
to Cook Street, and through that street to its eastern extension in Wabansia, thence on a direct line toward Ohio Street to Kinzie's Addition,
thence eastwardly to the lake shore, thence south with the line of the
beach to the northern United States pier, thence northwardly along
said pier to its termination, thence to the channel of the Chicago River,
thence along said channel until it intersects the eastern boundary line

of the town of Chicago as laid out by the canal commissioners, thence
southwardly with said line till it meets Jackson Stre t, thence westwardly along the line of Jackson Street until it reaches the point of
beginning.

In 1832 the total collection of taxes amounted to $357.78, the
most of which came from licenses to keep tavern and sell goods. At
that period there were no mail routes or post roads in this section, and
of course no postoffice in Chicago. The only method of getting mail
was to send a half-breed Indian once in two weeks to Niles, in Michigan, and he was always instructed to get possession of all the newspapers available, and bring them back to Chicago. The trip was made
on foot, and usually occu-
pied a week. The promi-
nent families here at this
time were those of James
Kinzie (son of the famous
John Kinzie), who lived at
Wolf's Point at the junction
of the North and South
Branches of the river; Elijah
Wentworth, who kept a tavern; William See, Alexander
Robinson, Robert A. Kinzie,
Samuel See, who lived on
the north side of the North
Branch, nearly opposite
Wolf's Point, and who, in
company with his brother,
John Miller, kept a tavern;
and Mark Beaubien, also a

SITE OF OLD FORT DEARBORN,
RIVER STREET AND MICHIGAN AVENUE.

tavern keeper, who lived on the east side of the South Branch just
above its junction with the North Branch. There was also an Indian
trader named Bourasso, and a family named Boliveu, who lived just
south of the fort. There were two or three other families, but the
preparation of a directory of Chicago, as it then was, would be a
work of but few minutes.

There was something of an Indian scare when Black-Hawk broke
loose from the south in 1832, and at one time there were several hundred fugitives in the fort, who fled there for protection against expected raids. It was in this war that Abraham Lincoln gained his

renown as a soldier, and many other heroes appeared who afterward reaped a generous reward from their grateful country. In the same year George W. Dole inaugurated the slaughtering and packing industry, by killing and packing 200 head of cattle and 350 head of hogs. This was but an humble beginning of what has grown to be one of the greatest industries of modern Chicago.

Meanwhile Fort Dearborn had been rebuilt, and a garrison occupied it until June, 1833, at which time there were about a dozen families settled about the fort. The site of the old fort is now occupied by a massive five-story business block, within the angle formed by the junction of River Street and Michigan Avenue. This building, which is shown in an accompanying illustration, bears on its north front a marble tablet with the following inscription:

THIS BUILDING OCCUPIES THE SITE OF OLD FORT DEARBORN, WHICH
EXTENDED A LITTLE ACROSS MICHIGAN AVENUE AND SOME-
WHAT INTO THE RIVER AS IT NOW IS.

THE FORT WAS BUILT IN 1803-4, FORMING OUR OUTMOST DEFENSE.

BY ORDER OF GEN. HULL IT WAS EVACUATED AUG. 15, 1812, AFTER
ITS STORES AND PROVISIONS HAD BEEN DISTRIB-
UTED AMONG THE INDIANS.

Very soon after, the Indians attacked and massacred about fifty
of the troops and a number of citizens, including women and children,
and next day burned the fort. In 1816 it was rebuilt, but after the
Black Hawk war it went into gradual disuse, and in May, 1837, was
abandoned by the army, but was occupied by various government officers till 1857, when it was torn down, excepting a single building,
which stood upon the site till the great fire of Oct. 9, 1871.

At the suggestion of the Chicago Historical Society this tablet was
erected, November, 1880, by   W. M. HOYT.

Mark Beaubien, the original tavern-keeper of Chicago, but a short time since yielded up a life of far more than average length. He came to Chicago from Michigan in 1826, and bought from John Kinzie a small log house which stood about where the corner of Lake and Market Streets is now located, paying $100 for it. This cabin was transformed into the famous "Sauganash" tavern, and was the humble pioneer of the Grand Pacific, Palmer, Tremont, Sherman, and

other palatial hotels of Chicago. In later years, in response to an
inquiry as to his manner of keeping tavern in the olden time, Mr.
Beaubien said: "I had no ped, but when traveler came for lodging, I
give him planket to cover himself up on the floor, and tell him to look
out, for Ingin steal it. Den when he gits to sleep I take de planket
way careful and give it to noder man and tell him same, so I always
have peds for all dat want em." He was the father of twenty-six children, of whom sixteen were by his first, and the rest by his second
wife.

On the 26th of November, 1833, there occurred an event which
was of more importance to the destinies of the coming city than all
that had before taken place. This was the establishment of a news-

CHICAGO IN 1845.

paper, the first enterprise of the kind, and known as *The Chicago
Democrat.* John Calhoun was the daring person who took this initial
step, and he is to the journalists of Chicago what Columbus is to
modern explorers. The place of publication was at the corner of
LaSalle and South Water Streets. The first number urged strongly the
beginning and completion of the Illinois & Michigan Canal, in order
to facilitate intercourse between Lake Michigan and the Mississippi
River, and added that, "with even the present limited system of navigation, goods have been transported from New York to St. Louis in
the short space of twenty-three days." The issue of April 16, 1834,
commenced a marine record, announcing the arrival of one schooner
from St. Joseph, and the departure of two others.

Wolf and bear hunting within the corporate limits of the town was

2

one of the amusements that were sometimes resorted to both for pastime and for the protection of the pigs, sheep, fowls, etc. In October, 1835, a bear was treed in the woods near what is now the corner of Market and Jackson Streets, and many wolves were killed the succeeding winter in the same locality. During the summer season of 1834, Chicago was visited once a week by a steamboat from Lake Erie, and the same year the schooner Illinois entered Chicago River, being the first vessel that performed this feat. Before, owing to a bar at the mouth of the river, vessels had to unload outside and handle their cargoes with lighters, but a freshet came, and opened a channel for the admission of this vessel. Considering the "bridge nuisance" of

OLD SALOON BUILDING.

to-day, there are many who will regret that a vessel was ever found to make the initial passage.

Chicago now had several taverns, a newspaper, a packing establishment, a ferry or two, and a marine list. In religious progress it was not behind. The Jesuits had preached to the Indians in the seventeenth century; and in 1833 no less than four of the principal denominations were represented, viz: Catholic, Methodist, Presbyterian and Baptist.

The year 1836 was a notable one in the history of Chicago. On the 18th of May of that year the first ship built here was launched amidst the rejoicing of the entire population of the village. July 4th of that year was not only the national anniversary, but was the day on

which the first soil was turned in the work of excavating the Illinois
& Michigan Canal. Such a thing as a railway connection with Chicago was not dreamed of at that time, and the future of the city was
supposed to depend on the water connection between the lake and the
Mississippi River. This year was also the one in which Chicago put
off her rural garments, and modestly but hopefully arrayed herself in
the garb of a young city. The actual and legal incorporation of the
city was not effected until a year later—March 4, 1837,—but in 1836
the necessary steps were taken by the people, and at that date, *de
facto* if not *de jure*, the city of Chicago became a fixed fact. At the
first city election William B. Ogden, the Democratic candidate, was
elected mayor, his opponent, John H. Kinzie, being the Whig representative. The entire vote was 706, of which Mr. Ogden received 469,
and Mr. Kinzie 237.

The map of that year gives the boundaries of Chicago as follows :
On the south by Twenty-second Street, on the west by Wood Street, on
the north by North Avenue and on the east by the lake. This boundary included the grounds of the fort and some land along the lake
shore extending a half mile north of North Avenue, which were
reserved.

The first meetings of the municipal authorities were held in what
was called the Saloon Building, on the southeast corner of Lake and
Clark Streets. Five years later the meetings were held in a private
building on the corner of LaSalle and Randolph Streets. The first
city hall was constructed in Market Building, a structure erected by
the city, and which stood in the center of State Street, with its south
front on a line with Randolph, and extending north toward Lake. The
lower floor was a market, and the upper floor was arranged for the uses
of the municipality. In 1851 a joint court-house was built by the
county and city on Court-House Square, the site of the present city and
county buildings, and was used until it was destroyed by the great fire
of 1871.

Chicago grew rapidly after its incorporation as a city, and it was
believed by those who had land to sell that in the future it would reach
a population of not less than one hundred thousand souls. The year
of its incorporation, however, it encountered its first serious obstacle
in the financial panic of that and the following year. The demand for
real estate fell off very heavily, as may be gathered from the sales of
the canal company, which in 1835 were over three hundred and seventy thousand acres ; the next year over two hundred and two thou-

sand, and in 1837 less than sixteen thousand acres. There was an improvement the succeeding year, when the sales mounted up to one hundred and sixty thousand. Many people left the city during the two years referred to, under the conviction that Chicago's day of prosperity was passed, and that it was doomed to extinction as a city.

Statistics show that from 1832 to 1853 real estate increased in value at a rate which is almost beyond belief. Lots 3 and 4 in block 31, for instance, were worth $102 in 1832, and sold for $108,000 in 1853. Several lots held by Beaubien and the Kinzies at $346 in 1832, were sold in 1853 at $540,000. The rise in general, during this period, was scarcely less on an average than that exhibited in the instances cited.

The next serious set-back Chicago had after the panic of 1837-38 was the flood of 1849, the consequences of which were serious. The inundation occurred in March and was produced by the overflow of the Desplaines River. The South Branch of the Chicago River was filled with ice, which was soon undermined by the flood from the Desplaines. There were many vessels in the river, and these were crushed in the advancing gorge of ice. The pushing mass included everything in its march, and this added to its deadly character. Some forty vessels were utterly destroyed, and the only bridge in the city was annihilated. The damage to the shipping, wharves and city generally was estimated at considerably over a hundred thousand dollars.

In 1850 Chicago had forty-two miles of railway on the Galena line, which was commenced in 1847. Two years later it was connected with the east by the Michigan Southern Railway, and from that time to the present its progress as a railway center has been without a parallel in modern civilization.

An event of considerable importance took place in 1855, when Dr. Levi D. Boone was mayor, having been elected on the Know Nothing ticket. One of his first official acts was to recommend to the common council that the license for saloons be raised from $50 per annum to $300, and that no license be issued for more than three months. This excited great opposition among the liquor sellers and their friends, who banded together to resist the movement. The attempt to collect the new license, and to enforce the Sunday law which had long been a dead letter, led to great excitement, and during the pendency of a trial of one of the offenders, a great crowd gathered on the corner of Randolph and Clark Streets, filling both thoroughfares and totally obstructing travel. In the afternoon the police and the mob came into

OLD BLOCK HOUSE AND LIGHT HOUSE IN 1857—THE LAST OF OLD FORT DEARBORN. SEE PAGE 16.

violent contact. There was a good deal of shooting on both sides, and
although the official reports show but one man killed on the side of
the rioters, it is believed that several were killed and carried off by
their friends, or else died later from wounds received in the melee.
A couple of pieces of artillery were brought out and placed in position
for service, but the police handled the mob, and dispersed it without
great difficulty.

The greatest event in the history of Chicago was the Great Fire, as
it is termed, which broke out on the evening of Oct. 8, 1871. Chicago
was at that time a city of wood. For a long time prior to the evening
referred to there had been blowing a hot wind from the southwest,
which had dried everything to the inflammability of tinder, and it was
upon a mass of sun and wind dried wooden structures that the fire

FIRST HOUSE ERECTED IN THE BURNT DISTRICT.

began its work. It is supposed to have originated
from the accidental upset-
ting of a kerosene lamp in
a cow-barn on DeKoven
Street, near the corner of
Jefferson, on the west side
of the river. This region
was composed largely of
shanties, and the fire spread
very rapidly, soon crossing
the river to the South Side,
and fastening on that portion
of the city which contained nearly all the leading business houses, and
which was built up very largely with stone and brick. But it seemed
to enkindle as if it were tinder. Some buildings were blown up with
gunpowder, which, in connection with the strong southwest gale, prevented the extension of the flames to the south. The fire swept on
Monday steadily to the north, including everything from the lake to the
South Branch, and then crossed to the North Side, and, taking in
everything from the lake to the North Branch, it burned northward
for a distance of three miles, where it died out at the city limits, when
there was nothing more to burn. In the midst of this broad area of
devastation, on the north side of Washington Square, between Clark
Street and Dearborn Avenue, the well-known Ogden House stands
amid trees of the ancient forest and surrounded by extensive grounds,
the solitary relic of that section of the city before the fiery flood.

The total area of the land burned over was twenty-one hundred acres. Nearly twenty thousand buildings were consumed; one hundred thousand people were rendered homeless; two hundred lives were lost, and the grand total of values destroyed is estimated at two hundred millions of dollars. Of this vast sum nearly one-half was covered by insurance, but under the tremendous losses many of the insurance companies were forced to the wall, and went into liquidation, and the victims of the conflagration recovered only about forty-four millions, or less than one-half of their insurance, and only about one-fifth of their aggregate loss. Among the buildings which were burned were the court-house, custom-house and postoffice, chamber of commerce, three railway depots, nine daily newspaper offices, thirty-two hotels, ten theaters and halls, eight public schools and some branch school buildings, forty-one churches, five elevators, and all the national banks.

If the Great Fire was an event without parallel in its dimensions and the magnitude of its dire results, the charity which followed it was equally unrivaled in its extent. Scarcely were the flames under way, and the extent of the destruction foreseen, when efforts for relief seemed to begin spontaneously wherever the telegraph carried the news. All the civilized world appeared to instantly appreciate the calamity. Food, clothing, supplies of every kind, money, messages of affection, sympathy, etc., began pouring in at once in a stream that appeared endless and bottomless. In all, the amount contributed reached over seven millions of dollars! Nothing so God-like in its grandeur as a practical illustration of human sympathy with misfortune was ever before or since known in the history of mankind.

It was believed by many that the fire had forever blotted out Chicago from the list of great American cities, but the spirit of her people was undaunted by calamity, and, encouraged by the generous sympathy and help from all quarters, they set to work at once to repair their almost ruined fortunes, merchants and manufacturers resuming business in private dwellings, or in temporary shanties put up on the sites of their burned houses, as soon as the debris could be cleared away. Rebuilding was at once commenced, and, within a year after the fire, more than $40,000,000 were expended in improvements. The city came up from its ruins far more palatial, splendid, strong and imperishable than before. In one sense the fire was a benefit. Its consequence was a class of structures far better, in every essential respect, than before the conflagration. Fire-proof buildings became the rule, the limits of wood were carefully restricted, and the value of the reconstructed portion immeasurably exceeded that of the city which had been destroyed. The commerce of the city increased by millions of dollars immediately after the fire, and, in fact, a magnificent new city grew up on the ruins of the old, and was, in all respects, incomparably the superior of the one that had been devoured by the flames.

In 1857 the grades of the city were at least eight feet below their present level. At that time the city was for many months of the year simply a huge mud hole. It was suggested by some engineering genius that the grades be raised. This met with most violent opposition, but the intent was persevered in, and finally carried into practice. It was contended that it would be impossible to procure the materials for filling, but the end justified the effort, and the streets now up to grade are dry and easily drained ; a system of practical sewerage has taken the place of the drainage ditches and gutters of early Chicago, and in that respect the city stands next to London and Paris. By the process of elevating the grades many buildings were left with their first stories almost hidden by the raised sidewalks and curbing. In some cases the stories thus affected were transformed into basements, and additional stories added above. In other instances the buildings were torn down, but where they were sufficiently valuable to justify the labor and expense, they were raised to the height required, and new foundations built. Entire brick blocks have been thus raised, and even moved laterally, without suffering the least injury.

Since the fire building operations have been officially supervised, and a high degree of excellence and safety has been reached. The area within which the erection of wooden buildings is forbidden reaches well away in every direction from the business centers, and thus renders impossible any such devastating fire as that of 1871. Not only is the use of wood for walls no longer tolerated, but there has grown up a rivalry among citizens for the construction of fire-proof buildings. Stone and brick are universally employed in walls, but wood, in a great many instances, scarcely enters at all into the composition of the best structures.

The panic of 1873 affected Chicago very seriously. although the ultimate result was that but little injury was done to legitimate interests. The failures were mainly among real estate speculators. At the beginning of the panic real estate, especially of the unimproved kind, was so high as to be substantially "out of sight." Prices of improved real estate are to-day well up, but in many instances they have not yet reached the altitude which they attained in 1873, nearly a dozen years ago. Some of the results of the panic were beneficial. Improvement was substituted for wild speculation, and residences and business blocks were built on lands that before were unoccupied and held for a rise in prices.

July 14, 1874, another fire broke out in the heart of the city, and swept over eighteen blocks, consuming 600 houses, and leaving blackness and ruin in its path. Fortunately the area ravaged by the destructive element was occupied mainly by wooden structures, and the loss was light compared with that of the previous conflagration, aggregating' only about $4,000,000. The splendid palaces of trade that had been reared on the ruins of 1871 were nearly all spared in this second visitation.

Despite the flat surface on which it stands, Chicago is one of the healthiest of the large cities of the country. Its highest death rate of late years was 20.29 per 1,000 of the population in 1875, and its lowest 15.70 in 1878. Compared with the mortality of many other cities, this is remarkable. In New York the rate per thousand per annum averages very closely on 30; in Boston from 21 to 25; in Philadelphia from 20 to 26; and in many of the great European cities from 25 to 45 per thousand. The winds from the southwest and those from the lake sweep alternately over the city, and constantly purify the atmosphere. The purity of the water, which is brought from a point two miles out in the lake, is also a potent factor in the reduction of the rate of mortality, and the sewerage system, which is much better than that in average use, is not without its effect in the same direction. The cholera made a visit to Chicago in 1866, but unlike its predecessor in 1852, it found its ravages checked by preventive sanitation. At present the sanitary condition of the city is such that epidemics of any kind are not regarded as among the probabilities.

The great labor riots of 1877, which originated in Pittsburg, extended to all important cities in the country, the agitation here lasting three or four days. The militia were called out, but their services were not required, except as guards of certain private property and public buildings that were threatened, the local police being equal to all the demands of the occasion. The number of killed and wounded was less than a score. Considering its extent and the heterogeneous character of its population, Chicago is one of the most orderly of modern cities.

On account of its lake breezes, enormous railway facilities and numerous and unequaled hotels, Chicago has long been a favorite place for summer conventions. For this purpose it possesses a special advantage in having, in the main hall of the exposition building, the largest place of assembly in the country, if not in the world. The convention which nominated Lincoln in 1860 met in Chicago, as did the national Democratic Convention of 1864, which nominated McClellan. Garfield was nominated here in 1880. Blaine was nominated in the Republican Convention held in Exposition Hall in June, 1884, and two weeks later Cleveland was nominated by the national Democratic Convention held in the same place. Many of the denominational conventions have made the city their place of meeting; and in the case of no national assemblage, political, religious, social or otherwise, has there ever been found any difficulty in caring for all who came, irrespective of numbers, and without inconvenience to other transient visitors, either as to hall or private entertainment.

The marvelous growth of Chicago in population, and the equally rapid expansion of the business interests of the city, have attracted universal attention and been the theme of admiring comment on the lips of all the world. Rising from seventy inhabitants in 1830 to 3,820 in 1836, and over 4,000 in 1837, when the town was organized as a city, the first three years of its existence in that more dignified capacity do not seem to have added much to its numbers, the census of 1840 showing only 4,853 inhabitants. From this time on the growth was rapid, the population increasing seven-fold in the next ten years, and numbering 29,963 in 1850. In 1860 it was 112,172 ; 298,977 in 1870 ; 503,185 in 1880, and in 1884 it was estimated on a fair basis of calculation at 650,000, of which 50,000 represents the increase during the previous years.

The material wealth of the city has kept pace with the population. Starting with a taxable valuation in 1837 of $236,842, which fell off in consequence of a panic to something over $94,000 in 1839-40, and made an astounding jump from $151,342 in 1842 to $1,441,314 in 1843, again doubling itself the succeeding year, the increase has since been rapid and steady. The total valuation was $7,220,249 in 1850 ; $37,053,512 in 1860, and $275,986,550 in 1870. In October, 1871, the great fire consumed $200,000,000 of property, yet notwithstanding this enormous loss the taxable valuation in May, 1872, only a few months after the fire, was $284,197,430, and it rose in the next two years to $303,705,140. Then the legislature passed a law transferring the duty of assessing and levying taxes to the county

authorities, their valuations being subject to revision by the State
Board of Equalization. The result was a contest between the counties
in the reduction of their tax lists, and the total valuation, in Chicago,
in 1875, was cut down to only $173,764,246, or something over one-
half that of the preceding year. In 1880 the total taxable valuation
was only $117,133,643, or less than one-half that of the year after the
losses of 1871, although the actual values had been multiplied by improvements. In 1883 the figures were $133,230,504. The revenues
of the city were further restricted in 1879 by a law prohibiting the
levy for municipal purposes from being raised above two per cent, on
the valuation. The tax-rate for all purposes is $3.41 on the $100, but
as that figure is considerably less than two per cent on the actual value
of property, one result of the present system is to give Chicago, which
really enjoys a very light taxation compared with other cities, a most
undesirable advertisement as a heavily tax-burdened city.

The bonded indebtedness is $12,751,500, having undergone a
gradual reduction from $14,103,000 in 1871, when it reached the
highest point ever attained.

The number of buildings erected in 1883 was 4,086, and their estimated cost was $22,162,610. The building operations the current
year promise to be of increased magnitude and interest.

All the great industrial, commercial and financial lines of enterprise
exhibit a growth proportionate to the remarkable increase of the population, until, as has been well said, the people themselves look with
wonder on the magnitude of the various interests that have grown up
under their efforts. Among the most extensive lines of business are
the handling and manufacture of food products, in all branches of which
there is an immense traffic. The receipts of cattle for the year 1882-
83 were 1,878,944, and the shipments 966,758. The receipts of
hogs for the same year were 5,697,163, and the shipments 1,363,759.
The number of cattle packed was 697,033, and the number of hogs
4,222,780. The total receipts of flour and grain, the former being
represented by its equivalent in wheat, amounted to 164,924,732
bushels. The receipts of lumber were 3,587,634,000 feet, and of
shingles 2,288,949,000. From the above figures it will be seen that
Chicago is the greatest market in the world for lumber and shingles,
grain, and hogs and cattle, besides being the greatest packing center
for the latter products.

In manufactures the demands of the trade with tributary regions
have caused a constant addition to the list of products and a steady

increase of facilities, until Chicago has become one of the leading manufacturing cities of the country. The United States census of 1880 makes the following exhibit of the industrial interests of the city: Number of establishments, 3,519; capital invested, $68,836,-885; hands employed, 62,431 men, 12,185 women, 4,798 children; annual wages, $34,653,462; value of materials used, $179,209,610; value of products, $349,022,948. The capital invested in slaughtering and meat packing is stated at nearly eight and one-half millions of dollars; in clothing, nearly six and one-half millions; in foundry and machine shop products, nearly four and one-half millions; in iron and steel production, nearly four millions; in brewing, over three and one-fourth millions; in agricultural implements, over three millions; in printing and publishing, nearly three millions; in furniture, nearly two and one-half millions; tanning, nearly two millions; carriages and wagons, over one and one-fourth millions; soap and candles, over one and one-fourth millions; sash, doors and blinds, nearly one and one-fourth millions; distilling, over one million. These statistics are, of course, only approximate, and for obvious reasons rather understate the facts; but since the date to which they relate, the interests they represent have grown rapidly, facilities being largely increased in all branches, and operations being correspondingly expanded so that it would be quite within the mark to add at least 50 per cent to the figures as given.

The Thoroughfares.

THE STREETS, AVENUES, BRIDGES, TUNNELS, SEWERS AND STREET RAILROADS.

THE facilities provided by public and private enterprise for the convenience of intermural transit compare favorably with those of other great cities.

The **Streets and Avenues** of Chicago originated in a road running from the town in a southwesterly direction, and branching after a short distance into two roads, one known in those days as the "Trail to the East," and the other as "Hubbard's Trail to Danville," or, farther out on the prairie, the "Road to Widow Brown's."

The plank-road was subsequently a feature in the history of the city. The first built was in 1848, and was known as the Southwestern; then came the Northwestern; next the Western; after which were the Southern, the Blue Island, and the Lake Shore. All of these were not only regarded as enterprises of great magnitude at the time, but were of material benefit in assisting the development of the city. It was believed by many at the time of their construction, and so urged in at least one of the public prints, that plank roads were of far more value to the city than railways. Indeed, there were those who urged that railways be kept out of the city, and the conveyance of passengers and the transportation of produce and goods be limited to plank roads. One writer says that on the plank roads, passengers are conveyed at the rate of ten miles an hour, which is as fast as they are taken on the Michigan Central Railway, and with ten times the safety. It was urged by this class of reasoners that the railways would take away all the profits of transportation, while, if the work were done by teams, the money would come to Chicago.

Originally the streets were simply mud roads, and during portions of the year were next to impassable, the worst places being planked when absolutely necessary. There was not much attempt at the construction of improved roadways until about 1864, at which time the

The raising of the grade of the streets has been noted in the opening chapter, on page 24.

"Nicholson" was laid down on Lake Street. From that time wooden pavement had a run, and in fact is yet in use on many of the principal streets. Within the past two or three years, in the business portion of the city, granite has been largely used. Macadam is used on the boulevards, and on some of the streets, notably Ashland Avenue and Jackson Street; the material, outside of the business portions, being largely wood. The wood now in use is mainly cedar blocks, which, with the improved method of laying them, are giving very satisfactory results. Asphalt has been used to some extent, but has not given entire satisfaction, and seems likely to be wholly abandoned. When completed, the paving system of Chicago, as now in use, will render it one of the best paved cities in the world. The entire length of the streets of the city is 650 miles. The length of the paved streets is about 200 miles.

The names of the principal streets generally indicate their origin. Many of them are named for the Presidents and others who were prominent in the nation or state ; the names of people more or less conspicuously connected with the history of the city, of the surrounding states, and other equally obvious sources, contributed to the nomenclature. The names of the Presidents and leading statesmen of the country will be readily recognized. Clark Street was christened in honor of Gen. George Rogers Clark, of Kentucky, who acquired military fame in the early contests with the French and Indians. Fifth Avenue was originally named in honor of Capt. Wells, who was one of the victims of the Indian massacre in 1812, and that portion of the street which lies in the North Division still retains the name. Ann Street was named after a daughter of the venerable Philo Carpenter ; Augusta after another daughter ; and so on of many other names of women. In this respect Chicago has shown no lack of gallantry.

The city is laid out in rectangular lines, with the exception of several streets which were constructed on the routes of the old plank roads, and which consequently radiate to the northwest and southwest. The principal business streets of the city lie on the South Side, where are congregated within a space of about ten blocks square nearly all the wholesale business of the city, and a large proportion of the retail trade. This area contains the palatial business houses, hotels and public buildings whose magnitude and architectural beauty have added so largely to the fame of Chicago. South Water Street, which lies next to and parallel with the main river, is largely devoted to the produce commission business. It is always almost impassable from the

MICHIGAN AVENUE, CORNER ADAMS STREET---PULLMAN BUILDING.

number of trucks, vans and carts which throng it and the boxes of
produce which encumber its sidewalks. Here are brought and distributed daily the various products of the market garden, orchard,
field and stream.

State Street is the great shopping street of the city, and on any fair
afternoon it can be seen thronged with pedestrians and carriages, and
presenting a scene of gayety, wealth and beauty such as is paralleled
only on Regent Street, London, or some of the more notable boulevards in Paris. It was originally much narrower and was widened to
its present handsome and attractive proportions by moving the houses
back along a stretch of three miles. Michigan Avenue, Wabash Avenue
and State Street, near the river, are all given up to wholesale houses.
Michigan Avenue, a few blocks from the river, loses its identity in
Michigan Avenue Boulevard (see chapter on "Parks and Boulevards"), the entire extension of which is a favorite residence street,
as are also Prairie, Calumet, Indiana and other avenues, containing
residences which are palaces in their cost and architectural design
and finish. State Street is traversed by the cable line of cars as far
south as Thirty-ninth Street. Twenty-second Street, running east and
west, and more than two miles from the City Hall, is for a dozen blocks
nearest the lake a busy, business thoroughfare. It has a bank and
many pretentious retail stores. Archer Avenue, branching from State
Street, between Nineteenth and Twentieth Streets, takes a southwesterly direction, crosses a branch of the Chicago River, and extends beyond the city limits. It has horse cars, and resembles in the character
of its buildings, shops, people, etc., Blue Island and Milwaukee Avenues, on the West Side. Wabash Avenue is traversed by a cable line
of cars from Madison Street south to Twenty-second Street. At
Twenty-second Street the cable car line runs east to Cottage Grove
Avenue, which it follows in its southeasterly direction parallel with,
and about two squares west of the lake shore, to the junction of Drexel
and Oakwood Boulevards, four and a half miles from the City Hall.
Cottage Grove Avenue is devoted principally to business purposes.

Madison Street is the great east and west thoroughfare of Chicago.
The eastern portion, or East Madison Street, in the South Division, is
splendidly paved, and is flanked on either side with wholesale and
retail establishments.

West Madison Street is the principal retail street of the West Side.
The street extends westward from the lake, passing in its course Garfield Park and the Chicago Driving Park, and is finally lost in an unim-

proved roadway in the open prairie, at a distance of over five miles. It is traversed by horse cars its total improved length. Randolph and Lake are the other leading parallel business streets of the West Division. Both have street car lines. Ogden Avenue, beginning in Union Park, takes a southwesterly direction, curving westwardly in its course, passes Douglas Park, and ends at Twenty-second Street, near the city limits. It long retained the appearance of a country road, being till recently unimproved and sparsely settled. A cedar pavement has just been put down, and stores and shops are rapidly appearing all along its line, and it is fast assuming a metropolitan air. It has horse cars, and in time will be a busy business thoroughfare.

The intervening streets between the river and Halsted Street are largely occupied by manufactories. In this section are found nearly all the great machinery, steam-engine, boiler and kindred iron-working concerns. Halsted Street is reached some five squares west of the Madison Street crossing of the river, and is the leading north and south thoroughfare of the West Side. It extends, in an almost straight line, entirely across the city. Its southern half is traversed by street cars direct to and from the Union Stock Yards, and is given up almost wholly to retail trade, by Irish, German and other foreign elements. The buildings after a few squares are principally wooden structures that escaped the great fire. They present a quaint and dingy appearance. Blue Island Avenue branches from Halsted Street, at the latter's junction with West Harrison Street, in a southwesterly direction to the great lumber district. The buildings with which it is densely lined are generally the poorest class of wooden structures in the city. The dingy-looking shops are kept by Irish and Germans of the lower classes, with here and there a Swede or Norwegian.

Milwaukee Avenue is distinctly the German business thoroughfare. It is lined with retail shops of every description, markets, saloons, etc. Many of the buildings are wooden ante-fire structures, and are as decidedly foreign in appearance as are their occupants. Beginning at the river and Lake Street, Milwaukee Avenue extends in a northwesterly direction away beyond the city limits, where it is merged in a country road in the open prairie.

Washington Boulevard is the leading residence street of the West Side. It belongs to the great boulevard system of the city, and has been referred to in the chapter on "Parks and Boulevards." West Monroe, Adams and Jackson, parallel with and south of Madison Street, are also popular residence streets, save a few squares occupied

3

by business and manufacturing establishments near the river. They are flanked by fine dwellings, churches, and lines of shade trees, interspersed here and there with little gems of parks of the brightest description. Ashland Avenue, running north and south, is splendidly paved and contains some of the handsomest houses on the West Side.

On the North Side, Clark Street is the leading business street, being occupied mainly by the smaller retail stores. It extends northward beyond Lincoln Park, and is a great thoroughfare. The streets lying near and parallel with the river are largely used by manufacturing establishments, and commission houses engaged in handling hides, leather, wool, etc. The preferred residence streets are LaSalle and Dearborn Avenues, Rush, State and Pine Streets, some of the residences being very elegant and artistic in architectural and other ornamentation. Chicago Avenue, from North Clark Street west to the river; Division Street, from North Clark to Clybourne Avenue; Clybourne Avenue, which here has its beginning and extends in a northwesterly direction to the city limits; and Larrabee Street, running north and south, are all business thoroughfares. They traverse a section of the city inhabited almost wholly by a foreign population--Scandinavian, German, etc.

The residences on the streets referred to as residence streets are generally built of superior materials. Red pressed brick is much used, but stone is the favorite. Of the latter there are many kinds, all varying in color, so that there is nowhere any sameness in the character of the coloring. There is equal diversity in the forms of the houses, there being but very little block building, each house, as a rule, being wholly independent in material, size, form and decoration. Joliet limestone, which is milky white at first, and after exposure becomes a rich, soft cream-color, is in large demand. The deep, rich brown of a sandstone from Lake Superior is also much used; there is also the close-grained dark gray of the Buena Vista quarries, and a dozen other kinds of material, including the cheerful cream-colored pressed brick of Milwaukee, all of which afford infinite variety of pleasing effects. The churches are generally constructed of rough-dressed limestone of a dark-grey, which is a color eminently in harmony with their purpose. The winds blowing alternately from the lake and from the land are sufficient to keep the city free from smoke, with the result that these richly-colored building materials are rarely obscured by stains, and the streets present always the striking effects flowing from the warm, bright, sympathetic colors.

The **Bridges** of Chicago are interesting, and many of them are important, features of its system of highways. Under the latter head must be classed the bridges over the Chicago River and its branches. These bridges, thirty-six in number, are built and owned by the city, being regarded equally with the streets as a public work, furnishing . necessary convenience of transit between the divisions. It has been jocularly said that the first bridge was a ferry, and it must be acknowledged that a number of the early devices to facilitate passage over the stream were a sort of cross between a ferry boat and a bridge. The first structure of this kind was a log float stretched across the river after the manner of a pontoon bridge, from which the idea was probably derived. Other bridges of the kind followed, and in some of them an improvement was introduced, the bridge being hinged on a pivot at one end, and a rope attached to the opposite end was used by means of a capstan and levers, to pull the float around, out of the way of passing vessels. A further improvement on these clumsy efforts at a drawbridge was made in the bridge erected over the river at the Dearborn Street crossing in 1834. This was the first drawbridge built in Chicago. The center span was made in two sections, hinged at the piers and meeting like an arch over the middle passage. The bridge was drawn by breaking the arch upward with a combination of ropes and pulleys, which lifted the meeting ends of the sections and made a space between them through which vessels passed. This structure so utterly failed to meet popular expectations that it was unanimously voted a nuisance, and when its removal was ordered, the citizens gathered and carried the order into effect by chopping the bridge down with axes. It was difficult to plan a structure that would meet the demand for convenient transit on the one hand, and for unobstructed navigation of the river on the other and, indeed, the satisfactory solution of that problem has not yet been practically accomplished. A nearer approach to it than was reached in any previous effort, was made in the construction of the first iron bridge in Chicago, at Rush Street, in 1856; but a number of cattle that happened to be on it when it was turned to allow a vessel to pass, crowded to one end or side and overturned it. The jealousies between the divisions, which had greatly interfered with the progress of these important public improvements, and the slow process of private subscription for their erection, were rapidly giving way to the growing needs of the situation, and in 1857 the city took hold of the matter and erected a bridge over the South Branch at Madison Street. This was the first bridge built entirely at the expense of the munici-

pality, and it was the inauguration of a municipal policy that has re-
sulted in the construction of a valuable iron bridge, swinging on a
central pier, at every alternate street reaching the river or either of its
branches, in the business portion of the city. The latest and best of
these structures is the new double roadway bridge at Rush Street—the
only one of the kind in the city, and the largest swing bridge in the
world. It is operated by steam and lighted by electricity, and was
built at a cost of $130,000. At its formal opening, August 7, 1884, it
bore a test weight of about 375 tons. For a time the present bridge
system was comparatively satisfactory, but the city has outgrown it, and
there is now a strong and growing demand for some plan by which
transit can be effected without being subject to the frequent annoying
delays caused by the necessity of opening the bridges for vessels, and
the accidents that result from that operation.

The Tunnels under Chicago River, two in number, one at LaSalle
Street, connecting the
South Side with the
North Side, and the
other at Washington
Street, connecting the
West Side with the
South Side, were con-
structed with the view
of supplying more
convenient passage
than the bridges af-
forded. The Washing-
ton Street Tunnel was
the first one construct-
ed, and was finished
and formally opened
to the public Jan. 1,
1869, at a cost of
$512,707.57. The La
Salle Street Tunnel
was completed and
opened July 1, 1871,

LASALLE STREET TUNNEL.

at a total cost of $566,276.48. It has some improvements in arrange-
ment and construction suggested by experience with the Washington
Street passage. The total length of the latter is 1,608 feet, and of

the LaSalle Street Tunnel 1,854 feet. Each has a double driveway and a separate foot-way on one side, which is reached by stairs. The tunnels are wide, lofty, well lighted and ventilated, and each is fairly drained by means of a sub-tunnel five feet in diameter, which is connected with a steam pump at one end.

The **Sewerage System** of Chicago is extensive, well arranged and efficient, despite the engineering difficulties in securing satisfactory drainage of a level area so slightly elevated above the waters of the river and lake. Brick or pipe is used for sewers, according to the character of drainage required. The total length of sewers of both kinds is about 400 miles, laid at a total cost of nearly six and a quarter millions of dollars, or an average of $15,493.58 per mile. They are kept clean and in repair at an average annual cost of $107.65 per mile. There are about 13,000 catch-basins and 15,000 man-hole chambers connected with the system. During the year 1883 about fourteen and a quarter miles of sewers were laid, and 835 catch-basins and 497 man-hole chambers constructed, at a total cost of $232,084.-33. The advantages of this important agent of cleanliness and sanitation are very evenly distributed among the three divisions of the city, according to their needs.

The **Street Railways** of Chicago all start from the business center of the city, and radiate to all sections promising traffic sufficient to maintain the lines in operation, thus giving the greatest public accommodation consistent with a reasonable care for the capital invested in such enterprises. The fare is universally five cents. The number of cars and the time-tables are arranged with due regard for public convenience. The first street railway in the city was laid along State Street, and was commenced in the fall of 1858. From that beginning the service grew rapidly to its present proportions. The railways are operated by three companies, representing three systems, which correspond with the divisions of the city. The oldest of these companies is.

The **Chicago City Railway Company** whose lines constitute the railway system of the South Side. This company has within the past two years largely substituted the cable plan of traction in the place of horses, and although there have been some difficulties and dangers attending its use, they have been largely overcome, and the success of the plan may be considered established. These lines alone now have an aggregate length of twenty miles, employ 100 "grip-cars," which do the work of 2,500 horses, and run an average of nine miles per hour, conveying 100,000 passengers daily. The total number of miles of track is seventy-seven; number of cars, 400; average distance traversed daily, 25,000 miles; average number of passengers carried daily, 120,000; number of horses, 1,200. The powerful engines which operate the cable system are located at the corner of State and Twenty-first Streets.

The North Chicago City Railway Company operates the North Side system of street railways. It was organized in 1859, and commenced running its cars on North Clark Street and Chicago Avenue in August, 1859. The capital stock of the company is $500,000; number of miles of track, thirty-four; total number of cars owned, 251; number of horses, 1,530; average distance traversed daily, 9,600 miles; average number of passengers carried daily, 60,000.

The Chicago West Division Railway Company was incorporated in 1863, succeeding to the franchises held by the Chicago City Railway Company on the West Side, and now operates the lines in that division. The capital stock of the company is $1,250,-000; number of miles of track, ninety-seven; total number of cars owned, 634; number of horses, 3,375; average distance traversed daily, 21,620 miles.

The Chicago Passenger Railway Company has opened up a new street car line which greatly adds to the facilities of transportation between the West and South Sides. The new line of cars runs on Harrison Street, from Western Avenue to Centre Avenue thence north to Adams Street and east to Franklin. Here the cars take alternately different directions around a "loop;" one car runs northward three or four blocks (to Washington Street) then east to Michigan Avenue, proceeding southwardly to Adams and back, to and past the Franklin Street turning, while the next car goes around the same loop in the reverse direction.

Transportation Facilities.

THE RAILROADS, LAKE MICHIGAN, CHICAGO RIVER, AND THE CANAL.

THE transportation facilities of Chicago are the most complete and extensive of any inland city in the world.

The Railroads are so intimately connected with the growth of the city that the history of one is practically the chronicle of the other. When Chicago first forged her way into the notice of the world, and began to foreshadow her present majesty, the railroad was a new thing, scarcely emerged from the shadows of uncertain experiment. Faith in it was far from general, and the cost of construction, equipment and operation was appalling to a new country rich only in the gifts of nature and in indomitable energy. Moreover, there was deep-seated prejudice in favor of water ways. In all the world there were not as many miles of railroad as Illinois now boasts. But destiny had marked out for the city a meteor course to empire, and she was early alive to the necessity for avenues for her commerce. Vast realms rich in all the treasures of nature lay at her feet, inviting conquest and inspiring enterprise. With the necessity came the men whose energy laid the basis for that magnificent system of iron roadways to which is chiefly due the marvelous development of the west and the northwest, and the greatness of the city. Before the close of the third decade of the present century, the practical advantages of railroads had begun to excite discussion in the city, and in January, 1831, a commission was appointed to investigate the relative value of a canal and railroad between the Chicago and Des Plaines Rivers. A multiplicity of schemes sprung up over the state, more or less connected with Chicago. The question of a road to be operated in conjunction with the Illinois & Michigan Canal was agitated, and a bill to charter such a road, under the title of the Illinois Central Railroad, was introduced into the state senate by Lieut-Gov. Jenkins, in 1832, but died in its incipiency. Many other enterprises were projected, but lay dormant. In 1835 a public letter from Sidney Breese, then circuit judge and afterward United States senator, revived the agitation of the Illinois Central

scheme. Meanwhile the city was pushing her way to the south and
the west, on paper at least. The first road chartered out of Chicago
was the Galena & Chicago Union, now a part of the Northwestern system. It was incorporated Jan. 16, 1837, with an authorized capital of $100,000, and permission to increase the same to $1,000,000,
and the charter contemplated propulsion "by steam or animal power."
Three years were allowed in which to begin work. The survey was
begun in 1837, but the financial panic of that year caused the collapse
of the enterprise, and it was not resumed until ten years later. By an
act of the state legislature, Feb. 27, 1837, the state undertook the
construction of 1,340 miles of railroad and the Illinois & Michigan
Canal. Work was begun at once in many quarters, but the magnitude
of the undertaking crushed it, and gave a blow which retarded progress in that direction for several years. In 1847 the work of constructing the Galena road was begun. On the 10th of October the
first engine ever run out of Chicago, named the "Pioneer," arrived via
brig "Buffalo," and was put to work on the part of the road then complete. This engine is still in existence. Nov. 20, 1848, the first wheat
ever brought to the city by rail was received. In 1852 this road was
completed to Elgin, forty-two miles, being laid with strap rails. The
Illinois Central was chartered Jan. 18, 1836, but the enterprise col-
lapsed, and was not revived till 1850, when the present charter was
granted. The incipient stages of railroad building were now past.
Capital, heretofore cautious to timidity, eagerly sought investment in
this direction, and henceforward roads were to seek the city, not the
city the roads. The first great east and west line to enter the city
was the Michigan Southern & Indiana Northern, now the Lake Shore
& Michigan Southern, Feb. 20, 1852. Just three months later the
Michigan Central was opened. This was followed by the Chicago &
Northwestern; the Chicago, Burlington & Quincy; the Chicago, Rock
Island & Pacific; the Pittsburg, Ft. Wayne & Chicago, and the various
other lines making up the grand system. On the first day of February,
1854, 1,785 miles of road terminated in the city. The total mileage
of the systems centering here now is about 32,285 miles.

The marvel of this system is the magnitude of the lines comprising
it, and the immense mileage controlled. Sweeping across the continent,
they give access to all the ports of both oceans, stretch southward to
the harbors of the Gulf, and, disregarding the boundaries of nations,
penetrate to the centers of Canada and the Mexican Republic. The
suburban systems of trains operated by these roads have created

a cordon of flourishing suburban towns around the city. During 1883 the average number of regular daily trains arriving were: Passenger, 123; suburban, 77; freight, 141; departing: Passenger, 122; suburban, 78, and freight, 124; total, 665. To these must be added a large number of irregular trains which, together with the natural increase, and the further increase due to the establishment of new lines, will doubtless swell the present aggregate arrivals and departures to fully 850. A peculiar feature of the railroad system of the city is the number of competing lines reaching to all important points, and producing a healthy rivalry, which inures to her benefit in cheap and abundant facilities for transportation. It is a notable fact, also, that while her sister cities have subscribed enormous sums toward their highways, Chicago, in her corporate capacity, has never given one dollar of aid, lent her credit, or taken a share of stock in any of the multitude of enterprises of this kind associated with her history.

The **Chicago & North-western Railway Company** operates 5,646 miles of roadway, tapping the chief centers and rich agricultural regions of Illinois, Wisconsin, northern Michigan, Minnesota, Iowa, Dakota and Nebraska, forming one of the principal commercial highways of the west. Its chief termini are Chicago at the east, Council Bluffs at the west, Pierre, Dakota, and St. Paul and Minneapolis at the northwest and Ishpenning at the north. It was organized June 7, 1859, by the creditors of the Chicago, St. Paul & Fond du Lac Railroad, who had succeeded to that property by foreclosure. The line then reached from Chicago north ninety-one miles to Janesville, and from Fond du Lac south twenty-eight and one-half miles. The Chicago, St. Paul & Fond du Lac Company grew out of a consolidation March 30, 1855, of the Illinois & Wisconsin and the Rock River Valley Companies, chartered respectively in Illinois and Wisconsin early in 1851. The policy of the new company was vigorous from the start. Before the close of 1859 through trains were running from Chicago to Fond du Lac, and an era of extension and absorption was inaugurated which has culminated in the present gigantic system. In 1882 the various companies whose lines had been absorbed were merged into the Chicago & Northwestern Company by formal proceedings. Since that time the Northwestern has acquired control of the Chicago, St. Paul, Minneapolis & Omaha Railway by the purchase of 147,000 shares of its stock, and of the Sioux City & Pacific Railway by purchase. The system is divided into five principal divisions or lines. Skirting the shores of Lake Michigan, the first of these penetrates, via Milwaukee, the Michigan peninsula. The second, passing more to the northwest, sweeps away through Madison, Beloit, and on to Minneapolis and St. Paul. Diverging from this line at Elroy, a third grand division takes a westerly course, crosses the Mississippi River at Winona, traverses Minnesota, and halts at Pierre, Dakota. The fourth line leaves Chicago, heads due west, crosses Illinois and Iowa, and terminates at Council Bluffs; and the fifth, leaving this line at Tama, 134 miles beyond the Mississippi, sweeps northward into Dakota. The equipment of the road includes 593 engines and 19,867 freight and passenger cars. The passenger station of the company at the southwest corner of Wells and Kinzie Streets is a massive structure of red pressed brick, with cut stone trimmings, in an attractive style of architecture. Adjoining on the south, and on North State, West Kinzie and at the corner of Canal and Sixteenth Streets, are located the freight depots. The general office is at 56 Kinzie Street. The principal ticket offices are at the depot and at 62 Clark Street.

The **Michigan Central Railroad** is the great central highway of Michigan, through which it ramifies in every direction, and brings tributary to Chicago the vast and fertile region bordered by the great lakes—Michigan, Erie and Huron. It is also a great thoroughfare to the east, especially favored by summer tourists because of its magnificent scenery and cool atmosphere. The construction of the main line, which runs from Detroit to Kensington, Ill., 270 miles, was begun in 1836 by the Detroit & St. Joseph Railroad Company, chartered June 29, 1832. April 22, 1837, that company disposed of its property and franchises to the state of Michigan, and under the auspices of the state the road was opened from Detroit to Ypsilanti, thirty miles, Feb. 3, 1838; to Ann Arbor, eight miles, Oct. 17, 1839, and in similar small sections annually to Kalamazoo, 144 miles, Feb. 2, 1846, when the legislature refused further appropriations for the work. In this year the present company was chartered and purchased the road, taking possession September 24th. The price paid was $2,000,000, entailing a loss of $500,000 to the state. In May, 1852, the line was finished to Kensington. From this point it enters Chicago, fourteen miles distant, via the Illinois Central track, over which it holds a lease, and uses as a passenger station the depot owned jointly with that road at the foot of Lake Street, the freight depots being located at the foot of South Water Street. The following are the lines operated by the company, including the Canada Southern and other leased roads : Chicago to Niagara Falls and Buffalo, 512.9 miles ; Lake to Joliet, 45 ;

Niles to Jackson, 103.4; Niles to South Bend, 11.1; Kalamazoo to South Haven, 39.5; Jackson to Grand Rapids, 93.9; Jackson to Bay City, 114.2; Bay City to Mackinac City, 182; Beaver Lake to Sage's Lake, 8; Pinconning to Bowen's Branch, 35; Detroit to Bay City, 109; Vassar to Saginaw City, 22.3; Lapeer to Five Lakes, 8.5; Vassar to Caro, 13; Detroit to Toledo, 59.3; Essex Center to Amherstburg, 15.7; Air Line Crossing to Courtright, 62.6; (Michigan, Midland and Canada Railway) St. Clair to Ridgeway, 15; Petrolea Branch, 5; Niagara Junction to Niagara, 27.7; Welland to Buffalo, 23; total, 1,506.1 miles. The line now crosses the Niagara River on its new cantilever bridge, just below the falls. The equipment of rolling stock comprises 396 locomotives and 11,362 cars of all kinds. The general offices are at Detroit. The Chicago offices are at 183 Dearborn Street.

The **Lake Shore & Michigan Southern Railway** was begun by the state of Michigan with the purpose of building a line through its southern tier of counties, connecting Monroe on Lake Erie with New Buffalo on Lake Michigan. Eighteen miles laid with strap rails were completed from Monroe to Petersburg in 1839, extended to Adrian in 1840, and to Hillsdale in 1843, when the state, being unable to secure funds for its further construction, sold the property in 1846 to the Michigan Southern Railway Company, organized in May of that year. In 1835 the Northern Indiana Railroad Company was chartered by the state of Indiana, as the Buffalo & Mississippi Railroad Company, and was organized two years later. The financial disasters of 1837 delayed the enterprise until 1849, when the property was acquired by the Michigan Southern Company, which decided to make Chicago the western terminus, and by which the work was pushed vigorously, the line from lake to lake, 243 miles in length, being opened May 22, 1852. In 1849 possession of the Erie & Kalamazoo, from Toledo to Adrian, thirty-three miles, was acquired by perpetual lease. This line had previously been laid with strap rails and operated with horse power. The Palmyra & Jacksonburg Railroad was opened to Tecumseh, thirteen miles, in 1838, sold to the state of Michigan for $22,000 in 1844, and was included in the sale by the state to the Michigan Southern Company, by which it was finished to Jackson. The Lake Shore & Michigan Southern Railway Company was organized under the laws of Ohio in 1869, and was formed by a consolidation of the system just described with the Cleveland & Toledo, a consolidation, Sept. 1, 1853, of the Toledo, Norwalk & Cleveland, and the junction railroads extending from Toledo to Cleveland; the Cleveland, Plainsville & Ashtabula, running from Cleveland to Erie, and the Buffalo & Erie Railroad. There were 927.23 miles of road included in this consolidation which has been increased, by purchase, lease and construction to 1,405.56 miles. The main line is from Chicago to Buffalo via Cleveland, 540.04 miles, and is double tracked throughout. The passenger depot is on Van Buren Street, corner Sherman. City offices at depot. General offices at Cleveland, Ohio. Controlling interest was recently acquired in the New York, Chicago & St. Louis Railway, and the two roads are now operated conjointly.

The **Chicago, Burlington & Quincy Railroad** stretches from Chicago to Denver, and envelops the states of Illinois, Iowa, Nebraska, Colorado, Missouri and Kansas in a net-work of roadways and branches aggregating upwards of 3,400 miles. It taps the coal fields at Streator, sweeps west and southwest to St. Louis, Kansas City, Leavenworth, St. Joseph, Atchison and Denver, Omaha, Lincoln, Des Moines, Burlington and Davenport. The road was chartered in 1852 as the Chicago & Aurora (from Chicago to Aurora, some forty miles), but was consolidated with the Central Military Tract Railroad and reorganized under present name July 9, 1856. The purchase of the Northern Cross Railroad, in 1860, extended the line to Quincy, and the Peoria & Oquawka two years later, gave it a through line to Burlington. In 1875 the Burlington & Missouri Road in Iowa, and in 1880 the same road in Nebraska, was absorbed. And thus the vast landed estate of the company in Iowa and Nebraska was obtained. From 1880 extensions and acquisitions have followed each other rapidly. The road is renowned for the excellence of its equipment. Principal offices, corner Adams and Franklin Streets. Passenger station, Union Depot, Canal Street. Perceval Lowell is General Passenger Agent.

The **Illinois Central Railroad** enters the city from the south over six tracks lying along the lake shore. It is a popular route of suburban travel, and has passenger stations at short intervals along the city and suburban portion of the line, which includes a branch from Park Side to South Chicago, 4.76 miles. The company was chartered in December, 1850; organization completed February 10th following. An act of Congress made a land grant to the road, conditioned on its completion within six years, and payment to the state of Illinois of seven per cent of the gross earnings. The latter is now a source of considerable revenue to the state. The entire line from Chicago to Cairo, 364.73 miles, and from Centralia to Dubuque, Ia., 340.77 miles, was opened for traffic Sept. 26, 1856. The Chicago & Springfield, a reorganiza-

UNION DEPOT, CANAL STREET, BETWEEN MADISON AND ADAMS STREETS.

USED BY: CHICAGO, BURLINGTON & QUINCY; CHICAGO, MILWAUKEE & ST. PAUL; CHICAGO & ALTON; PITTS-
BURGH, FT. WAYNE & CHICAGO, AND CHICAGO, ST. LOUIS & PITTSBURGH RAILROADS.

tion of the Gilman, Clinton & Springfield Road, 111.47 miles, was leased in 1877. The Kankakee & Southwestern, from Otto to Chatsworth, was built the following year, and was subsequently extended to Normal Junction, 79.46 miles. A branch from Kempton to Kankakee Junction, Ill., 41.8 miles, and from Buckingham to Tracy, ten miles, were also added. The Dubuque & Sioux City, the Iowa Falls & Sioux City, and the Cedar Falls & Minnesota Roads, having a total of 402.16 miles, are operated under lease. In 1882 almost the entire stock of the Chicago, St. Louis & New Orleans Railway was acquired, and the control of the system extending from Cairo to New Orleans, 548 miles, with branches from the main line to Kosciusko and Lexington, Miss., 30.30 miles. In 1884 a branch was opened from Jackson, Miss., to Yazoo City, 45.34 miles, and from Kosciusko to Aberdeen, 86.67. Total number of miles in the system, 2,064.76. General office, 78 Michigan Avenue. Depots, foot of Lake Street.

The **Chicago, Rock Island & Pacific Railway** was the first road to reach the Mississippi from Chicago. Originally organized as the Rock Island & LaSalle Railroad in 1847, it was reorganized and chartered as the Chicago & Rock Island Railroad, Feb. 7, 1851, and the line was opened to the Mississippi River July 10, 1854. Upon consolidation with the Mississippi & Missouri Railway Company Aug. 20, 1866, the present title was assumed. The extension to the Missouri River, and to a junction with the Union Pacific Railroad was completed in 1869. The Kansas City extension, built by the Iowa Southern & Missouri Northern Railway Company, was subsequently purchased, and the Hannibal & St. Joseph, the Peoria & Bureau Valley, and the Keokuk & Des Moines Roads were leased. June 4, 1880, a formal consolidation was effected, absorbing the following roads: South Chicago Branch, Washington Branch, Iowa Southern & Missouri Northern Railroad, Atchison, Des Moines, Indianola and Winterset Branches, Newton & Monroe, Atlantic Southern, Avoca, Macedonia & Southwestern, and the Atlantic & Audubon Roads, making the total mileage owned 1,120.9, exclusive of side tracks, and an aggregate of 1,796 miles operated. Among the chief terminal points are: Chicago, Peoria, Kansas City, Rock Island, Council Bluffs, Atchison, Davenport, Des Moines, Leavenworth and Keokuk. Control of the "Albert Lea Route," acquired in 1881, greatly augmented the mileage and furnished an inlet to Minneapolis and St. Paul. Freight depots, Fourth Avenue and Twelfth Street. Passenger depot, Van Buren Street, between Pacific Avenue and Sherman Street. E. St. John is general passenger agent.

The Chicago & Alton Railroad, with its leased lines, forms a grand trunk system spanning the states of Illinois and Missouri, and connecting the cities of Chicago, St. Louis and Kansas City, via Joliet, Bloomington and Springfield. The total length of line operated is about 1,050 miles. The main line proper reaches from Joliet to Alton. It was chartered as the Chicago & Mississippi River Railroad Feb. 27, 1847, and opened for traffic in 1855. It was reorganized as the St. Louis, Alton & Chicago Railroad in 1857, and the main line extended from Alton to East St. Louis two years later, giving it a total length of 243½ miles. The present company was formed Feb. 16, 1861, and came into possession, by foreclosure, in the year following. Entrance into Chicago was secured by a lease in perpetuity of the Joliet & Chicago Railroad, thirty-seven miles in length. In 1879 the Chicago & Illinois River Railroad, now operated as the Coal City Branch, was purchased, and in the same year the Kansas City, St. Louis & Chicago Railroad, just completed, was acquired by perpetual lease. In 1872 the Louisiana & Missouri River Railroad, and in 1877 the Mississippi Bridge had been similarly acquired, as had also the St. Louis, Jacksonville & Chicago Railroad, since consolidated with the controlling company. The Upper Alton line was extended to Milton in 1882. The equipment embraces some 220 engines, and about 6,200 cars of all kinds, including dining, sleeping, parlor and reclining chair cars. The freight depots are at the corner of West Van Buren and South Canal Streets. Passenger trains use the Union Depot on Canal Street. The general offices are located at the northwest corner of Dearborn and Adams Streets. The ticket office is at 89 South Clark.

The Pittsburg, Fort Wayne & Chicago Railway is a part of the great Pennsylvania system. It is over this line that the limited express, composed entirely of palace sleepers, runs between Chicago and New York, in twenty-five hours. The company is successor, by consolidation Aug. 1, 1856, of the Ohio & Pennsylvania Company, chartered in Ohio Feb. 24, 1848, and in Pennsylvania April 11th of the same year; the Ohio & Indiana Company, chartered in Ohio March 20, 1850, and in Indiana Jan. 15, 1851, and the Fort Wayne & Chicago Company organized in Indiana Sept. 22, 1852, and in Illinois Feb. 5, 1853. The entire line from Chicago to Pittsburg, 468.39 miles, was opened for business Jan. 1, 1859; sold under foreclosure Oct. 24, 1861, and reorganized under the present title Feb. 26, 1862. On the 27th of June, 1869, the road was leased in perpetuity to the Pennsylvania system, to which it has proved profitable, at a rental of 7% per annum on the capital stock. Depots and local offices, corner Canal and Madison Streets. General offices at Pittsburgh.

The Chicago & Eastern Illinois Railroad Company succeeded the Chicago, Danville & Vincennes Company, which was organized Feb. 16, 1865. The road was sold under foreclosure Feb. 9, 1877, and present company was organized in August following. Main line extends from Danville, Ill., to Dolton, seventeen miles south of Chicago, whence cars enter the city over the Chicago & Western Indiana. The Evansville, Terre Haute & Chicago Road is operated under a 999 years' lease. Freight trains are run over the Indiana, Bloomington & Western Railway to Covington, Ill., and thence over its own line to Coal Creek, nine miles. A branch, thirteen miles, extends from Wellington to Cisna Park, and another from Danville to Sidell, twenty-two miles, through the Grape Creek coal fields. From Otter Creek Junction a leased line extends to Brazil, Ind. General offices, 123 Dearborn Street.

The Chicago, St. Louis & Pittsburgh Railroad succeeded to the franchises of the Columbus & Indianapolis Railroad, a new company being formed April 2, 1883. A direct line from Chicago connects with the Pittsburgh, Cincinnati & St. Louis Railroad at Columbus, Ohio, and another to Indianapolis, Ind., connects with the Jeffersonville, Madison & Indianapolis Railroad. The main line, 187.15 miles, is from Columbus to Indianapolis. From Bradford Junction, Ohio, a branch, 230.98 miles, extends to Chicago, and from Richmond, Ind., a branch, 102.22 miles, extends to Anoka Junction. A third branch, 60.19 miles, runs from Peoria Junction, Ind., to Illinois State line—making a total length of roadway of 580.54 miles. Union Passenger Depot, Canal Street. Freight depots, corner Carroll Avenue and North Halsted Street, and Carroll Avenue and Clinton Street. The Pennsylvania Company holds a majority of the stock and operates the road.

The Chicago, Milwaukee & St. Paul Railway sweeps westward in four great parallels, the first of which crosses the state of Illinois via Elgin, spans the Mississippi at Savanna, throws off branches southward to Rock Island, Davenport and Ottumwa, and stretches on to Council Bluffs. The second line leaves Milwaukee via Madison and Prairie Du Chien, throws branches to Sioux City, Yankton and Running Water. The third parallel passes north via Milwaukee, thence west via Portage and La Crosse, traverses southern Minnesota and penetrates far into Dakota. Leaving the first line at the Mississippi River, the fourth grand division follows the Father of Waters north past Dubuque, crosses the second line at Prairie Du Chien and the third at La Crosse, strikes direct for St. Paul and Minneapolis, and runs thence to Ellendale and Aberdeen, Dakota, and continuing south to Mitchell it strikes the Iowa and Dakota division. The intermediate territory between the parallels is filled with branches and minor lines which increase the total mileage operated to 4,804.6 miles. The company, which holds a charter from the state of Wisconsin, its chief offices being at Milwaukee, was formed by a consolidation in 1873 of the Milwaukee & Waukesha, the Madison &.Prairie Du Chien, the La Crosse & Milwaukee, and the St. Paul & Chicago companies, with a total of 1,399 miles of track, which was augmented in 1878 to 1,539 miles. In the next year 535 miles were added by purchase and construction, 143 of which were in Dakota, the purchases including the Western Union, the Davenport & Northwestern, the Minnesota Southern, and the Minnesota Extension railroads. In 1880 349 miles of road were built and 1,193 miles purchased, and in the next year 442 miles of road were constructed. During 1882 the total mileage was increased to 4,520 miles, which, up to July 15, 1884, had been further augmented to 4,804.6 miles as above stated. The equipment of the road is very complete, numbering 626 engines and 19,018 cars of all classes. Passenger trains use the Union Depot at Canal and Madison Streets. The freight depots are at the corner of Carroll Avenue and North Union Street. Grain elevators are at the corner of North Canal Street and Carroll Avenue. Ticket offices are at 63 Clark Street and at the Union Depot. F. A. Miller is the general agent in Chicago. The general office is at Milwaukee, Wis.

The Louisville, New Albany & Chicago Railway, better known as the "Monon Route," traverses the entire length of the state of Indiana from north to south and has for its termini Chicago, Louisville, Indianapolis and Michigan City. It owns a one-fifth interest in a leasehold of the Chicago & Western Indiana Railroad, over whose line it enters the city from Hammond, Ind., and uses jointly with other roads the new passenger station of that company at Polk Street and Fourth Avenue. It also holds a one-fifth interest in the Belt Railway of Chicago. The original line was chartered by the state of Indiana, Jan. 25, 1847, under the name of the Louisville, New Albany & Chicago Railroad, and sold under foreclosure and reorganized by the first mortgage creditors under its present name, Dec. 27, 1872. It was opened July 4, 1852, and extended from Michigan City to New Albany, 288 miles. On the 10th of July, 1881, it was consolidated with the Chicago & Indianapolis Air Line Railroad, which was a reorganization of the Indianapolis, Delphi & Chicago, under the charter of which the com-

4

pany completed its line from Delphi to Hammond in January, 1882, crossing the main line at Monon. Later in the same year a contract was concluded with the Pennsylvania Company whereby that company doubled its track between the junction of the two roads and the Louisville bridge, and track privileges were secured over the same by lease for ninety-nine years, and an entrance into Louisville gained. The track from Chicago to Louisville, 317 miles in length, is now operated as the main line. The line from Monon to Michigan City, fifty-nine miles, is known as the Northern division, and the branch from Monon to Indianapolis, ninety-four miles, opened for traffic March 25, 1883, as the Indianapolis division. A feature of the route is a through line of sleepers from Chicago to Jacksonville, Fla. By an arrangement now in effect with the C. H. & D. R. R. a through line of Pullman buffet sleepers, parlor chair cars, in fact, solid train service is being performed between Chicago and Cincinnati via Indianapolis, and by similar arrangements with the Chicago & Indiana Coal Ry., through coach service is in effect between Chicago and Brazil, Ind., via Fair Oaks. The equipment embraces sixty engines and 2,400 cars of all descriptions. The freight depots of the Western Indiana Railroad at the corner of Polk Street and Fourth Avenue are used. The ticket office is at 73 Clark Street, and the general offices are at 183 Dearborn Street.

The **Chicago & Grand Trunk Railway** now forms the western extension of the Grand Trunk Railway of Canada by which it is operated, and with which it forms a continuous line from Chicago through Indiana and Michigan and Canada to Portland, Me., and the Atlantic coast, embracing, with branches and auxiliary lines, a total mileage of 3,330 miles. Its termini are Montreal, Detroit, Niagara Falls, Buffalo, Chicago, Goderich, Quebec and Portland. The main line of the Chicago & Grand Trunk Railway extends from Chicago to Port Huron, Mich., a distance of 335 miles. It also operates four miles of the Grand Trunk Junction Railroad, and four and a half miles of the Western Indiana Road, over which it enters the city from Forty-ninth Street, running into the Union Depot of that road at Third Avenue and Polk Street, which it uses as a passenger station. The company is the result of a consolidation, effected April 7, 1880, of the Port Huron & Lake Michigan, opened in December, 1871, and the Peninsula Railroad, opened in 1872 (which were consolidated under the name of the Chicago & Lake Huron Railroad, in August, 1873, and extended to Valparaiso, Ind.), with the line between Lansing and Flint, Mich., built by the Northwestern Railroad Company, and the extension from

New Passenger Depot, Corner Fourth Avenue and Polk Street.

USED BY THE CHICAGO & GRAND TRUNK; CHICAGO & ATLANTIC; CHICAGO & EASTERN ILLINOIS; LOUISVILLE, NEW ALBANY & CHICAGO, AND THE WABASH, ST. LOUIS & PACIFIC RAILROADS.

Valparaiso to Chicago, built by the Northwestern Grand Trunk Railway Company, and opened Feb. 8, 1880. The rolling stock of the Chicago & Grand Trunk proper consists of 135 locomotive engines and 1,169 cars for all purposes. The Grand Trunk system, however, of which it forms the western division, owns over 21,000 cars and some 700 locomotives. The freight depots are at Twelfth Street and Third Avenue. The ticket offices are at 103 Washington Street, and at the depot. The main offices are at Port Huron and Detroit, Mich. The Chicago office is in the First National Bank building.

The Wabash, St. Louis & Pacific Railway is a vast system of connecting lines formed by consolidation, purchase and lease of its various parts, aggregating 3,601.2 miles. It is an important highway. The main line of the road, 712.2 miles long, extends from Toledo, Ohio, via St. Louis to Kansas City. Other principal lines reach out to Chicago, Burlington, Council Bluffs, and less important termini. The Chicago line is formed of the Chicago & Strawn Railroad from Strawn, Illinois, to a junction with the Chicago & Western Indiana Railroad near Chicago, 97.8 miles, whence it enters the city via the latter road, 1.9 miles, making use of the terminal facilities of the Chicago & Western Indiana, including the Union Depot at Fourth Avenue and Polk Street. The Chicago & Strawn Road was acquired by purchase Aug. 1, 1880, and the Chicago & Paducah, 165 miles, April 1, 1880, and merged into the main corporation. The other terminal facilities include the use of the freight depot of the Western Indiana Company at Twelfth Street and Fourth Avenue. The rolling stock consists of 614 engines and 20,177 cars of all descriptions. On the 10th of April, 1883, the road and property of the company were leased for 99 years to the St. Louis, Iron Mountain & Southern Railroad which was itself leased to the Missouri Pacific Railroad Company, which thereby came into control and with which close connections were formed advantageous to through traffic to the Pacific slope. The principal offices are established at St. Louis. In the summer of 1884 Solon Humphreys and Thomas E. Tutt were appointed receivers. The local ticket office is at 109 Clark Street. The local freight offices are at the freight depot corner of Twelfth Street and Fourth Avenue.

The Chicago & West Michigan Railway, whose main line extends from La Crosse, Ind., to Pentwater, Mich., 208.74 miles, with branches ramifying through the adjacent territories and making up a total mileage of 409.74 miles, has recently secured an entrance into Chicago over the Michigan Central Railroad, whose depots at the foot of

South Water Street it uses, and it constitutes with its connections a through line to Manistee, Ludington, Grand Rapids, Muskegon, Grand Haven, and all points in western Michigan. Parlor and sleeping cars are run on all trains. This company was formed Oct. 1, 1881, by the consolidation of the Chicago & West Michigan Railroad, from New Buffalo to Pentwater, 170 miles, with branches 91.9 miles; the Grand Rapids, Newaygo & Lake Shore Railroad from Grand Rapids to White Cloud, forty-six miles, organized Sept. 11, 1869; the Grand Haven Railroad from Allegan to Muskegon, fifty-seven and a half miles, and the Indiana & Michigan Railroad, of Indiana. The company first named was organized Jan. 1, 1879, as the successor of the Chicago & Michigan Lake Shore Railroad Company, which was organized April 24, 1869, opened its main line July 1, 1873, and was sold under foreclosure and reorganized Nov. 16, 1878. In 1882 the Indiana & Michigan Railway was opened to La Crosse. By a recent arrangement the company now runs through daily trains from Grand Rapids to Cincinnati over the tracks of the Cincinnati, Indianapolis, St. Louis & Chicago Railway. The equipment includes some thirty engines and 900 cars of all classes. The general offices and address of the road is at Muskegon, Mich. The local ticket office is at 67 Clark Street.

The Chicago & Western Indiana Railroad was organized under the statutes of Illinois June 6, 1879, for the purpose of leasing its road and terminal facilities in the city and vicinity to other companies. It owns the splendid new Union Depot now in process of construction at Fourth Avenue and Polk Street, together with freight depots and warehouses at Twelfth Street and Third Avenue, which, together with the track, are used jointly by the Chicago & Eastern Illinois, the Wabash, St. Louis & Pacific, the Chicago & Grand Trunk, the Chicago & Atlantic, and the Louisville, New Albany & Chicago Companies. It also owns an elevator on the Chicago River near Eighteenth Street with capacity of 1,500,000 bushels. The road was opened in May, 1880, and in the following year the company was consolidated with the South Chicago & Western Indiana Railroad Company, whereby access to the iron and lumber interests at South Chicago was secured, and with the Chicago & Western Indiana Belt Railway Company affording connection for the transfer of cars with the various roads centering in Chicago. The Belt division is leased by the Belt Railway of Chicago. The track owned by the company includes the line from Polk Street to Dalton, Illinois, 16.69 miles, the Hammond extension, 10.28 miles, and the Belt division, 24.68 miles, making a total of 51.69 miles. The annual rental is $760,000. The rolling stock includes 12 locomotives and 155 cars, principally platform cars. The company also owns sixty-seven acres of land within the city limits, and 146 acres in the immediate suburbs, including some very valuable wharf property. The principal offices are at 94 Washington Street.

The Cincinnati, Indianapolis, St. Louis & Chicago Railway, popularly known as the "Big Four," or the "Kankakee Route," constitutes a through line between Chicago, Indianapolis, Louisville and Cincinnati, and at the last two places forms through connection for all points in the south. The company grew out of a consolidation in 1866 of the Cincinnati & Indianapolis and the Lafayette & Indianapolis Railroads, taking at that time the title of the Indianapolis, Cincinnati & Lafayette Railroad, and operated the main line from Cincinnati to Lafayette, 174.90 miles, until sold under foreclosure, Feb. 2, 1880. It was then purchased in behalf of those formerly interested in it, and a new company organized, which took possession March 6th of the same year. The Cincinnati, Lafayette & Chicago Railroad (Lafayette to Kankakee, seventy-five and a half miles,) was leased Sept. 1, 1880, and incorporated into the main line, and an entrance from Kankakee into Chicago over the line of the Illinois Central was acquired by contract. This contract also secured the use of the terminal stations of the latter road at the foot of Lake and South Water Streets. The company owns a half interest in and operates the Kankakee & Seneca Railroad between the points named, 42.32 miles, and a branch to Lawrenceburg, Ind., 2.60 miles. It also operates, under perpetual lease, a line from Valley Junction to Harrison, Ohio, 7.40 miles; another from Fairland to Martinsville, Ind., 38.30 miles; and a third from Greensburg to North Vernon, Ind., 44.39 miles, making the total lines operated 385.41 miles. The rolling stock consists of seventy-five engines and 3,173 cars of all kinds. The general offices of the road are at Cincinnati. The local ticket office is at 121 Randolph Street, and the local freight office 130 Washington Street.

The New York, Chicago & St. Louis Railway, better known as the "Nickel Plate," was organized as a competing line for the traffic formerly controlled by the Lake Shore & Michigan Southern Railroad, with which it runs parallel through the same territory a few miles to the south. The company was organized April 13, 1881, under the laws of New York, and began work in the same year. The line stretching from Chicago, via Ft. Wayne, along the' shores of Lake Erie to Buffalo, 513.28 miles, was opened for business Oct. 23, 1882. The roadway is laid with steel rails, and the line is some twenty-five miles shorter than the "Lake Shore Route." Recently control of the line has been obtained by the Lake Shore & Michigan Southern Railroad Company through the purchase of some $26,530,000 of its stock, and it is now operated in conjunction with that road, and uses the same depots in this city.

The Baltimore & Ohio & Chicago Railroad forms a part of the great Baltimore & Ohio system, the picturesque and popular through line to the Atlantic border. It was chartered March 13, 1872, as the Baltimore, Pittsburg & Chicago Railroad, and opened for traffic in November, 1874. The line, which was built and is owned by the Baltimore & Ohio Company, extends from Chicago Junction, Ohio, to Parkside Junction, Illinois, on the Illinois Central Railroad, 262.60 miles. From Parkside Junction it enters the city over the track of the road last named, a distance of eight and a half miles, making use of a temporary passenger station at the foot of Monroe Street, adjoining the Exposition building on the north. An extension of the line is also in progress to Pittsburg. The present title was adopted in 1877. The principal offices are located at 83 Clark Street, the resident officers of the road being A. P. Bigelow, general agent, and T. H. Dearborn, general northwestern passenger agent. The general officers are those of the Baltimore & Ohio Company. The chief ticket office is also at 83 Clark Street. The freight depots are at the foot of South Water Street. The rolling stock of the road is that of the Baltimore & Ohio system, and is unsurpassed in point of excellence. This is the only through line east from Chicago via Washington City.

The Belt Railway Company was chartered Nov. 22, 1882. May 1, 1883, under lease from the Chicago & Western Indiana Railroad Company, it assumed control and commenced to operate what is now known as the Belt Railway of Chicago, a track beginning at South Chicago and extending west about eleven miles, thence north about eleven miles to a connection with the Chicago, Milwaukee & St. Paul Railway, and connecting between those two terminal points with all railroads entering the city. This road does a general transfer or switching business between the various railroads, and to and from the industries located on its own line. It is situated outside the city limits, on the open prairie. It is equipped with nine powerful locomotives, and 130 flat cars. The total length of the line is 22.20 miles. The office of the company is at 94 Washington Street.

The Chicago & Western Railroad is a local line for switching purposes, extending from Morgan Street to Ada Street, Chicago, 1.44 miles, and forming a connection between the Chicago, Milwaukee & St. Paul and the "Pan Handle" tracks, with a number of coal and lumber yards, elevators and warehouses. The road-bed and tracks operated were acquired by lease, Oct. 5, 1881, for 99 years, from the Chicago & Eastern Illinois Railroad Company. The office is at 87 Dearborn Street.

The Chicago & Atlantic Railroad runs across the northern portion of Indiana, south of the "Ft. Wayne Route," 269 miles to a junction with the New York, Pennsylvania & Ohio Railroad at Marion, Ohio, in connection with which it is operated, and forms an additional through line to the Atlantic coast. The company is the outgrowth of a consolidation June 19, 1873, of the Chicago & Atlantic Railroad Company, organized as the Chicago, Continental & Baltimore Railroad Company Dec. 1, 1871, and the Chicago & Atlantic Extension Railway Company, formed March 15, 1873. Into the company thus formed was also merged, July 15, 1873, the Baltimore, Pittsburg & Continental Railroad Company, which had been organized Nov. 18, 1871. Track laying was completed in 1882, and the road was formally opened on the 17th of June of the following year. The main line of the road extends from Marion, 257 miles, to a junction with the Chicago & Western Indiana Railroad, 19.5 miles from the city. The latter road is thence used into the city, together with its terminal facilities. The general offices of the company are at the corner of Clark and Fourteenth Streets.

The Chicago & Evanston Railroad Company is organized under a charter granted Feb. 16, 1861. The authorized capital stock is $1,000,000, of which $565,700 are paid in. The road is completed to Calvary, a distance of about nine miles, and will probably be in operation to Evanston very early in 1885. The piece of road from Wabansia Avenue along Hawthorn Avenue to Larrabee Street is owned jointly with the Chicago, Milwaukee & St. Paul Railway Company. The company proposes to construct a track from Larrabee Street to the Union Depot on Canal Street. This road has encountered many difficulties that have greatly retarded its construction. The office of the company is at No. 8 Ashland Block.

Lake Michigan, one of the chain of great inland seas which, with their connections, form a grand internal and international waterway, was, until within the past half century, practically the only commercial highway of the city, and still continues, despite the fierce competition of railroads, one of the great arteries of her trade and an important agent in her prosperity. Along its shore came first the light canoes of the Indians, to barter with the traders at the primitive post. With increasing traffic grew up a demand for heavier boats, which was met by the "Mackinaw" barges used largely in the fur trade. These did not wholly disappear from the lake until 1830. As the commerce of the city widened, the lake constituted the sole avenue to the east, and over its bosom and through the straits came and went the first cargoes. Then, as the natural resources of the country were developed and cultivated, it brought within the city's reach the iron and copper and timber of the north, and the products of its bordering fields, and bound her in close connection with the thriving communities on its shores. It is now the avenue of a splendid commerce, extending to Manitoba in the far northwest, through the straits to the busy cities on the eastern lakes and the shores of the picturesque St. Lawrence, giving direct communication with Milwaukee, Erie, Buffalo, Cleveland, Detroit and other important points, and access via the Erie and Welland Canals to the Atlantic seaboard and European ports. Over the lake passes a large percentage of the direct imports and exports of the city, which amounted in 1841 to $1,848,362, and in 1883 to $13,647,551, exclusive of duty. The lake also provides a cheap route to the coal fields of Pennsylvania and the lumber regions of the north, and has made Chicago the distributing point for these commodities for the great northwest, and the greatest lumber market in the world.

The first vessel to arrive at Chicago was the schooner "Tracy," in 1803, bringing soldiers and supplies for the fort. At that time, and until 1833, there was no harbor, and a bar across the mouth of the river prevented access to it. Vessels were anchored off shore, and unloaded or loaded by lighters. In the year named, after long and patient effort, Congress was induced to appropriate $25,000, and the building of the present magnificent harbor was begun, access being gained to the river in the following spring. Lighthouses were built but found ineffective, and the harbor was unprotected until 1870, when the present breakwater, now approaching completion, stretching across the inlet and enclosing the spacious inner harbor, with its lighthouse, was begun. In 1835 some 212 vessels arrived in port. From 1832 occasional steamboats touched at Chicago, but it was not till 1830 that the first regular line was established. This line of boats plied between the city and Buffalo. In 1856 the first clearance for Europe direct was made by the steamer "Dean Richmond," and the

first direct arrival from abroad did not occur till the following year.
The total arrivals in port in 1883 were 11,967 vessels, having a tonnage of 3,812,464 tons, and the total clearances were 12,015 vessels,
with a tonnage of 3,980,873 tons.

The Chicago River is properly an internal waterway of the city,
intimately connected with the lake and constituting an essential part
of the harbor. Its shores are continuous lines of docks bordered by
mammoth warehouses, elevators and yards for heavy traffic in coal,
lumber, etc., and giving anchorage to the multitude of vessels plying
the lake. As it now is, the river is more a creation of man than of
nature. The original bed was comparatively shallow and narrow, and
near its mouth turned abruptly southward, entering the lake by a tor-
tuous channel, over a bar which blocked the passage of vessels. As
early as 1805 an agent of the government suggested the cutting away
of the bar, but his idea only contemplated the clearing of a passage
for the admission of the Mackinaw trading crafts, and was not given
attention. The first vessel to enter the waters of the river was the
" Westward Ho," which was hauled over the bar by oxen in 1833. In
March of the same year work was begun on the Government piers, and
before the close of the following year both the north and south
piers had been pushed out some 500 feet, cutting off the old tor-
tuous channel to the south. In the spring of 1834 a freshet did
the work of dredging, and vessels of heavy burden entered the river
for the first time. The timbers for piers were first rafted from the
Calumet River, and the stone was procured some three miles up
the South Branch. Later the timbers were brought from Wisconsin
and Michigan. Up to 1838 the piers were annually pushed further
into the lake, but the continuous formation of bars at the mouth of
the channel by the lake currents destroyed the practical benefits of
the work, and in this year the course of the piers was deflected
twenty-five and a half degrees to the south. Work continued inter-
mittently until 1857, when the north pier extended into the lake
2,800 feet, and the shore line at the mouth of the river had pushed
itself out several hundred yards. The channel between the piers was
then 200 feet wide, and had been dredged to a depth of eight to
twelve feet. In 1854 it was determined to create an interior basin,
and the river was widened for the purpose. In October of the same
year a ship canal was dredged through the bar. The wharfing privileges, which had occasioned much dispute, were defined in 1833, and
the wharfs were sold or leased in perpetuity, in consideration of a

CHICAGO RIVER FROM LAKE MICHIGAN.

payment of their value and an annual rental of one barleycorn. It was specified in all cases that a substantial dock, three feet high and five feet wide, should be built and maintained in perpetuity. In 1857 only six miles of dock had been built. At present there are twelve miles of slips and basins, and twenty-nine miles of river front mostly docked.

The **Illinois & Michigan Canal** tapping the Chicago River at Bridgeport, four miles south of its mouth, extends to a junction with the Illinois River at LaSalle, ninety-six miles distant, whence, by the improvement of the latter river, access is had to the Mississippi.

Wisconsin Central Line, composed of the Wisconsin Central R. R. and its controlled and leased roads, forms a grand through line from Chicago to St. Paul and Minneapolis, Minn., and from Chicago to Ashland, Wis.; also from Milwaukee to the same points, there being no direct Chicago and Milwaukee connection. On completion of the Wisconsin & Minnesota R. R. from Schleisingerville to Chicago, the Wisconsin Central R. R. between Abbottsford and Neehan, and the Milwaukee & Lake Winnebago R. R. became parts of the through line, which was opened July 26, 1886. The total length of line operated is 600.62 miles, as follows: Chicago to Schleisingerville, 122 miles; Wisconsin & Minnesota R. R., 55 miles; Minnesota, St. Croix & Wisconsin R. R., 98 miles; Stevens Point, Wis. to Menasha, Wis., 64.70 miles; Portage City branch—Stevens Point to Portage City, 71.70 miles; Ashland branch—Stevens Point to Ashland, 188.47 miles; Rib Lake branch—Chelsea, Wis., to Rib Lake, Wis., 5.60 miles, and the following leased branches and spurs: Milwaukee and Lake Winnebago R. R., 87.30 miles; the Packawaukce & Montello R. R., 7.75 miles.

It has joint track facilities with the Chicago, Milwaukee & St. Paul Railway, at Milwaukee, and runs its own freight and passenger trains solid in and out of that city, connecting at Rugby Junction (27.5 miles) with the main line. The general offices of the road are in Milwaukee. The local ticket office, H. C. Fuller, agent, is at 205 S. Clark Street, and the passenger and freight depots are on the corner of Polk Street and Fifth Avenue.

The Public Buildings.

THE CITY, COUNTY AND UNITED STATES GOVERNMENT BUILD-INGS AND THE POSTOFFICE.

CHICAGO is very little, if at all, behind contemporary cities in the number, character, architecture, and general details of her public buildings, and in some of these particulars the public buildings surpass those of any other municipality in the country.

The County Court House and City Hall may well stand for an example; notwithstanding the fact that, through economy or lack of taste, the original design was changed by leaving off the domes and other upper structures that would have greatly added to the appearance of the building. It is a dual structure, occupying the square bounded by Clark, LaSalle, Washington and Randolph Streets, giving it a frontage of 340 feet on the east and west sides, and 280 feet on the north and south. It is located in the business center of the city, and is by far the most massive and elaborate public building in Chicago. The style of architecture is the modern French *renaissance.* Above the sub-building is a colonnaded double story with Corinthian columns thirty-five feet in height, which gives to the entire structure a lofty, yet solid and imposing appearance. These immense columns of polished Maine granite support an entablature at once mathematical and elegant in proportions, and divided into architrave, frieze and cornice. An attic story enriched by the sculptor's chisel with allegorical groups representing Agriculture, Commerce, Peace and Plenty, Mechanical Art and Science Art, surmounts the entablature and completes the grandeur of the noble outlines. The materials are principally upper silurian limestone, from the quarries along the Desplaines River in this state. The columns, pilasters and pedestals are of Maine granite. The building is fire-proof throughout, and the total cost is nearly $6,000,000. The work of construction was begun in 1877, and the court-house division, which fronts on Clark Street, was completed and occupied by the county officials in 1882. The apartments assigned to the County, Probate, Superior, and Circuit Courts are capacious and convenient, amply provided with

private rooms for judges, jurors, offices of the court attaches, and
huge fire and burglar-proof vaults for the preservation of judiciary
records, while each suite is fitted up in a style plain but very rich,
which is at once appropriate to the character of the edifice and com-
mendable to good taste. The Sheriff, Coroner, and Recorder of Deeds
occupy the extensive basement, and the County Clerk, Board of Commissioners, and Board of Education, together with a host of other
officials, find conveniently arranged quarters within its spacious walls.

The City Hall division, fronting on LaSalle Street, is similar in its
architectural features to the county portion of the building, and was
intended to be its complement, except for such variations in ornamentation as were required to avoid monotony and introduce a distinctive
element into its appearance. The interior is finished in white oak.
The police and fire departments and the City Electrician are located in
the spacious basement story; the water, building and special assessment departments, and the offices of the Mayor, Comptroller, and
City Treasurer, in the first story; the numerous offices of the department of public works occupy the second story; and the law, health
and educational departments, the city council and working committees
and the numerous other offices of the city government, are all allotted
ample and convenient quarters. A large portion of the interior of the
upper stories is still unfinished. The settling of the foundations from
the immense weight has caused the cracking of some stones in both
the city and county buildings, but as yet has not injuriously affected
either the durability or safety of the structures.

This is the second joint structure built by the county and city for
administrative use, and the third city hall erected by the municipal
authorities. When Chicago became a chartered city the "Fathers"
leased a hall in the old "Saloon Building" (shown in illustration on
page 18), said to have been the finest public hall west of Buffalo at
the time. It was located at the southeast corner of Lake and Clark
Streets, and was a square three-story frame, having its first floor
devoted to store purposes, the second to offices, and the third floor
occupied by a public hall. In 1842 a building at the corner of LaSalle
and Randolph Streets was secured and occupied until the first municipal structure erected in Chicago was completed. This was called the
Market Building, and was situated in the center of State Street, fronting forty feet on Randolph, and extended north toward Lake Street 180
feet. It was a plain two-story stone and brick structure. The first
story was divided into thirty-two stalls and leased for market purposes.

NEW COUNTY COURT HOUSE AND CITY HALL, CLARK, WASHINGTON, RANDOLPH AND LASALLE STREETS.

The upper story contained four rooms used for city purposes. It cost $11,000, and was first occupied Nov. 13, 1848. In June, 1851, the county and city decided to erect a joint building on the public square, and Sept. 11, 1851, the corner-stone was laid with appropriate ceremonies. As at first constructed, it had two stories and basement. The main part was 100 feet square, and had four narrow wings projecting

THE SECOND COURT-HOUSE IN CHICAGO—BURNED BY THE GREAT FIRE.

from the sides. It was first occupied Feb. 7, 1853. A third story and two wings were afterward added. The grounds contained graveled walks, grass plats, trees, shrubbery, etc. The building was destroyed by the great fire in 1871. The east wing, however, was left in such a condition as to be again made habitable and, in part, served the wants of the city officials until the erection of the present edifice on the same site necessitated its demolition. The city administration then fell into its old itinerant habits, and drifted about until it found lodgings in the "old tank," or "rookery," as the make-shift for a city hall is familiarly styled, on the corner of LaSalle and Adams Streets. This homely-looking structure, which has a history of its own, was in its original state a huge iron water tank, or reservoir, belonging to the old water works service on the South Side, prior to the great fire. The municipal government seized upon it and made it the nucleus of a temporary abiding place. Surrounding it with a hastily erected squatty two-story brick building, and transforming the tank itself into safety vaults, it was dignified by the appellation of " City Hall."

The Criminal Court and County Jail Buildings consist of three buildings grouped together. They occupy about two-thirds of the square between Michigan, Illinois and Clark Streets and Dearborn Avenue, an alley forming the west boundary line. The Criminal Court building has a frontage of 140 feet on Michigan Street, and sixty-five feet on Dearborn Avenue. It is constructed of limestone. The main entrance on Michigan Street is through a broad portico with massive fluted columns. A wide entrance from Dearborn Avenue, through a hallway, leads also to the center, or court, into which the main entrance opens, and from which stairways ascend to the court rooms above. The Criminal Court of Cook County occupies the entire upper portion of the building. The sessions of the court commence the first Monday in each month, and are presided over by the Judges of the Circuit and Superior Courts of Cook County in alternation. Adjoining on the north is a two story and basement building which fronts directly upon Dearborn Avenue, giving an "L" shape to the eastern exposure of the court building. This is occupied in part by the north town officials, the county utilizing the remainder. This building, which is of brick with stone trimmings, extends 137 feet on Dearborn Avenue to the corner of Illinois Street, on which it fronts forty-three feet. It is entered from both thoroughfares by plain iron balcony stairs rising from the sidewalk to the main floor. In the space or yard formed by the rear of these two structures with Illinois Street on the north and the alley on the east, the county jail is located—the frontage on Illinois Street being 141 feet. It is in no wise connected with the other buildings except by a narrow bridge, enclosed with heavy corrugated sheet iron, which leads direct to the "criminal box" in the court room. It contains one hundred and thirty-six cells in the male wards, forty-eight in the female and fourteen in the juvenile wards. It is a plain, substantial structure of brick and iron, and is in marked contrast with the architecture of the court building. This group of buildings was erected in 1873 by the county at a cost of $375,000.

5

The United States Government Building (Postoffice and Custom House), completed in 1880 at a cost, including grounds and surrounding street improvements, of $6,000,000, is one of the handsomest government edifices in the country. Its base dimensions are 342 by 210 feet, which leaves spacious elevated lawns, surrounded by heavy coping. It occupies the square bounded by Dearborn, Clark, Adams and Jackson Streets, and is three stories in height, with base-

U. S. GOVERNMENT BUILDING — POSTOFFICE AND CUSTOM-HOUSE.

ment and attic. The style of architecture is known as the Romanesque, with Venetian treatment. It is almost entirely of iron and stone, and is fire-proof throughout. The basement and first floor are occupied exclusively by the Postoffice Department. In the basement, reached by an inclined driveway on the west side, extending from Adams Street through to Jackson, all mail matter is received and dispatched. The first floor is devoted to the general delivery, carriers, money order, registry and stamp divisions, and executive purposes. The interior of the building above the basement forms a court, 83 by 198 feet. This court is covered by an immense skylight at the second story, being an open court above. The second floor is used by the Collector of Customs, Internal Revenue Collector, Sub-Treasurer, Commissioner of Pensions and special mail agents. The third floor is occupied by the various United States Courts and offices connected with the Interior and Law Departments. The interior of the building is exceedingly rich in finish. The floors are all in tiling of black and white marble. The grand staircases in the north and south halls are especially notable, being of solid iron, artistic in design, and painted to represent wood, with steps laid in small parti-colored tiles. The building is furnished with four elevators and every improved convenience of the age, and is heated throughout by steam from engines in the basement, the temperature being regulated to 60° the year round. The approaches are from each of the four streets; they are exceedingly spacious, and are made uniform with the broad sidewalk surrounding the square, which is covered to the curb with massive stone flagging. Each of the four streets forming the square were also paved to the center by the government. The prominence of the building is made more imposing by the appearance of isolation given it by its surroundings, which throw it out in bold relief. Large as the building is, the postoffice department is already crowded, such has been the growth of the business since it was occupied. Eight branch offices, located in different parts of the city, each with its corps of clerks and carriers, help to relieve the pressure; but by far the largest portion of the work is done from the main office, among the large business houses situated within its immediate delivery district. The total number of carriers employed is 317; number of clerks, 480; total number of pieces delivered in 1883, 78,754,271; total receipts for the year ending June 30, 1884, $1,-892,241. The amount of duties collected in the customs department in 1883 was $4,075,166.85, on merchandise valued at $10,453,701. The internal revenue collections for the fiscal year ending June 30,

COLLECTOR'S OFFICE—U. S. CUSTOMS.

U. S. SUB-TREASURY OFFICE.

1883, were $9,118,191.   On the lawn plat formed by Clark and Adams Streets, and facing their intersection, stands a monument seven feet in height, bearing this inscription :

TO THE MEMORY

OF

GEORGE BUCHANAN ARMSTRONG

FOUNDER OF THE

RAILWAY MAIL SERVICE

IN THE

UNITED STATES;

BORN IN ARMAGH, IRELAND,

OCTOBER 27, A. D. 1822.

DIED IN CHICAGO

MAY 5, A. D. 1871.

ERECTED BY THE CLERKS

IN THE SERVICE

1881

A life size bust of Mr. Armstrong surmounts the pedestal of polished dark marble which rests on a base about three feet square.

The **Other Public Buildings**, including hospitals, asylums, infirm-aries, police stations, engine houses, and school-houses, have been noted in appropriate chapters.

The City Government.

THE VARIOUS DEPARTMENTS OF THE CITY GOVERNMENT, THE MAYORS, AND THE WATER SYSTEM.

THE City Government is reasonably well organized in both its legislative and executive branches. Police, fire, health, law, finance, education and other objects of municipal attention, are allotted to proper control, and then almost everything else is thrown into a sort of *omnium gatherum* entitled the Department of Public Works.

The Legislative Power is vested in the Mayor and Board of Aldermen, commonly called the City Council. The Mayor's term of office is two years. The board has thirty-six members—two from each of the eighteen wards, elected in alternate years for a term of two years each. The Mayor presides over the deliberations of the body, or, if he be absent, a member from the quorum present is called to the chair.

The following is a complete list of the mayors and the dates of their election :

William B. Ogden, .	. May	2, 1837	Thomas Dyer, .	. .	Mar. 10, 1856
Buckner S. Morris,	. Mar.	6, 1838	John Wentworth,	.	Mar. 3, 1857
B. W. Raymond,	. Mar.	5, 1839	John C. Haines,	. .	Mar. 2, 1858
Alexander Lloyd,	. Mar.	3, 1840	John C. Haines, .	.	Mar. 1, 1859
Francis C. Sherman,	. Mar.	5, 1841	John Wentworth, .	.	Mar. 6, 1860
Benj. W. Raymond,	. Mar.	7, 1842	Julian S. Rumsey,	.	Apr. 16, 1861
Augustus Garrett, .	. Mar.	7, 1843	Francis C. Sherman,	.	Apr. 15, 1862
A. S. Sherman,	. . Mar.	7, 1844	Francis C. Sherman,	.	Apr. 21, 1863
Augustus Garrett,	. Mar.	5, 1845	John B. Rice,	. .	Apr. 18, 1865
John P. Chapin,	. . Mar.	3, 1846	John B. Rice,	. .	Apr. 16, 1867
James Curtiss, .	. . Mar.	2, 1847	Roswell B. Mason, .	.	Nov. 2, 1869
James H. Woodworth,	Mar.	7, 1848	Joseph Medill,	. .	Nov. 7, 1871
James H. Woodworth,	. Mar.	6, 1849	Harvey D. Colvin, .	.	Nov. 4, 1873
James Curtiss,	. . Mar.	5, 1850	Monroe Heath,	. .	July 12, 1876
Walter S. Gurnee, .	. Mar.	4, 1851	Monroe Heath, .	. .	Apr. 3, 1877
Walter S. Gurnee,	. Mar.	2, 1852	Carter H. Harrison,	.	Apr. 1, 1879
Charles M. Gray,	. . Mar.	14, 1853	Carter H. Harrison,	.	Apr. 5, 1881
Isaac L. Milliken,	. Mar.	13, 1854	Carter H. Harrison,	.	Apr. 3, 1883
Levi D. Boone,	. . Mar.	8, 1855			

In 1863 the term of office of mayor was extended from one to two years. In 1869 the time of holding the city election was changed from April to November, and the persons then in office were continued until the first Monday in December. The city was reorganized under the general incorporation act in April, 1875, and consequently no election was held in November of that year, but the persons in office held over until July, 1876. In that year the City Council provided for an election for city officers under the new incorporation, but omitted all reference to the office of mayor. Nevertheless, a popular vote was taken for mayor at the election, and Thomas Hoyne received 33,064. The canvass of the returns being made, the Council disregarded the vote for mayor, but the new Council canvassed the returns and declared Mr. Hoyne elected. Mr. Colvin, the incumbent, declined to yield possession, and the matter was taken to the courts, where the case was decided against both contestants. A special election was then ordered by Council and held July 12, 1876, resulting in the election of Mr. Heath to serve till after the next regular election.

Measures can be passed over the mayor's veto only by an affirmative vote of two-thirds of the board. The regular meetings are held every Monday evening. The other city offices filled by general election are : Clerk, Treasurer, and City Attorney. The heads of all the other departments, and the occupants of minor positions in the municipal service, are appointed by the mayor, with the approval of the council.

The **Law Department** consists of a Corporation Counsel, City Attorney and Prosecuting Attorney.

The **Department of Finance** is under the City Comptroller, City Treasurer, and City Collector.

The **Building Department** is supervised by the Commissioner of Buildings, assisted by a secretary and six inspectors. The building laws require plans and specifications of all structures to be filed in this department, and a permit issued by it, before the work of erection shall begin. All fire escapes and elevators are also subject to inspection and control by this department.

The **Department of Public Works**, the most ponderous bureau of the corporation government, is under the supervision of a commissioner, who is supported by a City Engineer. The heads of the sub-departments are Superintendent of Sewerage ; Superintendent of Streets, with a corps of street engineers; Superintendent of Maps, and Superintendent of Water Collections, each being provided with the number of assistants requisite to the proper direction of the host of minor employes. The labors of the department of public works are many and difficult.

The City's Water System affords notable evidence of the high order of ability and engineering skill engaged in it. The peculiar and stupenduous mechanism of the system by which Chicago obtains her abundant supply of water, was first conceived by El- lis S. Chesbrough, then city engi- neer, in 1863, and under his person- al supervision the entire work of construction was executed, and the system put in op- eration. His plan to obtain pure water through a tunnel extended two miles under the bed of the lake was then gen- erally regarded as a visionary scheme, that would entail end- less expense with- out benefiting the city. The contractors for constructing the great tunnel and crib were Messrs. Dull & Gowan, of Harrisburg, Pa., and the contract price was $315,139. Work on the tunnel began March 17, 1864, and the last brick was laid Dec. 6, 1866, rapid progress having been made from the lake end to a junction with the shore end from the time the "crib" was finished and placed in position. The crib, which was built on shore

NORTH SIDE WATER WORKS TOWER.

and launched like a sea-vessel, is sixty feet high and constructed in pentagonal form within a circumscribed circle of ninety-eight and one-half feet diameter. It has three walls—the outer, the center and the inner—which are firmly braced and bolted together, forming one great structure. Each wall was calked and tarred like the hulk of a vessel, before the three were joined together. White-oak timbers twelve inches square were used for the upper twelve feet, and white pine of the same dimensions for the remaining forty-eight feet. These timbers are bolted together with square rods of iron. The bottom is composed of three layers of twelve-inch timbers bolted together in an equally firm manner. The crib contains fifteen water-tight compartments, the "well," through which a hollow iron shaft nine feet in diameter goes down thirty-one feet below the bottom of the lake, being in the center. It was towed to its proper position in the lake, and there sunk and weighted in its place with heavy stones. The tunnel, which is five feet in diameter and two miles long, is sixty-six feet below the surface level of the lake at the crib. It taps the shaft in the well at a point which gives the water a "head" of eighteen feet, with a velocity of four and two-tenths miles per hour, and will deliver 57,000,000 gallons daily into the great well under the water-works building. From this well immense engines lift the water into the stand-pipe, or "water tower," 175 feet high, whence by its own weight it is distributed throughout the city. There are four engines at these works which have, combined, 3,000 horse-power. The largest one—of 1,200 horse-power, with fly-wheel twenty-six feet in diameter—has a capacity for pumping 2,750 gallons of water at each stroke. It cost $200,000. These are the main works of the system, though generally termed "North Side Water Works," and are situated at the foot of Chicago Avenue. The first works erected were totally destroyed by the fire of 1871, but they were speedily replaced by the present enlarged constructions. A second and similar tunnel was constructed from the crib to the new pumping works established on the West Side at the corner of Ashland and Blue Island Avenues. This tunnel runs in a southwesterly direction under the city, passing twice under the bed of the river, and is six miles in length. The system, as a whole, is conceded to be one of the grandest triumphs of modern engineering, and is capable of furnishing the city with 104,000,000 gallons of water daily, through over 500 miles of main and distributing pipes. It supplies the fire department with an abundance of water through 4,144 fire hydrants. It has been perfected at an expense of about $10,000,-

000. The crib is in charge of a keeper, who, with his family, resides in a comfortable cottage erected on it. It is connected with the City Hall by telephone, and is a notable stopping place for excursion boats in the summer season. The North Side works are also a favorite resort for thousands, being at the north terminus of Pine Street where terminates, for the present, the Lake Shore drive which passes through the handsome grounds of the works.

The Police Department is under the control of a General Superintendent, appointed by the Mayor and subject to removal at any time. The city is divided into five police precincts, which are subdivided into sixteen districts—the first precinct containing four districts and the remaining four precincts three districts each. General headquarters are at the central station, located in the City Hall. The detail for each precinct is under a captain, and each station is in charge of a lieutenant with one patrol sergeant and two desk sergeants or station keepers. The central detail, located at central station, is distinct from the precinct commands, and is under a captain with sub-officers of like rank as the district officers. The secretary is also the inspector of the department. Jan. 1, 1884, the total number of men constituting the police force, including officers, was 637. Of this number forty-seven are officers, fifty-three occupy subaltern positions, twenty-two are in the detective service, eighty-four in the signal service, forty-eight on special detail, seventy-one on permanent post duty and 307 are patrolmen—eighty on day duty and 227 on the night force. The remaining five are classed as disabled. The "central detail" was recently increased by forty picked men from the different precincts, and now numbers 100 experienced policemen. This branch is imperatively demanded in order to protect life and limb and regulate teams in the crowded thoroughfares of the city's business center. The men are on permanent post duty at street crossings, bridges, tunnels, markets, railroad depots and public buildings, a few being detailed to travel the commercial heart of the city and enforce the ordinances relative to street and sidewalk obstructions. They are distinguished from other branches of the department by the device on their helmets, consisting of a wreath encircling the initials " C. D ;" by the absence of club and belt, or even cane, and by their white-gloved hands and polite attention to pedestrians—ladies especially. The uniform of the entire force is of dark navy blue cloth frock coat, buttoned from waist to collar, vest and pants of the same, black belt, and helmet (or hat) bearing the patrolman's number or designated rank of an officer. The ratio of the entire force to the population is one policeman to each 1,050 inhabitants, or one night patrolman for each 3,000 and one day patrolman for each 9,000 of the whole population. The average area assigned to each night patrolman is eighty acres, and there is one day patrolman for every 240 acres; the average number of buildings to be guarded by one night patrolman is 350; by each day patrolman, 1,050. This lack of numerical strength, however, is more than counterbalanced by the efficiency of the police telephone and signal system. This valuable acquisition is strictly a Chicago invention, having been suggested by A. J. Doyle, chief of the police department, and devised by the city electrician, Prof. John P. Barrett, and first introduced in the department in the fall of 1880. The results of the first experiment in the West Twelfth Street district were so satisfactory that the system was adopted, and is now in general use throughout the department. The various districts are all connected by an electric current with the general headquarters, and

THE POLICE PATROL.

from 375 patrol or street boxes, placed at the most prominent street corners, there is a current going into the station of the district in which each box is located. These street boxes are octagon-shaped, with a gas-light on top, thus taking the places of ordinary iron street lamp-posts. The interior contains the electric alarm box, which in turn contains the chief principle of the system—the signal box, and also the telephone. The signal box is provided with a dial, similar to that of a clock, with eleven spaces marked "fire," "murder," "thieves," etc. When the pointer is placed on a space and the signal current turned on, the station, through a companion device, is at once apprised of the nature of the case, and the "patrol wagon" responds fully prepared for the work on hand. The patrol wagon is a police wagon and ambulance combined; a hospital stretcher, hand-cuffs, lantern, blankets, medicine-chest, and coil of rope for use at fires, being constantly carried. Patrolmen are required to communicate with their station by means of the telephone in the box, at stated periods. The same description of signal box is placed in private residences, banks, business houses, hotels, etc., and connected with the nearest station on the same circuit as the street patrol box. The total valuation of the property belonging to the police department is $353,419.09. The total expenditures of the department during the year 1884 were $703,579.66. Police courts are established in each police precinct except the fourth, which was very recently created out of the third and the old fourth—now the fifth—precincts. The court rooms are located at the principal district station house in each precinct, and a session is held every morning. The four police magistrates are appointed by the Mayor of the city, subject to confirmation by the City Council.

The **Fire Department**, as first organized in Chicago, was a "leather bucket corps." In the Historical Society's rooms can be seen the only one of the buckets now in existence. The owner's initials, "C. S."—Clement Stose—are still upon it. That beginning was in 1835. The present superbly appointed department is the growth of the paid service first organized in 1858. The Chief Engineer of the depart-ment then, is the efficient Fire Marshal now—Dennis J. Swenie—who for thirty-five years has been a competent member of the city's fire force. The "Long John," named after Hon. John Wentworth, was the first steamer placed in commission, and dates her entrance into the service Dec. 25, 1858. Marshal Swenie was superseded in com-mand in 1859, through the influence of the "old volunteer boys," who opposed the pay system. Twenty years after, in 1879, he was ap-pointed by the present Mayor to the position of Fire Marshal and Chief of Brigade. The brigade comprises seven battalions, and the uniform force consists of one Fire Marshal, one First Assistant Fire Marshal, one Assistant Fire Marshal and Secretary, seven Assistant Fire Marshals and Chiefs of Battalions, eighty-eight company officers and 282 men, a total of 380. The Fire Alarm Telegraph Corps, num-bering two officers and twelve men, together with two Clerks and one Veterinary Surgeon, gives, as the total working force of the depart-ment, 397 members. The apparatus is as follows: Thirty-three En-gine Companies, nine Hook and Ladder Companies (two of which operate a one-horse, two-wheeled, single tank chemical engine), and three Chemical Engine Companies. Each engine is attended by a hose cart. There are in the service twenty-five two-wheeled carts, each drawn by one horse, and fourteen four-wheeled carts, drawn by two horses each. A notable feature in the way of special apparatus is a portable standpipe and water tower, which can be raised to the height of sixty-five feet, to reach fires in the upper or remote parts of buildings. There are 189 horses in the department; the quantity of hose on hand amounts to 37,782 feet; and the total length of ladders is 2,115 feet. The real estate is valued at $215,000, the thirty-eight buildings at $304,650, and the apparatus at $568,878, making the total valuation of all property in use by the department $1,088,528. The cost of maintenance in 1883 was $556,551. The Fire Alarm Telegraph, first introduced June 2, 1865, is now embraced in the city telegraph system, which comprises all lines, telegraph and telephone, in the police and fire service and the various other departments of the city government. John P. Barrett is Superintendent.

The Health Department is under the Commissioner of Health. His chief aids are three Medical Inspectors, one in each division of the city; a Registrar of Vital Statistics, Small-pox Hospital Physician, Chemist, Chief Tenement and Factory Inspector, Secretary and Clerk. The small-pox hospital work is lessened by house to house visits for the purpose of vaccinating those who have not undergone that precautionary treatment. The department also keeps a careful supervision over the arrangements for safety and health of inmates of domiciles as well as workshops. The law imposes a penalty for the erection of any building without the Health Commissioner's approval of its plans for ventilation, light, drainage and plumbing. The effect of this is a marked increase of attention to sanitary arrangements on the part of builders and owners of houses, and a low rate of mortality. The authority of the department has a wide range, however, and the results of its well directed labors in all branches of its jurisdiction are clearly shown by the general improvement in the sanitary condition of the city. A great deal of valuable work is done by the inspector of meats and stockyards, whose condemnations represent an important contribution to the stock of public health ; as are also the operations of the sanitary police, the scavengers, and others working under the direction and control of this department. Oscar C. De Wolf, M. D., has been Health Commissioner since 1879.

The Educational Department has been duly noted in the chapter on the "Educational Institutions."

The Militia.

THE NATIONAL, STATE AND INDEPENDENT MILITARY COMPANIES.

CHICAGO had some warlike training in the days of her pioneers, and suffered at least one serious disaster, which is recorded in the account of the massacre of Fort Dearborn.* The occupation of the fort probably had some influence in nourishing the military spirit, as there are accounts of early militia organizations, and the city does not seem to have been without something of the kind from the time the population was sufficient to form even a Falstaffian company. Her volunteers took a fair part in the Mexican war, and bore their full share in the late war of the rebellion. Indeed, few centers of population played so conspicuous a role in that bloody drama. From the first call for volunteers her young men responded freely, and when the draft came she supplied a large quota. The county and city were united in the drafts, but much the largest portion was of course always drawn from the city. The aggregate drafts were for 24,069 men, and when the war ended 22,436 of those had been furnished, with one draft held in abeyance. In bounties, $2,571,272 had been paid out; $90,809 had been distributed among the families of soldiers; and the Board of Trade had distributed $220,000, and the Merchants' Association $75,000 in the same way, besides sending out a battery of artillery each.

The total actual cost to Chicago and Cook County was over $4,000,000, and the share of the city and county in the total general expenses of the war is estimated at $58,000,000. Below the then southern limits of the city, on the lake shore, were situated the prisons of Camp Douglas, where so many thousands of Confederate prisoners were confined during the conflict. The ground on which the camp stood is now covered with fine residences, and is one of the most pleasant of the resident portions of the city. The great national sanitary fair was held in Chicago during the war, and an immense sum was accumulated for the use of the sick and wounded Federal soldiers. The military spirit

* See first chap'er in this volume.

is not dead among the people, although the parsimonious course of the
state toward military organizations is well calculated to starve it out.

The Division of the Missouri, U. S. A., including the states lying
west of the Mississippi River and cast of Utah, together with Illinois
and Wisconsin, is under the command of Maj.-Gen. John M. Schofield,
who took command on the first of November, 1883, upon the removal
of Lieut.-Gen. Sheridan to Washington. The headquarters, which were
for a long time located in the Honore Building, 204 Dearborn Street,
were removed May 1, 1884, to the fourth floor of the new Pullman
Building, corner of Adams Street and Michigan Avenue. There are no
troops stationed here, excepting a few on detail as clerks to assist Gen.
Schofield and the other officers. There is a recruiting office for infantry
at No. 9 South Clark Street, with a few men under Capt. Chas. W.
Miner, of the Twenty-second
Infantry, and one for cavalry
under First Lieut. Gustavus C.
Doane, Second Cavalry, at No.
18 South Clark Street. The
Department of the Missouri,
which belongs to the Division
of the Missouri, and of which
the state of Illinois is a part, is
under command of Brig.-Gen.
Auger, with headquarters at
Fort Leavenworth, Kan.

The Illinois National Guard
is composed of two brigades of
infantry with cavalry and battery attachments. The law for
their organization and government went into effect in July,
1877. The First Brigade has
its headquarters in Chicago,

FIRST REGIMENT (INFANTRY) ARMORY, 24 JACKSON ST.

under command of Brig.-Gen. Chas. Fitz-Simons. His staff is composed of an adjt.-general, a judge advocate, inspector general, quar-
termaster general, commissary general, inspector of rifle practice,
surgeon, and two aides-de-camp. The brigade is composed of the
First Regiment of Infantry, Col. E. B. Knox; the Second Regiment
of Infantry, Col. H. A. Wheeler; the Third Regiment of Infantry, Col.
C. M. Brazee; the Fourth Regiment of Infantry, Col. Fred L. Ben-

net; the First Regiment of Cavalry, Lieut.-Col. Dominick Welter; Battery C, Maj. Wm. M. Wood; Battery D, Maj. Edgar P. Tobey. The armory of the First Infantry is at No. 24 Jackson Street, where drills are held nightly by one or the other of the companies. The building is of stone, rather massive in appearance, but not large enough to properly accommodate the regiment in drill. It is occupied on a ten years' lease. The Second Infantry occupy rooms at No. 179 Randolph Street. The armory of Battery D is a building 140×200 feet in size, at the corner of Michigan Avenue and Monroe Street. It was built by Battery D with contributions from citizens, and is well suited for their purpose. The armory of the First Cavalry is of the same size as that of Battery D, and adjoining it on Michigan Avenue. The brigade headquarters are also located in offices in this building. The State Guards hold a brigade encampment once a year. The brigade numbers about 2,500 men, about 1,500 of them located in Chicago. The state furnishes the guns and accoutrements, and allows each man $1 per day for four days' encampment, every year, and pays the armory rents. Further than this it does nothing, but the regiments and companies have held together in the hope that an appropriation would be secured, similar to those of New York and Pennsylvania. The local commands are largely composed of young men of excellent families. The Second Brigade, with headquarters at Springfield, consists of about the same number of men as the First Brigade, but has only one battery of artillery and no cavalry.

The **Chicago Light Infantry** (colored) was organized in 1879, and has been partially uniformed and equipped by the state. It consists of about sixty-five men at present, with Alex Brown as captain. The commanding officer of the State Guard has so far refused to recognize the company as a part of the regularly organized State Guard, principally on the ground of the disreputable character of its members.

The **Other Military Companies** are wholly independent organizations. Of these the

Hibernian Rifles are the oldest and decidedly the st ongest in numbers, consisting at present of seven companies, aggregating about 500 men, all of Irish descent and members of the Ancient Order of Hibernians. The headquarters are at No. 192 East Washington Street. The organization partakes largely of a social nature. John Kinsella is Lieut.-Col. commanding.

The **Clan-Na-Gael Guards** were first organized in 1875; afterward disbanded, and reorganized in 1882. They are now in a prosperous condition, own appropriate uniforms and guns, and have a balance in the treasury. Aside from its military character, the company looks to the social and benevolent interests of its sixty-eight members, who, like the Hibernian Rifles, are all Irishmen. Drills are held at 192 East Washington Street. The Captain is L. P. Buckley.

The Lackey Zouaves were organized by G. W. Lackey, who was colonel of an Illinois regiment in the late war, and from whom the Zouaves took their name, in May, 1877. Soon after the company's organization it was ordered to the assistance of the First Regiment of the State Guard, in the July riots of that year. Failing in health, Col. Lackey was succeeded as captain of the company about two years ago by W. W. Hammell. The latter gave up the position some months ago and at this writing (Sept., 1884,) the company is without a commander, and is practically inactive, though it is intact, and financially prosperous. There are at present thirty-five men, uniformed and otherwise equipped. The headquarters at present are at the office of J. Dalton, 181 Mnroe Street.

Parks and Boulevards.

THE PUBLIC AND PRIVATE PARKS AND SQUARES, THE BOULE-VARDS, AND DOUGLAS MONUMENT.

THE parks and boulevards of Chicago supply the great need of her teeming population for healthful recreation amid attractive surroundings, which all may enjoy with a feeling of common proprietorship. The smaller parks, although very beautiful and useful in their way, could not meet the wants of a city which had outgrown their capacity, and out of the demand for something larger and grander grew the magnificent system of parks and boulevards that to-day almost encircle the city. The initial steps toward this system, which was conceived on a scale of great magnitude, were taken some eighteen years ago, although no decisive measure was reached till some time later, when, through the efforts of public spirited citizens, the legislature began to pass bills for the establishment, control and maintenance of the parks, and the people, entering into the spirit of the improvement, accepted the burden of expense. From that time the development of the system, although not yet complete, has been one of the most remarkable of the many wonderful growths of Chicago, and but for the interruption of the great fire it would be much farther advanced than it now is. The system comprises a chain of parks, including Lincoln Park on the North Side, Humboldt, Garfield and Douglas Parks on the West Side, and Washington, Jackson and Gage Parks and Midway Plaisance on the South Side. The latter four and the northern portion of Lincoln Park lie outside of the present city limits. The combined area of these parks is 1,879 acres, and they are connected by boulevards complete or contemplated. Most of the land taken for this system of parks was located on the open prairie, with only bits of stunted timber here and there, and without natural advantages that could be utilized in preparing the attractive features of the landscapes. The lakes were dug, the variations in the surface were laboriously made, and, in fact, all the artistic designs are of artificial construction, and were wrought out with much toil and painstaking. Nearly all of the varied vegetation was procured by the transplanting of trees, plants and grasses from

C

other points, in many cases from other states, and it is only by constant labor under the direction of the highest skill that the parks have grown from a dead level of a treeless soil into landscapes of infinite variety and surpassing beauty. The boulevards are of uniform construction, paved with macadam, as a rule. Most of them are bordered with elms which have been taken from their native habitat and replanted here. The trees ranged from thirty to sixty feet in height at the time of their transplanting, and have since required infinite care to secure them against injurious effects from the change of soil and climate and prairie winds. They are generally set in grassy strips along the borders of the boulevards, between the outer edges of the sidewalks and the curbing, and when full grown will give the drives the appearance of broad country lanes. None of the parks, and but few boulevards are yet completed, although they are well advanced, and steadily progressing toward completion; but there are fountains and statuary, and many other features of ornamentation to be provided, and large unimproved portions of the parks to be brought under the hand of the landscape gardener. The boulevard park system consists of three divisions, corresponding to the divisions of the city in which they are located, each supported in whole or in part by a tax on its division, and managed by commissioners appointed by the state from among citizens of the highest standing in the community.

Lincoln Park, the oldest of the boulevard parks, lies in the North Side, between the lake and North Clark Street, stretching along the lake shore from North Avenue on the south to Diversey Avenue on the north, a distance of about one and a half miles. Twenty years ago the old Chicago Cemetery occupied the southern portion of the land, but as it was encroached upon by the city the ground was condemned for park purposes, and the bodies removed, as noted in the chapter on "The Burial Places." On a wooded knoll west of the main drive stands a square stone vault or mausoleum, enclosed with an iron fence and having over its somber portal the single word:

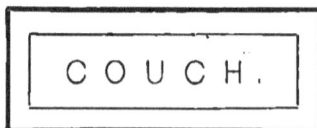

```
C O U C H .
```

Not far from this, and hidden amid shrubbery, is a family lot with broken gravestones and trampled mounds, the whole enclosed with

heavy stone curbing.   On a prostrate slab one reads this tender record
of a young mother and her child :

> REBECCA,
> WIFE OF
> ELIJAH PEACOCK.
> DIED
> FEBRUARY 10, 1850,
> Æ. 29 YEARS.
>
> ALSO, WILLIAM,
> THEIR SON,
> DIED FEB. 19, 1850, Æ. 8 MOS.
>
> SHE DIED IN BEAUTY, LIKE A ROSE
> BLOWN FROM ITS PARENT STEM;
> SHE DIED IN BEAUTY, LIKE A PEARL
> DROPPED FROM SOME DIADEM.

These are about all that remain to indicate the former use of the
ground.   The park at first contained about sixty acres, but it has since
been gradually extended until its area has grown to 250 acres.   Its
connection with the boulevard system dates from 1869, when the legislature provided for its maintenance and improvement, and appointed
its first Board of Commissioners.   The park has eight miles of drives,
nine miles of walks, seven bridges, two tunnels and twenty acres of
lake surface.   From the magnificent lake shore drive, which extends
from Oak Street to the northernmost limit of the park, the panorama
on either side is one of unrivaled beauty.   On the west is the park
with its succession of landscapes, each different from the others, yet
perfect in itself, and on the east is the lake flashing its ever-changing
hues upon the vision, its rippled surface dotted with sails and steamers,
and at night the red gleam of the lighthouses in the distance, and the
lights of the vessels that move fitfully about, and the weird moonlight
that, falling upon its dimpled face, is shivered into millions of radiant
beams.   There is a long artificial lake of some twelve acres in the
southern half of the park, and a smaller one of eight acres in the
northwest section.   The zoological department contains an interesting
collection of animals and birds.   The list embraces sea-lions, prairie
dogs, several varieties of bears, antelopes, buffalos, deer, foxes, rac-
coons, wolves, etc.   A young buffalo was born recently and this is said
to be the only known event of the kind while the mother was in cap-
tivity.   The floral department is a striking and attractive feature.

About 100,000 plants of different colors are displayed in beds artistically shaped and arranged, and the conservatories contain a large array of the most beautiful and curious tropical plants and flowers. A striking Indian group in bronze, life size and standing upon a massive granite pedestal, is the gift of Mr. Martin Ryerson. The Lincoln monument, provided for by the munificent legacy of $50,000 left by the late Eli Bates, of this city, is in progress under the able hands of Mr.

A SCENE IN LINCOLN PARK.

St. Gaudiens. When completed, it will be given a central location. It is conceded by judges of art who have inspected the design, that this will be one of the finest works of the kind ever erected to the memory of the eminent Illinoisan. The refectory, semi-Swiss in design, is located near the boat landing on the north border of the larger lake, on the line of the main drives. The park has a system of water-works of its own, which supplies a large and handsome drinking fountain for horses in the northern part, another on the lake shore drive, and innumerable hydrants and springs at almost every turn. There are two artesian wells, one near the animal quarters and the other on the northwest side. The park is illuminated at night by fifty arc electric lights, placed upon high poles. The music stand is located east of the ridge drive, and the expense of occasional summer concerts is defrayed mainly by contributions of citizens of the North Side. The south lawn is used for base-ball, cricket, lawn tennis, archery and military and police drills and parades. Along the west line is a fine promenade of granolith sixteen feet wide and 3,000 feet in length.

Humboldt Park is the most northern park in the city. It is situated four miles northwest from the City Hall, between West North Avenue on the north and Augusta Street on the south, with North Kedzie Avenue on the west and North California Avenue on the east. It is reached from the city by the Milwaukee Avenue and West North Avenue horse-car line; from the north by Humboldt Boulevard, and from the south by Central Boulevard. Lying out on the prairie, it is swept by the southwest winds which for so much of the year play over the city. It contains 200 acres and in many respects is one of the most charming parks in the city. It is densely covered in places with groups of trees, which show between them lawns and meadows in pleasing variety. The lakes are a special feature. They cover a large portion of the area, and afford excellent rowing. The boat landing is near the refreshment pavilion, and the band stand is conveniently situated for rowing parties to enjoy the Sunday concerts that constitute one of the great attractions of the park during the summer. There are a conservatory, cascades, grottoes and drinking fountains for men and animals. An artesian well 1,155 feet in depth yields water of high medicinal qualities, similar in many respects to the mineral waters of Garfield and Douglas Parks. The following is the analysis of a wine gallon of the water:

Chloride of Magnesium,	7.702 grains.		Carbonate of Iron, . . .	0.065 grains
Sulphate of Soda,	. . 23.211	"	Silicate of Soda,	, . . 0.763	"
Sulphate of Magnesia, .	4.132	"	Alumina,	. , ... traces.
Sulphate of Lime, . .	10.229	"	Sulphuretted Hydrogen,	faint traces.
Carbonate of Lime,	, 12.131	"	Organic Substances, . .	none.

TOTAL. 58.233 grains.

Free Carbonic Acid, ... 11.13 cubic inches.
Temperature at the Well, ... 63.5° Fahrenheit.

The lands for the park cost $241,157, without improvements.

Garfield Park was formerly known as Central Park, but after the death of President Garfield, that name was changed to the present one as a tribute to the memory of the illustrious dead. It is the most western park of the great encircling system, and lies from four to five miles west from the City Hall, stretching between Colorado Avenue on the south and West Kinzie Street on the north. It is reached by the Madison Street, Lake Street and Randolph Street car lines, and by Washington Boulevard. It contains 185 acres of ground, which cost, unimproved, $456,596. The seventeen-acre lake in the central part of the grounds has two miniature islands. The refreshment pavilion has breezy balconies and piazzas affording fine views. The boat landing is 300 feet in length. Over 30,000 plants are propagated in the conservatory every year. There is a handsome drinking fountain for horses, which was presented by the Illinois Humane Society, the cost of its construction being contributed by Mrs. Mancel Talcott. The artesian well, sunk to a depth of 2,200 feet, is a center of attraction. Hundreds of visitors go daily to drink the water, and many carry it away in bottles and jugs for home consumption. It is saline and chalybeate, and possessed of valuable medicinal properties for cases of anæmia, indigestion, diseases of the urinary organs, rheumatism and kindred complaints. The following is the analysis:

Chloride of Magnesium,	8.352 grains.		Sulphate of Soda,. . .	13.645 grains.
Chloride of Sodium, .	87.491	"	Silicate of Soda, . . .	0.508 "
Bromide of Magnesium,	0.301	"	Alumina. , , , . . .	traces.
Sulphate of Lime, . .	1.114	"	Organic Substances. . .	none.
Carbonate of Lime, . .	14.802	"	Sulphuretted Hydrogen,	none.
Carbonate of Iron, . .	0.712	"		

	TOTAL, 146.925 grains.
Free Carbonic Acid, ...	13.44 cubic inches.
Temperature at the Well, ...	71.4° Fahrenheit.

Water flows from the well at the rate of 150 gallons per minute. A pretty sight is a small cataract known as "miniature Niagara," falling from a basin on the top of the rocky grotto at the mouth of the well. There are wooden, stone and iron bridges, and different shaped lawns, with walks and drives, all of which are bordered with trees, beds of flowers, and all the other accessories of the landscape gardener's art. There are three miles of foot-paths and a driveway of about two miles. The southern portion of the park grounds, comprising sixty-seven acres, lying just south of Madison Street, is as yet unimproved, and has long been occupied as a driving park by the Central Driving Park Association.

Douglas Park, four miles southwest of the City Hall, lies on the open prairie. It is slightly smaller than either of the other West Side parks of the system, containing only 180 acres. It is west of

SCENES IN WASHINGTON PARK.

California Avenue, between Twelfth Street on the north and Nineteenth Street on the south. It is reached from the city by the Madison Street and Ogden Avenue horse-cars. Douglas Boulevard forms a connection with Garfield Park on the north. The park itself has numerous attractive features. The artesian well in an embowered grotto, feeds the lake, and is visited by many on account of the medicinal properties of its water, which is not, however, considered as valuable in that respect as the water from the well in Garfield Park. An analysis of the water shows that a wine gallon is composed as follows :

Chloride of Magnesium,	3.236	grains.
Chloride of Sodium, .	2.320	"
Sulphate of Soda, . .	28.321	"
Sulphate of Lime, . .	6.422	"
Carbonate of Lime, . .	11.149	"

Carbonate of Iron, . . .	0.103	grains.
Silicate of Soda, . . .	0.731	"
Alumina, ...	traces.	
Sulphuretted Hydrogen,	faint traces.	
Organic Substances, . .	none.	

TOTAL,	57.282 grains.
Free Carbonic Acid, ...	10.22 cubic inches.
Temperature at Well, ...	57.1 ° Fahrenheit.

The conservatory and propagating houses are spacious ; over 60,000 plants are transplanted from them every year. Grassy lawns are used for base ball and croquet playing. From the balconies of the unique refectory is had a fine view of the lake, eleven acres in extent, and the most striking vistas of the grounds. It is in Douglas Park that the Chinese congregate in the month of August to perform one of their religious ceremonies, which is celebrated by the flying of kites of the most curious shapes and patterns, many of them representing animals, which, perhaps, never existed save in the excited imaginations that pictured them. The original cost of the lands of Douglas Park was $241,157.

South Parks is the name by which Washington and Jackson Parks, connected by Midway Plaisance, are collectively known. The total cost of the ground for these parks, including expenses of quieting title, and ground for connecting boulevard, was $3,208,000.

Washington Park lies between six and seven miles south of the City Hall, and extends from Fifty-first to Sixtieth Streets, between Cottage Grove and Kankakee Avenues. It is more than a mile from the lake shore, contains 371 acres, and is reached by the State Street and Wabash Avenue cable-cars, over Indiana and Cottage Grove Avenues, by Michigan Avenue, Drexel and Grand Boulevards, and by the phaetons and the dummy line from Oakwood Boulevard. The artesian

THE STABLES

"THE CONSERVATORY"

"THE MOUND."

Scenes in Washington Park.

well is 1,643 feet deep, and the water is somewhat similar to that
of Garfield and Douglas Parks. It supplies a large portion of the
water required, some being drawn from Hyde Park. The conservatory
is a very handsome structure, 40×120 feet, containing a splendid collection of tropical plants, and there are nine spacious propagating
houses, and a cactus house. About 170,000 plants are set out annually.
One of the attractions of this park is the "Meadow," which contains
about 100 acres, and is belted by beautiful lines of timber. The
"Mere" is a winding lake of thirteen acres. The Park Retreat is a
wooden building three stories in height. It is of ornamental architecture, and is used as a restaurant, and for the offices of the local
management. The stable is one of the attractions. It is built of
stone in the form of a Greek cross, is 325×200 feet in its greatest
diameters, and will accommodate 100 horses. The portion allotted
to the horses is said to be the most complete thing of the kind in the
world. It is in the form of a circle, and the stalls are ranged in two
concentric rings with an alley between. The phaetons used for the
transportation of visitors to and through the parks are kept in this
building. The cost of the unique structure was $40,000. The phaeton
horses are all iron-gray, and are selected with a careful eye to their
beauty of form and adaptability to the service. Both Grand and
Drexel Boulevards are traversed by the phaetons, which make regular
trips at short intervals to Oakwood Boulevard for passengers, and the
number of persons carried during the season has reached 45,000,
and is steadily increasing. A prominent feature near the entrance of
Drexel Boulevard is a large drinking fountain for horses. Permits for
base ball, croquet, archery, etc., are always granted on proper application.

Jackson Park lies along the shore of Lake Michigan, between seven
and eight miles from the City Hall. It contains 593 acres, of which
84 are improved, and extends from Fifty-sixth to Sixty-seventh Streets,
Stony Island Avenue forming the western boundary. It is reached by
the dummy engine from Oakwood Boulevard, and by the phaetons
from the same point, all of which connect with South Side horse-cars,
and also by the Illinois Central trains. There are two broad covered
dancing platforms in the unimproved portion for picnic parties. The
system of interior lakes, covering 165 acres, is connected with Lake
Michigan by an inlet north of the pier. The lakes are of sinuous outline, with many small bays and inlets extending into the surrounding
grounds, and when finished as designed, will constitute the prominent

SCENE IN UNION PARK, WASHINGTON BOULEVARD AND OGDEN AVENUE.

feature of the park. The main entrance is at Fifty-seventh Street, where the visitor leaves the depot of the Illinois Central Railroad at South Park Station, and at once confronts the most charming scene, —spreading trees and beds of flowers in the summer, with a broad, open meadow beyond. From many points there are fine views of the park, and of Lake Michigan and its hundreds of amphibious craft. A break-water is in process of construction for the protection of the shore from erosion by the waves, and the beach is being laid with stone block pavement for the same purpose. The occasional summer concerts draw many visitors. Jackson is destined to be one of the finest and most attractive, as it is now the largest, of the boulevard parks.

Midway Plaisance extends from Jackson Park to Washington Park, between Fifty-ninth and Sixtieth Streets. It was intended to connect the two parks both by boulevard and basin, the latter uniting the lake systems of the parks, but it will be years before the costly design of the basin can be completed. It is one and one-tenth miles in length, and contains eighty acres. It is to be handsomely improved, and will be one of the pleasantest portions of the South Parks division.

Gage Park, the smallest of this system, is a neat park of twenty acres situated about four miles west of Washington Park, at the junction of Garfield and Western Avenue Boulevards.

The Other Parks are under the management of the city government. They are distributed miscellaneously throughout the city. In the West Division are Union, Jefferson, Wicker, Vernon, Congress and Campbell Parks. Union Park is nearly two miles west of the City Hall, on the line of Washington Boulevard, on the east side of Ashland Avenue and the south side of West Lake Street. It contains fourteen and four-fifths acres. It has a small lake, mounds, a fountain and several cages of animals, the most conspicuous of which is a monstrous grizzly bear. The park is not in good repair, owing to neglect, but is still an interesting place of resort. A movement is extant to have its management transferred to the West Chicago Park Commissioners, when it is hoped that its pristine beauty will be restored. Jefferson Park is about one and a half miles south and west from the City Hall, occupying one large block of five and a half acres, bounded by Adams, Throop, Monroe and Loomis Streets. It has a lake, a fountain and a grotto, and is a very charming little feature of the vicinity. Vernon Park lies nearly two miles southwest of the City Hall, stretching along the north side of West Polk Street, between Center Avenue and Loomis Street, and contains nearly four acres. Wicker Park lies three miles northwest of the City Hall, and one block south of Milwaukee Avenue, within the angle formed by the junction of Park, North Robey and Fowler Streets, and contains four acres attractively arranged. Congress and Campbell Parks contain seven-tenths and one-half acre, respectively. In the North Side, Washington Square, containing two and a quarter acres prettily laid out, lies between North Clark Street and Dearborn Avenue, and Washington and Lafayette Places. Union Square contains a half acre. It forms the northwest quarter of the block bounded by Goethe, Scott, Astor and Stone Streets. In the South Side is Lake Park, the largest of the city parks. It extends from Randolph to Twelfth Street, between Michigan Avenue and the strip of ground along the lake shore occupied by the Illinois Central Railroad. It contains forty-one acres, has some small trees and some walks and benches, but is not much frequented except by idlers. Dearborn Park is simply an open half-square without cultivation, on the west line of Michigan Avenue, between Washington and Randolph Streets. Groveland and Woodlawn Parks are contiguous, lying between Cottage Grove Avenue and the lake,

DOUGLAS MONUMENT.

near Thirty-fifth Street, and each contains four and a half acres of ground. The former is a picturesque wood of ancient-looking elms, vine-covered and threaded with shady walks. Opposite these parks, on the west side of Cottage Grove Avenue, are the grounds of the Chicago University, which, together with those of the parks, were donated by that gifted citizen of Illinois, Senator Stephen A. Douglas, whose family mansion occupied the immediate vicinity for many years prior to his death. The mausoleum containing the remains of the Senator is located on a plat of ground bordering upon Woodlawn Park, near the eastern terminus of Douglas Avenue, and overlooking Lake Michigan. Towering above the mausoleum to the height of 104 feet is a noble monument in memory of the distinguished statesman, orator and citizen. Surmounting this is an admirable and very life-like bronze statue of Mr. Douglas, executed by the Chicago artist, Leonard Volk. The mausoleum and shaft are of granite. At the corners are four bronze female figures, seated on granite pedestals, each inscribed with the character respectively represented, viz: "Illinois," "History," "Justice," "Eloquence." The marble sarcophagus in the crypt bears on its side the following inscription: ·

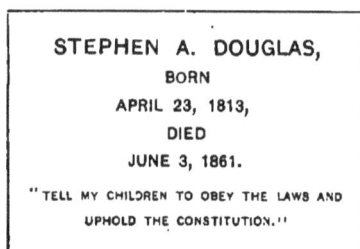

STEPHEN A. DOUGLAS,
BORN
APRIL 23, 1813,
DIED
JUNE 3, 1861.

"TELL MY CHILDREN TO OBEY THE LAWS AND
UPHOLD THE CONSTITUTION."

The cost of this magnificent tribute of respect was about $100,000. Ellis Park is a pleasant little place of three and three-eighths acres, lying four miles south of the court-house, between Cottage Grove and Vincennes Avenues, at the Thirty-seventh Street crossing. Aldine Square, at Thirty-seventh Street and Vincennes Avenue, is an enclosed park of one and a half acres, handsomely arranged, and, like Groveland and Woodlawn Parks, surrounded by elegant and costly mansions. All three, too, are maintained in the same manner, viz: by special tax levied for the purpose on abutting property.

Michigan Avenue Boulevard commences at Jackson Street and extends south for about three and one-fourth miles to Thirty-fifth Street. It is 100 feet wide and is completed its entire length. It is a fashionable drive, one of the finest in the country, and runs through one of the richest residence sections of the South Side.

Thirty-fifth Street Boulevard commences at the south end of Michigan Avenue Boulevard, and extends eastward about one-third of a mile, where it connects with Grand Boulevard. It is sixty-six feet wide, and is completed its entire length.

Grand Boulevard commences at its junction with the east end of Thirty-fifth Street Boulevard, and extends directly south for a distance of two miles, where it enters the northwest corner of Washington Park. It is 198 feet wide and has a broad central driveway which runs between wide grass-strips bearing double rows of trees. Outside of these are roadways thirty-three feet wide, the one on the east being for traffic and that on the west for equestrians. Along the outer borders of the roadways are strips of grass bearing single rows of trees, and outside of these are the footways with a line of trees along the outer

THE COTTAGE.

border of each. There are many handsome residences along the boulevard, and others in course of construction, and in favorable weather it is thronged with people of both sexes on horseback and in vehicles.

Oakwood Boulevard commences at Grand Boulevard and Thirty-ninth Street, and extends eastward a half mile to the north end of Drexel Boulevard. It is 100 feet wide, and is completed its entire length. At its junction with Drexel Boulevard stands "The Cottage," a very handsome building erected by the South Park commissioners as a waiting-room for passengers desiring to take the phaetons or the dummy train for South Parks.

Drexel Boulevard is the gem of the boulevard system. It commences at the east end of Oakwood Boulevard and running south parallel with Grand Boulevard to Fifty-second Street, turns east for one block and enters Washington Park one square south of its northern boundary. It is 200 feet wide and 1.48 miles long, and has 3.05 miles of completed driveways. There is a broad central strip throughout the entire length, planted with trees and shrubbery, and ornamented with sinuous walks and grass plats and beds and borders of flowers, and foliage plants, in various designs, among which a magnificent flower-decked elevation known as "The Mound," shown in the illustration on page 89, attracts universal attention. There is also, near the park end, a wonderful triumph of the florist's art in the shape of an elephant, composed of growing cacti, and remarkably correct in outline. At Fifty-first Street stands the splendid fountain donated by the Messrs. Drexel, of Philadelphia, in honor of whom the boulevard was named. Along either side of the central space is a broad driveway as level and smooth as a floor, and thronged on pleasant evenings with vehicles containing representatives of the wealth and fashion of the city, many of them occupants of the handsome villas

DREXEL FOUNTAIN.

along the boulevard, or owners of others that are being erected there. Drexel Boulevard was modeled after Avenue l' Imperatrice, Paris, and with the highest order of taste in design, and of skill in execution, nothing has been omitted that could add to its attractiveness, and it is conceded that it surpasses its prototype.

Garfield Boulevard is planned on a grand scale. Its design is similar to that of Grand Boulevard, having a broad central driveway with a row of trees and grass plats and shrubbery on either side, outside of which are roadways for traffic and for equestrian exercise, the whole plan being laid with'n a lane of elms. It is 200 feet wide, and has a total length of three and one-half miles, and the ways thus far completed aggregate three and three-fourths miles in length. It leaves

Washington Park at Fifty-fifth Street, and extends west along the line of that street to Gage Park, through which it connects with

Western Avenue Boulevard, which is also planned on a similar scale and of kindred design with Grand Boulevard. It is 200 feet wide, and runs directly north from Gage Park to the Illinois & Michigan Canal, a distance of nearly three miles, but only a little over three-fourths of a mile of roadway is completed. The plan contemplates its extension from its present terminus north to Thirty-first Street, west to California Avenue, north to Laughton Street, west to Sacramento Avenue, and north to Douglas Park, thus completing the connection between the South Side and West Side divisions of the system by a line of boulevards, which, when finished, will not have its equal in the world. Negotiations are in progress for the purchase of the ground for this extension.

Douglas Boulevard, "L" shaped, 250 feet in width and one and three-fourths miles in length, connects Douglas and Garfield Parks, entering the former from the west and the latter from the south. Its plan is essentially the same as that of Central Boulevard. The driveway has been completed, but few shade trees have yet been set out, and floral ornamentation has not been introduced. Open prairie abounds along its entire length. The original cost of the land was $27,569. Improvements are constantly being made, and Douglas promises to become one of the most fashionable and popular boulevards on the West Side.

Central Boulevard constitutes the connecting link between Garfield and Humboldt Parks. It is a little over a mile and a half in length, and has an average width of 250 feet. The completed driveway, thirty-eight feet wide, is bordered on either side by a slender lawn, with a "bridle path" running along within its outer edge, and fringed with rows of elms. The viaduct arching the tracks of the Chicago, Milwaukee & St. Paul Railway, affords a good view of the surrounding country.

Humboldt Boulevard is as yet little more than a country road. It has been partially graded by owners of adjoining property, and a few trees have been set out, under the direction of the park commissioners. The boulevard proper is 250 feet in width, but it embraces in its plan Palmer Place, 400×1750 feet and Logan Square, some 400×800 feet. Its total length is about three miles. It connects Humboldt Park with a proposed boulevard from Chicago River to Lincoln Park. The land was acquired at a cost of nearly $32,000.

7

Washington Boulevard was constructed upon that portion of Washington Street extending from Halsted Street through Union Park to Garfield Park, a distance of about three and one-fourth miles. It is bordered for nearly its entire length with handsome residences, many of them having fine lawns and rows of shade trees in front. It is 100 feet wide in its western extension, and is a fine, broad driveway in all i s parts, although not of uniform width. It is to the West Side what Michigan Avenue Boulevard is to the South Side, being the most popular drive in its section of the city.

Lake Shore Drive, though not a boulevard in the strict sense of the term, is a part of the boulevard system. It extends from Oak Street, a little north of the North Side water works, to Lincoln Park, of which it really forms a part, and thence it continues along the lake shore to the northernmost park limits. It is three-fourths of a mile in length to its entrance into the park proper. Its total width is 200 feet, and the driveway, completed, 100 feet. It will be extended south from Oak Street to the river, as a boulevard, grants for that purpose having passed the Common Council and been accepted by the park commissioners.

Charity and Benevolence.

THE HOSPITALS, ASYLUMS, HOMES, AND OTHER CHARITABLE, BENEVOLENT AND HUMANE ORGANIZATIONS.

WITH all her pride of power and material wealth, Chicago does not neglect the claims of humanity, but cultivates the various lines of humane endeavor as ardently as if they were channels of trade, and endows them as liberally as if they were commercial institutions. This is demonstrated by her great public charities, and by the number of her organizations for special relief purposes. There is scarcely any form of human suffering or need, present or contingent, but finds its remedy in her hospitals, dispensaries, asylums, homes, or one of the many associations for the help of others or for mutual aid.

The **Chicago Relief and Aid Society** was organized under special act of the legislature in February, 1857. The main object was to aid such of the poor as through sickness or other misfortune require temporary assistance. It was not the intent to extend aid to the permanently needy, nor to assist any until proven worthy. Able-bodied applicants are assisted in finding employment, and in other cases money and clothing are provided. Rules of the society provide that no loan shall be made from the funds; that no person who receives aid shall ask alms of the public; and those receiving aid shall be regarded as entitled to assistance until careful investigation shall prove to the contrary. The affairs of the society are managed by a board of directors selected from prominent business men, and this board reports annually to the City Council. It owns the Chicago Relief and Aid Society Building, in which its offices are located. During the period of extreme suffering which followed the great fire of 1871, the society found its energies taxed to their utmost capacity, and its system of relief subjected to the severest possible test, but, although the scope of its operations was extended considerably beyond the original purpose of the organization, it passed the ordeal with remarkable success. The millions which flowed into the city in the shape of money and supplies, from all civilized portions of the globe, were mostly turned over to the society for distribution, and it thus had over one hundred thousand homeless people to provide with shelter and food, and extensive needs in other directions to supply. An executive committee and sub-committees were organized, and the great work was commenced and carried on systematically. The labor was incessant, but the service was marked with surprising celerity, considering the care necessary to insure a judicious execution of the trust. In less than three years the society disbursed nearly four and a half millions of dollars. Of this the shelter committee expended nearly one million in building and furnishing more than 9,000 houses; $250,000 were paid out for sewing machines, and tools for mechanics and laborers; $300,000 for fuel for families; and more than $500,000 were distributed by the medical department and the committee on charitable institutions. May 1, 1874, there was left of about five millions received for the aid of the victims of the conflagration, something over a half million of dollars. This has been quietly and carefully disbursed, and when the final account was rendered Jan. 1, 1884, not a dollar of the vast sum commonly known as "the fire fund," was reported lost or misappropriated. The society then announced that, its stewardship of this fund having ended, it must thereafter confine its operations within the original scope of its organization. Charles G. Truesdell, the superintendent, has for many years ably filled that difficult and responsible position.

The Old People's Home was founded in 1861, as the "Old Ladies' Home," through the efforts of Miss Caroline Smith, who afterward bequeathed to it about $1,000 and two lots of ground. In 1864 a house was purchased, but it afforded accommodations for only eleven inmates, and after the fire of 1871 it was totally inadequate to the legitimate demands upon its room. The Chicago Relief and Aid Society then came to its assistance with a donation of $50,000, stipulating that there should be no discrimination as to sex, race, nationality, or religious belief, and that the donors should have the right to name one inmate for every $2,500 given. The conditions were accepted, and the institution was accordingly reorganized in May, 1872, under its present title. A commodious three story building was erected on Indiana Avenue near Thirty-ninth Street, and was occupied, with nineteen old ladies, Nov. 25, 1874. It has capacity for eighty inmates, and the average number in the Home is sixty-six. The value of this property is $70,000; of the property previously occupied, $5,000; there are endowments amounting to $34,857; and the institution is free from debt. Its annual expenses are something over $10,000, the bulk of which is met by contributions. All the inmates are old ladies, the plan being to erect a duplicate building for the use of old men. Admission is restricted to persons of good character, who have been residents of Chicago for two years, are sixty years of age, in indigent circumstances, and have no children able to provide for them. In special cases persons fifty-five years of age are admitted by a vote of the board of managers. All admissions are on six months' probation, at the expiration of which permanent residence may be accorded or refused, and if granted is liable to be canceled at any time, for cause. An admission fee of $300 is required in each case, and inmates must furnish their own rooms. The board of managers consists of thirty ladies of high social standing, and there is a board of nine trustees composed of citizens prominent in charitable work. There are also a matron, and a physician and assistant physician.

The Foundlings' Home is one of the most noted charities in Chicago. It had its birth in the humane impulses of Dr. Geo. E. Shipman. On the 31st of January, 1871, the Home was opened at No. 54 South Green Street. Two months later a removal was effected to roomier quarters at Sangamon and Randolph Streets, and in May, 1872, a donation of $10,- 000 was accepted from the Chicago Relief and Aid Society, the Home was incorporated, and the present main building commenced. It is on Wood

FOUNDLINGS' HOME.

Street, just south of Madison, and cost, with the ground, about $50,000, the Relief Society adding $20,000 to its previous donation. It was occupied in May, 1874. It is built of light brick, is cruciform, with a front of 40 feet and a depth of 60 feet, is three stories in height with attic and basement, and contains about forty rooms. In 1883 a new wing was built on adjacent grounds. It is of red brick, sixty-two by forty feet, five stories high, and connected with the main building by an annex. It contains nine dormitories, eight rooms for hospital purposes, the rooms of the superintendent and his family and of the lady assistants, etc. These buildings have a capacity for more than 100 inmates. Many of the babies are adopted into reputable Christian families, eighty-two being so placed last year. Of about 5,000 infants received since the Home was opened, 890 were adopted, 1,097 were returned on the application of their parents, and 2,992 died. Nursing mothers are also given shelter. The current expenses are about $6,000 per annum, the money for which, as well as for the grounds, buildings, etc., is all received by voluntary contribution. The founder, George E. Shipman, M. D., is secretary and superintendent.

The **Servite Sisters' Industrial Home for Girls** was established by the Servite Sisters in a small way, in May, 1877. The location is 1396 West Van Buren Street. The object is the care of homeless and destitute children from nine to eighteen years of age, who come of their own accord or are brought by parents or sent by the courts. They are taught all kinds of work for which they have capacity, in the forenoon, and in the afternoon they are taught the common English branches. The building is a substantial brick of five stories and basement, with three wings two and three stories high. It cost, with the grounds, about $40,000, and belongs to the Sisters who occupy and manage it. The institution is supported by contributions of money and clothing, by the sale of manufactured articles, and by interest on invested funds, each of the eighteen Sisters having $2,000 or upwards in United States bonds, the income from which is devoted to that purpose. The average number of non-paying inmates is about thirty-five. Some 300 have passed through the Home, three having died. Sister Mary Francis is Mother Superior.

St. Joseph's Home for the Friendless and Industrial School for Girls, is located at 409 and 411 South May Street. It was founded and incorporated in 1878, as a place of refuge for respectable young girls who are temporarily out of employment. It is a Catholic institution, and is supported mainly by the laundry, the dress-making department, and the income from those who are able to pay their board. The building is the property of the association, is of brick, four stories in height, with a basement and capacity for the accommodation of 100, which is about the average number of inmates. The value of the property is $14,500; the annual expenses $11,000; and the number of inmates received per annum about 1,000.

The **Chicago Hospital for Women and Children,** corner of Paulina and West Adams Streets, was founded in February, 1865, mainly through the efforts of Dr. Mary Harris Thompson. Its objects are to afford a home for women and children among the respectable poor in need of medical and surgical aid; to treat the same classes at home by an assistant physician ; to afford a free dispensary for the same, and to train competent nurses. The hospital passed through many vicissitudes, including the great fire, after which it located on its present site, purchased for it by the Chicago Relief and Aid Society at a cost of $25,000, and given on condition that twenty-five patients, named by the society, should be cared for free of charge. The grounds are spacious, measuring 150 by 80 feet, but the house, formerly a private residence, is only large enough to accommodate twenty-five patients and the necessary attendants. Some $30,000 have been raised and work commenced on a new building on the same lot, to accommodate eighty to one hundred patients. There is a free dispensary, and many thousands of patients have received treatment, in the hospital and at their homes. The institution is not endowed, but is supported through the unselfish efforts of the lady managers, aided by small sums received from paying patients and the proceeds of occasional entertainments. It is out of debt and has a balance in its treasury. It is conducted wholly by women. The "Board of Councilors," or managers, is composed of thirty prominent ladies; the medical staff consists of experienced lady physicians, with Mary Harris Thompson, M. D., at the head, and there is a consulting staff of gentlemen well known as able practitioners. Mrs. J. C. Hilton is president.

The Newsboys' and Bootblacks' Association was founded in 1868 for the purpose of supplying a Home for such of the indigent boys of the streets as were disposed to earn their own living. The association was incorporated in December, 1874. The building is at 146 Quincy Street. The funds for its construction were raised by subscription. It is of brick, four stories in height, with a basement, and contains offices, dining-room, wash-rooms, rooms for officers, and dormitories with single beds for 100 boys. There are two schools, one in the daytime for the smaller boys, and one in the evening for the larger ones. A special feature of the institution is the Newsboys' Sunday school, at which the average attendance is 235. The property is held in the name of three trustees, and the Home is supported by small sums paid by the boys for food and lodging, and by contributions from various sources. The average number of boys in attendance is fifty, and the average annual cost of the maintenance of each boy is about $150. W. H. Rand is president.

The Chicago Home for the Friendless was founded for the purpose of extending assistance to worthy indigent women and children. The association was organized in March, 1858, and incorporated in February, 1859. · It first occupied a frame building on West Randolph Street, but in 1869 was removed to its present location at the corner of Wabash Avenue and Twentieth Street. Jonathan Burr donated one lot, and George Smith two, for the site of the building, and liberal contributions enabled the association to erect the structure. In 1868 an addition was built, Jonathan Burr contributing $5,000 toward the cost and subsequently $5,000 more to furnish it. In 1880 the Home

HOME FOR THE FRIENDLESS.

received the munificent bequest of $87,000 from the estate of H. H. Taylor, deceased, with a portion of which another addition was built, and is known as "The Taylor Memorial." The building and its additions are quite extensive. They are of red brick, have four stories and an attic, and contain upwards of 100 rooms, including dormitories, work-rooms, school-rooms, kindergarten, play-room, nurseries, bath-rooms, lavatories, literary department, domestic department, infirmary, dispensary—in fact they are in every respect admirably arranged for the purpose they were intended to serve. A fire-escape communicates with every floor. The Home school, which has an industrial class, is supported mainly by the income of a bequest of the late Jonathan Burr, of which the Home is trustee. Particular attention is paid to instruction in household work. Children of proper age who have been surrendered to the Home, or are otherwise entirely at its disposal, are, on application, placed in Christian families where ample assurance is given that they will be kindly treated and properly reared. The management is under a numerous board of managers, composed of six ladies from the city and one or more ladies from the congregation of each of the city churches, except Catholic. A recent report shows that the number of admissions for the year was 1,802, of which 1,072 were adults, and 730 were children. The number of children surrendered to the Home was 173, and the number placed in permanent homes was 105. The expenses for the same year were $16,962.74, of which $13,102 were paid from the proceeds of investments. A little paper, called the *Home Visitor*, is published in the interest of the institution. Much outside work is also done under the supervision of the Home patrons. Sick and needy are visited and assisted. Temperance movements are encouraged, etc., etc. Mrs. M. H. Moudy is matron and superintendent.

The **Burr Mission**, which consists of an "Industrial School, Mission School and Free Chapel," was founded by the late Jonathan Burr, in 1868, and was first located at the corner of Fourteenth Street and Third Avenue. In 1880 it was removed to the corner of Twenty-third Street and Wentworth Avenue, a new and commodious brick building having been erected for it, with large chapel and Sabbath-school accommodations, at a cost of $11,500. There is a spacious reading-room, stocked with magazines and newspapers, and the day school is in a very flourishing condition, the enrollment for 1883 showing fifty-one boys and sixty-three girls, with an average attendance of fifty. A kindergarten was successfully opened in the same year. The Chicago Home for the Friendless is the trustee for the Mission in perpetuity, and the latter is under the sole management of the officers of the Home. The objects of the Mission are the religious and secular education of the poor.

The **House of the Good Shepherd**, under charge of the Sisters of the Good Shepherd, is an asylum for women and female children. The building stands in a large enclosure, on the corner of North Market and Hurlbut Streets. It is five stories in height, and well arranged and equipped for the work. The asylum was established in May, 1859. The first building was destroyed by fire, and the present building was erected at a cost of $70,000. In a niche in the front stands a stone figure of heroic dimensions, representing the Good Shepherd carrying the lost sheep. The total value of the property is $200,000. The work of the institution is largely reformatory. There are five departments, each kept apart from the others, viz: The penance reformatory for grown persons; the juvenile reformatory for young persons; the industrial school; the Magdalen asylum, and Our Sisters' community. School and religious exercises are held daily in each department. There are accommodations for 400 inmates, and an average attendance of about 350. All are received, whatever their record; some at their own request, and others sent by friends or the city. The institution is self-supporting, apart from the trifle it gets from the city, and small amounts paid by boarders, earning its income with the laundry and the needle. Subscriptions are very rarely solicited. There are some fifty-five children between the ages of five and ten years, and about thirty old women who are unable to do any work. The annual expenses are $31,000. There are thirty-six Sisters engaged in the establishment, of whom Sister Angelique is Mother Superior, and Sister Mary, of the Nativity, assistant.

The **Orphan Asylum of the Guardian Angel** was established in 1867 by a German Catholic orphan society organized in 1865. In 1872 the "Guardian Angel German Catholic Society" was incorporated and took charge of the institution. The building was burned Oct. 23, 1879, and the present structure was erected on the site at a cost of $35,000. The grounds embrace forty-nine acres, and the property is valued at $50,000. The asylum has 130 inmates, and is managed by a sisterhood known as the "Poor Handmaids of Jesus Christ." A monthly publication, conducted by Mr. L. Biehl, is issued in behalf of the institution. Rev. J. Essing is president.

The **Michael Reese Hospital** is maintained and managed by the Hebrew Relief Association. It is located on the corner of Twenty-ninth Street and Groveland Avenue, and is a very handsome and capacious structure, with four stories and basement. It was erected from a fund provided by the will of the late Michael Reese. This fund amounted to $90,000, of which $40,000 were devoted to the building, and the remainder invested as an endowment. There is no test of faith in admissions, and both male and female patients are received. Over 500 are admitted to the hospital annually. The first hospital of the Association was erected in 1866, at the corner of LaSalle and Chilli Streets. It was destroyed by fire in 1871, and until the present building was occupied in October, 1881, the association placed its patients in other hospitals.

The Illinois Charitable Eye and Ear Infirmary was founded in 1858 by Dr. Edward L. Holmes, who has been professionally associated with the institution ever since. It was incorporated in 1865, and up to the period of the fire was a private charity, aided by small annual appropriations from the state. Among the incorporators were

THE ILLINOIS CHARITABLE EYE AND EAR INFIRMARY.

some of the best known philanthropists of Chicago. It was first located on East Pearson Street, but after its destruction, the Chicago Relief and Aid Society gave the present site on the corner of West Adams and Peoria Streets, and the state appropriated the necessary funds for the erection and equipment of the institution, on the trustees conveying to it the entire property. It was opened to the public in 1874. The object is to provide gratuitous board and medical and surgical treatment for indigent residents of the state who are afflicted with diseases of the eye and ear. The building is a four-story brick, 104 × 50 feet, with basement, and an L about 40×30 feet. The chapel, stables, and wards for contagious diseases occupy detached positions. The main building contains a complete domestic department, office, laboratory, clinical, operating, public and private rooms, wards for patients, etc. The institution will accommodate about 150 inmates at a time, and over 400 are admitted annually. There is a dispensary provided for the gratuitous treatment of outside eye and ear patients, in which between 2,000 and 3,000 persons are treated annually. The daily average of the infirmary and dispensary combined is nearly 150 patients, and the total number of treatments since the institution was established is about 100,000. The surgical and medical departments of the infirmary are in charge of competent and experienced medical gentlemen. E. C. Lawton is superintendent.

The **Chicago Orphan Asylum,** 2228 Michigan Avenue, is popularly known as the Protestant Orphan Asylum. It is under Protestant management, but children are admitted without regard to creed. It is one of the oldest charitable institutions in the city, and was organized Nov. 5, 1849, to relieve, protect, educate and provide means of support for orphaned and destitute children. The present location was occupied in 1853. The building was erected by subscriptions at a cost of about $20,000, and has 192 inmates. Recent additions give accommodations for 250 children. There is a day school divided into primary, secondary and and kindergarten departments. Children may be given out for adoption, or, after reaching the age of twelve years, may be indentured to any respectable service. The institution is supported by contributions and by the rentals of eight handsome brick dwellings on the grounds, and by the income from invested funds and minor resources. Among the handsome donations and bequests it has received was $12,000 for the additions to the building above mentioned, from Mrs. Mary H. Talcott, and an endowment of $5,000 from the same liberal hand to provide shoes for the children. Also bequests from the late Jonathan Burr of $11,760; Flavel Mosely, $10,000; Col. J. L. James, $5,000; Allan C. Lewis, $4,000. William A. Brown and Thomas Church have each given $1,000, and the Chicago Relief and Aid Society donated $10,000. A board of eleven trustees, with an advisory board, manage the general business, while the internal management is directed by a board of forty ladies. A competent medical staff looks after the physical welfare of the children without charge. Mrs. Norman T. Gassette is president of the lady managers; Mrs. Henry S. Fitch and Miss Sarah M. Horton, secretaries; Mrs. B. W. Kendall, treasurer.

The **Home for Incurables** was incorporated May 26, 1880, and was opened for the reception of patients in January, 1881. The building, a two-story brick, was formerly a private residence. It stands on a lot of two acres at the corner of Racine and Fullerton Avenues. The institution provides a home for all classes of incurables. About thirty-five patients can be accommodated at a time. Those who are unable to pay are admitted free. Applicants must have resided in Cook County for at least twelve months. The Home is supported mainly by voluntary contributions.

The Hospital of the Alexian Brothers, 569 North Market Street, represents the first establishment of the order in America. In 1866 the Brothers occupied a small frame at Dearborn and Schiller Streets, and in 1869 moved into a larger frame they had built on the present site, which embraces ten lots, extending back to Franklin Street.

THE HOSPITAL OF THE ALEXIAN BROTHERS.

After the fire of 1871 the spacious building now occupied was erected at a cost of $45,000. It has ample accommodations for 100 patients, and 115 to 120 have been cared for at one time. The average number of inmates is ninety, and over 1,000 are received annually. Only men are admitted, but there is a dispensary in connection which is open to the sick and needy of both sexes. There is no discrimination as to creed or nationality. Many patients are sent in by the city, but the expenses, which amount to about $18,000 per annum, are met wholly by subscriptions solicited by two of the Brothers. The entire property, valued at about $75,000, belongs to the Alexian Brothers. Bro. Philip Kraener is rector and superior.

Uhlich Evangelical Orphan Asylum (German) had its inception about fifteen years ago, having been established in 1869 through the efforts of the Rev. Joseph Hartman, the present president. The asylum was first located on North Clark Street, but was swept away by the fire of 1871. Soon afterward the buildings now occupied, at the corner of Burling and Center Streets, were erected, the Chicago Relief and Aid Society contributing $20,000 for the purpose. There are two buildings. The asylum proper is a three story structure with base dimensions of 50×75 feet. A one story building, 25×50 feet, is used for dining-room and other purposes. The spacious grounds, consisting of eleven lots, constitute play-grounds for the children. About sixty German orphans, of both sexes, at present find homes at the institution, this being the average number of inmates. The asylum property is valued at $46,000, and the annual expenses are $6,000. The well-known philanthropist, Carl Gottfried Uhlich, who had been its most liberal supporter, made a valuable donation of forty-eight city lots to the asylum, the revenues from which aid materially in its maintenance. Christian Mauermann is the superintendent.

The Woman's Hospital of Chicago, 118 Thirty-fifth Street, was founded in 1870 as the "Woman's Hospital of the State of Illinois," by Dr. Reeves Jackson, who was its surgeon-in-chief for about ten years. The property occupied is leased, but a fund is being raised for the erection of a building at the corner of Rhodes Avenue and Thirty-second Street, where a large lot has been purchased, and another adjoining is in negotiation. The institution is specially devoted to the treatment of the diseases and accidents peculiar to women, irrespective of creed, color, or condition in life; the clinical instruction of students in medicine, and the practical training of nurses. Patients are treated in the hospital and outside, and the expenses, amounting to about $9,000 per annum, are met by paying patients' fees and donations. It has accommodations for about thirty-five patients, with an average of thirty, and an annual aggregate of 208 inmates. The Board of Trustees and Board of Managers are both composed of ladies of social prominence, and there is an able medical staff of seven visiting members. Miss E. Lunt is matron.

The Maurice Porter Memorial Hospital, at the corner of Belden Avenue and North Halsted Street, was founded in 1882 by Mrs. Julia Porter, in memory of her dead son. Its object is the care of sick and injured children, for whom it has accommodations to the number of ten. The cost is all borne by Mrs. Porter. Miss Jennie Gilmore is matron.

The Home for the Aged of the Little Sisters of the Poor was founded in 1876, with the view of providing a home for destitute men and women over sixty years of age and of good moral character. It was incorporated in 1881. No distinction is made as to creed or nationality. The building, which was erected in 1880, occupies a large lot at the corner of Throop and Harrison Streets. It is four stories in height, has well-furnished accommodations for 140 persons, and averages about 125 inmates. The male and female departments are separate. The Home is supported by contributions, and the property is nearly paid for. Sister Mary, of St. Helena, is Mother Superior.

St. Joseph's Hospital, established by the Sisters of Charity in 1869, is located at 360 Garfield Avenue. The building, which was erected in 1872, is a four story brick, with accommodations for eighty patients and an average attendance of about sixty. No applicant is barred on account of sex or creed, the hospital being arranged in male and female departments. Patients who are able are expected to pay for admission and treatment ; otherwise they are received free. Patients are sometimes sent by the city, but the institution is supported by the pay patients, from contributions and from occasional fairs. The medical staff is composed of eminent physicians and surgeons. Sister Mary Cephas is in charge.

ST. JOSEPH'S HOSPITAL.

St. Luke's Free Hospital, one of the noted institutions of the city, originated with a few benevolent ladies, during the civil war, in an effort to care for the sick prisoners and soldiers at Camp Douglas. In 1864 it was started as a free hospital for the sick poor, and has reached its present eminence and prosperity after many trials and removals. It is under Episcopalian control and management, but no distinction is made in admission on account of sect, sex, or nationality. In May, 1871, a location was purchased at 1434 Indiana Avenue. A year later the Chicago Relief and Aid Society donated a considerable sum and a tract of ground on State Street near Thirty-seventh. In 1881 Mr. N. K. Fairbank gave 100 feet on Indiana Avenue adjoining the hospital grounds on the north, which was extended back to seventy feet frontage on Michigan Avenue by subsequent purchases from contributions. The erection of a spacious new hospital on the Indiana Avenue front was at once commenced. It consists of four handsome buildings, costing $130,000, on the ground donated by Mr. Fairbank, all connected by corridors, and a fifth to be hereafter erected on the old hospital site adjoining. These are to be followed by a building on the Michigan Avenue front, which will be allotted to the administrative department of the institution, and constitute the main entrance. In addition to the wards in the new building, the plan provides for a chapel, amphitheaters for clinics and autopsies, and all the accessories of the best modern hospitals. Large subscriptions have been made to the building fund by many well-known citizens, the largest amounts being $25,000 from Tolman Wheeler, and $25,000 from the W. B. Ogden estate. Six of the beds are permanently endowed with interest-bearing investments of $3,000 and upwards each, and eighteen are supported by annual contributions of $300 each from various sources. Annually on St. Luke's Day a collection is taken up for the hospital in all the Episcopal churches of the city. The management have $32,381.77 at interest, and the property is valued at over $185,000. A recent annual report places the receipts at $17,094.75 ; expenditures, $15,413.49 ; patients admitted, 403 ; discharged, 360 ; deaths, 35 ; births, 33 ; and 1,372 patients were treated the same year in St. Luke's Free Dispensary, which was opened in the hospital building in 1871, and is under the same management. The medical staff of the hospital and dispensary is composed of men of high standing in the profession, who give their services gratuitously. Rev. Clinton Locke, D. D., is president and superintendent.

The **Lakeside Summer Sanitarium**, at the foot of Twenty-fifth Street, was founded in 1883 by the president, Mrs. B. Shoeneman. It provides nursing and care for infant children of the poor, during the hot days of summer, while teething, and suffering with diseases peculiar to their age and the season. Proper food and baths are given, also experienced medical attention, and clothing when necessary. Nearly 1,000 children were cared for during the summer of 1884. The institution is supported by voluntary contributions. Mrs. N. R. Stone is secretary and treasurer.

The **Floating Hospital Association** has been in operation since 1876, the purpose of its work being to furnish lake excursions for fresh air to sick children and other invalids among the poor. During about nine weeks in the hottest portion of the summer, a steamer is chartered to make three excursions daily, except Saturdays and Sundays, from Clark Street bridge to North Avenue pier at Lincoln Park.

The pier is covered and provided with a large number of hammocks for the use of the children. As many as 600 are taken out at one trip. The cost of this charity is about $1,200 per annum, which is raised by subscription. Competent medical attendance is provided. No one afflicted with contagious diseases is allowed to go on board the vessel. Dr. C. L. Rutter, 182 N. State Street, is secretary.

Mercy Hospital, corner of Calumet Avenue and Twenty-sixth Street, was founded about 1848–49 by the Sisters of Mercy, and was incorporated in 1852 as "Mercy Hospital and Mercy Orphan Asylum."

MERCY HOSPITAL, CALUMET AVENUE AND TWENTY-SIXTH STREET.

A building at the present location was first occupied in 1863. In 1864 the orphanage was transferred to the Sisters of St. Joseph, and the institution was confined to hospital work. In 1869 a capacious wing was constructed and equipped, and the sisters moved the hospital into it, and established the House of Providence in the main building. The objects are, first, to take care of the sick poor, and then of as many who are able to pay as can be accommodated. The building is a three story brick, with basement, and is provided with an amphitheater, sick wards for males and females, private rooms for paying patients, and the usual domestic and sanitary conveniences. It has comfortable capacity for 180 patients, and an average of 175 inmates. It is managed by thirty-four Sisters, at an annual expense of $26,000, which is met by voluntary contributions and the sums received from pay patients. The entire property is valued at $260,000, but is encumbered with a mortgage debt.

8

Cook County Hospital occupies an entire block, embracing twelve acres, bounded by Wood, Harrison, Lincoln and Polk Streets. It was founded in 1865 as an independent hospital, and was then located at the corner of Arnold and Eighteenth Streets. Later it fell into the hands of the county authorities, and has since steadily grown to its present magnificent proportions. The buildings are all of red brick, trimmed with stone, built in the pavilion style, with courts between, and well-lighted corridors connecting the four main structures. The latter are four stories in height, with attics and basements, and are provided on every floor with accommodations for thirty to forty patients, besides smaller rooms for private patients, or cases that demand isolation. There are a kitchen, dining-room, bath-rooms, closets, etc., on each floor, and rooms are conveniently located for the resident attaches. An air-shaft rises through the center of each building, from the sub-basement to the roof, connecting with air-chambers between the floors, and a coil of steam pipe in each shaft heats the air as desired to create a draft. By this means the atmosphere of the rooms is constantly changed. The rooms and wards are warmed by indirect heat from a regulator in each apartment. These arrangements give complete ventilation, and command a perfectly even temperature at all seasons. In the center of the group of buildings is the amphitheater for surgical operations and clinics, with a seating capacity for 600, for the use of students of the medical colleges of the city. A smaller amphitheater is provided for autopsies held by the professors for the instruction of students, and in the basement beneath it is the public morgue of Chicago. A large kitchen, bakery, dining-rooms, and dormitory for the help employed in the hospital, occupy special quarters near the store-room and laundry. There are also storage for ice, barns for horses, provender, vehicles, etc., on the ground. One of the most striking features is the new building, surmounted by a tower, erected on the Harrison Street front. It constitutes the main entrance to the institution, and is five stories high, the two upper stories being allotted to private patients, and the remainder occupied by the administrative department, with admission, reception and examining rooms, laboratory, drug and dispensing rooms, lavatory, offices, committee and family rooms. Altogether, there are comfortable and convenient accommodations for over 500 patients. The stairways are all broad and of gradual ascent, and elevators afford easy access to the upper floors. A recent annual report gives the daily average of patients as 353; inmates, including employes and physicians, 448; daily cost of

each, 64 cents. Receipts from private patients were $1,886.50; from
sale of clinic tickets, $1,540. The total number of patients treated
was 5,194, of whom 508 died, 2,252 were discharged recovered, and
there were 121 births. The current expenses were $104,795.
The finishing and furnishing of the hospital throughout are of a superior order, and in its elegant and strikingly diversified style of architecture, and the perfection of its sanitary arrangements and appliances, it is unsurpassed by any institution of the kind in the country
—perhaps in the world. W. J. McGarigel is warden ; Miss M. E.
Hempel, matron of the Training School for nurses, is head nurse.
The resident staff of physicians and surgeons is supplemented by the
faculties of the medical colleges.

The **Washingtonian Home** had its origin in a movement instituted
by the Good Templar lodges in Cook County. In 1863 they secured
from their grand lodge a donation of their fees and dues for the succeeding year, as the nucleus
of a fund for the establishment of a reformatory for in-
ebriates. In the following
January the Washingtonian
Home Association was organized and incorporated. A
building at 547 State Street
was occupied for about a year,
when the property at 566 to
572 West Madison Street,
known as the Union Park
Hotel, and previous to that
noted as the Bull's Head
Tavern, was purchased for
$10,000. In 1867 a special

THE WASHINGTONIAN HOME.

charter was obtained from the legislature, giving the Home ten per
cent of the revenues of the city from licenses for the sale of intox-
icating liquors. To the income derived from this source was added a
bequest of $19,000 from Jonathan Burr, and by January, 1875, the
directors found their treasury in a condition to justify the erection
of the present spacious building on the site then occupied by the
Home. This building is an imposing structure of four stories, with
mansard and basement, and has a front of 106 feet on Madison
Street. It was erected at a cost of $56,489, and the furnishing cost

over $6,000. It contains sleeping rooms for 111 persons, convalescent and amusement rooms, padded rooms for patients with delirium, chapel, hospital and well arranged laundry and culinary departments. Free patients are received in certain cases, but the majority are expected to pay a small charge for board and attendance. The number of admissions in 1883 was 927, and the total number since the Home was opened is 6,120. There is a board of thirty directors and a staff of six physicians. Daniel Wilkins, A. M., is superintendent.

The **Martha Washington Home** is a supplementary institution to the Washingtonian Home, established by the association for the reformation of inebriate women. It is under the same control and is similarly organized and managed. It occupies the handsome buildings and grounds of the old military school on Graceland Avenue, which were purchased and refitted for the purpose at a cost of $15,-829.24, and was formally opened in July, 1882. A total of 146 inmates had been received at the beginning of 1884. Miss M. M. Gray is the matron.

St. Joseph's Orphan Asylum, Nos. 3 and 5 Douglas Place, was founded in 1864, and after many removals was finally established in its present permanent and beautiful home. The building is a five-story brick, with basement and two wings, one of three stories and the other of four. It has accommodations for 250 children, and an average attendance of 220. Its object is the care of destitute children, and their proper education. Boys are taken from four to eight years of age, and transferred to the Christian Brothers at Feehanville, where they are provided for. Girls are received during the same age, and are kept until homes are secured for them, or may remain in the institution if they prefer. The asylum is maintained by a monthly allowance from the ecclesiastical government. It is managed by the Sisters of St. Joseph. The property is valued at about $60,000, and the annual expenditures are about $9,000. The average number of inmates annually is about 600.

Saint Vincent's Infant Asylum of Chicago, formerly known as Saint Vincent's Foundling Asylum and Lying-in-Hospital, is located at 191 LaSalle Avenue, and was established in July, 1882. It has room for about fifty children, and admits children, including foundlings, under the age of six years. Some of these are boarded at the asylum by their parents, and others are brought in by the police and charitable persons. The institution is supported by donations and what is paid by parents and friends of inmates. The number of children cared for in 1883 was 370, and the expenditures amounted to $6,554. At six years of age the children are given to persons who adopt them, or otherwise placed where their future will be properly cared for. Sister M. Julia is the Mother Superior.

The **Chicago Nursery and Half-Orphan Asylum** is located in a three story brick building at 855 North Halsted Street. It contains school-rooms, play-rooms, nurseries, hospitals, bath-rooms, dormitories, etc. The asylum was opened in 1860 for the care of children of poor women, while the mothers are seeking or actually engaged in

THE CHICAGO NURSERY AND HALF-ORPHAN ASYLUM.

employment. The plan was afterward extended so as to include the care and maintenance of children deprived of either parent. A small house was secured, and parents were permitted to bring their children in the morning and take them away at night, paying five cents per day for each child. The charge is now gauged by the wages earned by the parents. The present building was erected in 1870. There is a day school with an average attendance of eighty-six, and vocal music is made a specialty. The average family is about 140. There is a board of trustees, and a board of managers consisting of thirty-eight ladies. Mrs. C. M. Blanchard is matron.

The German Society extends a helping hand to German immigrants, principally in aiding them to secure employment, and providing temporary support. It also aids poor German residents, especially widows and orphans and the sick. Employment was obtained for over 5,000 persons during 1883; assistance and advice were given to nearly 4,000 others. The society was organized in May, 1854, and was first known as the "Deutche Gesellschaft von Chicago." It experienced two or three changes in name, and was finally reincorporated under the present title Dec. 5, 1883. The new charter was procured to enable the society to hold land which had previously been donated and was held in trust for its use. Its income is derived from invested funds of $12,000, dues from members, and from contributions. The German Ladies' Society was instituted by this organization, and works in co-operation with it. The management of the German Society is vested in a board of fifteen directors. The office of the society is at 49 LaSalle Street. William A. Hettrich is President; Max Eberhardt, 9 South Canal Street, Secretary; Conrad L. Niehoff, Treasurer.

The German Ladies' Society was organized in 1878 as the Ladies' Club of the German Society, but has since become measurably an independent organization, with its own officers, directors and committees, all composed of German ladies. It continues to co-operate in the work of the German Society, but its main object is to erect a home for old, helpless and needy Germans, toward which end it is accumulating a fund from contributions, the proceeds of festivals, picnics and other entertainments. The office is at 49 LaSalle Street.

The Erring Woman's Refuge was organized in 1863 for the relief, protection, care, and reformation of such erring women as may voluntarily place themselves under its care, or may be so placed by any lawful authority. Work was started in a little cottage in the North Division, and then a somewhat larger building was obtained on the South Side. In 1865 the managers purchased a building on the corner of Indiana Avenue and Thirty-first Street, where the institution is now located. The present building was erected and occupied in the winter of 1876. It will accommodate about forty persons, besides officials and attendants. The value of the property of the society is about $40,000, and there is an endowment by bequest of the late Jonathan Burr amounting to $21,261. The annual receipts and expenditures each aggregate about $8,000. The sum of $2,234 was received in 1883 from the work of inmates; $721 from city fines, and $4,359 from rents and interest. The total number of women received into the Refuge for that year was 119, and the average cared for during the year was fifty-three and one-half. About 1,100 women, mostly under twenty years of age, have been under the care of the institution, which provides for the inmates for two years, and secures suitable means of support for the worthy on leaving. Its affairs are directed by a board of thirty-nine lady managers. Mrs. Helen Mercy Woods is superintendent.

The **United States Marine Hospital**, on the lake shore, six miles north of the city, succeeded a smaller marine hospital which stood near the Rush Street bridge for nearly twenty years. The area of the

UNITED STATES MARINE HOSPITAL.

grounds is about ten acres and the building is a handsome four-story granite structure, 300×75 feet, with a basement, having accommodations for 150 patients, the average number cared for being about sixty-four. It is the largest hospital of the kind in the country, and cost complete, $450,000, being provided with every modern improvement in arrangement and equipment. It has a dispensary from which over 3,000 patients are treated annually, the large majority being outside applicants for medical aid. The maintenance of the hospital is provided for by a tax on the tonnage of all vessels. All American seamen are entitled to admission free of charge, and foreigners upon the payment of a small sum. T. W. Miller, M. D., is surgeon in charge. Applicants can be examined at the city office, Room 20, Post-office building, Chicago.

The **Presbyterian Hospital** affords medical and surgical aid and nursing to sick and disabled persons, of every creed and nationality. The building adjoins Rush Medical College on Wood Street, and forms two wings of the hospital as it will be when fully completed. It is four and a half stories in height, and of red pressed brick with stone trimmings. Internally it is provided with every modern convenience for serving the needs and comfort of the sick. Over $45,000 (wholly contributions) were expended in erecting and furnishing the building. At present all inmates are required to pay for board and treatment, but free beds for the worthy indigent will be added as soon as practical. Rooms are also provided for private patients. The hospital was opened Aug. 20, 1884, and a total of twenty-seven patients had been admitted Oct. 1, of the same year. The total capacity of the portion of the hospital already completed is eighty beds. The nursing is under the direction of a graduate of the Illinois Training School for Nurses, and a board of twenty-eight managers direct the affairs of the institution. Dr. E. P. Davis is the resident physician.

Cook County Insane Asylum is located on the county poor farm. The insane were formerly sent to the Infirmary, but in 1870 the present structure was erected near the Infirmary, for that class of patients, and in 1873 it was enlarged. It now has accommodations for 400 inmates, but an average of about 600 is crowded into it and a new building is now being erected. Of the inmates only seventy-two are native born. Over fifty-three per cent are females. Forty-eight per cent of the insanity is due to inherited and fifty-two to acquired defects. Henry Varnell is warden, and James G. Kernan, M. D., medical superintendent.

The **Chicago Eye and Ear Infirmary**, 2813 Groveland Park Avenue, was incorporated in 1882. It furnishes gratuitous advice and medicine to the poor, afflicted with diseases of the eye and ear, and also cares for those who are able to pay for this class of treatment; and gives clinical instruction to students in those branches of practice. It is sustained partly by fees from patients who are able to pay, and by voluntary contributions, but mainly by the manager, Dr. C. H. Vilas.

Hahnemann Hospital, 2813 Groveland Park Avenue, is the clinical annex to Hahnemann Medical College. After the fire of 1871 it received $15,000 from the Chicago Relief and Aid Society, and was opened to the public in a separate and suitable building. The amphitheater was burned Oct. 21, 1883, and a new and commodious structure is in course of construction on the opposite side of the avenue.

Cook County Infirmary is located twelve miles from the city on the county poor farm, a tract of 160 acres of fine y-cultivated land in Norwood Park Township, on which is also the Cook County Insane Asylum. There are nine buildings arranged in a semi-circular group, and connected by corridors. The building allotted to the administrative department is 48 by 52 feet; and there are four dormitories each 32 by 120 feet, besides hospitals and dining-rooms. These structures are of brick, in the Gothic style of architecture, with interior finish of natural oak. They were completed in 1882, at a cost, including furniture, of $183,000, and have capacity for 1,000 patients. The average number of inmates is 700, and the total number admitted annually is about 1,700. The institution is reached from the Madison Street depot of the C. M. & St. P. R. R. J. C. L. Frey is warden, and Dr. G. A. Hoffman, physician in charge.

Bennett Hospital is a four-story brick building in the rear of Bennett Medical College. Each floor is divided into four wards, and there are accommodations for fifty patients, twenty being the average number of inmates. The hospital is owned and managed by the college.

The American Humane Association is an organization of considerable importance at this great center of the live stock trade. It is national in character, and was organized in October, 1877. It is intimately associated with various local and state humane societies throughout the country, and aims to secure humane treatment to live stock while in transit. Its work has so far been almost entirely directed toward securing improvement in transporting cattle on railroad trains, and it has succeeded in causing improved cattle cars to be placed upon many of the railroads, so that cattle are now fed and watered while en route, and consequently make the journey with less suffering than was formerly the case. The society meets annually at such time and place as may be designated by the body in session. Edwin Lee Brown, Clinton Street, corner Jackson, is president.

The Relief Works were organized and incorporated in 1883, under the auspices of the Society for Ethical Culture. The purpose is to furnish trained nurses to act in connection with the free dispensaries, and visit the sick who apply to the dispensaries for medicine. These nurses made during the first year a total of 1,773 visits. A Ladies' Auxiliary Union was also organized for the purpose of providing clothing for distribution by the nurses, and a large quantity was thus distributed during the year. W. M. Salter, No. 83 Madison Street, Hershey Music Hall, is president.

The United States Life Saving Station, shown in the illustration on the opposite page, is located on a strip of land at the mouth of the Chicago River, known as Illinois Central Railroad Pier No. 1. It is accessible by the viaduct at the foot of Randolph Street. It was established in 1875 simply as a life-boat station, by a volunteer crew whose support was derived from an allowance, by the government, of $10 for each life saved. The volunteer service was supplanted in 1878 by a paid crew, under the maintenance of the general government. A new station was built and all the modern appliances for saving lives have been introduced. The crew consists of a keeper and eight men. One man is kept on watch day and night, and during foggy or stormy weather two men patrol the beach for four miles in either direction from the station. The station is kept open during nine months of the year, beginning with the first day of April and continuing till the last day of December.

The American Association of the Red Cross was founded upon the "Geneva Treaty" of 1864, and has for its object the relief of sufferers from war, pestilence, famine and other national calamities. It operates, with its auxiliaries, under the provisions of the Geneva treaty, which has been signed by all the great nations of the earth, President Arthur signing for the United States in 1882. The association has accomplished an untold amount of good in the judicious distribution of the vast sums of money and supplies which have been voluntarily contributed for its disposal in the hours of great national or "providential" calamities. The Central organization, Clara Barton, president, at Washington City, is under the immediate control of the highest government officials, the President of the United States being president of the Board of Consultation. The Chicago Branch was organized in 1882, and has its headquarters at Room 1, Central Music Hall Building. It did a noble work in sending supplies to the recent Ohio and Mississippi River flood sufferers. Rev. E. I. Galvin is superintendent. Mrs. Mary Weeks Burnett, M. D., is secretary.

The Prisoners' Aid Association of Illinois is an outgrowth of the Prisoners' Aid Association of Chicago. Its efforts are mainly devoted to the improvement of prison influences and the reformation and assistance of discharged prisoners. A recent report shows that 448 persons were furnished with employment, or otherwise aided, during the year. The Chicago association, which was incorporated Feb. 21, 1882, was changed to a state organization in March, 1884. There are now about 150 members. J.W. Plummer, 52 East Lake Street, secretary.

U. S. Life Saving Station, Near Mouth of Chicago River.

The **Western Seamen's Friend Society** was organized Nov. 10, 1830, to promote the spiritual and temporal welfare of seamen and boatmen and their families on the western lakes and rivers. It is the oldest charitable organization in the city, and is the parent society of the chain of local organizations which constitute the Bethel Mission system of the west, still maintaining an active interest and participation in their work. The supply of missionary service and the establishment of Bethel homes and schools at suitable points is encouraged and assisted; current moral and religious literature is circulated; the Scriptures are distributed; shops and prisons visited and appropriate books and papers placed in the hands of inmates; a gospel ship is maintained to organize Sunday schools and hold religious services in isolated neighborhoods on the islands and along the shores of the lakes; and all other efficient and available agencies employed in promoting the mission of the society. Its affairs are under the management of a board of directors. B. Frankland, 32 North Desplaines Street, is general superintendent.

The **Chicago Bethel**, at the northwest corner of Randolph and Desplaines Streets, embraces the "Mariner's House" of the Western Seamen's Friend Society, the Bethel department for transient meals and lodgings, and the Bethel mission and school. The Mariner's House is for the better class of seafaring men and others who desire a quiet home. The Bethel department furnishes meals and lodging to transients at nominal prices, or free to the really needy on proper recommendation, and fully 18,000 men are received in this department annually. The Bethel school has an enrollment of about 300, and an average attendance of 175. The nightly gospel meetings are well attended. The relief department distributes 1,600 articles in an average year. The annual expenditures in the Chicago district amount to over $6,000, part of which is met by contributions and part by receipts from the business of the Home. The Bethel is under a heavy debt, which it is gradually reducing.

The **Illinois Humane Society**, organized in 1870 for the prevention of cruelty to children and animals, is one of the most important agencies in the city for the relief and prevention of suffering. It pays special attention to educating children in the law of kindness, seeking thus to rear a humane generation. This work is prosecuted in the public schools, and 1,065 "Bands of Mercy" have been organized, with 67,120 members. A recent report of the outside work shows that 2,632 cases were investigated during the year, and 1,467 children looked after and relieved, 251 being placed in charitable institutions. There were 753 cases of cruelty to animals, 432 teamsters reprimanded, 251 prosecutions, resulting in fines aggregating $3,512, and 273 horses laid up from work, 187 abandoned horses killed, and ninety-six removed by ambulance. Eight inebriates were sent to the Washingtonian Home. The society is supported by contributions from the public. The directors include some of the leading citizens of Chicago. John G. Shortall is president; Henry W. Clarke is secretary; O. L. Dudley is chief of special agents. Office, 113 Adams Street.

The Woman's Christian Association aims to promote the general welfare of women, especially such as are dependent on their own exertions for support. It was incorporated in April, 1877, and is located at 1516 Wabash Avenue. The board of managers consists of 100 ladies from the various churches. It is supported in part from its own earnings, and in part by membership fees and private subscriptions. It affords a boarding-house for young women, and has an employment bureau for women seeking situations, or others desiring female help. About a thousand young girls have been sheltered under its roof. The building provides ample accommodations for fifty inmates. A free dispensary for women and children at 182 Dearborn Street is also conducted by the association. The library has some 450 volumes and 600 periodicals. Flowers, reading matter, childrens' toys, etc., are distributed in the county hospital weekly, and papers and tracts among the inmates of the jail.

The House of Providence adjoins Mercy Hospital, on the corner of Calumet Avenue and Twenty-sixth Street. It affords a home for distressed women of good character, and young girls out of employment. It is sustained by those of the inmates who are able to pay from two to three and a half dollars a week for their board. No one having a good character is refused admission. The building is of brick, with three stories and basement, and has capacity for fifty to sixty persons. The property belongs to the Sisters of Mercy, and is managed by two from that order.

The Charity Organization Society was organized in November, 1883, to help the able-bodied poor to be self-sustaining, reclaim the pauperized poor, stop street-begging and prevent imposition and fraud. It has established the Provident wood-yard at 395 North Clark Street, where the hungry may always earn a meal, if able to work. The main office is at Room 14, 129 Dearborn Street, and branch offices are located at 430 North Clark Street and 2207 Michigan Avenue.

The **United Hebrew Relief Association** of Chicago was established in 1859, to assist the needy of the Hebrew faith. to make them self-sustaining, to see that no children grow up to be paupers, and to provide hospital facilities for the sick and disabled. The association is the result of the amalgamation of several Hebrew relief societies which existed prior to 1859. It manages and supports the Michael Reese Hospital. Over 5,000 persons receive assistance annually. A list of regular beneficiaries is kept, and aid extended monthly as needed. Residents and strangers are alike assisted, shoes and clothing distributed, and transportation furnished where advisable. About $10,000 are annually disbursed in this work. The office is located at No. 200 LaSalle Street. Isaac Greensfelder is president.

The **Deaconess Institute and Hospital** of the Swedish Evangelical Lutheran Church was organized in 1882 as a charitable institution. In May, 1884, hospital work was taken up with the view of forming the nucleus of an establishment to meet the needs of the denomination in the northwest. It occupies a small building at 151 Lincoln Avenue, with beds for fifteen persons, and is maintained by the St. Augustine Synod of the Northwest. C. B. L. Boman is secretary.

The **Central Free Dispensary** occupies the whole of the first floor of Rush Medical College, corner of Harrison and Wood Streets. The rooms are elegantly fitted up and provided with every convenience for treatment of patients and for clinical instruction, which is here given to the students of the college. The Dispensary has been in active operation at its present location since the fall of 1876. It is the result of the union of two dispensaries—the "Brainard" and the "Herrick." It is sustained by the interest of a fund donated by the Chicago Relief and Aid Society shortly after the great fire, by a small annuity from Cook County, and by voluntary contributions. It also receives the income from a fund of which the trustees of the college are custodians, and which was bequeathed by a wealthy and kind-hearted Scotchman, John Phillips, deceased, for the purpose of establishing and maintaining a free dispensary in West Chicago. About twenty thousand patients receive treatment yearly. The dispensary is open every day except Sunday. A staff of attending and visiting physicians is provided.

The **South Side Free Dispensary** is one of the oldest institutions of the kind in Chicago. It has been in existence about a quarter of a century. It was for a time a part of Mercy Hospital, under the name of the Davis Free Dispensary, but is now located at the corner of Twenty-sixth Street and Prairie Avenue. One of its features is a provision for visit'ng those who are unable to come to the dispensary.. For this purpose the South Side is divided into twelve districts, each of which is assigned to a graduated physician who gives his services free. Over 8,500 prescriptions are filled annually, and about 3,000 visits made to patients at their homes.

The **Central Homœopathic Free Dispensary** was organized in 1876, by the ladies, wives and friends of the faculty of the Homœopathic Medical College, and is located in the college building on the corner of Wood and York Streets. It is virtually a part of the college. It furnishes medicines and surgical assistance free to the poor, and attends to obstetric cases gratis. It is sustained by subscriptions and the proceeds of entertainments. The noted "butterfly ball" netted $5,000. It has an average of about one hundred applicants a day for relief.

Hahnemann Hospital Dispensary was organized in May, 1859. Its several departments, medical and surgical, are in the charge of the faculty of Hahnemann Medical College. Its location is in the hospital building, 2813 Groveland Avenue, and it is open every day except Sundays. It averages 30,000 gratuitous prescriptions annually. It is supported by voluntary contributions and from the treasury of the hospital.

The **West Side Free Dispensary** was established and incorporated Sept. 9, 1881, as a clinical annex of the College of Physicians and Surgeons, and for the gratuitous treatment of the deserving poor. The dispensary is located on the first floor of the college, corner of West Harrison and Honore Streets, and was opened to the public in November, 1882, since which time about 7,000 treatments have been given, and over 10,000 prescriptions filled.

The **Bennett Free Dispensary** is at Bennett Medical College, 511 State Street, and is under the management of the officers of the college. It is open from 1: 30 to 3 P. M. daily, except Sundays.

The **Police and Firemen's Relief Fund** is under the control of a board of trustees consisting of the mayor, the chief of police, the chief of the fire department, the chairman of the committee on police, city comptroller, the city treasurer, and the committee on fire and water of the City Council. The fund is provided under a special act of the state legislature, from certain specific taxes, fines, etc., and from the two dollars' initiation fee and an annual assessment of $3 from each member of the police and fire departments. The fund is for the relief of all disabled members of the two departments named.

The **Chicago Exchange for Women's Work**, popularly known as the

" Women's Exchange," was organized March 1, 1879. It is benevolent in intent, its object being to provide a depot for the reception and sale of any marketable article a woman can make in her own home, or any valuable article her necessities oblige her to dispose of, thereby assisting needy women to turn to personal profit whatever useful talent they may possess. The " Exchange " is conveniently located at 219 Wabash Avenue. In addition to the sales department, there is a restaurant supplied with home-made and home-cooked food. There is also a school under the charge of Mrs. J. S. Robinson, devoted to instruction in embroidery and various kinds of needle-work. There were 11,839 articles, of a total value of over $12,000, sold at the exchange during the year 1883. Any person subscribing $5, may become a member of the association. Each depositor of articles for sale is required to pay an annual fee of $1 and a commission of 10 per cent on all sales. There are now nearly 250 subscribing members of the association.

The **Societa Operaia Italiana** was founded by Italian mechanics and laborers, to educate their children, paying the expenses out of the society funds when necessary. It also helps needy Italians in this country, principally by obtaining work for them, and especially aims to disabuse Americans of the idea that Italians are a class of mendicants, and invokes Italian organ grinders and beggars to abandon their lazy employment. A weekly allowance of $5 is made to a sick member, and at death $100 is paid to the widow. The society was organized Sept. 18, 1881, and incorporated Feb. 24, 1882. The membership is about 100. Meetings are held monthly at 54 Lake Street. S. G. Meli is president.

The **Deak Verein** is a Hungarian benevolent society, whose meetings are held monthly at the office of the Hebrew Relief and Aid Association Room 5, No. 200 LaSalle Street. It assists needy Hungarians in all parts of the world. It sent $700 to the flood sufferers of Hungary in 1883, and aided indigent Hungarians to the extent of $1,000.

The **Schweitzer Benevolent Association** has sixty members, all .natives of Switzerland. It was organized in 1872, chiefly for the relief of distressed Swiss immigrants, but also to provide for destitute Swiss people living in this country. The Swiss republic and several of the Swiss cantons aid it with an annual donation. Regular meetings are held monthly at Uhlich's Hall. L. Boerlin, Swiss Consul, is president; Alfred Bucher, 168 Market Street, is secretary.

St. George's Benevolent Association is one of the oldest benevolent organizations in the city, and its good work has been widely felt. It gives advice to English immigrants, and grants relief to persons of English parentage, not members of the association, who are of good moral character. It visits the sick, buries the dead and cares for the widows and orphans of deceased members, and performs other mutual offices of benevolence. There are about 300 members enrolled. Meetings are held monthly at the Sherman House.

The **Scandinavian Emigrant Relief Society** was organized May 5, 1881, to look after the interests of Scandinavian immigrants, and give them such information and assistance as they may require. The office is at No. 183 North Peoria Street, where an agent of the society is ready to respond to calls. O. L. Stangeland, 239 West Erie Street, president.

The **Svea Society** is a Swedish organization, dating from Jan. 22, 1857. It is devoted to literary and benevolent objects. It occupies a suite of rooms at the corner of Chicago Avenue and Larrabee Street, which include a library with 1,600 volumes, meeting room, etc. Each member is entitled to $6 per week when sick, and upon death his heirs receive $100. There are 175 members. Axel Chytraus, Room 17, No. 80 Dearborn Street, is secretary.

The **Chebra Kadisha Ubikur Cholim** is a Jewish benevolent organization. It holds religious services on the holidays; relieves the sick and gives deceased members ritualistic burial. It was organized in 1861. Its monthly meetings are held on the first Sundays at the corner of Clinton and Randolph Streets.

The **Western Society for the Suppression of Vice** (Chicago branch) was organized in 1878, since which time its influence has been largely felt. It aims to secure the enforcement of the laws for the suppression of obscene literature, illustrations, advertisements and articles of indecent and immoral use. During the year 1883 fourteen dealers were arrested, with convictions and pleas of guilty in twelve cases, sentences to imprisonment aggregating six years and six months, and fines amounting to over $1,500. A large quantity of obscene matter was captured. The branch has a membership of 200. The office is at 6 Arcade Court. W. W. Vanarsdale is secretary.

The **Young Men's Hebrew Charity Society** has been in existence about three years. It gives a "charity ball" annually, the proceeds of which are given to the various charity societies of the city, without regard to sect. About $10,000 have been distributed in this way. Levi A. Eliel, 53 Dearborn Street, is secretary.

The **Schwaben Verein** is a German society of 250 members, organized March 1, 1878, for social and benevolent purposes. It has held seven annual festivals, which have yielded some $20,000, out of which

9

about $3,000 have been given for charitable purposes. These festivals are usually held at Ogden's Grove, in August of each year. The society has had plans and drawings made, and will erect a monument to the poet Schiller, in Lincoln Park, and at a cost of $15,000, for which $3,000 have already been set aside.

The Irish Catholic Colonization Association of the United States is a stock company, organized March 17, 1879, with a capital of $100,-000, divided into 400 shares. It is composed of prominent Irish Americans, and has for its purpose the colonization of Irish immigrants in the western states and territories. It has been fairly successful in its work, and has planted a number of flourishing colonies in Minnesota, Nebraska and Dakota. The headquarters in Chicago are at the office of the vice-president, W. J. Onohan, City Hall.

The Danish Veteran Society is composed of veterans who fought for the cause of Denmark in the Dano-German wars of 1848-49-50 and 1864. It extends a helping hand to any member in need of substantial aid. It was incorporated in 1874.

The Society for Home Teaching of the Blind was organized in 1883 by a number of young married couples. It maintains a free lending library for blind people at No. 4 Arcade Court. The library contains nearly 300 volumes of the choicest books, printed in raised letters, and a large number of blind persons go to the rooms every Saturday afternoon for books, and to meet in social converse; and a missionary is employed to teach the blind to read at their own homes. C. H. Adams is president and H. H. Bradley is secretary and treasurer. Mrs. Victor Lawson is chairman of the board of managers.

Benevolent and Mutual Aid Societies not heretofore mentioned are: Hotel Men's Mutual Benefit Association, organized in 1879; Postoffice Employes' Mutual Aid Association, 1874; Letter Carriers' Relief Fund Association, 1876; Policemen's Benevolent Association, 1868; Benevolent Association of the Paid Fire Department, 1863; Firemen's Benevolent Association, 1847; Mutual Benefit and Aid Society (German), 1871-74; First German Christian Aid Society, 1859; Cristoforo Columbo Mutual Aid Society, 1879; Cambrian Benevolent Society, 1848; Northwestern Traveling Men's Association, 1875; Societa Italiana Di Unione E Fratellanza, 1868; German Mutual Benefit Association, 1875; Societe Francaise De Secours Mutuals; Bavarian Verein; Deutcher Krieger Verein; Chebra Gemiluth Ubikur Cholim.

The numerous secret and fraternal life assurance societies are omitted from this volume for want of space.

The Clubs and Societies.

LITERARY, SOCIAL, POLITICAL, SPORTING, PLEASURE, AND OTHER CLUBS AND SOCIETIES.

THE clubs and societies present numerous and varied features of the social side of life, and afford an interesting field for the study of human nature, representing as they do its gregarious elements. The principal clubs are purely social, providing the enjoyment of the amenities of social intercourse for hours that would otherwise be laden with ennui instead of winged with refreshment. Other associations are devoted to the prosecution of some special purpose, either as a diversion, or for mental or physical exercise in some particular line, or for mutual improvement or assistance in the prosecution of a common purpose. Chicago is abundantly supplied with all classes of these organizations.

The **Chicago Literary Club** is the leading literary organization in the city, and ranks among the highest in the country. Its membership includes some of the brightest minds of the age, men whose reputations are international, such as Rev. Robert Collyer, Rev. David Swing, Rev. R. A. Holland, Prof. Louis Dyer, of Harvard University, Thomas Hughes, M. P., Seymour Haden, the famous etcher, Lieut. Gen. Sheridan and others. The club was organized April 21, 1874, for the purpose of discussing topics of interest in essays, conversations, etc. It has a membership of about 200, probably one-third of the members being non-residents, and occupies a fine suite of rooms on the sixth floor of Portland Block. In addition to the rooms usually required for club purposes, there is an auditorium for the weekly discussions which take place on Monday evenings. The following is a list of the presidents of the club since its organization : Rev. Robert Collyer, Hon. Charles B. Lawrence, Dr. Hosmer A. Johnson, Daniel L. Shorey, Edward G. Mason, William F. Poole, Rev. Brooke Herford, Edwin C. Larned, George Howland, Maj. Henry A. Huntington. Only gentlemen are admitted to membership. The annual dues are $24. Dr. Charles Gilman Smith is president; Fred W. Gookin, secretary and treasurer.

The **Fortnightly of Chicago** is composed exclusively of women.

It was organized by the late Mrs. Kate Newell Doggett, June 4, 1873, for the purpose of social and intellectual culture. The club soon gathered many of the brightest intellects of Chicago. It has ample rooms in the Art Institute building, on Michigan Avenue and Van Buren Street, in which afternoon meetings are held semi-monthly, except from May to October. The afternoon meeting of the fourth Friday in October is supplemented by a reception in the evening. The membership is limited to 175, and there are now 140. The admission fee is $10, and the annual dues $10. The tendency of thought, as exhibited in the essays, is philosophical in the modern sense of the word, and much of the work done by the association is of the highest literary character. Mrs. Mary H. Loomis is president; Mrs. Helen S. Shedd, secretary; Mrs. Drusilla Wilkinson, treasurer.

The Chicago Women's Club was founded by Mrs. Caroline M. Brown, for the purpose of securing mutual sympathy, counsel and united effort toward the progress and higher civilization of humanity. It was organized in 1875, with Mrs. Brown as president. Among the practical results of its labors are the appointment of a woman physician on the medical staff of the Cook County Insane Asylum, and of a night matron in the woman's department of the jail, and the support of a charity kindergarten near the corner of Arnold and Butterfield Streets. There are classes in art and literature, and efforts are being made to establish classes in kitchen gardening. Each branch of the work is placed in charge of a committee. The rooms of the club are in the Art Institute building at the corner of Michigan Avenue and Van Buren Street. Regular meetings are held semi-monthly. Mrs. Henry L. Frank is president; Mrs. Helen C. Pierce, secretary; Mrs. H. B. Stone, treasurer.

The Press Club of Chicago was organized and incorporated in January, 1880, for the purpose of securing a closer intimacy among members of the journalistic profession in Chicago, and affording them a place of rest and recreation during their unemployed hours. The club now has about 170 members, and is probably the only unmixed newspaper club in the country. Nobody is eligible to membership who has not been for at least one year prior to his application, connected in a literary capacity with a Chicago newspaper, or who shall not have been engaged in purely literary work for the same length of time. The rooms are on the third floor of 113 Madison Street, and include a library and reading room, an assembly room, a billiard room, a pooltable and bar, and a card room. The last Saturday night in each month is termed " Fourth Night," and is devoted to a reception of the members of the club, their friends, and ladies. In the autumn of each year there is a grand benefit performance in some leading place of amusement, the proceeds of which are contributed to the library fund. Some of the best operatic and dramatic talent of both continents has appeared at these annual entertainments. On the anniversary of the organization, a grand banquet is given by the club at one of the principal hotels, to which distinguished literary men are invited and entertained as guests. The membership fee is $15 ; the annual dues, $12. The club has the portrait of each president done in oil at the close of his term. F. B. Wilkie, one of the main organizers of the club, was its first president and James R. Bradwell, of the *Legal News*, is the present presiding officer.

The **Chicago Club** is one of the oldest and most fashionable clubs in the city. It owns its building, has its own cuisine, and is modeled in many essential respects after the established clubs of the old world. It was founded in 1869 by very prominent citizens, among whom were Philip Wadsworth, Chas. B. Farwell, Octavius Badger, G. H. Wheeler and others. The club house was for a time on Michigan Avenue, but having erected the handsome building it now occupies on Monroe Street, opposite the Palmer House, the club moved into it in 1875. The house is of red brick with tasteful stone trimmings, and is five stories in height with a basement. Following the French plan the culinary department is placed on the fifth floor. The private and

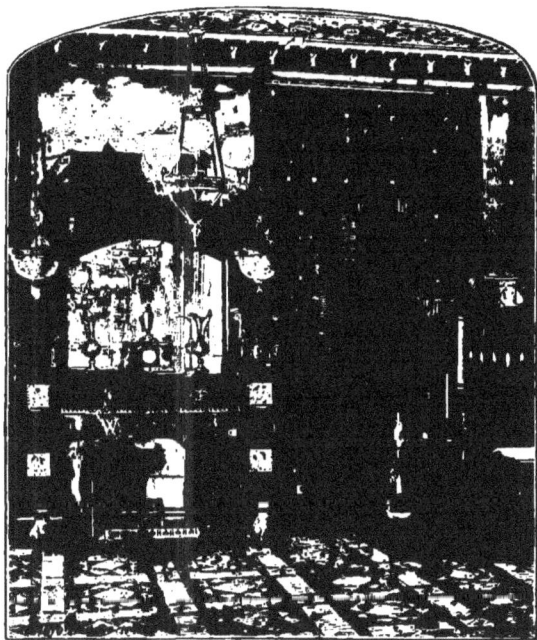

INTERIOR VIEW CHICAGO CLUB HOUSE.

general dining-rooms, on the next floor below, are so arranged that they can all be thrown into one when necessary. The third floor is occupied by sleeping-rooms, and the second story by the library, card and directors' rooms, and a fine billiard room. The reception rooms, cafe and reading rooms, on the first floor, are entered through an imposing hall. All the rooms are artistically finished, and there are many excellent paintings, among which is a portrait of President Fairbank, by the well-known Healy. The club is a purely social organization. The membership numbers over five hundred; the initiation fee is $300, and the annual dues $80. N. K. Fairbank is president; Thomas S. Kirkwood, secretary and treasurer.

The **West Side Club** was founded in November, 1882. It occupies a fine three-story club house at 451 Washington Boulevard, which contains parlors, reception, library, card and billiard rooms, and all other necessary appointments. The club is social in its purpose, and gives literary and musical entertainments which are of an excellent character. There are 125 members. Philip Stein is president.

The **Calumet Club**, located on Michigan Avenue and Twentieth Street, is probably the largest social organization of the kind in the west, and enjoys the possession of a building which, in extent, convenience and elegance of finish and furnishing is not surpassed by that of any similar institution. The Calumet is regarded as the most aristocratic club in the city. It was organized April 4, 1878, and was instituted under its charter with Gen. Anson Stager as president; Charles J. Barnes as vice-president; and F. B. Tuttle, treasurer and secretary. A spacious dwelling at the corner of Michigan Avenue and Eighteenth Street was the home of the club until it completed the palatial structure it now occupies. The building is of red brick with terra-cotta trimmings, covers an area 81×183½ feet, and its height of ninety feet is divided into five stories and a basement. The main entrance is a massive doorway, which opens into a hall of striking dimensions and decoration. On the left of the hall there is a fine old-fashioned fireplace, with andirons and other ancient fixtures. Opposite the entrance rises the principal stairway, at the first landing of which a large window presents a view of Calumet Lake in stained glass. The main reading-room is one of the most elegant apartments in the city, with carved furniture, and walls adorned with full-length portraits of many distinguished citizens, among them Hon. John Wentworth, Gen. Anson Stager, Edson Keith, and Gen. Phil. Sheridan. The billiard-room and the cafe in the rear are handsomely fitted up, and the assembly room is remarkable for its size, and for its artistic frescoes. The card-room is superbly furnished, the ceiling beautifully frescoed, and the stained glass windows hung with rich and costly curtains. The "Old Settlers' Room" is one of the most interesting in the building, containing a large collection of portraits of prominent men and pioneers, and curiosities and relics of early Chicago. An entresol between the second and third floors is allotted to members' sleeping-rooms. The dining-

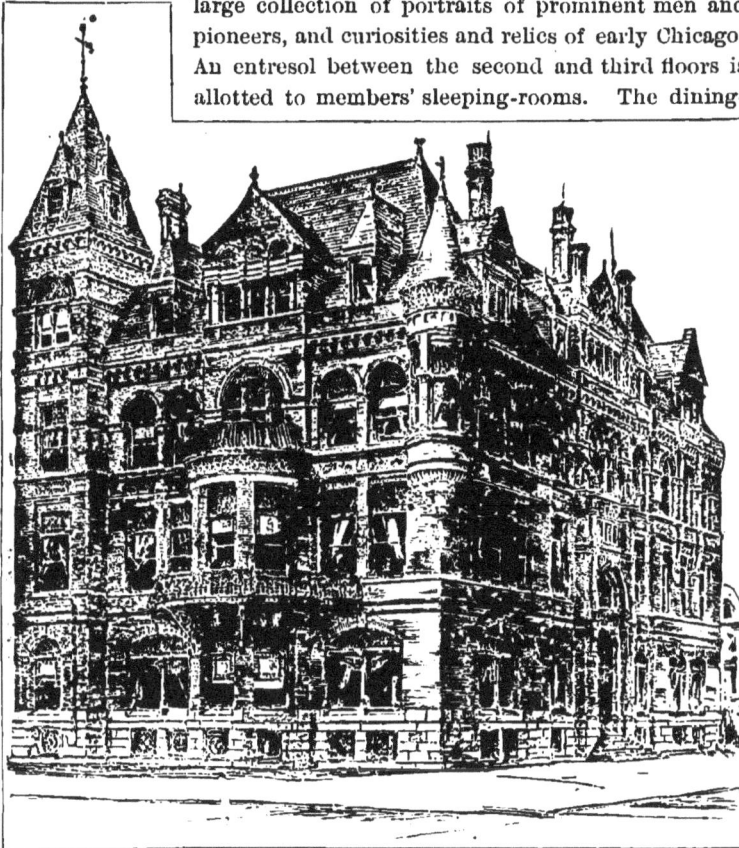

CALUMET CLUB HOUSE.

hall is capable of seating 300 people, and three private dining-rooms connected with the hall can be thrown into one with it. The cuisine is noted for its excellence. There are 721 members, most of them leading business men of the city. The membership fee is $250, and the annual dues $80. J. W. Doane is president; T. R. Jenkins, secretary; C. J. Blair, treasurer.

The **Commercial Club of Chicago** was organized Dec. 27, 1877, for social purposes, and to promote the commercial interests of the city. It is composed of gentlemen prominently representing those interests. The membership is limited to sixty. It has no club house, but meets monthly, except during the summer, and gives a grand annual banquet in January. It entertains distinguished commercial men from abroad in regal style, and is an organization of high character and great usefulness. John M. Clark is president; A. F. Seeberger, treasurer; George C. Clarke, secretary.

The **Standard Club** occupies a high position as a social organization. It was instituted April 5, 1869. Its club-rooms are at 1302 Michigan Avenue, and are handsomely fitted up. The members number 190, nearly all of the Jewish faith. Charles H. Schwab is president; E. Hoffman, treasurer; B. Mergentheim, secretary.

The **Chicago Merchants' Club** was started Jan. 29, 1884, for social purposes and to aid in maintaining the dignity of mercantile avocations. It purchased the elegant apartments at the southwest corner of Clark and Madison Streets previously occupied by the Chicago Mercantile Club, which had fitted them up at a cost of $15,000. They include all the usual reception, sleeping, refreshment and amusement rooms. The dining-room is capable of seating 125 persons. The attractive cuisine of the club is much resorted to by the members, who are 150 in number, and many of them resort to it for one or more of their daily meals. Ladies are admitted to the club-rooms on Saturdays. The membership fee is $50, and the annual dues $60. L. H. Bisbee is president; John W. Hepburn, secretary; Albert Seckel, treasurer.

The **Heather Club** has forty members, principally Scotchmen. It was organized in the spring of 1881, for the purpose of literary and social intercourse. Weekly meetings are held at the club rooms, No. 153 Clark Street. George Handy is secretary.

The **Union Club** is to the North Side what the Calumet and Chicago Clubs are to the South Side. It is an aristocratic institution, its membership of 500 being drawn from the highest social circles. It was organized in February, 1878; located at State Street and Chicago Avenue for about eighteen months; then for three years in the well-known Ogden House, opposite Washington Square. In November, 1883, it moved into the premises now occupied, which are owned by the club. The building is a massive structure 80 × 86 feet, and stands on a lot 110 × 147 feet. The material is a fine brown sandstone from

Massachusetts, rough dressed, and the style of architecture is original and imposing. The design was by Messrs. Cobb & Frost, architects. The interior finish throughout, except the parlor, is oak, and very rich. The main entrance opens into a large square hall, resembling a baronial hall of the times of " good queen Bess." The hall has a wide old-fashioned fire-place for burning cordwood. The stairway leading up from this hall is very elegant. The reception room is on the left of the entrance, and the office on the right. The double parlor on the same floor is finished in mahogany, the division being marked by a mahogany arch of elaborate design. The walls are decorated with choice

UNION CLUB HOUSE.

pictures. The cafe is quite unique, resembling the interior of an old English inn. The large *salon*, or assembly room, and the library, card and directors' rooms, are on the second floor, and the third floor is devoted to lodging rooms for members. The location at Dearborn Avenue and Washington Place was happily chosen, being in every way favorable for the purpose. The entire property cost $150,000. The membership fee is $100, and the annual dues $40. The officers are A. A. Carpenter, president; L. J. Gage, vice-president; H. A. Keith, secretary; and A. W. Cobb, treasurer.

The **Bankers'** Club is an organization of the leading bankers of the city, to promote social intercourse and advance the interests of the members and of banking generally. The club was instituted early in 1883, and numbers some seventy members. The meetings are held quarterly, and the business of the sessions is usually followed by a banquet and general sociability and good fellowship.

The **Illinois** Club is the fashionable social organization of the West Side, its membership being composed principally of prominent business men who are residents of that section of the city. The club was organized in April, 1878, and occupies a two-story stone front mansion at 154 South Ashland Avenue, one of the finest of the West Side thoroughfares. The premises were designed for a fine residence, and cost $40,000, and the house was refitted for club purposes at a cost of $10,000. An addition is now in course of construction which will cost, with furniture, $30,000 more. The art gallery of the Illinois Art Association will occupy a portion of the new building. The furnishing throughout—billiard, card and reading rooms, parlors and all other apartments—is both elegant and substantial; the decoration is of a highly artistic order. The walls are hung with many choice works of art from the most noted studios of Europe and America. The receptions and musicales given by the club are delightful entertainments, and the club house is thronged with representatives of the world of fashion on such occasions. The membership fee is $100, and the annual dues $40. There are 300 members, to which number the club is limited. The institution is well managed and prosperous, having a surplus in the treasury. J. H. Bradley is president; Fred. K. Morrill, secretary; W. A. Hammond treasurer.

The **Union League** Club was organized in 1879 as the Chicago Club of the Union League of America. It is both social and political in character. one of the conditions of membership being absolute and unqualified loyalty to the government of the United States. Its membership is limited to 1,000, and now numbers 850, and includes many prominent citizens. It occupies its handsome new club-house on the corner of Jackson Street and Fourth Avenue, which was erected at a cost of $150,000, not including the expensive and luxurious furniture and fittings. The club formerly occupied apartments in the Honore building, corner Dearborn and Adams Streets, and removed to the present location in 1886. A feature of the club is its excellent cuisine, and many of its members resort to it for dinner and luncheon daily. J. McGregor Adams is president.

The **Lakeside Club** is the youngest of the Chicago clubs, dating from June 2, 1884. It occupies two finely furnished mansions on Wabash Avenue and Thirtieth Street. It has about 120 members, and is preparing to build a club house at a cost of some $50,000. The membership fee is $25, and the annual dues $50. Morris Beifield is president; Jacob Kahn, treasurer; N. A. Mayer, secretary.

The **Iroquois Club** is a social and political organization, instituted by leading Democrats during the Hancock campaign of 1880. It was at first called "The Chicago Democratic Club," and held its meetings in the Palmer House. In October, 1881, it was reorganized and incorporated under its present title. Politically it limits its field to national politics. It has fitted up in elegant style six stories of Haverly Theater building, which it occupies under a lease for five years. There are reception, reading, smoking, bar, card, billiard, dressing, cafe and toilet rooms; private dining rooms, and a main dining hall elaborately finished and hung with pictures, three spacious rooms which can be thrown into one for use as the general assembly room, and give seating capacity for 500 persons, with a raised platform overlooking the hall thus formed; and there are also a well provided culinary department and other conveniences. The membership fee is $50, and the annual dues $40. The number of members exceeds 500. The club has made itself a power in the Democratic party, and has a national reputation and influence. Erskine M. Phelps is president; Walter Mattocks and Frank G. Hoyne, secretaries; J. H. McAvoy, treasurer.

The **Saracen Club** was organized in 1876 by Mrs. Fernanda Jones, for the purpose of promoting social and intellectual culture among its members. It is a mixed club of ladies and gentlemen. The meetings are held on the first Thursday evening of every month at the residence of some one of the members. The membership is limited to fifty. The annual meeting takes place on the first Thursday in May. Henry W. Fuller is president; William M. Payne, secretary and treasurer.

The **Chicago Liberal League** was organized in 1881, and now has a membership of nearly 100 persons. Its main object is to secure and maintain a complete separation of church and state in all things; and to promote this end it holds regular Sunday evening meetings at Odd Fellows' Hall, corner of Halsted and Madison Streets, for the free discussion and agitation of the subject. E. A. Stevens is president; Mrs. L. M. Swank is recording secretary, and Henry Borg is treasurer.

The **Society for Ethical Culture** was incorporated in April, 1883. Its object is to find and disseminate "a truer philosophy of life and a

higher ideal of duty " than are presented in the speculative philosophy
and dogmatic theology of the day. To this end the society provides
weekly lectures and discussions for adults, classes for the instruction
of children, and normal classes for older students. It has also instituted a system of Relief Works, which has been incorporated and is
one of the active relief agencies of the city. Among the 100 members of the society are some of the most prominent gentlemen in the
literary and social circles of Chicago. A. B. Hosmer, M. D., 170 State
Street, is secretary ; W. M. Salter, 83 Madison Street, lecturer.

· **The Moral Educational Society** is composed of ladies, assisted by
an advisory board of ladies and gentlemen. It was founded Nov. 13,
1882, for the dissemination of elevated ideas relative to marriage and
parenthood, the abolition of vice, and the moral training of youth.
The meetings are held monthly at the Grand Pacific Hotel, and are
open to all ladies desiring to attend. The society also holds public
meetings occasionally. Some thirty-six members are now enrolled.
Miss Mary Dye, 383 Washington Boulevard, is secretary.

The Margaret Fuller Society seeks by discussion and study to
advance the education of women in political economy and the principles of government. It was instituted Aug. 3, 1880, and is the first
society of the name. It is composed of ladies, gentlemen being admitted only as honorary members. Some forty names are on the rolls.
The society holds its meetings semi-monthly at the Grand Pacific
Hotel, and its proceedings are published from time to time. Miss
Louisa Burpee is secretary.

The Unity Club was organized on the 10th of January, 1883,
by Rev. Jenkin Lloyd Jones, pastor of All Souls' Church. The
purpose is to study and discuss the writings of Robert Browning,
and other literary works and art subjects. There are forty members,
mainly of the church congregation. The meetings are held monthly
in All Souls' Society Hall. Rev. J. L. Jones is president ; Miss Eva
Manierre, secretary ; Charles Ware, treasurer.

The Illinois Association of the Sons of Vermont is one of the largest
state clubs in the west. It grew out of a centennial celebration held
Jan. 17, 1877, by natives of Vermont, in commemoration of the formal
declaration of the people of Vermont at Westminster Court-house that
they were an independent commonwealth. A permanent organization
was effected on the 22d of the following month. Regular meetings
are held semi-annually in Room 70, Government Building. The club
seeks to promote a more cordial interest and sympathy among natives

of the Green Mountain state who reside in Illinois, and gives a grand annual banquet at the Palmer House on the 17th of January, which is usually attended by 400 or 500 people. It has 300 members. Elbridge G. Keith is president; E. B. Sherman, Room 70 Government Building, secretary; H. H. Nash, treasurer.

The **Channing Club** is an organization of Unitarians, for social purposes and the general advancement of Unitarian interests in Chicago and the west. It meets monthly, except in July, August and September, at the Union League rooms. The programme of exercises embraces essays, papers and general discussion, preceded by a collation. The club rooms, at 135 Wabash Avenue, include offices for organizations engaged in Unitarian work in the west, and pleasant reception rooms where visitors to Chicago interested in the Unitarian cause are cordially received. Eric Winters is secretary and treasurer.

The **Garibaldi Legion** is an Italian society with purely social and literary objects. It was organized in 1882, soon after the death of the Italian statesman whose name it bears. There are about seventy-five members. Meetings are held on the second Friday of each month at Uhlich's Hall. John G. Riggio is president, and John Ginochio is secretary. .

The **Plattsdeutschen Verein** was organized Nov. 15, 1874, and incorporated on the 26th of March the following year. It membership is composed entirely of "Low Dutch," and its object is to encourage and keep in practice the customs and usages of the mother country, and especially to keep fresh the "Low Dutch" literature and language. The society has a small library. Meets at Uhlich's Hall Thursday evenings.

The **Virginia Society** is a club established in 1880 to promote social intercourse among natives of Virginia and their descendants. Among its founders were the late Cyrus H. McCormick, who was the first president; the late Gen. N. B. Buford, Judge S. M. Moore, and Judge John G. Rogers. Four meetings are held each year, at the Palmer House, subject to call. O. W. Nixon is president; H. L. Mason, secretary; S. G. Seaton, treasurer.

The **Citizens' Association of Chicago** was organized in 1874, to promote municipal reforms, rectify and prevent abuses, sustain popular rights against encroachment, secure the enactment and enforcement of good laws, encourage desirable enterprises, and generally to assist in advancing the interests of the city and the people in respect to order, justice, and the development of industry and trade. It does not engage in any enterprise for any religious denomination, political organization, or organization interested in promoting temperance or sumptuary legislation. It keeps vigilant watch over every public interest, and promptly interferes upon every reasonable occasion. It has over 900 members, who are divided into committees having special departments to look af er, such as finance, military, theaters, tenement houses, street obstructions, railway crossings, fast driving, education, adulteration of food, civil service reform, taxation, city and county legislation, judiciary, elections, water supply, pavements, etc. The rooms of the association are at 35 Merchants' Building, 92 LaSalle Street. J. C. Ambler is secretary. .

The Sons of Maine is the title of a club composed of natives of the state of Maine, who hold social reunions and in other ways unite in keeping up a patriotic pride in the Pine Tree state. It was organized in April, 1880, and has about 200 members. Regular meetings are held semi-annually, generally at the Palmer House. The first meeting of the year is always on the 20th of March, the date of the admission of Maine into the Union. George M. How is president ; Newton Goodwin, secretary ; William Sprague, treasurer.

The Illinois St. Andrew's Society, one of the oldest social and benevolent associations in the city, was organized in January, 1846, and chartered in 1853. It takes kindly care of those of the Scottish nationality who need its aid and counsel, and has a burial place in Rose Hill, where are interred those Scotchmen who die destitute in Chicago. A monument designates the ground, and over each grave is a plain stone which records the name, etc., of the stranger. The society derives its funds from initiation fees of $2 each, membership fees of $3 per annum, the proceeds of the annual dinner on St. Andrew's day, and the yearly balls given for the benefit of the ladies, who do not attend the anniversary dinners. George Anderson, Esq., is the only survivor of the original organizers, and his recitation of "Tam O'Shanter" is always a feature of the anniversary banquet. Andrew Wallace is president, 95 Dearborn Street.

The Chicago Bar Association, incorporated in 1874, was organized to maintain the honor and dignity of the profession of the law, to cultivate social intercourse among its members, and to increase its usefulness in promoting the due administration of justice. The incorporators were : Charles M. Sturges, James P. Root, C. B. Lawrence, Charles Hitchcock, Robert T. Lincoln and Ira O. Wilkinson. The annual meeting of the association is held on the second Saturday in January. The membership fee is $15. The board of managers meet monthly, except in July, August and September, at Room 71, County·Building. F. Q. Bull is president; George W. Cass, secretary, and Robert E. Jenkins, treasurer.

The **Cook County Teachers' Association** is composed of teachers engaged in the practice of their profession, in the school districts outside of the city. The total number of teachers so engaged is 650, and there is an average attendance of about 300 at the meetings, which are held monthly from October to May, inclusive, in Methodist Church Block. A growing interest is manifested in the programme of exercises, which embraces addresses by prominent educators, essays and discussions, all bearing upon the work of the members. The association was organized in 1878. William H. Ray, Hyde Park, secretary.

The **Chicago Turngemeinde** is the oldest and strongest German society in the city. It dates its organization from 1853, and now has a membership of over 400. It owns Turner Hall at 255 North Clark Street. The corner stone of the building was laid in the summer of 1872, and the official opening of the hall took place Jan. 1, 1873. The property has now a value of fully $175,000. The main hall has a floor space of 75×125. The gymnasium is thoroughly equipped, and the library, reading and meeting rooms are appropriately arranged. The library contains over 3,000 volumes, and includes many standard German works. The reading-room is supplied with the leading German periodicals. At an evening school, conducted in the building, instruction is given in the languages by competent teachers. There are also a school of short-hand and classes in drawing, free to members of the society. About 500 children, of both sexes, are instructed in gymnastics. The first Turner Hall, occupied in 1863, was destroyed by the great fire, and the present building was erected on its site. The president of the society is L. Nettelhorst; the financial secretary is H. Heinemann, and the treasurer is E. Fielder.

The **Turn Verein Voerwarts** has about 250 members. It formerly owned the West Side Turner Hall, 251·West Twelfth Street, and although it become necessary, through financial embarrassment, to sell the property, the society still occupies the hall. The gymnasium has an excellent equipment. Senior classes are taught in the evening, and juvenile classes in the afternoon, Prof. W. Zoller being the instructor.

The **Bohemian Gymnastic Association** ("Sokol") is the "central union" of thirteen branch societies, distributed among the leading American cities. Four of these branches are in Chicago. The membership of the association is composed of delegates from the branch societies. Its main object is to promote the mental and physical culture of the Bohemian people in this country. It meets on the first Friday of each month at 74 West Taylor Street. J. B. Belohradsky is president, and George Hajek, secretary.

The Aurora Turn Verein was organized Feb. 22, 1864. It formerly owned Aurora Turner Hall, corner of Huron Street and Milwaukee Avenue. Becoming financially embarrassed the hall was sold, but the society continues to occupy it. The gymnasium, which is the leading feature, is well equipped with devices for gymnastic exercise, and there are senior and juvenile classes, for the boys and girls. The library contains several hundred books, mostly German, and the reading-room is supplied with the leading German periodicals. The membership numbers about 270, and the society is flourishing. William Legner is president; Prof. Aug. Zaph, teacher.

The Military Order of the Loyal Legion of the United States, organized in 1867, has its headquarters for the state of Illinois in this city. Its members are, or have been commissioned officers of the United States army and navy, who made honorable records during the late war. The Illinois membership numbers about 175, mostly in Chicago. Meetings are held monthly at the rooms of the Chicago Literary Club, in Portland Block, at each of which some member reads a paper on some battle or campaign. Gen. Sheridan commanded here until his removal to Washington. He was succeeded by Col. John Mason Lewis.

The Eighty-second Illinois Veteran Society was organized in October, 1881, to keep up good fellowship among comrades of the regiment, to relieve distress, and to bury dead brethren when necessary. The members are Germans and Scandinavians. The meetings are held monthly at No. 171 North Clark Street. Joseph Reilling is president; Geo. Vocke, secretary; Peter Lauer, treasurer.

The Nineteenth Illinois Infantry Volunteers Veteran Club numbers fifty members, and was organized in the summer of 1880, to promote reunion and mutual good fellowship. Regular meetings are held monthly at No. 106 Randolph Street.

The Veteran Union League is composed of old Union soldiers of any regiment or state, honorably discharged, together with a limited number of their friends. It was organized for social and political purposes, and dates from June, 1880. It has a total of 175 active and honorary members, including some of the best citizens of Chicago. It is an offshoot of the Chicago Union Veteran Club, its members being also members of the latter organization. The League has handsomely furnished apartments at No. 185 Clark Street, a whole floor being fitted up for its use. Regular meetings are held here monthly. W. S. Scribner is president ; W. W. King, treasurer ; W. H. Coulston, Matteson House, secretary. A growing interest is minifested in the affairs of the League, and it promises to increase in influence from year to year.

The **Union League of America** was founded the first year of the late civil war, for the purpose of supporting, protecting and defending the constitution and government of the United States against all enemies. It had many stirring assemblies during the years of the great conflict, and did incalculable good for the country. The nucleus of the organization was formed at a meeting of eleven patriotic persons in Cleveland, Ohio. The work of organization spread rapidly, and in May, 1863, the national council met for the first time, with eighteen states represented. From that time the league gained rapidly in strength, and soon extended its beneficent influence over the entire country, counting its members by the millions. It has little more than a nominal existence at present, though the organization is still intact. The Grand Council of the State of Illinois has its headquarters at Room 415, First National Bank building. George Harlow is president ; Henry S. Hawley, secretary, and John C. Baker. treasurer.

The **Thirteen Club** was organized April 13, 1883, to combat the superstition as to the unlucky character of Friday, of the number Thirteen, and other relics of folk lore. There is also provision for assisting members or their families in case of sickness or death among them. The number Thirteen is introduced in every possible way. At all banquets each table must contain exactly thirteen, and the regular meetings are held on the thirteenth of each month. in Room 13, at the Grand Pacific Hotel. The exercises are social and literary. The club now c ntains two groups of thirteen, or twenty-six members in all. Francis H. Hill is chief ruler ; William C. Duncan, scribe ; W. H. Bolton, receiver.

The **Canadian Club** is a social organization instituted in 1880. It has two classes of members, the leading class being native Canadians and their descendants, and the other such persons of other nationalities as the club may see fit to admit to membership. The latter class is limited to 100. The entire membership is 125. The club gives an annual dinner. E. J. Ogden is president ; E. R. Ogden, treasurer ; W. G. Richardson, secretary.

10

The Washington Park Club was organized in 1883. Though one of the newest, it is one of the most aristocratic club organizations. It was modeled after the American Jockey Club of New York City, and famous European jockey clubs. It opened its splendid race course—for running races—June 28, 1884, with a brilliant and successful meeting. The grounds, lying just south of Washington Park, contain eighty and one-half acres. Nearly $450,000 have been spent on the grounds and improvements. The track is eighty feet in width, and a mile in circuit. The infield is ornamented with two small lakes. The club house is palatial. It covers 80×125 feet of ground and cost over $60,-000. It is open to members the year round. The grand stand, 55×504

WASHINGTON PARK CLUB HOUSE.

feet, is three stories high and will seat about 10,000. The stables will accommodate 500 horses. The club has over 600 members. The entrance fee is $150, and the annual dues $40. The capital stock is $250,000. Gen. P. H. Sheridan is president; John R. Walsh, treasurer; and John E. Brewster, secretary.

The Chicago Union Veteran Club is a strong political organization numbering 1,875 active and associate members, among whom are many prominent and influential men. It was organized in September, 1876, to "uphold the principles of the Republican party," but "reserving the right to act independently where the interests of the Union veteran soldiers are involved;" to procure employment for Union soldiers and sailors, and to cultivate good fellowship among the members. It was incorporated Dec. 6, 1880. Sons of deceased Union soldiers may become active members, and sons of living veterans associate members, if of age. The annual picnics of this club are always largely attended. The club exerts a powerful influence in local politics. The regular meetings are held monthly at the office of the secretary. James A. Sexton is president; John L. Manning, 163 Washington Street, secretary; William H. Bolton, treasurer.

The **Chicago Board of Trade Battery Association** was organized July 3, 1865. It is composed of members of the old Board of Trade Battery, banded together for mutual benefit and to perpetuate friendships formed while in active service. All members of the battery are considered members of the association. There are ninety-five of these living whose residences are known, and eighty-five who may be living, but whose residences are not known. The annual meeting for reunion is held at the Palmer House club room, on the first Monday in April.

The **Twenty-fourth Illinois Veteran Society** was organized in 1868, for social and commemorative purposes, and to relieve needy regimental comrades. It has sixty members, and holds monthly meetings at No. 171 North Clark Street. Charles Hagemann is secretary.

The **Chicago Veterans of the Mexican War** is an association composed of soldiers, sailors, mariners and teamsters who served in the war with Mexico, and were honorably discharged. The general objects are social and commemorative, but its special purpose is to aid in placing the surviving veterans of the Mexican war on the pension rolls of the government, as a just and proper recognition of their services. The association, which was formed in November, 1876, now numbers about sixty members, nearly all of them residents of the city. Regular meetings are held quarterly at No. 106 Randolph Street. James R. Huegunin is secretary.

The **Irish-American Club**, one of the most popular Irish organizations in the city, was founded in 1881, for social, literary and national purposes. It has about 300 members, and is the oldest club of the kind in the country. It occupies very neat and convenient rooms on the third floor of Nos. 88 and 90 Washington Street, which include a general meeting hall, reception room, billiard room, reading room and library.

The **Chicago Mercantile Battery Veteran Association** was formed in 1867, disbanded by the great fire of 1871, and reorganized in 1877. It now has about 100 members, chiefly residents of the city and suburbs. Its purpose is to bring together socially those who served during the war in the Mercantile Battery, so named because it was raised by the efforts of the " Mercantile Association" of the city. The present members are all that survive of the 300 who served with the battery. An annual reunion is held by the society.

The Irish-American Council, which was organized in 1869, has a membership numbering 195, composed of three delegates from each of the sixty-five Irish-American societies in the city. Its office is to arrange for the celebration of St. Patrick's and other Irish national days. The meetings are at the call of the president. William Curran is president.

The Fritz Reuter Club was organized for social objects in 1881. Its membership is restricted to Germans engaged in mercantile pursuits, and is limited to seventy-five. Seventy members are now enrolled, and until recently its club rooms under McCormick's Hall, were open four days and evenings of each week. At present meetings are held on Wednesday evenings only, at Uhlich Hall.

The Chicago Association of Ex-Union Prisoners of War was first organized in April, 1880, as the Prisoners of War Union of Chicago. Upon the reorganization of the National Association in September, 1883, the Chicago subordinate association was also immediately reorganized. The main object is to secure national legislation for the benefit of ex-union prisoners of war. Several bills for this purpose have already been introduced in Congress, but none of them have yet been passed. Meetings are held on the second Friday of each month at No. 106 Randolph Street. There are nearly 200 members enrolled.

The Chicago Photographic Association has for its object the advancement of photography, mutual instruction and social good fellowship. It was organized in 1871, and meets monthly at 229 State Street. Prof. H. D. Garrison is president, and F. H. Davies, 88 Walton Place, is secretary and treasurer.

The Chicago Yacht Club is the only yacht club in the city. Its club house is at 189 Michigan Avenue, near the anchorage of the fleet, which consists of twenty-four vessels, and is harbored behind the government pier. The yachts are the individual property of the members. Among the most noted are the "Wasp," the largest sloop in fresh water, owned by Capt. Prindeville, the projector and first commodore of the club, and the schooner "Idler," owned by vice-commodore Fisher, and believed to be the fastest yacht in the world. At the regatta of the New York Yacht Club, June 8, 1876, she made the fastest time ever made by any yacht. She has won more prizes than any other yacht in America. The club has an annual summer cruise to Milwaukee, attended by a cup race, and social festivities on board, the families and friends of many of the members accompanying them on the cruise. The summer, and fall reguttas on the lake near Chicago are events of public interest. The club signal is a swallow-tailed red pennant, with a diagonal blue band half the width of the head, the upper margin of the band being a straight line from the lower point to the upper clew. The club house walls are ornamented with marine pictures and models. This club has been the inspiration and support of yachting interest in this section, and since its organization has not lost a life in any of its cruises or contests. It was organized in 1875, and incorporated in 1882, and has 150 members. The officers are : A. J. Fisher, commodore ; E. W. Syer, vice-commodore ; R. F. Pettibone, rear commodore ; Harry Duvall, recording secretary ; A. P. Seymour, 162 Washington Street, corresponding secretary ; F. W. S. Bramley, treasurer ; F. B. H. Bonter, measurer ; W. Blanchard, M. D., fleet surgeon ; C. E. Kremer, judge advocate ; Jos. Ruff, time-keeper.

The **Farragut Boat Club** is the oldest club of the kind now in existence in Chicago, and one of the most prominent and influential in the amateur boating circles of the United States. It was organized March 10, 1872, and incorporated July 1, 1875. On three occasions the boat house of the club was destroyed by lake storms—at the foot of Twenty-first Street in 1874 ; at the foot of Thirteenth Street in 1877 and at the foot of Twenty-fifth Street in 1882. In the latter case the house, a commodious structure of brick and stone, was entirely destroyed together with eighteen valuable boats. A temporary house of brick was immediately constructed and fully equipped with new boats, and the club at once purchased valuable building lots on Lake Park Avenue, near Thirty-first Street, and at this writing (October, 1884,) is actively engaged in the arrangements for the erection of a club house to cost $20,000. The working plans indicate a very elegant and substantial structure, two stories high, over a fine basement which will contain the bowling alleys, boat room, and gymnasium. The main floor is devoted to parlors, library and club rooms. The third floor will contain a fine private theater and dancing hall. Owning but one boat in 1872, the club now possesses twenty-five of the most expensive boats, including a number belonging to members. The entire club property is valued at $20,000. The membership includes 160 of the representative young men of Chicago. The club has now over fifty hard fought victories in aquatic contests, and many flags and gold medals attest its prowess in this direction. It is a member of the "National Association of Amateur Oarsmen," of "The Mississippi Valley Amateur Rowing Association" and of the "Northwestern Amateur Association." The receptions and entertainments given by the Farragut Club during the winter season are regarded as among the leading social events. The officers are: Lyman B. Glover, president; Clinton B. Hale, vice-president; George R. Blodgett, secretary; Frank M. Staples, treasurer; George A. McClellan, captain; Charles S. Downs, commander; W. R. Collins, Lieut. commander; W. V. Booth, ensign.

The **Pullman Athletic Association** was incorporated in February, 1883, as a joint stock company, with a capital stock of $10,000. Its buildings are located on Athletic Island, Pullman, on the shore of Lake Calumet. In addition to a boat house there are two fine grand stands commanding a running track and also the rowing course on the lake. On the mainland there are cricket and base ball grounds, controlled by the club. Athletic games are given under the auspices of the club every spring and fall, and several notable regattas have been given by it. In 1883 a notable event on the Pullman rowing course was a regatta in which Edward Hanlan, John Teamen and all the other leading professionals of this county participated. The same year the annual regatta of the Mississippi Valley Amateur Rowing Association was held on the same course. The membership of the club includes many living both in Chicago and Pullman. The president is Mr. E. W. Henricks; secretary, W. R. Harper; treasurer, John Hopkins.

The **Evanston Boat Club** is composed of business men of Chicago, who reside in Evanston. It was organized in 1880 and now has sixty-five active and seventy-five honorary members. Its club house, located at Evanston, was erected at a cost of about $6,000, and its boats and other club property are valued at $4,000. The club house is one of the best in this section. It contains club rooms, toilet and reception rooms, and a spacious dancing hall. The club parties, readings and other entertainments given by the club are among its leading features. It belongs to the Mississippi Valley Amateur Rowing Association, but has only taken part in one contest. H. M. Winnie is president; F. K. Stevens, treasurer; F. J. Kitchell, secretary; E. S. Sherman, captain.

The **Catlin Boat Club** was organized April 7, 1882, with seven members. A boat house was immediately erected at Cedar Lake, Ind., thirty-eight miles from Chicago, which was replaced in 1883 by a larger and better structure. It is 28×44 feet, has two stories and is provided with reading, sleeping and other rooms. The club now numbers fourteen members. It belongs to the Mississippi Valley Amateur Rowing Association, but has only rowed in one race, and has not yet won any prizes. The membership fee is $20, and the annual dues $12. Charles Catlin is president; Robert Meyers, treasurer; Thomas P. Hallinan is secretary; and Thomas W. Reading, captain.

The **Delaware Boat Club** was organized in October, 1880. Its club house is located on the lake shore, near the North Side water works. It is equipped with the usual club conveniences, and a creditable gymnasium. The first entry in the Mississippi Valley Amateur Rowing Association regattas was in 1883, at Pullman, where the Delaware's four-oared crew took fourth place. And in 1884, the club won the junior and senior double scull races of the same association at Moline, Ill. The club has thirty-two active, associate and honorary members.

The **Ogden Boat Club** was the first boat club organized on the North Side and dates its existence from 1881. It was chartered in 1883, and now has a membership of thirty, all young men of high social and business standing. It is the strongest boat club in the North Division. Its boat house at the foot of Superior Street is transformed into a gymnasium during winter months. The rowing exercises take place in the lake. S. H. Kerfoot, Jr., is president; Edward Dickinson, secretary.

The **Chicago Canoe Club** is composed of about sixty prominent business men who practice canoeing for exercise and pleasure. It was organized Jan. 11, 1884. Short annual cruises are made by the club or in smaller parties. The headquarters of this club are in rooms at the Academy of Sciences, 263 Wabash Avenue.

Tippy Canoe Club is a private canoe club of eighteen members from the Chicago Canoe Club. It was organized in 1884, and has a small boat house at the foot of Thirty-fifth Street.

The **Iroquois** is a boat club of recent organization on the North Side.

The **Cumberland Gun Club** is devoted to the preservation of game and the enforcement of the game laws, and to hunting and fishing, and kindred sports. It controls, by lease and purchase, seven and one-half square miles of marsh land in Lake County, Ind. The club house, known as "Cumberland Lodge," is six miles from Lowell, on the Louisville, New Albany & Chicago Railroad. A keeper is in charge of the club house the year round. A gamekeeper and constable are also employed during the shooting season. The membership is limited to seventy-five, and the membership fee is $75. Semi-annual meetings are held at the Sherman House, in January and July. John M. Smyth is president; Chas. K. Herrick, secretary, and John Heiland, treasurer.

The **Tolleston Club** was formed in 1871 by a number of gentlemen of Chicago, who for years had resorted to the marshes of the Little Calumet River for duck and snipe shooting. It was incorporated under the state law of Illinois, March 27, 1873. The tract of marsh land owned by the club, comprising some 2,100 acres, lies in Lake County, Ind. It is surrounded by a wire fence and is under guard of efficient gamekeepers. The club house is located on the north bank of the Calumet River, nearly in the center of the extensive marshes. It is provided with ample conveniences for sportsmen, and for the social entertainment of the members of the club. The club property is valued at $75,000. There are over 100 members. F. A. How is president; Edward Starr, secretary; and C. D. Peacock, treasurer.

The **Audubon Club** was chartered Jan. 21, 1876, and has for its objects the enforcement of the laws for the protection of game, the education and advancement of its members in the art of wing-shooting, and the collection and preservation of ornithological specimens. It has no special place for shooting, but generally meets in Kleinman's Park, at Grand Crossing. The annual meeting of the club is held at the Sherman House, the second Tuesday in January. There are thirty-five active members. Charles Kern, 110 LaSalle Street, is president.

The **Chicago Sharpshooters' Association** has over 150 members, nearly all Germans, and is the oldest German shooting club in the city. It was incorporated Feb. 16, 1865, by act of the legislature which gave it the powers of ordinary business corporations, and summary powers in dealing with delinquent members. It is devoted to rifle target practice. The range, two hundred yards long, is in "Sharpshooters' Park," an eighty acre tract of land owned by the association, and valued at about $50,000, about two miles southeast of Washington Heights, on which are a club house and hall.

The **Mak-Saw-Ba Club** took its name from one of the early Indian chiefs of this region. It was organized and incorporated in 1878, and is recognized as one of the leading organizations of the kind in this locality. It owns over 3,000 acres of land situated in Starke and La Porte Counties, Indiana, sixty-four miles from Chicago, especially adapted to hunting and fishing, and kindred sports. Its spacious club house was erected at a cost of $2,800, and its membership, including many prominent men of the city, numbers seventy-five persons. The rules adopted for the government of the club prohibit the sale of intoxicating liquors on the grounds, and exclude gambling in any form. No loaded gun is allowed in the club-house, and the firing of guns is

expressly prohibited on the Sabbath day. Semi-a█████████usiness meetings are held at the Sherman House on the seco.█████ay of December and June, respectively. George G. Newbury is president; William
E. Chamberlin, treasurer; and Charles D. Newbury, secretary.

The Fox Lake Shooting and Fishing Club was incorporated in June,
1879. Its membership is limited to seventy-five, and over fifty are
now enrolled. The club property is located on the west shore of Fox
Lake, McHenry County, Ill. It consists of several acres of land having

CLUB HOUSE.

ample shore line, with broad, clean, pebbly beach. The entire grounds
are fenced in a substantial manner, and rise from the water's edge to
the height of eighty feet. There are swings and hammocks, and all
necessary provisions for croquet and tennis. The main club-house
stands on a terrace, commanding a beautiful view of the lake. The
building is a two-story frame, three sides having broad balconies, over-
grown with woodbine. On the crest of the hill in the rear, and shaded
by trees, is "Pullman Cottage," a bachelor retreat for the gentlemen of
the club. At the foot of the bluff is the boat house, the upper story of
which is devoted to billiards. The club owns several hunting and fish-

ing boats, tw███████ sail boats, six row boats, and a large yacht, perfect in model, ████ing and finish. The cost of the grounds and improvements was $14,500. C. F. Hills is president, and Philo J. Beveridge, secretary. J. M. Miller, 85 Washington Street, is manager.

The Diana Hunting Club owns 2,600 acres of land at Thayer, Indiana, fifty-three miles from Chicago, on the line of the L. N. A. & C. Railway. Twenty acres of the land are under cultivation. The club-house contains thirteen rooms and accommodations for forty-five persons. The club was incorporated in December, 1881. F. Freudenberg is president; J. A. Kreutzberg, 86 Oak Street, secretary; and E. E. Roehl, treasurer.

The South End Shooting Club, organized in 1873, and subsequently incorporated, is confined to trap shooting. Four contests are held each year at Watson's Park, Grand Crossing, for a medal, which becomes the property of the member who wins it three times. George T. Farmer, 130 LaSalle Street, is secretary.

The Sportsmen's Club of Chicago was organized nearly twelve years ago, and has at present thirty members, the limit provided by the constitution. Its club house and grounds are at Water Valley, Indiana, on the Kankakee River, fifty-six miles from Chicago. C. A. Orvis is president, and J. J. Flanders, secretary and treasurer.

The North Chicago Sharpshooters' Association, composed mostly of Germans, was incorporated in August, 1879. It has a membership of about 125, including many prominent persons. It owns a tract of twenty-five acres of land in the southeast corner of the town of Jefferson, on which is a fine range, 200 yards in length, and a large hall used for club purposes. Matches are held every Sunday between April 15 and September 1.

The Lake View Rifle Club is now in the seventh year of its history, having been organized in February, 1877. Its range is 200 yards in length, and is said to be one of the finest in the west. The grounds, which are known as the old Lake View House grounds, are nicely situated, and are well shaded by large forest trees. The club house is neat and appropriate. Regular shoots are held every Saturday during seasonable weather, commencing at 2 P. M. There are thirty-five active and fifteen honorary members. Seth F. Hanchett is president; Henry C. Bradley, secretary and treasurer; John Macauley is captain.

The Chicago Shooting Club, the largest trap shooting club in the city, was incorporated twelve years ago with but seven members. It holds four shooting contests each year at Kleinman's Park, Grand

Crossing, a medal being awarded to the victor and becoming the individual property of any member who may win it three times. The club now has a membership of sixty-five.

The **Southwest Chicago Sharpshooters' Association** has a range at the corner of Halsted and Fifty-second Streets, the grounds being known as the Southwest Chicago Shooting Park. The park is open every day for the pleasure of the members, and the association has regular shooting practice every Sunday during seasonable weather. It is composed wholly of Germans. It was incorporated March 6, 1877, as the "Southwest Chicago Schuetzenverein."

Other **Sportmen's Clubs** include the English Lake Shooting and Fishing Club ; Lake George Sportsmen's Association ; Vermillion Gun Club and Geo. H. Thomas Rifle Club.

The **Chicago Bowling Club** was organized and incorporated in 1871. It now has a membership of fifteen persons. The club house and bowling alley, located at 500 North Clark Street, are owned by the club, and valued at $6,500.

The **Chicago Curling Club** was organized about twenty-five years ago, for the purpose of keeping up an interest in the old Scotch game of curling, which is played on ice during the winter months. The lakes at Lincoln Park have been used for that purpose for years past, but the club has recently purchased property on York Street, near Ashland Avenue, at a cost of $20,000, for a club house and an artificial pond. There are about 100 members, the majority being natives of Scotland.

The **Chicago Cricket Club** usually plays its games in Lincoln Park on Tuesday, Thursday and Saturday of each week during the season, which extends from May 15 to October 1. Its membership, numbering 150 persons, active and associate, includes many fine players, and the club is generally recognized as the strongest in the west. It was organized in 1876, since which time a greater local interest has been manifested in the old English game than ever before. Its roll of honorary members contains the names of such well-known persons as P. D. Armour, Gen. P. F. Sheridan, Mayor Carter H. Harrison and others. E. J. Ogden, M. D., is president ; R. P. Palmer, 150 LaSalle Street, secretary ; E. R. Ogden, M. D., 1636 Michigan Avenue, treasurer.

The **Other Cricket Clubs** are all of recent organization. The Wanderers and the St. George's Clubs were each organized in 1883. Both are strong clubs. The Wanderers has about fifty members. Its playgrounds are at the corner of Thirty-seventh Street and Indiana Avenue.

F. Rayfield is secretary. The St. George's Club plays at Lincoln Park four days of each week. It has about seventy playing members. W. J. Dowse, 154 Center Street, is secretary. The Albion Club plays at Douglas Park. The Millard Avenue and the Rovers are new clubs on the West Side. The Pullman Club, at Pullman, is a very strong club.

The **Chicago Racquet Club** is an association organized in 1880, with the view of encouraging a taste for racquets and other similar diversions tending to muscular development. The club is located at 185 Michigan Avenue, in the same building-with the bicycle club. It has a membership of about fifty. The initiation fee is $25, and the annual dues $25. Samuel Johnson is president.

The **Chicago Bicycle Club** was organized in September, 1879. It has sixty-five active members, and an associate membership consisting of friends of the club who are not bicyclists. It uses the club house at 185 Michigan Avenue, jointly with the Racquet Club. The club house is provided with a gymnasium, bowling alley, baths and an apartment for bicycle practice. Rules of the club provide for five-miles contests every thirty days, and annual contests for championship medals. A medal is awarded for the greatest number of miles traveled by bicycle each year.

The **Hermes Bicycle Club** is composed of about twenty young men of the South Side, under twenty-one years of age.

The **Armory Bicycle Club** has about twenty-five members, most of them also members of Battery D, State Guards. Headquarters at Battery D Armory.

The **Union Riding Club** is a fashionable society of ladies and gentlemen, and the only riding club in the city. It was organized and incorporated in 1882. Its spacious and handsome club house, provided with all the requisites of a first-class riding club, is located at 529 North Clark Street. A proficient riding-master instructs the members in the equestrian art. The membership numbers 130 persons, all stockholders in the club.

The **Chicago Base Ball Club** was first organized in 1870, and was a member of the National Association of Base Ball Clubs until that organization disbanded in 1876. Since that time it has been a member of the National League, and is now the only professional ball club in the city. It won the championship in 1876, 1881 and 1882. The year after the great fire it had no team in the field. A. G. Spalding is president.

The **Polo Clubs** play polo on roller skates only. The Chicago Polo Club is the oldest. It was organized in February, 1884, and incorporated the following May. Its members are patrons of the Casino Roller Skating Rink. The club has played against some of the best clubs in the country, and has gained considerable reputation for proficiency. It has nicely fitted up club rooms in the Casino Rink for the entertainment of visitors and friends. The Princess Polo Club was organized in June, 1884, from the best skaters of the Princess Rink. Its match games have so far been confined to contests with the Chicago Club.

The **Dania Society,** Kinzie and Desplaines Streets, was organized Nov. 23, 1862, as the "Society Dania," and reorganized and incorporated under its present name in August, 1865. It admits males only to membership, and now has about 120 on its rolls. It gives substantial aid to members when sick ; has a commodious hall and a comfortable library and reading room, well supplied with Danish and American publications. The reading room is open from 3 P. M. till midnight every day for the accommodation of members.

The **Chicago Medico-Historical Society** meets at the rooms of the Medical Press Association, No. 188 Clark Street, annually, on the last Friday in April, and quarterly thereafter. It was organized in 1844. It collects and publishes data having reference to the medical profession, and publishes annually a list of physicians in good standing. Dr. P. S. Hayes, secretary and treasurer.

The **Chicago Dental Society** was organized in 1864. Its special object is to promote dental science and to afford social opportunities to its members. At a recent annual meeting Dr. G. V. Black was admitted as the first honorary member. Dr. J. G. Reid is secretary.

The **Chicago Academy of Homœopathic Physicians and Surgeons** is the oldest homœopathic society in the city. It was established in 1869, and its aim is the advancement and improvement of homœopathy and the collateral branches of medical science. It has a membership of fifty, and holds monthly meetings at the Grand Pacific Hotel. C. E. Ehinger, secretary and treasurer.

The **Chicago Eclectic Medical and Surgical Society** was organized in 1870. Mutual benefit in the promotion of professional interests, the communication and development of useful and scientific knowledge, and the cultivation of fraternal sentiment, are the special objects of the society. Monthly meetings at the Grand Pacific Hotel. E. F. Rush, M. D., is secretary.

The **Chicago Medical Press Association** is an incorporated joint stock company. It provides a library and reading rooms, at 188 Clark Street, with a valuable collection of medical and scientific books, periodicals, etc., for the use of the stockholders, who must be members of the medical profession in good and regular standing. Dr. J. H. Etheredge is secretary, and Dr. J. N. Hyde, editor.

The **Chicago Medical Society** meets semi-monthly at the Grand Pacific Hotel. Its chief object is mutual improvement in the discussion of professional and scientific matters. It is the oldest general medical society in the city. It has a membership of 250. L. H. Montgomery, M. D., secretary.

The **Women's Homœopathic Medical Society** meets at Room 43, Central Music Hall, on the second Wednesday of each month. It was organized in 1879. Dr. Jennie E. Smith is secretary.

The **Chicago Gynecological Society** was organized in October, 1878, and incorporated in 1880. Its object is the discussion and consideration of all subjects legitimately connected with obstetrics, gynecology and pediatrics. Its meetings are held monthly at the Grand Pacific Hotel. E. W. Sawyer, M. D., is secretary and treasurer.

The **Woman's Physiological Institute** was organized in the summer of 1880, and is an outgrowth of the Chicago Woman's Club. Its purpose is to disseminate knowledge relating to the human system, particularly with reference to anatomy, physiology, hygiene, the training of children, etc. Mrs. Helen Shedd, 3759 Vincennes Avenue, is president.

The **Medical Science Club** was organized by a number of young physicians, July 10, 1883, to furnish able and energetic young physicians an opportunity to exchange information in regard to their investigations and discoveries in their respective specialties. Its meetings are held semi-monthly in Room 38, Central Music Hall. F. R. Day is secretary and treasurer.

The **Clinical Society of Hahnemann Hospital** holds monthly meetings at the Grand Pacific Hotel. The membership numbers about 300, composed of local physicians and the alumni of Hahnemann Medical College and of colleges of the same school in various parts of the country. The proceedings of the society are published in the *Clinique*, a monthly medical journal. Dr. A. K. Crawford is secretary.

Other Clubs and Societies, including art, musical and scientific organizations, will be found in more appropriate chapters. The church societies and literary clubs, all the temperance and secret societies, the trade and labor unions, and organizations partaking more of a state or national than a local character, and many minor local organizations, have been omitted from this volume.

The Burial Places.

THE BURIAL PLACES OF EARLY CHICAGO, THE NEW CEME-
TERIES, AND THE TOMBS.

THE burials of early Chicago were generally made near the residences
of the friends of the deceased. The first dead of the fort were
buried on a quiet spot of ground near the river on the North Side, and
not far from the residence of Mr. Kinzie, the pioneer settler, and who,
upon his death in 1828, was interred in the same vicinity. Later,
those dying at the fort were buried along the sandy shore of the lake
on the south side of the river. The soldiers who died of cholera in
1832 were interred very near the present foot of Lake Street. And
the lake shore, from Lake Street southward for a distance of several
squares, seems to have become a general burying ground of the embryo
city. Many of the graves there were afterward washed out by the lashing
waves of the lake. There was also a small burying ground on the West
Side, near the forks of the river. It is thought that but few interments
were made in it. In 1835, under the direction of the town authorities,
two cemeteries were laid out, one on the South Side and the other on
the North Side. The former was located on the lake shore, a short distance south of where Eighteenth Street now reaches the lake. The
latter lay on the lake shore just north of the Chicago Avenue of to-day,
and east of State Street. The North Side water works occupy a portion of the grounds. The South Side cemetery seems to have been
more used at first, but few, if any, burials took place in it after 1837.
Interments were made in the North Side cemetery as late as 1841 or
1842. The venerable citizen, J. Young Scammon, had a child buried
there, and friends and relatives of other honored and well-known citizens still living, rested for a time beneath its sod. The rapid growth
of the city, however, soon encompassed these cities of the dead, and
the sleeping inhabitants were removed to the cemetery which was
located on what is now the south end of Lincoln Park. But even here
the sacred precincts of the grave were invaded by the resistless march
of the city. Soon after the close of the late war the grounds of the
cemetery were condemned for park purposes, and most of the bodies

were taken up and reburied in the newer cemeteries which had been located miles out amid the country solitudes, "far from the maddening crowd's ignoble strife."

Rosehill Cemetery, located some six and one-half miles north of the City Hall, and about one and a half miles west of the lake, takes rank with the Campo Santo of Pisa, or Mount Auburn, Laurel Hill and Greenwood of this country. It is the largest of the cemeteries connected with Chicago, and possesses a site on a rolling upland from thirty to forty feet above the level of the lake. It encloses a space of about 500 acres, nearly one-half of which is improved. Approaching it from any direction, it stands out in alto relief from the level prairie, showing in the summer a mass of beautiful green. The main entrance to the grounds is through a stately and impressive castellated stone structure which contains a chapel appropriately arranged for funeral services. Within the grounds the winding and spacious macadamized walks and broad carriage drives are hard, smooth and noiseless. The slender lakes are bordered with spaces devoted to lawns and exquisite evolutions of landscape gardening. The lakes are filled with water from an artesian well 2,279 feet deep. There are spacious greenhouses and conservatories for propagating plants, shrubs and flowers for funeral or grave decoration. The receiving vault, embedded in the side of a large grassy mound, is very complete in all its arrangements. One of the first memorials which attracts attention, upon entering the cemetery, is an obelisk designating the family lot of the late P. F. W. Peck, who was a well-known and wealthy citizen of Chicago. It is of a dark-colored granite, plain, rich and massive. To the west is the beautiful memorial shaft, with broken top, heavily veiled, erected to that gallant soldier, Gen. Edward Greenfield Ransom, who died in the service of his country. His memorial stone tells the story of his soldier's career. On the pedestal is chiseled:—

CHARLESTON, MO.

FORT DONELSON.

SHILOH.

CORINTH.

CHAMPION HILLS, MISS.

VICKSBURGH.

PLEASANT HILL, LA.

The monument to Geo. S. Bangs, the originator of the fast mail service

VIEWS IN ROSEHILL CEMETERY, LOOKING EAST TOWARD THE ENTRANCE.

in this country, is one of the most unique and attractive in Rosehill. It is a massive tree, in gray stone, with top and several branches broken off; near the base, in the opening of a tunnel, is seen the rear of a mail car. A massive granite block, some three feet square, marks the resting place of Gen. B. J. Sweet, who was commander of Camp Douglas during the civil war. I: was " erected by his daughter, Ada." The monument to Mrs. H. O. Stone is very interesting. It represents a lady reclining at full length on a couch and playing with her child. The latter lies on one arm of the mother, whose other arm is thrown back over her head. The figures are in the finest Italian marble, and are masterpieces. The Masons, Odd Fellows, Good Templars, Firemen's Benevolent Association, Typographical Union, St. Andrew's and St. George's Societies, Batteries A and B, and Bridges' Battery are among the benevolent and patriotic associations which are represented. The soldiers' monument is one of the most imposing and characteristic memorials on the grounds. On the summit of the lofty shaft is a life-size figure of a federal soldier, with full accoutrements; and on the faces of the shaft are bronze castings, each indicative of some phase of soldier life. The Egleston and Staubro lot is noticeable for its elegant monumental piece, which consists of a square block of stone raised on a heavy pedestal, and crowned with a life-size female figure, her eyes fixed upon the sod and in her hand a wreath of immortelles. This beautiful cemetery was dedicated in the presence of nearly 10,000 persons, the corner stone being laid by the Masonic orders with all the impressive ceremonies peculiar to their organization. The stone, of Athens marble, bears the legend : "This stone was laid July 28, A. D. 1859, A. L. 5859, by the Masonic Order. M. W. I. A. W. Buck, Grand Master." On July 11, 1859, the first funeral cortege entered the cemetery, bearing the remains of Dr. J. W. Ludlam. Since that date over 20,000 interments have taken place. Rosehill Cemetery Company was incorporated in 1859. The board of managers is composed of prominent citizens. Frederick Tuttle is president; Hon. Van H. Higgins, treasurer; and Joseph Gow, secretary. The city office is at Room 29, No. 159 LaSalle Street.

Calvary Cemetery, the principal Catholic burying ground, is situated about ten miles north of the City Hall on the lake shore. It was laid out in November, 1859, and down to the present time nearly 40,-000 interments have taken place. Among the distinguished dead in Calvary, Bishop Quartiers and Col. James A. Mulligan were perhaps the most prominent. The remains of the former lie in the vault, it never yet having been decided where to bury them. The citizens of the city and state have just erected a befitting monument to the gallant soldier, Col. Mulligan. Handsome memorials have recently been placed on the family lots of M. and W. Devine, and of Chas. J. O'Neil, John D. Tully and Philip H. Murphy. The graves of Mrs. John Hogan, P. W. Snow and David Thornton are each surmounted by graceful monuments. Richard M. Hooley has erected a costly family mausoleum of a unique southern design. The P. J. Sexton mausoleum is also rich and costly. The monumental sarcophagus for J. A. Wolford and wife is the most elaborate memorial of the kind in the cemetery. The majority of the memorials, however, are of the plainer and simpler descriptions. The cemetery contains 100 acres.

Graceland Cemetery lies north of the city, about two miles from Lincoln Park, between the lake on the east and Clark Street on the west. It is about six miles from the City Hall, and is reached by a broad drive along the lake shore through Lincoln Park and thence by North Clark Street, or by horse cars on Clark or State Street. The Chicago & Evanston Railroad, in course of construction, when completed will carry passengers direct to the cemetery entrance. This beautiful city of the dead occupies 125 acres of land at a point where the shore of the lake rises into an upland of swelling ridges, whose undulating surface presents a varied and attractive site. It is laid out in broad and winding avenues which are so arranged as to develop all the stronger of the landscape effects, which consist of sinuous lakes, clumps of woodland, stretches of lawn and meadows, grassy depressions, parterres exquisite in coloring, all harmoni us, appropriate, and in keeping with the solemn purpose of the inclosure. Although a beautiful and picturesque spot in its primitive state, with its wealth of native forest trees and luxuriant foliage, vast sums of money have been expended in bringing Graceland to its present perfection. The sewerage system insures the thorough drainage of every part of the spacious grounds. The main sewer, leading to Lake Michigan, was constructed at a cost of over $10,000. The beautiful artificial gems of water—Lotus Pond, Willowmere and Hazelmere—are supplied from living springs, and by a system of steam pumps water is carried through a net work of iron pipes to all parts of the cemetery. During dry seasons the grassy lawns and flower covered mounds are kept green and fresh by frequent and plentiful sprinklings. The avenues and drives have been macadamized, and expense and labor have not been spared to make Graceland one of the most attractive burying grounds in the country. The new depot of the

ENTRANCE TO GRACELAND CEMETERY.

A.N. MARQUIS & CO.

Chicago & Evanston Railway stands at the eastern entrance of the cemetery, and from its platform a fine view of the grounds is obtained. The depot itself is an attractive feature. It is a compact, one-storied frame building, with many suggestions of Swiss architecture in its steep, overhanging roofs, and in the breezy openness of its columned platform. It nestles in a dense grove of evergreens, which enclose it on all sides save that fronting the cemetery. It not only furnishes every convenience for passengers, in waiting and other rooms, but is sufficiently capacious to supply the cemetery company with required office accommodations. The road, when opened to traffic, will prove of the greatest value in furnishing a much-needed transportation on the line of its extension. The entrance to the grounds, at the junction of North Clark Street and Graceland Avenue, shown in the illustration on page 164, is a graceful piece of architecture of rough-finished gray stone.

One peculiarity of Graceland is that it everywhere presents suggestive features, which, while not inharmonious with the purpose of a necropolis, are cheerful, quieting and restful. They mitigate the sombre atmosphere which envelops always the resting place of the dead. Standing anywhere on the banks of the miniature lakes, there are seen in every direction landscapes of varied outlines, vegetation reflected in the peaceful mirror of the waters, all of which might be mistaken for the interior of an ornate park, were it not that here and there the glint of a marble column is caught. In fact, the whole has a park-like appearance; and in this direction there is developed a beautiful effort to relieve to the utmost possible extent the extra solemnity which usually broods over places of sepulture. The glories of spring, and the rich fruition of summer are full of suggestions to the mourner who wanders through the shaded aisles, of a possible spring and summer which have no autumn nor winter. Here, too, may be seen what loving hands can do to surround the homes of the dead with expressive tributes of regretful remembrance by which even the grievous pangs of separation are ameliorated, the memories of dear ones tenderly preserved, and much of the gloom of the grave dissipated. Many of the historic names of Chicago are to be found on the tombs of Graceland, and in the long list of lot owners. The remains of John Kinzie, the pioneer citizen of Chicago, find a resting place here, after several disinterments and removals from one place to another. Col. John H. Kinzie was buried here in 1865. John H. Kinzie, Jr., who was killed at the taking of Fort Charles, White River, June 18, 1862, sleeps at

his father's side, and other members of this noted family occupy adjacent graves. No stately monument marks their last earthly home ; but
unpretentious headstones silently proclaim that they have long since
ended the journey of life. Many members of the well-known Ogden
family are buried in Graceland; and Judge George Manierre, Justin
Butterfield, H. H. Magie, Walter Newberry, Alexander Fullerton, N. B.
Judd, W. F. Coolbaugh, Dr. Daniel Brainard and E. G. Hall, all of whom
were honored and revered citizens, lie beneath its hallowed sod. The
remains of John Calhoun, the founder of the first newspaper in Chicago, rest here in peaceful silence. Near to the main entrance stands
the monument to the late Eli B. Williams, a wealthy and respected
citizen, who died in Paris, France, but whose remains came back to
sleep in the city of his adoption. The monument is a lofty shaft of
granite, surmounted by an emblematic figure indicative of the
faith of the living, and the future of the dead. To the right is the lot
of the Armour family, in which rests George Armour, a well-known
merchant. A plain, granite column with an urnal top marks the spot,
characterizing it with elegant simplicity.

Strolling on the visitor encounters other graves, often of well-known
citizens, as those of Mr. and Mrs. Wesley Munger. A sightly shaft,
impressive in dimensions and outlines, forty-three feet in height, is, in
its severe plainness and simplicity, characteristic of the men
whose memory it perpetuates. It is the monument of the Sherman
family, whose head, Francis Cornwall Sherman, now resting within the
shadow of this stern shaft, was the founder of the hotel bearing his
name, and was thrice mayor of Chicago. A Corinthian column with
fluted shaft, its entablature serving as the pedestal of a female figure
bearing a cross and book, marks the last home of Azariah R. Palmer, late
of the firm of Palmer, Fuller & Co. It is a handsome work in itself, and its
effect is increased by the environment. A square shaft, some twenty-
five feet in height, and bearing on its top a female figure—one of the
most attractive works in Graceland—is reared over the grave of E. H.
Haddock, one of Chicago's wealthy citizens. The Allan Pinkerton lot
contains the newly-sodded grave of America's famous detective, and a
plain headstone which marks the grave of Timothy Webster, one of
Pinkerton's men, an Englishman, who was hanged as a spy by the Con-
federates, in Richmond, Va. One of the most conspicuous monuments
in Graceland is a granite obelisk, some forty feet in height, without
decoration of any kind, which marks the resting-place of Washington
Smith, once a wealthy business man of Chicago.

THE TAYLOR MAUSOLEUM.

THE ALLERTON MONUMENT.

A. N. MARQUIS & CO.

SCENES IN GRACELAND CEMETERY.

THE BATES MONUMENT.

The massive memorial shaft of the "Peabody of Chicago," Jona han Burr, is of Quincy granite. It is not as imposing as many others; but Burr does not need granite or marble to perpetuate his memory. There is scarcely an educational or charitable institution in Chicago which does not possess a monument of him, in the nature of generous endowments more lasting than granite. In an open space, on a low mound of green, rises a tall granite column finished with a pointed, ornamental cap, at whose base rests Eli Bates, the philanthropist. The situation is a charming one, although there is a hint of isolation which is not in harmony with a life which was largely composed of close intimacy with humanity.

On the smooth, velvety lawn, is the mausoleum of H. H. Taylor, formerly one of Chicago's leading citizens. It is a superb piece of mortuary architecture. The walls are of rough-finished stone. It is shown in an illustration on page 167. Five persons are now enclosed within its solid walls, or rather in the catacombs to which it leads. The Medill family lot contains the graves of W. H. Medill, of the Eighth Illinois Cavalry, who died of wounds received in battle; of James C. Medill and of Samuel J. Medill, late managing editor of *The Chicago Tribune.* A plain but impressive monument rises above the spot.

Perhaps the most elaborate and costly monuments in Graceland are those on the family lots of J. V. Farwell and William M. Hoyt. The former is of Scotch granite, capped with an urn, and from its massive dimensions is the most conspicuous memorial on the grounds. The Hoyt monument consists of a heavy granite base, supporting three figures, emblematic of Faith, Hope and Charity.

The lot of W. A. Fuller has a massive block of polished granite which serves as the pedestal for a female figure wrapped in a classical robe, standing with bowed head, the left arm resting gracefully on the right and the right hand holding stalks of wheat. The monument on the lot of T. M. Avery, one of Chicago's oldest citizens, has a massive pedestal from which rises a circular shaft, with an Egyptian capital. On this capital stands a female figure holding in her hands a trumpet, and gazing far into the distance as if waiting for the dawn of the moment that will permit her to signal the resurrection. The lot of William Blair contains a chaste monument in the form of a tomb. It is massive, solid, with decorated frieze and pediments, and panels ample for the mortuary records of the future. That of. G. T. Abbey, a granite column surmounted by a figure of "Glory." That of Samuel Allerton is shown in the accompanying illustration; the two female figures represent

Grief and Consolation. That of one of Chicago's oldest and most respected citizens, Philo Carpenter, is de ignated by a plain column of Italian marble.

Among other lot owners, the names of many prominent people are found, and many of the lots are ornamented with beautiful memorials. Some of the most prominent of these are Seth Wadhams, Mayor Harrison, Judge Drummond, N. K. Fairbank, Wirt Dexter, Joseph Medill, Keith Bros., Jerome Beecher and S. B. Cobb, L. J. McCormick, Albert Keep, T. W. Harvey, John De Koven, Henry W. King, Lorenz Brentano, Volney C. Turner, Daniel A. Jones, Edwin H. Sheldon, the heirs of the late Cyrus H. McCormick, Elisha Eldred, D. O. Shipman, S. D. Surdam, Chas. W. Sanford, O. W. Potter, Hiram Wheeler, Frank Parmalee, A. F. Otto, Dr. Byford, J. H. Dunham, R. W. Roloson and H. H. Magie. The oldest monument in the cemetery is that of Daniel Thompson. It is a dark granite pentagonal shaft.

Graceland was founded in 1861 by Thomas B. Bryan, and contained at first only eighty acres. The first interment took place on the 13th day of April, 1860, since which time about 40,000 persons have been buried there, the number exceeding that of any other cemetery in America except Greenwood, near New York City. Graceland is controlled by Graceland Cemetery Company, of which Bryan Lathrop is president.

By provision of the charter, ten per cent of the gross receipts from the sale of lots is set apart to form "The Graceland Cemetery Improvement Fund," which is safely invested, and will draw compound interest until such time as the interest on the fund becomes available under the terms of the charter. This fund insures the perpetual maintenance and preservation of the cemetery. It is held and managed by the following Board of Trustees, who are themselves lot owners, and are among the ablest and most responsible men of Chicago, viz.: William Blair, J. W. McGennis, Daniel Thompson, Marcus C. Stearns, E. W. Blatchford, Hiram Wheeler, George C. Walker, Jerome Beecher, Edwin H. Sheldon, A. J. Averill, John De Koven and Henry W. King.

The city office of the cemetery is at 115 Monroe Street, Montauk Block.

Oak Woods Cemetery is located on the east side of Cottage Grove Avenue, at Sixty-seventh Street, three and one-half miles south of the city limits. The plan of the cemetery was modeled after the famous Spring Grove Cemetery, at Cincinnati, and the grounds were laid out under the personal direction of Adolph Strauch, superintendent of that beautiful home of the dead. The design is on the lawn system, and the grounds are divided into sections, each with mounds of various forms and sizes, and here and there are scattered shade trees and clusters of shrubbery. A superintendent's house, a chapel, four greenhouses and an ample receiving vault, have been provided. Three beautiful artificial lakes, each from three to four acres in extent, have been completed, and a fourth is nearly finished. Oak Woods contains the graves of some of Chicago's oldest settlers, and of many prominent citizens. The unmarked grave of Jas. H. Woodworth, twice mayor of Chicago, and member of Congress, is found in a secluded spot. One of the most conspicuous monuments in the grounds is that rising above the grave of William Jones, an old settler and wealthy citizen. Other well-known names are those of Dr. C. E. Dyer and Charles Hitchcock. The latter was an eminent lawyer, and president of the last constitutional convention of Illinois. A plain granite monument marks the grave of Col. W. J. Foster, the geologist, and author of various works on the prehistoric races of America. The monument recently erected to the wife of Hon. Van H. Higgins is perhaps the most striking memorial in Oak Woods. A heroic figure of a soldier on guard, in pure white marble, looks down upon the graves of some sixty soldiers who were inmates of the old Soldiers' Home, and who died in that institution. At each of the four corners of the lot is a large cannon, placed there under the direction of Robert T. Lincoln, secretary of war. In the southern portion of the cemetery are buried over 6,000 Confederate dead, who died prisoners at Camp Douglas. An occasional unpretentious headstone is the only record of the men who sleep beneath. The first interment in Oak Woods was made in 1864. The entire number of burials at the present time is nearly 17,000. The city office of the cemetery is at Room 22 Union National Bank Building. Marcus A. Farwell is president of the Association.

Mount Greenwood is one of the newest burying places, having been laid out as late as 1879. It is about eight miles south of the city limits and contains eighty acres. The land has a sandy, undulating surface and is dotted here and there with ancient forest trees. A heavy rustic fence completes the enclosure, and rustic seats have been placed at convenient points throughout the grounds. A large vault—said to be the largest in the state—has been constructed. But few burials have yet been made in Mount Greenwood, the number being about 550. The first interment was made April 28, 1880. The Association was incorporated July 26, 1879.

Concordia Cemetery, nine miles west of the city, and two miles west of Oak Park, contains about fifty-eight acres. It was laid out in 1871 and is the burial place of seven Evangelical Lutheran churches. Concordia is practically the successor of the Wunder, or German Evangelical Lutheran Cemetery, just east of Graceland. About 10,000 interments have taken place in Concordia.

The **German Evangelical Lutheran Cemetery** is popularly called Wunder Cemetery, in honor of the well-known German divine, Rev. Henry Wunder. It was laid out in 1860, and contained only four and one-half acres. In 1866 it was increased to fourteen and one-half acres. But few burials are made in it now, all the lots having been taken twelve years ago.

Waldheim Cemetery contains eighty acres. It was laid out in 1873 and the first interment took place July 16, 1874. Nearly 7,000 burials have since been made, principally Germans. The grounds are well improved. The receiving vault has capacity for 500. There is also a chapel and a local office. The city office of the association is at 78 Fifth Avenue.

Forest Home Cemetery was laid out in 1877. It contains eighty acres. The site is a portion of the old Haase farm. It is about four and one-half miles from the city limits, on the Desplaines River. About 1,000 interments have been made.

St. Boniface Cemetery is the burying ground of the German Catholics. It is situated on Green Bay road, three miles north of the city limits.

The **Jewish Cemeteries** of the city are generally burying places owned by the respective Jewish congregations, although some congregations lay their dead to rest in sections of the general burying grounds. The Kehilath Anshey Maarab Congregation Cemetery is situated about five miles north of the city, on the Green Bay road, and near Graceland. This congregation formerly had a burying ground in what is now a portion of Lincoln Park, but the bodies were disinterred and removed when the property was taken for park purposes. The general appearance of this cemetery is similar to that of Graceland. There are but few striking monuments, one of the most conspicuous being that erected by the Greenbaum Brothers over the graves of their parents. In the same locality are the cemeteries of the Hebrew Benevolent Society, established in 1855; the Chebrah Gemiluth Chasadim (association for charitable work); the Chebra Kadisha Ubikur Cholim, B'nai Sholom, all small in dimensions, containing but one acre each. The monuments and gravestones are generally plain and simple in design and execution, though there are a few exceptions. The grounds overlook the lake and are covered with a fine second growth of timber, and are generally of a level character. Sinai and Zion congregations have a united body of lots in the center of the western portion of Rosehill. The monuments are generally tasteful in appearance, but still of a plain character. That over the grave of Mrs. S. Hyman, in the Sinai division, is perhaps the most elaborate of all. The cemeteries of the Beth Hemidrash Hagadol congregation (Russian), the North Side Hebrew congregation and B'nai Abraham congregation are at Waldheim, ten miles west from the city, near Forest Home and Waldheim cemeteries (general burying grounds). The cemetery of the society of the Free Sons of Israel and that of the congregation of Ohabey Emunah are also in this locality. They occupy portions of the old Haase farm, formerly the property of Frederick Haase, and are favorably situated and well improved.

The Religious Institutions.

THE CHURCHES AND THEIR PASTORS, AND THE OTHER RELIGIOUS ORGANIZATIONS.

FATHER Jacques Marquette, a Catholic priest, was among the first white men known to have visited this locality; and the next was Rev. Claude Allouez, in March, 1676, more than two centuries ago. The next visit was made in 1699 by Revs. Pinet and Bineteau, one of whom, at least, resided here for some time. Then there is an interval of nearly a century, when the religious history of Chicago is resumed. Rev. Stephen Badin, said to be the first Catholic priest ordained in the United States, visited this point in 1796, and returned in 1822, when he baptized Alexander Beaubien, which was the first occurrence of the kind in the place. In 1825 the first Protestant minister made his appearance in the person of Rev. Isaac McCoy, a Baptist, who preached to the Indians the first sermon ever preached in Chicago, so far as can be learned from history or tradition. The first Sunday school in Chicago was organized in 1832, in which the venerable Philo Carpenter, who is still living, was an active participant. At the first quarterly meeting in 1833, Henry Whitehead was licensed to preach, and he is believed to be the first Chicago licentiate. During the development of the trading post into a great metropolis, the building of churches has generally led in the march of improvement. After the great fire which annihilated so many edifices devoted to church purposes, they rose again with magic celerity, and most of them came up in a splendor and strength unknown before.

The First Baptist Church is the parent of a number other churches of that denomination in the city, which were founded by colonies sent out from the congregation of the First Church, and have, in many instances, outgrown it in membership. The building now occupied is a fine stone edifice at the corner of South Park Avenue and Thirty-first S reet, and was erected in 1876 at a cost of $80,000. The history of the church is remarkable for its vicissitudes. It was organized by Rev. Allen B. Freeman, Oct. 19, 1833, with nineteen members, and services were for some years conducted in what was termed "Temple Church," used by all the early denominations. The financial troubles of 1837 prevented the construction of another building, and a workshop was transformed into a house of worship for the congregation. In 1844 a brick building, with basement, Ionic portico of six columns, and spire 112 feet high, was erected at the corner of Washington and LaSalle Streets. This was destroyed by fire in October, 1852, and a new building was erected on its site the succeeding year at a cost of $30,000. In 1864 the ground was sold to the Chamber of Commerce association for $65,000, of which $15,000 was given to other Baptist churches in the city, and the house to Tabernacle Church, and a commanding edifice was built, at a cost of $175,000, on Wabash Avenue near Hubbard Court. After the great fire the lecture room was used for relief purposes, over 12,000 meals being given in it. But it escaped the great conflagration only to fall by the lesser one of 1874, after which the present building was erected. Among the noted men who have held its pulpit are Rev. J. C. Burroughs. D. D., Rev. William Everts, D. D., and Rev. Geo. C. Lorimer, D. D. The time of its greatest strength was in the administration of Dr. Everts, when it had over 2,000 members. The present membership is 850, with 750 pupils enrolled in the Sunday school. Nearly 6,000 persons have been

THE FIRST BAPTIST CHURCH.

received into membership since the organization, about one-third of them by baptism. The pastor is Rev. P. S. Henson, D. D.

The **Second Baptist Church,** corner of Monroe and Morgan Streets, ranks among the very largest in point of membership and seating capacity, and is probably the largest Baptist church in the country. The building is a plain, sombre-looking, but very commodious and durable brick edifice, 60 by 110 feet, with needle tower and a bell. The auditorium is encircled by a gallery, and altogether will hold 1,800 people. The walls and ceiling are handsomely frescoed. The large lecture room in the lower story will seat 600, and the small one 150. The class rooms, culinary department, etc., are also in this story: The membership numbers 1,200, and there are 1,250 pupils in the home and mission Sunday schools. The church was organized Aug. 14, 1843, as the Tabernacle Baptist Church, by members of the First Baptist Church, who separated from that congregation on the slavery question. They subsequently undertook a movement against secret societies, and expelled one of their members for being connected with the Odd Fellows. In 1864 the First Church, in disposing of its property at LaSalle and Washington Streets, retained the lot, which it sold to the Chamber of Commerce, and allotted the building to those of its members living on the West Side who joined the Tabernacle and formed the Second Church, and the building was removed to its present site. Under the able ministry of the present pastor, Rev. Wm. M. Lawrence, D. D., the church has prospered and largely increased its membership.

Immanuel Baptist Church, Michigan Avenue near Twenty-third Street, is one of the prominent churches of Chicago. The building is perhaps the finest belonging to that denomination. The walls are of Illinois limestone and ornamented with Ohio freestone, the architecture being in the fifteenth century Gothic style. The tower ends in a spire 216 feet high. The interior is artistically finished and richly furnished, some novelties being introduced among the accommodations usually found in a church auditorium. The pulpit and platform are remarkably unique in design. A Gothic arch above the platform, surmounted by a cross, is forty feet high. The emerald green curtain of silk chenille, which hangs in the arch, was woven to order in Glasgow, Scotland. The curtains hanging from the canopy over the platform surround the baptistery, and are drawn aside during baptism. The pews, arranged in semi circle form, are of butternut and poplar, with black walnut ornaments and finish. The gallery, encircling the room, slopes down to the pulpit platform on either side. The vault of the ceiling is colored in blues, and the whole room is treated ecclesiastically in the Gothic style, copied in part from one of the chapels of Notre Dame Cathedral in Paris. The seating capacity is about 1,800. There are anterooms, lecture rooms, Sunday school rooms and all other appointments requisite to a modern church structure. Immanuel Church proper, was organized May 10, 1881. It is the outgrowth of Edina Place Church, founded in 1856, afterward removed to the corner of Wabash Avenue and Eighteenth Street, the name changing to Wabash Avenue Church. In 1868 or '69 Wabash Avenue Church was removed to Michigan Avenue, the site now occupied by Immanuel Church, and took the name of Michigan Avenue Church. The building having been destroyed by fire in February, 1881, the congregation, with about 150 members from the First Baptist Church, organized Immanuel Church, and rebuilt the present church edifice at a cost of $70,000. Rev. Geo. C. Lorimer, D. D., of the First Church, who had been active in the movement, was called to the pastorate. Prior to this the names of Revs. Robert Boyd, E. G. Taylor, D. D., Samuel Baker, D. D., Jesse B. Thomas, D. D., F. M. Ellis and J. W. Curtis, D. D.,appeared on the list of pastors. Immanuel Church was dedicated on Christmas Day, 1881. It is located in the midst of an attractive residence section, noted for its wealth and refinement. The membership now numbers over 600 with about 500 children in the Sunday school. Dr. Lorimer remains in charge. He ranks among the most noted orthodox ministers of the country.

The **Central Baptist Church** was organized June 23, 1873, and reorganized Oct. 10, 1877, to receive some members and property of the North Church, when it assumed the name "Central." Services have been mainly conducted in the chapel, No. 290 Orchard Street, but a new building is in course of erection on Belden Avenue, on a lot 75 by 125 feet. This building, which is shown in the accompanying illustration, will cost about $40,000. The church has a membership of 225; has 330 children in its Sunday school, and 200 in an industrial school. Rev. C. H. DeWolf was the first pastor. Rev. E. O. Taylor, the present pastor, has occupied the pulpit since July 19, 1877.

The **Fourth Baptist Church**, corner of Washington Boulevard and Paulina Street, is the outgrowth of a mission Sunday school on West Lake Street, near Bryan Place, and was originally called Union Park Church. The building is a plain frame with an unfinished spire. The main auditorium is neatly but plainly furnished, and there is a commodious lecture room in the basement. The membership is 450, with 450

CENTRAL BAPTIST CHURCH.

pupils in its Sunday school, and 250 pupils in Trinity Mission Sunday school at Indiana and Lincoln Streets. Centennial and Western Avenue churches are offshoots of this congregation. During the pastorate of Rev. Florence McCarthy, from 1860 to 1863, a schism occurred, a number of members withdrawing and forming a separate church. The breach was measurably healed, however, and the congregations were united July 8, 1874, under the present name. The pastor, Rev. J. Spencer Kennard, D. D., an able and popular divine, took charge Jan. 1, 1882.

Centennial Baptist Church, corner of Jackson and Lincoln Streets, is the aggregation of several detached Baptist elements on the West Side. The building was erected by seceders from Union Park Church, who organized under the name of Ashland Avenue Church. When the breach was healed, a few who remained with the Ashland Avenue Church, were joined by some unaffiliated Baptists on the West Side, a new organization was effected, and the present name adopted. The edifice is a plain brick structure, Gothic in style, the main building 42×85 feet, with a rear extension 26×50 feet for lecture and infant class rooms. The interior is neatly frescoed, and will seat 500 people. The pastors have been Revs. N. E. Wood, C. E. Hewitt, D. D., and A. H. Parker. Mr. Parker still occupies the pulpit.

The Central Church of Christ (Christian), corner of Indiana Avenue and Twenty-fifth Street, was formed by consolidation of the First and South Side Christian Churches, in August, 1882. The united congregations worshiped for a time in a building at the corner of Prairie Avenue and Thirtieth Street, removing to the present location Jan. 1, 1883. The building is a frame, with stained glass windows, and has seating capacity for 500 persons. The membership, largest of the denomination in the city, is 160. The Sunday school has an enrollment of about 300 pupils. Rev. Henry Schell Lobingier is pastor.

St. James' Church (Episcopal), at the corner of Cass and Huron Streets, is the oldest church of its denomination in Chicago. The building, which was erected in 1873, is a splendid structure. The width of transept, north and south, is 109 feet, and the depth of the nave 173 feet. In the vestibule is a beautiful monument to the memory of those of the parish who died in the war. There are some handsome windows and mural brasses, and in the tower is a fine chime of bells, the gift of the Carter family. The number of communicants is about 700. In the Sunday school there are between three and four hundred pupils, and the Bible class for young men numbers more than one hundred. The first service in the history of the congregation was held

Oct. 10, 1834, by Rev. Palmer Dyer, when the nucleus of a parish organization was formed by W. H. Egan, Dr. Philip Maxwell, Gordon S. Hubbard, John S. Kinzie and others. This service was held in the Presbyterian church at the invitation of the pastor, Rev. Jeremiah Porter. The organization as St. James' Church was effected in 1835, Rev. Isaac W. Hallam being the rector. Tippecanoe Hall, at the corner of Kinzie and Wolcott (now State) Streets, was occupied for a time but a building was erected at the corner of Clark and Illinois Streets on two lots donated by Mr. Kinzie, and was occupied March 26, 1837, and formally dedicated by Bishop Philander Chase, June 25, 1837. It was the first brick church edifice in Chicago, and in the belfry was placed the first church bell brought to Chicago, and which had been first rung here on Christmas morning, 1836. Twenty years later, in 1857, the parish built a

ST. JAMES' EPISCOPAL CHURCH.

handsome stone edifice at Cass and Huron Streets, at a cost, exclusive of ground and tower, of over $80,000. A rectory was erected at the same time. Subsequent enlargements and improvements brought the cost to nearly $200,000 at the time of the fire of 1871, when the whole was destroyed, only the monument above mentioned being saved. The vestibule, however, was sufficiently restored to be used as a chapel until the erection of the present edifice was commenced. Many distinguished divines have held the pulpit of St. James. Rev. Robert Clarkson had been rector for seventeen years, when he was called to the bishopric of Nebraska. Rev. J. H. Ryland, D. D., was rector for four years, during which the noble vestibule, tower and chapel were completed in time to feed the conflagration. Rev. H. M. Thompson, now Assistant Bishop of Mississippi, was rector at the time of that calamity. Rev. Arthur Brooks succeeded, and was followed by Rev. Dr. Harris, now Bishop of Michigan. The present rector, Rev. Wm. H. Vibbert, D. D., succeeded Rev. Dr. Courteney, in January, 1883. Under his rectorship the debt of $35,000 which rested on the parish was paid in April of that year, and the church was consecrated May 31 of the same year. A surpliced choir was introduced May 4, 1884, and the parish seems to have entered upon a new era of prosperity.

Trinity Church (Episcopal) grew out of the desire of a number of members of St. James' parish to have a church located on the south side of the river. The entire territory of the south division of the city was allotted to the new parish, and the church was organized Aug. 1, 1843. It occupied a fine stone edifice in 1871, and lost it in the great fire. Nov 22, 1874, the present handsome stone structure at the corner of Michigan Avenue and Twenty-sixth Street was occupied. It is Gothic in style, and has seating capacity for over 1,000 persons. The church has a membership of 457, and the Sunday school an enrollment of more than 800, with an average attendance of over 600. The names of the late Bishop Whitehouse and Rev. R. A. Holland, S. T. D., appear in the list of rectors. The parish contributes about $20,000 annually to missions and charities. Among the organized agencies are St. Luke's Hospital Society and Trinity Guild. The present rector, Rev. L. S. Osborne, took charge Jan. 1, 1884.

The Cathedral of SS. Peter and Paul, corner of Peoria Street and Washington Boulevard, is the cathedral church of the Episcopal see of Illinois. It was organized March 18, 1850, as the Church of the Atonement, with nineteen members. The first meetings were held in Temperance Hall, at the corner of Randolph and Canal Streets, but in 1851 the present location was secured. Rev. Dudley Chase, son of the late Rt. Rev. Philander Chase, first bishop of the diocese of Illinois, was the first rector. On his resignation, in 1857, the property passed into the hands of Rt. Rev. Henry J. Whitehouse, successor of Bishop Chase in the see of Illinois, and by him the building was enlarged and beautified, and at first was known as the "Bishop's Church." He inaugurated the modified cathedral system of the American church, which now numbers some fifteen cathedrals, this church being, in 1867, formally designated a cathedral, and so recognized by the diocesan convention. The Bishop appointed and gazetted Revs. J. H. Knowles, C. P. Dorset and Geo. C. Street, as canons. The building, having been freed from debt, was solemnly consecrated Dec. 10, 1879. It is a very unique stone structure in the extreme Gothic style, and is especially attractive in the interior, having a beautiful altar of pure white marble and a handsome reredos. There is also a commodious brick building in the rear, intended for a "clergy house" and other purposes connected with the cathedral work. Canon Knowles, who faithfully administered the affairs of the congregation, and under whom the large surpliced choir of men and boys attained the great excellence in the choral rendering of the church service for which the cathedral is noted, resigned in May, 1884, to take charge of the new mission of St. Clement, on the South Side, which has been inaugurated under very promising auspices. Bishop McLaren is the present diocesan.

Grace Church Parish (Episcopal) was organized May 19, 1851. Rev. Cornelius Swope, now assistant pastor of Trinity Church, New York, was the first rector. A church was built on the northwest corner of Dearborn and Madison Streets, seating about 300. Mr. Swope was succeeded June 25, 1854, by Rev. Louis L. Noble, the well-known art critic, who remained only a year, and was succeeded June 9, 1856, by Rev. Jno. W. Clark. Under Mr. Clark's rectorship the church was removed to the corner of Peck Court and Wabash Avenue, and greatly enlarged. A chapel was also built on the rear of the lot. Mr. Clark remained until June 12, 1859. In July of that year Rev. Clinton Locke, D. D., the present rector, was called to the charge. There were then about eighty communicants. In 1863 a handsome parsonage was built in the rear of the church edifice. In July, 1864, the building was again enlarged. In 1867 the lot for the present structure on Wabash Avenue between Fourteenth and Fifteenth Streets was purchased, the Peck Court property sold, and the new church was finished, and opened on Easter Day, 1869. In May, 1876, a cyclone blew off the steeple and damaged the church to the amount of $14,000. In the summer of 1882 the vestry purchased twenty-two feet north of the church, and on Easter Day, 1884, the whole remaining debt of the church, $20,-000, was paid. In January of the same year, Dr. Locke celebrated the twenty-fifth year of his rectorship and was made the happy recipient of many flattering testimonials of respect and affection, not only from his own congregation, but from his fellow citizens, his bishop and brother clergymen. In July, 1884, the church was thoroughly redecorated and put in repair. It is a handsome stone edifice of French

Gothic architecture, with uncompleted tower and spire. It is sixty-six feet wide and 130 feet long, with chapel in the rear, seats 1,000 persons, has about 600 communicants, a Sunday school of 800, and an industrial school of 250 children. It takes a very active part in the support of St. Luke's Hospital, which was founded by it.

The Church of the Epiphany (Episcopal) was organized in the fall of 1868, and the parish took possession of its first house of worship, on Throop Street between Adams and Monroe, on Epiphany Day, 1868. Rev. R. T. Sims was the first rector. The parish has about 110 families, with 375 communicants, and a Sunday school numbering about 300 children and teachers. The parish owns the property on Throop Street and 100 by 150 feet on the southeast corner of Ashland Avenue and Adams Street, on which a large and permanent church edifice will be erected, the present building being wholly inadequate and unsatisfactory. The rector, Rev. Theodore N. Morrison, came to the charge in December, 1876.

Christ Church (Reformed Episcopal), at the southeast corner of Michigan Avenue and Twenty-fourth Street, was organized Nov. 1, 1855, and has grown from seven communicants to 575, with 1,000 pupils enrolled in its Sunday school. The edifice, which is of stone and has seating capacity for 1,000 persons, was erected in 1865, and has since been several times remodeled, and is now one of the most attractive places of worship in the city. The style is a simple Gothic, the west front presenting very happy effects of broken masses, and light and shade. There is a central porch, or vestibule, flanked on either hand by a tower; that on the northern corner being in campanile form, and rising to a height of 100 feet. The interior is finished in a very artistic manner, the roof open timbered, and the walls beautifully tinted, especially in the chancel. After the organization the pulpit was temporarily filled by various clergymen, but the first permanent rector was Rev. Charles Edward Cheney, who came to the church in March, 1860, and still holds the rectorship. The views of rector and people have always been decidedly "Low Church," or evangelical, and the refusal of the rector to use certain expressions in the baptismal office, which he believed to be contrary to the Word of God, led to a long controversy with Bishop Whitehouse. Dr. Cheney was tried and deposed from the ministry, but his trial and sentence were declared of no effect by the Supreme Court of the State, so that he is still, in the eye of the law, a presbyter of the Protestant Episcopal Church. His church refusing to give up their rector, pastor and people became for a time practically independent, and so remained till in December, 1873, Bishop G. D. Cummins founded the Reformed Episcopal Church. The new organization fell in exactly with the views of Christ Church, and on Dec. 2, 1873, Dr. Cheney was elected, and soon after consecrated, a bishop of the new church. Feb. 18, 1874, Christ Church was formally reorganized as a Reformed Episcopal Church. Rev. J. W. Farley is assistant minister.

St. Paul's Church (Reformed Episcopal) was organized in 1873, with Dr. Samuel Fallows as its rector. After his election to the missionary bishopric, the pulpit was occupied successively by various ministers. At the fourth general council of the Reformed Episcopa Church, held in Ottawa, Canada, in July, 1876, Dr. Fallows was elected bishop of the jurisdiction of the West and Northwest, and three years later again resumed the rectorship of St. Paul's, in connection with his duties as bishop. The membership of the church numbers 460, and of the Sunday-school about 250. The new church edifice is on the corner of Adams Street and Winchester Avenue. It is one of the most beautiful churches on the West Side. It will accommodate 800 people. The interior is beautifully finished. The building formerly occupied was on the corner of Washington Boulevard and Carpenter Street.

Grace Church (Evangelical Lutheran) was organized Sept. 3, 1882. It occupies a portion of its unfinished building at Chicago Avenue and Franklin Streets, which has seating capacity for 400 people. It has a splendid memorial window of stained glass, forty-four and one-half feet high and containing 412 square feet, and, with two smaller ones, bearing the names of Melchior Muhlenberg, founder of American Lutherism, and of others prominent in the church. The number of members is seventy, and of Sunday school pupils 200. The pastor, Rev. Lee M. Heilman, was the organizer of the church.

The First Congregational Church, corner of Washington Boulevard and Ann Street, is the oldest Congregational Church in the city. It was instituted May 22, 1851, the membership being at first composed of Presbyterians who withdrew from that denomination on the slavery issue, in which the church afterward took a prominent part. It had several removals and was twice burned out before settling in its present commodious edifice. A church building erected in 1868 was partially destroyed by fire, and was rebuilt, the side walls being used in the present structure, which is a massive stone edifice, plain Gothic in style, and cruciform. It is 165 feet deep, and the extreme width of the transept is 100 feet. The interior decoration is artistically elegant, the finish being of black walnut and oak. The nave and transept contain 14,000 square feet, the roof being a clear span, and, with the gallery, seats over 2,000 people. The three large triangular windows contain elaborate allegorical ornamentation in stained glass. The front window represents the firmament, having numerous stars among its artistic tracery, and bearing appropriate inscriptions. One of the transept windows represents the crucifixion, and the other the resurrection, each having suitable inscriptions and emblems. The pastor's study is on the main floor. The spacious lecture, Sunday school, class, library and dining rooms, and the culinary department, are all in the basement, and very conveniently arranged and completely furnished. The infant class room is a model, the seats being placed like those of an amphitheater. Immediately after the great fire the building was used for a time as the headquarters of the city government. This church is indefatigable in religious and philanthropic work. It sustains several branch churches, a mission school, and two industrial schools. It has received 2,948 persons into membership since its organization, and now has a membership of 1,309. Rev. W. W. Patton, D. D., was pastor for over eight years, including the period of the war, during which the church was active in support of the Union cause, sending sixty-nine of its members to the army. The present pastor, Rev. Edward P. Goodwin, D. D., was installed Jan. 10, 1868.

The **New England Church** (Congregational), corner of Dearborn Avenue and Delaware Place, was formally instituted June 15, 1853. The building was erected on the site of one built by the church in 1865, and destroyed by the great fire. It is an elegant cruciform structure of stone, and contains memorial stones from Delft Haven, Scrooley and Plymouth, and a stone baptismal font from Scrooley. It cost about $150,000, and was completed in the winter of 1875. The church has received about 1,000 members since its organization, and now has about 475 members, and 900 pupils in its Sunday schools. Lincoln Park Congregational Church was built up by it, and it has just expended some $13,000 in erecting a mission chapel on Sedgwick near Blackhawk Street. Rev. Leander T. Chamberlain entered the ministry as pastor of this church, and remained in charge about eight years. Rev. Arthur Little, the present pastor, was installed early in 1878.

Union Park Congregational Church, corner of Ashland Avenue and Washington Boulevard, has 830 members, with 1,300 pupils in its Sunday schools. The building, which was completed and dedicated in the fall of 1871, is one of the largest church edifices in the city, covering 100×125 feet of ground. It is Gothic in style, built of rough-dressed stone, and cost over $200,000. The nave is an amphitheater, with an extensive gallery, giving a seating capacity of 2,200. The basement contains a spacious Sunday school and lecture room, with seats for 1,000 people, two Bible class rooms, library, study and parlors. The spire is 175 feet high. The church was organized May 22, 1860, by the faculty of the Chicago Theological Seminary, and the pulpit was for some years occupied by professors from that institution. Soon after its organization a mission Sunday school, which was organized by the First Congregational Church in June, 1858, united with it, largely increasing its

UNION PARK CHURCH—FROM UNION PARK.

strength and support. Rev. Chas. D. Helmer was pastor for nine years. The present pastor, Rev. Frederick A. Noble, D. D., took charge April 20, 1879.

Plymouth Congregational Church, Michigan Avenue near Twenty-sixth Street, ranks among the leading churches of the city. It was organized in December, 1852, by members of the First Presbyterian Church who were dissatisfied with the mild course of the denomination on the slavery question. The church edifice is a graceful stone structure, the interior artistically decorated, and the whole costing, with the organ, about $150,000. It has a frontage of 110 feet, and a depth of 160 feet. The main auditorium, which is finished in black walnut throughout, seats 1,400 persons comfortably. The rear portion of the building, containing lecture room, Sunday school rooms, committee room, cloak room, parlor, pastor's study and janitor's apartments, is divided into three stories. It was occupied for the first time on July 4, 1875. The minarets formerly on the church will soon be replaced by more appropriate ornaments. The church membership numbers over 700, and the Sunday school has over 1,100 pupils. The church is noted for the excellence of its choir. It is located in one of the best residence portions of the city. It sustains a prosperous local mission church, and in part a mission church and school. The pastor is Rev. Henry M. Scudder, D. D., a minister of national reputation. He has been in charge since Nov. 19, 1882.

Tabernacle Church (Congregational), corner of Morgan and Indiana Streets, was a mission school of the First Congregational Church, and was formally organized as a church Oct. 9, 1866. The building is a plain brick structure, with seating capacity for 1,200 people. The auditorium was recently raised, and a lecture room built underneath. The church has 468 members, and the Sunday school 1,200. Becoming burdened with debt some years ago, the church withdrew from the Congregational Association for a time, but returned after a large part of its obligations was cleared off. Rev. F. E. Emerich is the pastor.

Lincoln Park Congregational Church, corner of Garfield Avenue and Mohawk Street, was originally a mission school of the New England Church, and was organized as a church June 25, 1867. The building is a plain but substantial structure, erected at a cost of $30,000, of which the late Col. Chas. G. Hammond gave $14,000. The membership is 342. Rev. Burke T. Leavitt is pastor.

Central Church, in Central Music Hall, is an independent congregation, established in 1877, in support of the ministry of Rev. David Swing. This famous divine is a native of Cincinnati, of German descent; was graduated from Miami University in 1852, and had spent less than a year in the study of theology when he returned to the university as its professor of Latin and Greek, a position he held for thirteen years, preaching occasionally. His first appearance in Chicago was in 1866, as pastor of the Westminster Church, then New School Presbyterian, and when the Fourth Presbyterian Church was formed, in 1870, after the reunion of the "schools," by the consolidation of Westminster with the North Church, which had been of the Old

School, he became pastor of the united congregations. When the great fire swept over the North Side, he lost the hoarded results of years of literary labor, and with his wife and daughter and many of his parishioners spent the night of October 9th on the open prairie. He immediately undertook the reorganization of his scattered flock, and preached for a year in Standard Hall, and then in McVicker's Theater until January, 1874, when, the church having been rebuilt, he returned to his pulpit. But the catholicity of his views, and the frankness, eloquence and force with which he gave them utterance, had commanded wide public attention, and often attracted larger congregations than could be accommodated. Some of his liberal theological opinions had been warmly controverted by ministers of the same denomination, and an intellectual contest was inaugurated which excited intense interest in religious circles throughout the country. Arraigned on the charge of heretical teaching, his trial was a *cause celebre*, in which he added largely to the area and splendor of his reputation as a great theologian and orator. He was acquitted, and continued his pastoral relations to the Fourth Church until December, 1875, when he resigned and began preaching in McVicker's Theater. In 1877 the present congregation was organized, with a guarantee fund of $50,000, and Central Music Hall was engaged for Sunday services. The church has 550 members, and an aggregate of 1,000 pupils in three Sunday schools, located on West Madison and South Halsted Streets and North Avenue respectively. The singing is congregational. Large as the hall is, it is always thronged before the hour for service, and hundreds are often turned away unable to find even standing room.

The **People's Church** is an independent organization formed in 1881, and holding services every Sunday in McVicker Theater. It seeks to "unite all in the great law and duty of love to God and man," and welcomes to its fellowship all, of whatever faith, who are in sympathy with its spirit and work. It was founded by Rev. H. W. Thomas, D. D., a prominent minister of the Methodist denomination, who was successively pastor of Park Avenue, First and Centenary Methodist Churches, and was cited before the conference while occupying the pulpit of the latter church, and tried and expelled for heretical opinions regarding future punishment and the nature of the atonement. Pending these proceedings he preached to the people at large, and at the time of his expulsion his work had grown to such dimensions that he could not conscientiously give it up. Hence, the organization of the People's Church, and the continuation of weekly services in the theater, the spacious auditorium of which is always so crowded on such occasions, and hundreds have so often to be turned away, that arrangements are being concerted for a larger hall to accommodate the audiences. The Sunday school, with over 200 pupils, is conducted in the Third Unitarian Church, corner of Monroe and Laflin Streets. Dr. Thomas is a fine theologian and a pleasing speaker, of very sympathetic address, his own liberal but earnest faith commanding the attention and respect of his hearers, whatever their belief.

Chicago Avenue Church (Independent), corner of Chicago and LaSalle Avenues, was originally a mission of the First Congregational

Church, but was organized as a separate congregation in 1858. The building, which was finished in 1875, at a cost of $70,000, covers 100 × 109 feet of ground, is 60 feet high to the eaves and has a mansard roof. It is a red brick edifice with stone trimmings, and has a circular bell tower at the southeast corner, at the base

CHICAGO AVENUE CHURCH.

of which is the main entrance, admitting to an iron stairway leading to the auditorium, and double doors opening into the lower story. There are three other entrances. The auditorium, including gallery, seats 2,000 persons. It is substantially finished in contrasting woods, excellently lighted and ventilated, and ornamented with artistic frescoing. Two Bible class rooms in the basement seat respectively 100 and 200, and the lecture room about 600. The membership is about 400. The Sunday school is the largest in the city, having about 1,500 pupils.

The church is popularly known as "Moody's Church." Much of the earlier portion of the now famous evangelist's career was devoted to work for this church. Under his labors the church membership reached 300, and that of the Sunday school 1,000. When the church building, erected on Illinois Street in 1863 at a cost of $20,000, was destroyed in the great conflagration, his efforts aided largely in raising funds for the present structure. Rev. Charles A. Blanchard, president of Wheaton College, has supplied the pulpit occasionally since March 1, 1883, and regularly since September of that year.

The **First Methodist Episcopal Church** is the oldest church organization in Chicago. It is the lineal descendant of a congregation formed in June, 1831, by Jesse Walker, presiding elder of the " Chicago mission district " of the Illinois conference, and Rev. Stephen R. Beggs. Elder Walker, who was "superannuated" in the winter of 1834-35, has been well styled "the apostle of the Northwest." The first house of worship built by the church was a small frame, erected in 1834 at the corner of North Water and North Clark Streets. In 1838 the building was moved across the river on scows, and located at the corner of Clark and Washington Streets, the site occupied by the present building. In 1857 the church obtained a charter and adopted the plan of building which it has since pursued, viz.: erecting a business block, and assigning the lower story to mercantile purposes for revenue to be devoted to the support of the church and the aid of other churches, and preparing the upper stories as a place of worship. Up to the time of the great fire, over $70,000 had been contributed to other churches of the denomination in Chicago from this source. Since that time over $120,000 more have been distributed in the same way. It requires some sterling qualities in a church membership to thus sacrifice the outward appearance of their house of worship for the general good of the cause. The present large four-story stone front building, known as Methodist Church Block, was erected at a cost of $120,000. It has seven business or store rooms on the ground floor, and about fifteen rooms for offices above. The portion reserved for church purposes is on the third floor. The auditorium, with the gallery, has a seating capacity of 1,200. There are also lecture and class rooms and pastor's study on the same floor. The membership is about 120, with 100 in the Sunday school. Many of the officers of the church have held their positions for more than a quarter of a century. The present pastor is Rev. R. M. Hatfield.

Centenary Church (Methodist Episcopal), West Monroe Street near

Morgan, is one of the leading churches in the city. It was organized in 1842, and then known as the Canal Street Methodist Episcopal Church. There were two changes of location, the last one being to settle in the present commodious edifice, which was commenced in 1866, the centenary of American Methodism, from which the church took its present name. The lecture room was occupied Feb. 17, 1867, and the building was completed the following year, at a cost of $75,000. It is an imposing stone structure, of Gothic-like architecture, ornamented with minarets. The body of the church, with a gallery on three sides, will comfortably seat 1,200 persons. The interior finish is in black walnut. There are large parlor, lecture, study and other rooms in the basement. The number of members is about 700, and of pupils in the Sunday school about 600. Wide public attention was attracted to Centenary Church in 1880, by the charges of heresy brought against its pastor, Rev. H. W. Thomas, whose trial and expulsion from pastorate and ministry created intense interest in church circles. Among the prominent ministers who have held the charge were Revs. T. M. Eddy, D. D., F. D. Hemenway, C. H. Fowler, Robert Bentley, Charles Shelling, R. M. Hatfield, J. O. Peck, S. H. Adams and H. W. Thomas. The present pastor is Rev. O. H. Swift.

Grace Church (Methodist Episcopal), corner of North LaSalle and White Streets, was organized in 1847 as the "M. E. Society of Indiana Street Chapel," and in June, 1863, adopted the present name at the suggestion of the ladies' society, which had raised most of the money necessary to build a new house of worship for the congregation. A building at the corner of Chicago Avenue and LaSalle Streets, costing, with furnishings, over $90,000, was destroyed by the fire, but sixty days afterward services were held in a temporary frame erected on the ruins, and arrangements for rebuilding were started. The present site was determined on ; the building was commenced in 1872, and in May, 1873, was partially finished and occupied, but the front was not completed till 1877. It is a plain Gothic structure, with gable front, and cost about $100,000. It will comfortably seat about 1,200 people. The interior wood finish is black walnut. The parsonage cost about $4,000. The church membership numbers 380, and that of the Sunday school 930. Among the prominent names connected with its history are those of Drs. Bugbee, Tiffany and Felton. The present pastor, Rev. Wm. Fawcett, entered upon his duties Oct. 16, 1881.

Langley Avenue Church (Methodist Episcopal), corner of Langley Avenue and Thirty-ninth Street, was organized March 7, 1869, as

Oakland·Methodist Episcopal Church. Its name was thrice changed, the last time in 1875 to the present title. It was removed to the present location in August, 1871. The building is a neat frame edifice, with capacity for 500 in the main auditorium, and handsome lecture, class and library rooms and study below. The windows of the nave are of stained glass, and the ceiling is prettily frescoed. The organ and choir occupy an alcove in the rear of the pulpit. The cost, including ground, was about $22,000. Among the pastors have been Revs. C. G. Truesdell, Lewis Meredith, W. C. Willing and T. C. Clendening. The present pastor is A. C. George.

Western Avenue Church (Methodist Episcopal), corner of Western Avenue and Monroe Street, dates back to 1866. The building is a many-gabled Gothic structure, unique and elegant in design, with four towers, in the bases of which are the entrances. The street fronts are of pressed brick with brown stone trimmings. The interior is 91 × 108 feet, and is divided into two rooms, viz., the main auditorium and the lect-

WESTERN AVENUE M. E. CHURCH.

ure and Sunday school room. The former is an amphitheater, with bowled floor and circular pews, and will seat 800 persons. There is a broad gallery, under which are class rooms. All the rooms can be thrown into one by means of sliding doors, giving an auditorium with comfortable seating capacity for 1,600. The parlors are in the basement story, and the pastor's study in the southeast corner. The total cost, with organ, is about $35,000. The church has about 300 members, and is very active in all branches of its work. The pastor, Rev. W. H. Burns, took charge in December, 1883.

Park Avenue Church (Methodist Episcopal), corner of Park Avenue and Robey Street, had its inception in prayer meetings held in 1858 among some Methodist families in the neighborhood. It was first established as Park Avenue Mission, in a building erected by the church extension society in 1861. The present building was erected in 1865, at a cost of about $10,000, and on occupying it assumed the present title. Among the prominent pastors have been Revs. J. H.

Bayliss, W. H. Thomas, N. H. Axtell and S. McChesney. The building is unpretentious but serviceable, and will seat 900 people. The church has 300 members, and 600 pupils enrolled in its Sunday school. Western Avenue and Fulton Street Churches have grown out of a mission school established by this church. The house, which escaped the fire, was used for a time as a distributing station by the Relief and Aid Society. The present pastor is Rev. S. M. Davis.

Trinity Church (Methodist Episcopal), Indiana Avenue near Twenty-fourth Street, is an offshoot of the First Church. It was born of a mission Sunday school, and began life on its own account April 10, 1864, in a frame building on Indiana Avenue and Twenty-first Street. The present edifice was commenced in November, 1870. The conflagration of the following year delayed the work. The lecture room was occupied in January, 1872, but the main auditorium was not opened for services until March 12, 1875. The cost, including ground, was $142,540. It is one of the handsomest church edifices in the city, both for architectural appearance and interior finish. The beautiful baptismal font is a memorial gift of the widow of Dr. Thomas M. Eddy. It has a membership of nearly 500. Its present pastor is F. M. Bristol.

The First Presbyterian Church is located at the corner of Indiana Avenue and Twenty-first Street. After the fire of 1871 Calvary Church, which had commenced the erection of the building, was united with the First Church, the edifice being completed by the united congregations. It is a handsome brick structure, 84×150 feet, fifty feet high to the eaves, and 100 feet to the ridge of the roof, and has a spire 260 feet high—the tallest church spire in the city. It is finished throughout in hard wood, principally black walnut, has seating capacity for 1,100, and cost, including the ground, $165,000. The First Presbyterian is one of the pioneer churches of Chicago. It was organized with twenty-six members, June 26, 1833, by Rev. Jeremiah Porter. The first building was a frame at the corner of Lake and Clark Streets, which was opened with services Jan. 1, 1834. This was removed to the corner of Clark and Washington Streets, and after being twice enlarged was superseded by a brick edifice 65×100 feet. In 1855 the house and ground were sold, and a fine new building erected on Wabash Avenue, between Van Buren and Congress Streets, and occupied in the fall of 1856. The cost was $131,000 for the house and lot. A brick chapel was erected in 1864 on Griswold Street, south of Van Buren, for the use of the railroad mission founded by the church. In 1865 a large brick chapel was erected adjoining the church,

FIRST PRESBYTERIAN CHURCH.

for Sunday school and church purposes. All was swept away by the fire of 1871. inflicting a loss of nearly $200,000. The church has a grand record of Christian work in the success of its missions. It sustains the Railroad Chapel and Mission which occupies a house on State Street south of Fourteenth that cost $70,000, and has an average school attendance of 500. It founded Foster Mission on the West Side, the Sands Mission on the North Side, the Archer Avenue Mission and the Indiana Street school. There are many names of note connected with its history, among them that of the founder, Rev. Jeremiah Porter, still living in Detroit; Rev. John Blatchford, of New York; Rev. Flavel Bascom, who was president of the first anti-slavery meeting held in Chicago; Rev. Harvey Curtis, Rev. Z. M. Humphrey, Rev. Arthur Mitchell, and others who have left the impress of their labors on its development. The membership is over 750. The pastor, Rev. John H. Barrows, D. D., is noted for his ability, energy and zeal. He is an eloquent preacher, and besides his regular pastoral labors, he preaches to large throngs on Sunday evenings in Central Music Hall.

The **Second Presbyterian Church,** corner of Michigan Avenue and Twentieth Street, has a membership numbering 735, and nearly 1,000 pupils in its two Sunday schools. It supplies officers for the Burr mission school, supports an industrial school for girls during winter, and has numerous active organizations for missionary and charitable work. The building, in the English-Gothic style, covers 109½×165 feet of ground, and is built of rock-faced prairie stone, except the clearstory, which is of wood. The "Armour memorial tower" is a massive stone tower and spire reaching 200 feet above the ground, and built at the cost of Mrs. Barbara Armour, widow of the late George Armour, as a memorial of her deceased husband. The tower is pure Gothic, and has a spacious belfry with a cathedral-toned bell, weighing, with the mountings, three tons, the gift of the children of Mr. Armour. The interior is elegantly finished throughout in black walnut, the pulpit exhibiting some fine carving. The main audience room is 70×85 feet, and seats about 1,500, with the gallery which extends all around it, and the short second gallery in the east front. The rear portion of the building on Twentieth Street is two stories in height, and has a lecture and Sunday school room 38×58, with gallery, library, study, etc. The church was organized June 1, 1842, by a colony of twenty-six members of the First Presbyterian. It occupied four different locations before settling in the present site, the last of the four being a handsome Gothic edifice that was destroyed by the fire of 1871, in which year the membership of Olivet Church was added to that of the Second Church. Rev. Robert W. Patterson, D. D., the first pastor, occupied the pulpit for thirty-one years. The present pastor, Rev. Simon J. Mc-Pherson, D. D., was installed May 6, 1874.

The **Third Presbyterian Church**, corner of Ashland and Ogden Avenues, has the largest membership in the city, and it is said to be the third largest Protestant church in the country, surpassed only by Plymouth Church, Brooklyn, and Brooklyn Tabernacle. It has nearly 2,200 members, and has established three churches out of its congregation, viz.: Reunion, Westminster and Campbell Park. It has a Sunday school library of over 1,000 volumes, and sustains a Sunday school of 850 pupils besides Noble Street and Foster missions, making a grand total of nearly 2,000 pupils. The church was organized July 18, 1847, with thirty-five members. A small frame building that stood in a corn-field on Union between Washington and Randolph Streets, was occupied for more than ten years. In 1850 a number of members withdrew on the question of fellowship with slaveholders, and organized the First Congregational Church. From 1860 to 1869, under the pastoral charge of Rev. Arthur Swazey, D. D., over 500 persons were admitted, and a debt of $45,000 nearly extinguished. June 13, 1870, the present pastor, Rev. Abbott E. Kittredge, D. D., was called from the Eleventh Street Presbyterian Church, New York City, and under his administration the elegant building which was destroyed by fire Oct. 9, 1884, was purchased, and occupied in 1877. The church edifice was at once rebuilt. Dr. Kittredge resigned the pastorate, in 1886, and Dr. Withrow took charge in January, 1887.

The **Fourth Presbyterian Church**, corner of Rush and Superior Streets, is one of the noted churches of the city. It is the result of a consolidation consummated Feb. 6, 1870, between the North (Old School) and the Westminster (New School) Churches. The former was organized Aug. 6, 1848, and the latter Sept. 18, 1855. The present building was erected on the site of the one occupied at the time of the great fire, in which not only was the church building lost, but the homes of 490 of its 500 members. It is a modest stone edifice, Gothic in style, and the interior is finished and furnished in a substantial and comfortable manner. The church has about 500 members, and the Sunday school about 300. It supports a mission school in Home Street with a membership of 675. Rev. David Swing was pastor of this church at the time of his celebrated trial for heresy, but withdrew from it although acquitted of the charge. Rev. Herrick Johnson, D. D., LL. D., resigned the pastorate July 1, 1884 (having been in charge over three years), to accept a professorship in the N. W. Theological Seminary.

The **Fifth Presbyterian Church**, corner of Indiana Avenue and Thirtieth Street, was organized Jan. 15, 1868, and took its present name June 24, 1870, when the Twenty-eighth Street and South Presbyterian Churches were consolidated with it. The church edifice is a T-shaped brick structure, neatly and comfortably furnished, and seats between 400 and 500 people. There is a very pleasant lecture room in the south wing, and a library and study in the north wing. The membership numbers 262. The pastor, Rev. W. G. Woodbridge, was formally installed in January, 1884. He is a native of Baton Rouge, La., a graduate of Princeton College, New Jersey, and of the Columbia, S. C., Theological Institute.

The **Sixth Presbyterian Church**, corner of Oak and Vincennes Avenues, was organized in 1875. In 1872 a colony from the Ninth Presbyterian Church organized Grace Church, but after about three years a reunion was effected, and the reunited churches reorganized under the present name. The building was erected at a cost of nearly $20,-000. It has seating capacity for about 850. The church membership numbers over 450. Rev. Henry T. Miller was the first pastor of the reunited congregation. He remained in charge for seven years, when he resigned, and was succeeded by the present pastor, Rev. John H. Worcester, Jr., who was installed Feb. 13, 1883.

The **Eighth Presbyterian Church**, at the junction of Robey Street and Washington Boulevard, originated in a neighborhood prayer meeting among Presbyterian families in 1864. It was organized December · 20, of that year, with twenty-five members, and built a plain wooden chapel, which was removed two years later, and the present tasteful frame structure erected in its place. It has a belfry, surmounted by a graceful steeple. The bell is named " The Children's Bell," having been paid for mainly by the pupils of the Sunday school. The building has seating capacity for about 650. The church membership is 609, and that of the Sunday school about 700. The " Onward Mission," at the intersection of Indiana Street and North Hoyne Avenue, was established by the church Nov. 1, 1868, and is maintained by it with a Sunday school membership of 250. The church has a fine library and reading rooms. The pastor is Rev. Thomas Edward Green, a young, eloquent and very popular preacher.

Jefferson Park Presbyterian Church, corner of West Adams and Throop Streets, fronts toward the beautiful park from which it takes its name. The church edifice and chapel in the rear occupy a lot 77×150 feet. The building is of red pressed brick with stone trimmings, built in the Gothic style of architecture. The entrances are adorned with polished Scotch granite columns. A handsome spire and corner towers surmount the whole. The interior is arranged with the pews in amphitheater style, all the aisles radiating from the pulpit. The walls and ceiling are elaborately frescoed, and light is admitted by large Gothic stained glass windows. The seating capacity is 1,000, including the gallery. The building completed, with its furniture, cost over $40,000. The membership of the church is about 350, and of the Sunday school 220. The congregation was an offshoot from the Reformed Presbyterian Church, and was organized Jan. 31, 1867, with Rev. Robert Patterson, D. D., as its first pastor. Subsequently Rev. Francis L. Patton was pastor for six years, during which the present edifice was built. The present pastor, Rev. Thomas Parry, came to the charge in January, 1884. He is a native of Wales, but educated in the United States, and is a graduate of Princeton College and seminary.

St. Mary's Church (Catholic), Wabash Avenue and Eldridge Court, was organized in May, 1833, by Rev. John Mary Irenæus St. Cyr, who was appointed for the purpose by Bishop Rosetti, of St. Louis, April 17th of that year. He arrived here May 1, said his first mass May 5, and administered his first baptism May 22, and in October following dedicated to the uses of his church the first building erected in Chicago for a house of worship. It was located on Lake Street, and was a plain wooden structure, 25×35 feet, and its belfry contained the first church bell heard in the settlement. After two removals, the substantial brick occupied in 1871 was burned, when the present edifice was purchased from the Unitarian denomination, and subsequently underwent some remodeling and improvement. It is a very substantial stone structure, comfortably and durably finished and furnished, and has seating capacity for about 800 people. May 27, 1883, the church held a semi-centennial celebration of its establishment, when an address was delivered by Wm. J. Onahan, Esq., and a handsome marble memorial-tablet was unveiled and placed in the wall of the vestibule. It contains the following inscription : "To the memory of the early Catholic missionaries of Illinois, sleeping in their unmarked graves, from Marquette to St. Cyr, on the 50th anniversary of the establishment in this city of St. Mary's Parish, and the erection of the first Christian Church, this tablet is reverently and gratefully erected by the pastor and flock, May 1, 1883." The pastor is Rev. J. P. Roles.

The Cathedral of the Holy Name (Catholic), corner of North State and Superior Streets, was commenced in 1874 and completed in 1882. There is a group of buildings which includes the cathedral proper, a parochial school, the academy of the ladies of the Sacred Heart, the presbytery, and others, occupying an entire block. The academy and school are of brick, and the cathedral and presbytery of stone. The first two stand on a half block donated by the late Hon. W. B. Ogden for school pur-

poses. The original cathedral and school buildings were consumed by the fire of 1871. The cathedral, which was built at a cost of $200,000, seats 1,800 people, is of the Gothic style, cruciform, with a tower surmounted by a spire, and is noticeable for its graceful architecture. The interior is finely finished, abundantly lighted with large stained glass windows, and has three beautiful

CATHEDRAL OF THE HOLY NAME.

marble altars. The organ is exquisitely finished, and is probably the most powerful in the city. The singing is usually by a quartette, but large choruses are added on special occasions. The Cathedral of the Holy Name was organized as the Church of the Holy Name in 1846. The present clerical personnel is as follows: Most Rev. Patrick A. Feehan, D. D.; Very Rev. P. J. Conway, V.G., rector; Rev. P. D. Gill, chancellor; Revs. F. S. Henneberry, J. J. Carroll, M. J. Fitzsimmons and J. J. Darcy.

The Church of the Holy Family (Catholic), corner of West Twelfth and May Streets, is a large and handsome brick structure. It seats about 2,000 people, and is remarkable for its superb stained glass windows, its number of fine statues and its massive bell tower and spire. It was built in 1857 under the renowned missionary, Rev. Arnold Damen, S. J., who has performed wonders in rescuing large areas of Chicago from what at times was simple savagery. His labors here, apart from his religious efforts, have been of inestimable benefit to the city. The affairs of the church are directed by ten Jesuit Fathers. Sodality Building, immediately in the rear of the church, is a spacious structure. It contains numerous rooms and spacious halls for the use of the various church sodalities, and two libraries with an aggregate of 2,400 books.

St. James' Church (Catholic), corner of Wabash Avenue and Thirtieth Street, occupies one of the finest church edifices in the city. It is a Gothic-like structure of stone, cruciform, compact and well proportioned, and has an uncompleted tower. The nave is finished in oiled light wood, and two rows of polished granite pillars support the roof. It is lighted by large and handsome stained glass windows, and three marble altars are to be put in. It will seat, with the two small galleries, about 1,600 persons. The building was erected during the pastorate of Rev. P. W. O'Riordan, now coadjutor archbishop of San Francisco. The present clerical staff is composed of Revs. Hugh McGuire, Lawrence A. R. Erhard, P. J. Fenan and D. Lyon.

St. Johns Church (Catholic), corner of Eighteenth and Clark Streets, was established June 29, 1859. The church edifice is a splendid stone structure, pure Gothic in style, and a model of architectural beauty. It is somewhat cruciform, having a short transept. The spire is unfinished. The interior, with its brilliant frescoes, beautiful stained glass windows and panels presenting representations of scriptural characters is well worthy of the strikingly handsome exterior. It will seat 1,600 persons. This building was completed and dedicated in 1881, and was built mainly through the efforts of Father Waldron, who is highly esteemed for the great work he has accomplished, and for his charitable efforts in behalf of the poor of his parish. The officiating priests are Rev. John Waldron, and his assistant, Rev. C. P. Foster.

The Society of the New Jerusalem (Swedenborgian) was organized in 1843 with three members. It held its meetings for a time in a public hall. Rev. J. R. Hibbard, D. D., the first pastor, was installed in 1850. In 1857 an old church building, originally built by the Second Presbyterian Church on Harrison Street, was purchased, and served as a place of worship until the erection of a new church on the corner of Wabash Avenue and Adams Street. Dr. Hibbard's health failing him, Rev. C. Day Noble was called as an assistant in 1870, and in 1871 the pastor was granted leave of absence and sailed for Europe just before the great fire, which destroyed the building. The society then undertook to erect buildings for a South Side congregation on the corner of Eighteenth Street and Prairie Avenue, and a West Side congregation on the corner of Washington Street and Ogden Avenue. On Dr. Hibbard's return from Europe there was a division of the society, a part of the South Side congregation organizing as a second society with Rev. C. Day Noble as pastor. The panic of 1873 completed the financial ruin of many of the leading members of the society, still further crippling the operations of the church. In 1877 a new union society was organized with Rev. I. P. Mercer as pastor, holding services in Hershey Music Hall, Rev. Dr. Hibbard resigning the pastorate of the Chicago society in the same year, and services were suspended on the South Side. In 1881 the Chicago society sold its lot on the corner of Prairie Avenue and Eighteenth Street, and a new building was erected on Van Buren Street east of Wabash Avenue. The members of the two societies united, and Rev. I. P. Mercer became the pastor. The society now numbers some 200. Rev. Geo. Nelson Smith is pastor of the North Side congregation (Lincoln Park Chapel) and the West Side congregation (Union Park Temple). Rev. I. P. Mercer remains in charge of the New Church Temple. The society maintains a New Church library and book room, for the sale and circulation of the works of Swedenborg and other New Church writings. It is located in the temple on Van Buren Street east of Wabash Avenue.

The Kehilath Anshe Maarab (Congregation of Men of the West), corner of Indiana Avenue and Twenty-sixth Street, is the oldest Hebrew congregation in the city. It adheres to the party of moderate reform. It was organized in 1846, and numbers about 120 families. There were several removals before the congregation settled in the modest wooden building it now occupies. The seating capacity is about 800. Dr. Ignatz Kunreuther, lately deceased, was the first pastor. Dr. Samuel Sale is the present minister

Zion Congregation, corner of Sangamon and West Jackson Streets, occupies a modest frame building, which was erected in 1869. It has three Sunday school rooms in the basement. The auditorium seats about 700. The membership includes about 100 families of Reformed Jewish faith. Services are held both Saturday and Sunday mornings. The congregat on was formed in 1864, by seceding members of Sinai

Congregatio , the founder and pastor of the latter, Dr. B. Felsenthal, becoming the minister of the new synagogue, which position he still holds.

Sinai Congregation, occupying Sinai Temple, corner of Indiana Avenue and Twenty-first Street, was organized in 1861, and is the leading church of the Jewish faith in the west. The temple was erected in 1876 at a cost of $100,000, including the ground The interior is elegantly finished in hard wood, and very handsomely furnished. The auditorium is arranged like an amphitheater, and with the gallery, recently added, affords seats for 1,400 people. After the fire the congregation temporarily occupied various locations until the erection of the temple. The membership includes about 150 families, and is Reformed Jewish in faith. Dr. E. G. Hirsch, who is widely known as a man of great learning and piety, is rabbi in charge.

SINAI TEMPLE. ADLER & SULLIVAN, ARCHITECTS

St. Paul's Church (Universalist), Wabash Avenue between Sixteenth and Eighteenth Streets, is the leading and oldest church of its denomination in the city. The building is a fine stone structure, of Gothic architecture, modified by Romanesque features. The interior finish is black walnut, and a good deal of excellent carving adds to the beauty of the work. It was built in 1873, the edifice previously occupied having been destroyed by the conflagration of 1871. The main auditorium seats 1,500, and on the floor below is a lecture room with seating capacity for 600, a library, parlor and other rooms. The church membership embraces about 150 families, and the Sunday school has 400 pupils. There is also an industrial school in the building, with seventy pupils. This church had its inception in 1841–42. Rev. W. H. Ryder, D. D., was the pastor for over twenty-one years, commencing in 1860. Rev. J. Coleman Adams is the present pastor.

The Church of the Messiah, or First Unitarian Association, corner of Michigan Avenue and Twenty-third Street, was formerly known as the First Unitarian Church, and is the pioneer church of that denomination in Chicago. It was organized June 29, 1836, and after various changes finally settled in the present building in 1873, the building previously occupied in another location having perished in the conflagration, as its predecessor had also fallen victim to that element. The edifice is of stone, surmounted by a low tower, and was erected at a cost of $50,000. The interior is handsomely finished in black walnut and pine. The seating capacity is 750. Rev. Robert Collyer was minister at large for a brief season in 1857. In 1866 the noted Rev. Robert Laird Collier became pastor, and during his incumbency of

CHURCH OF THE MESSIAH.

nearly ten years, gave the church a national fame. After the death of his wife, he resigned his charge in 1875. She was a daughter of Hon. Hiram Price, of Iowa, Commissioner of Indian Affairs, and a woman of exceptionally noble mind and character. A fine two-story memorial structure called "Mary Collier Chapel," was erected in the rear of the church building at a cost of $30,000. It contains the pastor's study and parlor, and a chapel for Sunday school uses. Rev. Brooke Hereford followed Mr. Collier, and the present pastor, Rev. David Utter, took charge Jan. 15, 1883. The church supports the Hereford Kindergarten on Twenty-second Street near Wentworth Avenue.

Unity Church, Dearborn Avenue, opposite Washington Square, is the largest of the Unitarian organizations in the city. It was organized Dec. 23, 1857, and held its first services on the last Sunday in May, 1859. Rev. Robert Collyer preached the first sermon, and continued in the pastoral charge for twenty years, his brilliant ability and liberal and humane theology commanding public attention, drawing hundreds to the membership, and spreading the fame of his church far and wide. Christmas eve, 1859, Rev. Dr. Hosmer, of Buffalo, preached the dedication sermon in the first building erected for the church. Nearly ten years later—June 20, 1869—Rev. Dr. Bellows, of New York, preached the dedication sermon in the second edifice, erected and furnished at a cost of $210,000. Dec. 7, 1873, Rev. Dr. Furness, of Philadelphia, preached the dedication sermon in the third building (the previous one having been burned in 1871), which had been erected at a cost of $97,737, using the walls and foundation of its predecessor. It has capacity for comfortably seating 1,500 persons. The building is of rough-dressed stone, renaissance Gothic in style, with two unfinished towers, to the completion of which $26,000 left by the late Eli Bates will be applied. A gallery extends around three sides of the nave, and the interior finish is of dark hardwood, oil polished. The acoustic properties are said to be perfect. The church pays a great deal of attention to social, charitable and missionary matters. An Industrial school for girls, in which sewing and the various forms of housework are taught, has been supported by the church for a number of years. A fine building has just been erected for the school, at a cost of $20,-000, from a fund bequeathed for this purpose by the late Eli Bates. In the summer of 1879 the church reluctantly accepted the resignation of Mr. Collyer. Rev. Geo. C. Miln was then installed, but after about one year retired. The present pastor, Rev. Geo. Batchelor, was installed the first Sunday in November, 1882.

The First German Baptist Church, corner of Bickerdike and West Huron Streets, was organized in 1858. The house is a plain wooden building with a seating capacity of 400. It has 300 members, a Sunday school of 300 pupils; an afternoon Sunday school in the Danish language, with fifty pupils; and a mission school on Burling and Willow Streets which has 150 pupils and occupies a brick building erected by the church at a cost of $13,000. The pastor, Rev. Jacob Meier, has officiated since 1878.

The Memorial Church (Baptist), on Oakwood Boulevard near Cottage Grove Avenue, was formerly University Place Church. The society was organized near the close of 1868, in the chapel of the Chicago University, and had for its first pastor J. A. Smith, D. D. Several distinguished divines subsequently filled its pulpit. During the pastorate of Rev. J. T. Burhoe the building was removed to its present location, about a mile south of its former site. Its membership includes many persons who were formerly members of the Indiana Avenue Church, which dissolved in 1875. Rev. N. E. Wood, D. D., the present pastor, took charge in 1883.

The Churches in Chicago represent most all the denominations. Only the leading churches of the various denominations have been noted in the preceding pages. The total number of duly organized congregations is 262. The number in each denomination is shown in the following table:

DENOMINATION.	NO.	DENOMINATION.	NO.
Baptist	24	Independent	4
Christian	5	Jewish.	14
Congregational	25	Methodist Episcopal	40
Dutch Reformed	2	Methodist Episcopal (Colored)	3
Episcopal	16	New Jerusalem(Swedenborgian)	4
Episcopal (Reformed) . . .	6	Presbyterian	16
Evangelical Association . .	7	Roman Catholic	35
Evangelical Lutheran . . .	33	Unitarian	4
Evangelical Reformed. . . .	2	Universalist	2
Evangelical United.	5	Miscellaneous	13
Free Methodist	2	Total	262

The Chicago Bible Society is a branch of the American Bible Society. Its object is to promote the wider circulation of the Bible, and its field is confined to Cook County, in which there are thirty-seven auxiliary societies. About 150 local agents are employed in canvassing the county, and the city and county have been thoroughly canvassed eleven times since the organization of the society, and over a half million copies of the Bible have been circulated. The depository is at 150 Madison Street.

The Young Men's Christian Association (Holland) has had merely a nominal existence for some time, and for nearly two years its regular meetings have been suspended. Latterly, however, interest has been somewhat revived and a re organization is proposed. The association has a library of over 300 volumes. Meetings were formerly held at the First Dutch Reformed Church, corner of May and West Harrison Streets.

The Scandinavian Young Men's Christian Association was first organized June 1, 1872, by the young men of Trinity Lutheran Church, corner of Indiana and Peoria Streets, the congregation of which is Scandinavian. A reorganization took place in 1873, but not much interest was manifested until 1883, when the work revived. The association now has 140 members, and occupies a hall at No. 183 Peoria Street, where it has a small library of Scandinavian books and English Bibles. O. L. Stangeland, 239 W. Erie Street, is president.

The Chicago Young Men's Christian Association was founded in 1858. It began with 151 members, had 355 at the end of its first year and now numbers upwards of 3,000. During the war it was active in missionary and relief work among the soldiers, and gave seventy-five men to the first call for volunteers. One hundred and forty-one of its members perished in camp and on the field. Jan. 7, 1868, its commodious building at 148 and 150 Madison Street was destroyed by fire, and a second one was lost in the great fire of 1871, the losses aggregating in the neighborhood of $100,000. The present building was dedicated Nov. 26, 1874, and remodeled in the summer of 1882. It is a substantial five-story structure, erected at a cost of $90,000, and valued, with the ground, at $250,000. The library contains 3,600 works, and is free to all members. The reading-room is open to the public, and is abundantly supplied with papers and

Y. M. C. A. BUILDING.

magazines. The parlors are handsomely furnished and inviting. The gymnasium has an average daily attendance of 275. The baths are excellent and well patronized, 340 lockers being provided. The sociables, receptions and lectures are popular and liberally attended. Railroad branches of the association have been established at the corner of Kinzie and Canal Streets, where there is a reading room, and at 4645 State Street and 141 Stewart Avenue, where both reading and bath rooms are provided, and at the latter, coffee and sleeping rooms are also established. The employment department is doing excellent work.

The Chicago Sabbath Association has been in active operation since 1879, first as a branch of the International Sabbath Association, and afterward as a separate organization. Its special mission is to protect the Sabbath as a day of rest and worship, and hence it opposes all unnecessary labor, traffic, public shows, etc., on that day, as interfering with its dedication to the purposes mentioned, and tending to degrade it in the eyes of youth. The society has held some popular meetings and circulated a large amount of literature. Wm. Niestadt, 57 Washington Street, is secretary.

The Cook County Sunday School Association dates its formation March 24, 1859, and includes all workers in the Evangelical Sunday schools in Cook County. It aims to promote interest in Sunday school matters, and to develop better modes of work. It distributes about $13,000 annually for benevolence, and about $1,000 for state and county work. The office is at 148 Madison Street. W. B. Jacobs is superintendent.

The American Sunday School Union organized its Chicago branch in 1855. The special work of this organization is to establish and assist Sunday schools, employing missionaries for the purpose, and supplying the schools with suitable literature. Sixteen of the vice-presidents of the union are pious citizens of Chicago. F. G. Ensign, 148 Madison Street, is the superintendent of the Chicago branch.

Educational Institutions.

THE PUBLIC SCHOOLS, UNIVERSITIES, COLLEGES, AND OTHER EDUCATIONAL INSTITUTIONS.

THE educational institutions of Chicago are well up to its necessities, save in the matter of public school buildings. It has been an impossibility to extend the public school facilities so as to keep pace with the demands of the growing population. But there is an ample supply of private educational institutions, such as seminaries, grammar schools, kindergartens, manual training schools and business and professional colleges. The aggregate of schools of all kinds and grades in and immediately about Chicago, makes it a great center of education. In the building up of these schools money has been supplied lavishly; endowments and funds have been profusely furnished; the important accessories of great libraries have already reached an extraordinary extent; and scholarships of the most liberal character abound in many of the institutions.

The Public Schools are arranged on the well-known graded system, and are divided into three departments, primary, grammar, and the high schools. The primary schools are those in which the first four grades are taught; the grammar schools take the pupils up to the eighth grade; and the high schools take them through still higher studies known as the ninth, tenth, eleventh and twelfth grades. There are three high schools, one in each division of the city, and located as follows: The South Division high school, corner of Wabash Avenue and Twenty-sixth Street; West Division high school, corner of Morgan and Monroe Streets; North Division high school, corner of Wendell and Wells Streets. The total attendance in the high school department during the year 1883-84 was 1.400, at a total cost per pupil of $48.22. The eight grades of the primary and grammar departments cover such an amount of ground, that, in graduating from the grammar schools, the pupils are fairly well prepared to enter the world without further school instruction. Evening schools have been opened in various school buildings, and one at the Newsboys' Home—in all, fourteen. One of these is known as the Evening High School, and is for the bene-

· fit of those who desire to study in the higher grades. There are also five deaf mute schools, having a total attendance of about sixty. The elementary studies in these schools are in the course provided, including geography in some instances, and instruction relating to morals and manners. There are also classes in articulation for teaching vocal speech. There are sixty-eight public school buildings in the city. These are nearly all brick structures, and those lately erected are provided with every modern improvement. The management of the schools is vested in a board of education appointed by the mayor, and confirmed by the city council. This board consists of fifteen members. The total value of the school sites occupied is $1,166,475 ; and the total value of the school buildings, including heating apparatus and furniture, is $2,- 530.825. The income of the public school system consists of the school tax from the state and city, the income of the fund derived from rentals and sales of school lands, and from several special funds, such as the Jonathan Burr, Newberry, Michael Reese, Moseley and other funds, some of which were given for the purpose of supplying the children of indigent parents with the necessary text-books.

The school fund property, consisting of real estate and the principal of the school fund, amounts to $2,841,791. The city tax for school purposes in 1883 was $1,375,437.15, at the rate of 10.325 mills on a total tax valuation of $133,213,688. The total cash receipts of the school board for the year 1883 were $1,434,571.32, and the total expenditures $1,327,837.63. The total number of children enrolled in the city during the year 1883–84 was 72,509, and the average daily membership of pupils during the same period was 55,890, thus leaving thousands who either attend private schools or the parochial schools of · the religious denominations, but comparatively few, it is believed, who do not enjoy school facilities of some kind. There were 1,195 teachers employed, and the total cost of the system for the year was $1,132,- 820, of which $771,000 was expended for tuition.

The University of Chicago originated with Hon. Stephen A. Douglas. In 1855–56, while a member of the Senate of the United States, Mr. Douglas proposed, as a mark of respect to the memory of his deceased wife, to endow an educational institution under the general control of the Baptist denomination. To this end he offered to donate the ten acres of land on which the University buildings now stand. Rev. J. C. Burroughs resigned the pastorate of the First Baptist Church, accepted a deed of trust of the property for the purpose named, and undertook the task of raising funds for the construction of the neces-

*During 1886 the University of Chicago lost its property by foreclosure, and the school has suspended.

sary buildings. The corner-stone of the south wing was accordingly
laid July 4, 1857. This wing afforded accommodations for the students for some years, but in 1865 the buildings were completed. In
1858 the preparatory department was organized, with the double view
of preparing students for admission to the college, and of providing
those who are unable to take the collegiate course with a first-class
academic education. In 1873, the office of chancellor was created, and
vested with the financial and general management, and Dr. Burroughs
was chosen to that post. He was succeeded in the presidency by Rev. Dr.

UNIVERSITY OF CHICAGO, COTTAGE GROVE AVE., NEAR THIRTY-FIFTH ST.

Lemuel Moss, who a year later was succeeded by Hon. Alonzo Abernethy,
who occupied the chair for two years, when Rev. Galusha Anderson, S. T. D., LL. D., was called to the position, the duties of which he
still fulfills. The university includes a preparatory department, a general collegiate department and the Union College of Law. The latter
is referred to in detail elsewhere. · The curriculum of the collegiate
department embraces a classical and a scientific course, and the standard of examinations is high. Students are also allowed to pursue an
elective course, subject to the regulations of the faculty, certificates of
proficiency being given in studies in which satisfactory examinations
have been passed. Ladies are admitted into both the preparatory and

14

collegiate departments on the same terms as the other sex. There is a valuable library, and an extensive museum, embracing a considerable collection of charts, models, specimens, skeletons, etc., illustrative of human anatomy, zoology, geology and numismatology, together with a well equipped herbarium, and a full supply of modern apparatus for the illustration of lectures on chemistry and natural philosophy. The buildings are strikingly handsome in architectural design. They stand in a grove of old trees on Cottage Grove Avenue near Thirty-fifth Street. Although started under the auspices of the Baptist denomination, there is nothing sectarian in the management of the University.

The **Northwestern University** occupies a group of buildings in Evanston, one of the most beautiful suburbs of Chicago. The grounds on which the buildings are situated consist of about thirty acres lying on the shore of Lake Michigan. The main building, called University Hall, shown in the illustration on the opposite page, was erected at a cost of $110,000. It is used only for chapel, library, museum and recitation purposes. The library contains about 26,000 volumes, and 8,000 pamphlets. It includes the Greenleaf collection of Greek and Latin literature, about 14,000 volumes, which is said to be one of the most complete classical collections in America. What is known as the Orrington Lunt library fund, amounting to considerably over $25,000, is set apart for library purposes. The museum contains valuable collections. There is a large and well appointed gymnasium on the grounds. The university embraces a college of liberal arts, providing classical, Latin and scientific courses, a course in modern literature and art, and special and elective courses; a college of medicine (Chicago Medical College); a college of law (Union College of Law); preparatory school, school of elocution, conservatory of music, department of art. The university is under control of the Methodist denomination, but is unsectarian. The university was incorporated in 1851. The entire property, which includes large real estate interests in Chicago, is valued at $1,500,000. Female students are admitted on the same terms as males, to the college of liberal arts, the Evanston College for Ladies having become a department of the university in June, 1873. They occupy a handsome building known as the "Woman's College," and used chiefly for study and lodging rooms. In 1883 the university had a total of 753 students. Rev. Joseph Cummins, D. D., LL. D., is president of the faculty.

Cook County Normal and Training School, Normalville, Stewart Avenue and Sixty-seventh Street, was established by Cook County for the

purpose of furnishing competent teachers for the public schools. There are a normal and a preparatory department. All applicants for admission to the normal department must declare their intention to teach in the public schools and to give the county the preference in all offers to secure their services; and are required to pass satisfactory examination in various common school branches—except those holding teacher's certificates or those who have graduated from a high school. Pupils are admitted to the preparatory department without examination. Tuition is free to residents of the county. Non-residents are required to pay $30 per year. The buildings were erected in 1874. The school was originally established at Blue Island in 1867. Francis W. Parker is principal.

The Union College of Law was organized in 1859 as the law department of the University of Chicago. About ten years ago the Northwestern University was admitted to an equal interest and joint management in the school. The full term of study occupies two years of thirty-six weeks each. Those entering are expected to have at least a good common school education. The diploma granted for a full course admits the graduate to the bar of Illinois, and attendance for a shorter period is credited to the applicant on examination before the Appellate Court. The college occupies rooms at Nos. 80 and 82 Dearborn Street. Hon. Henry Booth, LL. D., is dean of the faculty.

St. Ignatius College, 413 West Twelfth Street, is conducted by the Fathers of the Society of Jesus. It was organized in 1869 and chartered a year later with power to confer the usual degrees. It embraces academic, collegiate, commercial and preparatory departments. The academic department is preparatory to the collegiate, but furnishes in itself a thorough high school education for those who have not the opportunity to take the collegiate course. The collegiate department comprises four classes: Philosophy, Rhetoric, Poetry and the Humanities. The commercial department embraces all the branches of a good English education. The preparatory class is for students not sufficiently advanced to enter the academic or commercial departments. In addition to the regular departments of instruction there are the Loyola Debating Society, for the promotion of eloquence and a taste for literary studies, and the Saint Cecilia Society, whose purpose is to improve its members in vocal music, and to contribute to the celebration of literary and religious festivals. In addition to collegiate studies the students are instructed in the doctrines and evidences of the Catholic religion. On completion of the collegiate course, the student receives the degree

of Bachelor of Arts, and by devoting one more year to the study of
philosophy, or two years to any of the learned professions, he may
receive the degree of Master of Arts. The college buildings are handsome and commodious. There are a staff of twenty professors, a fine
museum, a library of 12,000 volumes, a laboratory, a conchological
collection, and, in short, all that is essential to a first-class educational
establishment. Rev. Jos. G. Zealand, S. J., is president of the faculty.

The German-American Young Ladies' Institute is a day and boarding school for girls. It was established in 1880, and, as an institution
for practical instruction, it has become well and favorably known. The
two buildings occupied at Nos. 605 and 607 North Clark Street, near
Lincoln Park, are very commodious. They provide accommodations
for ten resident (boarding) students, and about seventy day pupils.
The course of study is divided into Junior, Intermediate and Senior
departments, and contemplates thorough instruction in all branches of
learning that may be essential to the pupil in after life, or that may add
to her accomplishments. It has always been the aim of the institution
to give pupils equal advantages in the German and English languages,
and special opportunities are now extended to boarding pupils in
acquiring the French language, there being two resident French
teachers. Pupils may enter the institute at any time. The faculty consists of ten instructors. Mrs. Amelia Ende is principal.

St. Xavier's Academy is conducted as a boarding school for young
ladies only, and is in charge of the Sisters of Mercy. It was first
opened in 1846, and was incorporated in February, 1847. In August,
1873, several changes in location having previously been made, the
pre ent splendid building, one of the handsomest devoted to educational purposes, on the corner of Wabash Avenue and Twenty-ninth
Street, was occupied. The course of study embraces the various
branches of solid and useful education.

The Chicago Manual Training School, Michigan Avenue and
Twenty-second Street, originated with an association of gentlemen
connected with the Commercial Club. It was incorporated in 1883,
and opened Feb. 4, 1884. Its object is to give instruction in mathe-
matics, drawing, and the English branches of a high school course, and
specially in the use of tools in shopwork of all kinds. The building
was erected by the association at a cost of $50,000. It is of pressed
red brick, five stories, and covers 80×100 feet of ground; and will
accommodate 300 pupils at study and work. The mechanical department is equipped with benches, lathes, tools, forges, engine, etc., and

the American Electrical Society's scientific library of nearly 500 volumes has been placed in the school, and other valuable books of reference have been donated.

The **Illinois Training School for Nurses** was instituted in 1881. The school occupies two wards in the County Hospital. Its object is not only to furnish trained nurses for the sick and wounded, but also to afford those who desire to become skilled nurses such facilities as will open to them a self-supporting and honorable profession. Pupils are required to undergo training for two years. The buildings and ground known as the Nurses' Home, are located at 304 Honore Street. They are the property of the society. The institution is supported by contributions, annual subscriptions, services to the hospital, private nursing and membership fees.

The **Illinois Industrial School for Girls** was chartered January, 1877, with a capital of $500 from the treasury of the disbanded Woman's Centennial Association. Its board of directors is composed of men and women from different parts of the state. It is located at South Evanston in the old Soldiers' Home building, which was remodeled and enlarged for the purpose. The specific object is the maintenance of a home and training school for neglected, dependent and homeless girls under eighteen years of age, until permanent homes and means of support can be secured for them. Mrs. Helen M. Beveridge is president.

St. **Mary's Training School for Boys** is a Catholic institution under the charge of the Christian Brothers, at Feehanville, Cook County. It was incorporated under the present name in 1882, a farm of 440 acres was purchased, and suitable buildings were erected.

The **Chicago Athenæum**, well called "The People's College," has its rooms at 48 to 54 Dearborn Street, occupying the three upper stories. It has for its purpose intellectual and physical training and has become a recognized institution of the highest educational value. It originated soon after the great fire, and was the medium through which relief, to the amount of $175,000, was bestowed upon the sufferers. It was then known as the Chicago Young Men's Christian Union, but three years later, the board of government, recognizing the need of practical educational work in a central location, the name was changed to the Chicago Athenæum. It includes day and evening classes, also a gymnasium. All the instruction of the Mechanics' Institute is given here. The curriculum is comprehensive, and withal notably practical. It includes drawing, music, elocution, mathematics, Latin, penmanship. lectures on English and American literature, book-keeping, short-hand and type-writing, French, German, and Spanish. It has a day grammar school and also a business school, open to both sexes, in which Munson's short-hand, type-writing, and German are taught. A ladies' class for the critical study of the best

English literature, especially Shakespeare, is held every Wednesday afternoon. An employment bureau furnishes clerks, mechanics, shorthand reporters and type-writers. . The Athenæum is wholly unsectarian, its only condition of memberbership being that of good moral character. The gymnasium is not the least important feature of the institution. It occupies a room 90×80 feet and twenty-seven

THE CHICAGO ATHENÆUM.

feet high, well-lighted and ventilated and equipped with every desirable accessory to such a place. It has a large active membership and gives several athletic exhibitions every winter to crowded houses. The number of people taught in the Athenæum is about 1,000 a year, a number very much greater than that of any academy or college in the state. Financially it is flourishing, and full of promise for the future. Its pressing need is a much larger building, with more class-rooms and a commodious hall for first-class lectures on art, science, and literature. Mrs. Mancel Talcott has given $5,000 toward a permanent fund, also $1,000 for the exclusive use of the library. The late Eli Bates left a bequest of $10,000 toward the same fund. The board of directors, of which P. B. Moulton, Esq., is president, and John Wilkinson, Esq., recording secretary and treasurer, is composed of sixteen prominent merchants and lawyers. A warm interest in the welfare of the Athenæum, is taken by the mercantile community. Mr. Edward I. Galvin is superintendent, and Mr. Joseph Silvers, assistant superintendent.

Rush Medical College is the oldest medical college in Chicago, and was the first educational institution incorporated in the Northwest. It was started in embryo in 1836 by Dr. Daniel Brainard, who for many years led the medical faculty of the west. Dr. Brainard, with Dr. G. C. Goodhue, of Rockford, Ill., secured an act of incorporation which was approved in 1837, but owing to the prevailing financial depression, the college did not organize until 1843, when two small rooms were fitted up on Clark Street, and a course of lectures delivered by the faculty, consisting of Drs. Brainard, Knapp, Blaney and McLean. In 1844 some North Side citizens donated a lot on which was erected a building costing $3,500. In 1855 this was remodeled and enlarged to accommo-

PRESBYTERIAN HOSPITAL.   RUSH MEDICAL COLLEGE.
RUSH MEDICAL COLLEGE.

date 250 students. In 1867 a new building was erected at a cost of about $100,000, but, on the fated 9th of October, 1871, the structure, with all its contents, disappeared in the flames. A temporary place was secured for lectures in the old County Hospital, and later a temporary structure was erected on Eighteenth Street. In 1875, the present building, at the corner of Wood and Harrison Streets was finished and occupied. It is one of the most complete institutions of the kind on the continent. It has two lecture rooms, each with a seating capacity of over 500 and thoroughly equipped. There are anatomical, physiological, clinical and chemical departments. The Central Free Dispensary is connected with the clinical department, and 2,000 cases are treated annually in the County Hospital. The value of the college property is about $125,000. The number of graduates per annum is about 175.

The Presbyterian Hospital, mentioned in the chapter on "Charity and Benevolence," was erected by the college, and then transferred to the Presbyterian Hospital Society—the faculty remaining in professional charge of the patients. The faculty is composed of twelve members. J. Adams Allen, M. D., is president.

Hahnemann Medical College is the oldest homœopathic college in the Northwest. It was incorporated in 1855, and lecture rooms were opened in 1859 at 168 Clark Street, with twenty-five students. The college building, at 2813 Cottage Grove Avenue, was erected in 1870. It is a brick structure with three stories and basement. The hospital is in the rear, one block away. There are two terms each year—a winter course, and a practitioner's course of six weeks in the spring. The plan of instruction is largely clinical and objective, the college course being the complement of the daily drill in the hospital. Female students are admitted on the same terms as males. Many students come from New York and New England to complete their course at this institution. The faculty consists of seventeen professors. A. E. Small, M. D., is president; R. Ludlam, M. D., is dean.

The Chicago Medical College, corner of Prairie Avenue and Twenty-sixth Street, was founded in 1859, as the medical department of Lind University, but in 1864 it was incorporated as a separate institution, and in 1869 it was adopted as the medical department of the Northwestern University. Its founders were Drs. H. A. Johnson, N. S. Davis, W. H. Byford, E. Andrews, R. N. Isham and David Rutter. It has a practitioner's course, a regular three years' course, and a fourth year for such as may desire to take it. The two large amphitheaters permit of lectures to two classes at the same hour. The laboratories are supplied with modern apparatus, and the museum contains an exceptionally large and useful collection. The college was the first in the United States to adopt a full graded system of medical instruction, and one of the first to require a fair standard of general education before entering the college. N. S. Davis, M. D., LL. D., is dean of the faculty; Walter May, M. D., LL. D., is secretary, and E. Andrews, M. D., LL. D., treasurer.

Bennett College of Eclectic Medicine and Surgery was inaugurated in 1868, and chartered a year later. The school was opened on Kinzie Street, between LaSalle and Fifth Avenue, with thirty students. The second course was held at No. 180 East Washington Street, and was interrupted, but only for a week, by the great fire. After moving once or twice after the fire, a site was obtained at 511 and 513 State Street,

on which was erected the present college building, a five-story structure, 40×100 feet, with accommodation for 250 students. Bennett
Hospital adjoins the college building in the rear. Ladies have been
admitted on the same terms as males, except during one or two sessions
of the school. The institution has graduated over 500 students. The
faculty consists of fifteen members. Prof. Milton Jay, M. D., is dean.

The **Woman's Medical College of Chicago** is located at 337 and
339 Lincoln Street, opposite the County Hospital. It owes its existence
largely to Dr. Wm. H. Byford, a local physician of eminence. It was
established in 1870, and is now on a permanent foundation, and owns
the brick building it occupies. There are a two and a three years'
course of study, and a select course in anatomy, physiology, chemistry,
or microscopy for ladies. The college is allopathic in its teachings,
and the only medical school in the West exclusively for women. The
faculty is composed of twenty-seven professors. W. H. Byford, A. M.,
M. D., is president, and Charles W. Earle, M. D., is secretary.

The **Chicago College of Pharmacy**, 415 and 417 State Street, was
founded in 1859. The war interrupted its progress after two courses of
lectures had been given, and nothing further was done until 1869,
when operations were again resumed only to be suspended by the fire
of 1871. The next year contributions from druggists and friends,
amounting to four or five thousand dollars, and some books having
been sent in, the lectures were once more resumed, and have continued
without interruption. The new college building was erected during
the summer of 1884. It is a handsome brick structure, and one of the
best equipped pharmacy colleges in the country. The lecture hall on
the first floor has seating capacity for 400 persons. The museum,
library and experimental laboratory occupy the second floor, and the
third floor is fitted up with an extensive pharmaceutical laboratory.
The curriculum embraces chemistry, pharmacy, materia medica and
toxicology, and botany. The college stands third in the United States
in point of attendance. Thomas Whitfield is president; S. L. Coffin,
secretary, and T. H. Patterson, treasurer.

The **Chicago Dental Infirmary**, Nos. 22 and 24 Adams Street, third
floor, was founded in 1882. Its purpose is to educate practitioners for
dental and oral surgery, to teach the science and art of dentistry to
medically educated students, and the treatment or extraction of teeth.
The institution is kept open the entire year for clinical instruction.
James A. Swasey is president; Edgar D. Swain, treasurer; Thomas W.
Brophy, secretary.

The Collegiate Department of the Chicago Dental Infirmary teaches the science and art of dentistry to medically educated young men who desire to practice that specialty. The degree of Doctor of Dental Surgery is conferred only on men having a degree in medicine from coleges recognized by the Illinois State Board of Health.

The Chicago College of Physicians and Surgeons (Allopathic), corner Harrison and Honore Streets, was organized in 1881. The building is a splendid stone structure four stories in height, with a tower 100 feet high. The architecture is the Queen Anne style. The amphitheater seats 475. The curriculum of the college is comprehensive. It is adapted to a two or three years' course. The faculty consists of thirty professors, lecturers and demonstrators. A. Reeves Jackson, M. D., is president; D. A. K. Steele, M. D., is secretary; Leonard St. John, M. D., is treasurer.

The Theological Schools are as follows : The Chicago Theological Seminary (Congregational) was founded in 1858. It occupies Carpenter & King's Halls and Hammond Library, corner Ashland and Warren Avenues. The library contains 6,000 volumes. The Presbyterian Theological Seminary of the Northwest, North Halsted Street and Fullerton Avenue, is the successor to a seminary originally established at Hanover, Ind., in 1830, removed to New Albany. Ind., in 1840, and to Chicago in 1859 on the offer of the late Cyrus H. McCormick to donate $100,000 for the endowment of four professorships. The buildings are spacious and handsome and the library contains 10,000 volumes. The Baptist Theological Seminary was organized in Chicago in 1865, and removed to Morgan Park in 1877. It has a Swedish department in which instruction is given in the Swedish language. The library, including the Huegestenberg and Ide collections, comprises about 20,000 volumes. The property is valued at $300,000. The Garrett Biblical Institute (Methodist Episcopal), occupies buildings erected on the grounds of the Northwestern University at a cost of $60,000. It was founded on a bequest of $300,000 worth of property by Mrs. Eliza Garrett. The Swedish Theological Seminary is under the supervision of the Northwestern Swedish M. E. Conference. It is exclusively a school for young men from the M. E. church. It was founded at Galesburg. Ill., in 1868, but removed to its present connection with Northwestern University in 1882.

The Chicago Mechanics' Institute was chartered in 1843. Its object is the diffusion of knowledge and information throughout the mechanical classes, and the formation of a library and museum for the benefit of mechanics. It does all its educational work through the Athenæum. Individual instruction is given through the classes of the Athenæum to mechanics and their children who are unable to pay for their tuition. The course of instruction includes reading, writing, arithmetic, geometry, and a complete course of free-hand and mechanical drawing. The average number of attendants during the past three years has been 140. This institute is a most valuable one, and is fully deserving of the sympathy and cordial support of the public. George C. Prussing is president; Murry Nelson, treasurer; Jos. Silvers, librarian, and John Wilkinson, auditor.

Schools not heretofore specially mentioned embrace every department of instruction, and are nearly all private enterprises. Many of the churches and charitable and benevolent institutions maintain general or industrial schools or kindergartens—see chapters on "Religious Organizations" and "Charity and Benevolence." Morgan Park Military Academy is located at Morgan Park, as is also the Chicago Female College, and the society of the American Institute of Hebrew, but are properly classed as Chicago institutions. Unity Church Industrial School has recently moved into its new building on Elm Street.

Music Schools are numerous, but all of a private character. The leading music schools are the Chicago Musical College, Central Music Hall; School of Lyric and Dramatic Art, Weber Music Hall; Hershey School of Musical Art, Hershey Music Hall.

The Art Schools are mentioned in the chapter on "Arts and Sciences."

The Private Schools, by which term all schools in the city, except public schools under the charge of the Board of Education, may be designated, numbered in May (1884) 156, with 33,874 pupils, as follows: Kindergartens, 26—with 626 female and 511 male pupils and 69 teachers; parochial, 73—with 15,036 female and 13,463 male pupils and 442 teachers; business colleges, 4—with 293 female and 748 male pupils and 37 teachers; all others, 57—with 2,274 female and 1,923 male pupils and 302 teachers.

The Libraries.

THE OLD AND NEW LIBRARIES, THE READING ROOMS, AND THE PRIVATE BOOK COLLECTIONS.

BEFORE the great fire of 1871 the principal libraries of the city were those of the Young Men's Association and of the Historical Society. The Young Men's Association was organized in 1841, and proceeded at once to make the first successful associated effort to establish a library in Chicago, and at the time of the conflagration had accumulated about 16,000 volumes, which were destroyed. The institution seems to have then and there received its death-blow, as it has never since been revived. There were several large collections of books on historical and other special subjects, owned by private individuals, but the two named were the only libraries open to general access. There was no public library, supported as a municipal institution by public taxation, and free to all.

The Public Library was originated by Thomas Hughes, M. P., of London, the well-known English author, soon after the great fire. Mr. Hughes issued an appeal to publishers, authors, librarians and others throughout Great Britain, asking for donations of books for the establishment of a free public library in Chicago, and in a short time more than 7,000 volumes were received in response to the appeal. The British Museum gave copies of all of its own publications, with other spare volumes, and its example was followed by Oxford University, the Commissioner of Patents, the Master of the Rolls and the leading English publishers, authors and owners of libraries. The Queen herself sent, "as a mark of English sympathy," a copy of her book on "The Early Life of the Prince Consort." At a public meeting Jan. 8, 1872, it was determined to make the library a public institution. A committee was appointed to draft a bill giving the city the authority to establish and maintain it, and the legislature promptly passed the measure. While the institution was taking on the form of organization, the books were temporarily placed in the immense iron tank at the corner of Adams and LaSalle Streets, which was formerly a part of the waterworks. A reading room was opened there in January, 1873. Early in

1874 library rooms were procured at the corner of Wabash Avenue and Madison Street. For public use the library was divided into two departments—the circulating department, from which books can be taken out under proper regulations, and the reference department, in which the books are open for examination, but are not allowed to be taken from the building. The circulating department was opened to the public May 1, 1874, the total number of volumes in the library at that time being 17,355. In May, 1875, the library was removed to the building at the southwest corner of Dearborn and Lake Streets, and in May, 1886, it was removed to the room now occupied on the fourth floor of the City Hall. Branch deliveries have been established at 124 East Twenty-second Street, 482 South Halsted Street, 409 Milwaukee Avenue, 817 West Madison, 349 E. Division, 233 Thirty-first, and 531 West Twelfth Streets. The following statistics for the year 1885-6 will give the reader an idea of the work of this library: Number of books in library, 119,510; expended for new books, $9,-405.38; circulation, 608,708; borrowers registered, 27,142; visitors to the reference department, 66.498; visitors to the reading-room, 655,816; periodicals on file, 325; newspapers on file, 156; cost of serials, $1,444.84; salary account, $32,202.76. Wm. F. Poole, formerly librarian of the Cincinnati Public Library, and previously of the Boston Athenæum, has been librarian since 1873. The library is open to the public every day from 9 A. M. to 10 P. M.

The Chicago Historical Society was organized in 1856. The first secretary and librarian was Rev. W. H. Barry. Nearly 100,000 volumes of books and a very large accumulation of manuscripts relating to the traditions and early settlement of Illinois, and a vast amount of valuable information concerning the civil war, including much that was rare and not otherwise obtainable, was secured and in the possession of the society before the great fire, and all was lost. Immediately after the fire, many collections were forwarded to the society from Europe and o'her sources, and reached here in time to be consumed by the fire of July, 1874. In the summer of 1877 money was raised to put up the present building, which was first occupied Oct. 15, 1877, with a collection of 703 bound and 998 unbound volumes and pamphlets. The building is located at 140 and 142 Dearborn Avenue. It is a plain brick structure, 40×60 feet, one story in height, and is but poorly adapted to the uses of the society. The library now comprises about 9,000 volumes and 28,000 pamphlets, including files of the daily newspapers; a splendid collection of the histories of the various counties of the northwest; over 100 volumes of manuscripts and manuscript letters, including the extensive collection made by Hon. E. B. Washburne during his long political life. The latter are kept in Mr. Washburne's private vault. There is also in the possession of the society every printed report of Massachusetts relating to agriculture, since 1837, and all the educational reports of that state for forty-five years; the reports of the asylum of the blind since February, 1829, which includes a report on the discovery of raised, printed letters for the use of the blind; and most of the reports of the charitable, reformatory and religious institutions of the same state since 1847. The historical matter relative to the early history of the northwest is very complete. There are portraits in oil of Gen. Grant, Columbus, Vespucius, Gen. Henry Dearborn, Edward Coles, the third governor of Illinois, Peter Menard, first lieut.-governor, W. B. Ogden, first mayor of Chicago, John Wentworth, John B. Rice, J. Y. Scammon, and others. The society owns 120×131 feet on the corner of Dearborn Avenue and Ontario Street, where the present building stands. It has had a fund of $62,000 bequeathed to it by Henry D. Gilpin, of Philadelphia, and another of $13,500 left by Miss Lucretia Pond, the income from which is to be devoted to the purchase of books, maps and historical paintings. The library rooms are open every day except Sunday for the benefit of the public. Elihu B. Washburne is president; Albert D. Hager, secretary and librarian; Henry N. Nash, treasurer.

The Union Catholic Library was established April 12, 1869, by a body of young men who formed a Catholic association for the purpose. It was first located in rooms in Oriental Block on LaSalle Street, and afterward in Kent Building on Monroe Street. The entire collection, except about 100 volumes, was burned in the fire of 1871. After the fire, rooms were secured in Pike Building on State Street, and a new collection begun. The library now contains about 3,000 volumes, and embraces books in all departments, save such as may conflict with the Catholic religion. The rooms of the association—consisting of suitable library rooms with a stage suitable for lectures and other entertainments—are at 121 LaSalle Street. They were occupied in May, 1885. The association now has about 460 members. Miss Mamie J. Graham is librarian.

The Chicago Law Institute Library belongs to the Chicago Law Institute, which was organized for the purpose of establishing a law library. It is located in handsome and commodious rooms on the fourth floor of the new county court-house. The institute was incorporated in 1857, mainly through the efforts of Hon. Elliott Anthony, the charter being modeled upon the charter of the New York Law Institute. The debris of an old law library were purchased and at the time of the great fire in October, 1871, the library contained about 7,000 volumes, valued at $50,000. After the fire the work of reconstruction was promptly begun, and rapidly carried forward. The library was moved into its present quarters May 2, 1881. It now comprises about 16,000 volumes, and is noted as bei g one of the. finest collections of legal works in the United States.

The Chicago Athenæum, 50 Dearborn Street, maintains a reading room and library for the benefit of its members. The reading room is provided with all the Chicago daily and several of the weekly papers, also the leading monthly magazines, and is open daily from 8 A. M. to 9:45 P. M. The library contains 1,050 volumes. During the past year 300 volumes of choice reference books and standard literature were added.

The Young Men's Christian Association Library, No. 148 Madison Street, comprises about 3,600 volumes, for the use of the members of the association. The reading room, supplied with daily papers, magazines and leading periodicals, is open to all.

The Private Libraries of Chicago include some of the most valuable collections west of the Alleghenies, both as to rarity and condition of the books collected. Some of the most noted collections have been made by E. G. Asay, Esq., a well-known lawyer, an unerring judge of works of value, and an untiring searcher after copies of rareness and exceptional worth. He was the pioneer book collector of the city, and at the present time is engaged mainly in accumulating works of the Elizabethan literature. He has now a library of nearly 1,800 volumes, including Shaksperian works, fine art works, and some famous illustrated copies. Many of these works are worthy of special mention. Among others, he has a set of Robert Burns extended from six to twelve volumes, with extra illustrations consisting of portraits and views, and including much other valuable matter, among which are twenty original songs and ballads in the autograph of the poet, and forty-seven letters by members of the Burns family. There is also a Shakspere extended from fifteen to thirty-six volumes by the addition of portraits, plates. drawings, water-colors, autographs and letters, among which is a letter written by Elizabeth to Henry of France; one by Bacon, and a large number commenting on Shakspere. There is a Moliere which is extended from six to twelve volumes with plates, portraits, and drawings;

and an edition of Scott extended from twelve to twenty-six volumes. A particularly valuable work is Lubke's History of Art, extended from two to six volumes by the addition of several hundred proof-plates. He has recently acquired a complete set of John Payne Collier's reprints. In addition to these, Mr. Asay has over one hundred very costly books on vellum; Don Quixote extended from six to eighteen volumes by the insertion of all the known illustrations, as well as the original drawings by Stothard. A Walton & Cotton's Angler is among the collection, which has been extended to six volumes by the addition of 430 plates. He has a set by Motley in which is a number of scenes of the period of the Spanish war, and a set of Prescott which contains, among other extra illustrations, a very curious document signed by Ferdinand and Isabella. The collection possessed by Mr. Asay represents a labor extending over a generation. Mr. George Armour probably has the most valuable private library in the city. It contains over 2,000 volumes, among which are very rare and unique works. In the main, the collection is made up of modern works, which are distinguished for the beauty of their paper, type, illustrations, and. binding. He has also a very valuable collection of etchings. Mr. E. B. McCagg has a fine and valuable library of a practical character. Mr. Perry H. Smith's library contains over 1,200 volumes, a great portion of which is devoted to the first Napoleon and his deeds and times. N. Q. Pope, Esq., has a library of over 2,500 volumes, inclusive of 400 books of rare old plays of the Seventeenth Century. Many of his books are superbly illustrated, and there are 500 volumes of old English literature, which include many volumes of the collection of the Duke of Hamilton, the collection of A. H. Griswold, New York, and other noted collectors. He has a remarkable Chaucer which was once in the possession of the Duke of Sussex ; an uncut folio of Beaumont and Fletcher, and original editions of Walton's Anglers, Spenser, Green, and Marlow, together with a perfect first-folio Shakspere, 1623. Many of his books are in fine bindings, by Bedford, Roger Paine, Reviere Matthews, and other noted binders. The collection of L. Z. Leiter is large, valuable, and made up largely of Americana and specimens of Elizabethan literature. John A. Rice once had what was claimed to be the largest collection of Americana in the United States. He is now at work on a library which is intended to be a very fine one. D. W. Irwin has a fine collection, which also includes a fine set of Dibdens. Mark Skinner has a large collection of rare American historical works. Henry Willing has an excellent collection of English litera-

15

ture and illustrated works. James B. Runnion has one of the finest collections of plays in the country, to which he is constantly adding. There are many other private libraries in the city, quite a number of which contain rare and valuable books. The collections here given represent a cash value of fully a half million of dollars.

Other Libraries, of both a general and special character, are numerous. Several of the public schools, and nearly all the private educational institutions (see chapter on "Educational Institutions") of importance, have good libraries—notably the University of Chicago, the Northwestern University, St. Ignatius College, Allen Academy, the medical colleges, the theological seminaries, and many Sunday schools, churches and church societies, and charitable institutions, as well as various scientific, social and religious organizations. Some of these, owing to their special character, are quite valuable. Among the leading libraries not already specially referred to in this chapter, are those of the Chicago Academy of Sciences, 1,000 volumes and 1,500 pamphlets; Dearborn Observatory, 1,000 volumes; Chicago Medical Press Association, 188 Clark Street; State Microscopical Society; American Electrical Society—library at Chicago Manual Training School; Svea Society (Swedish), 1,600 volumes; Plattsdeuchen Verein, Low Dutch; Chicago Turngemeinde, 3,000 volumes, mostly German; Irish-American Club; Dania Society. The Art Institute has recently begun the collection of works on art. The society for the Home Teaching of the Blind, No. 10 Arcade Court, has 300 volumes in raised letters. The Board of Trade has a library of 300 volumes; the Young Men's Hebrew Society, 3,000 volumes; the College of Pharmacy, 5,000 volumes.

Arts and Sciences.

THE ART AND SCIENTIFIC INSTITUTIONS, AND THE PRIVATE ART COLLECTIONS.

THE aspirations as well as the progress of Chicago in the higher walks of culture are well illustrated in the numerous organizations which may be considered schools of art and science. And the architectural splendor of many of her buildings, the scenery of her parks and boulevards, her high standard of musical effort, and her liberal patronage of all that is improving and elevating, are among the many tangible results of cultivation in these lines.

The Art Institute, formerly known as the Chicago Academy of Fine Arts, was incorporated May 29, 1879, and is now located in a handsome brick building at the corner of Michigan Avenue and Van Buren Street—the property of the association. Nearly all the art societies in the city occupy rooms in the building, or in some way make it their headquarters. It may, in fact, be termed the home of art in Chicago. The land, 54×170 feet, with the building originally upon it, cost $45,-000, but an addition was built to the Van Buren Street front at a cost of $22,000. The objects are to maintain schools of art and design, form art collections, and generally to promote art culture. The members are of two classes, viz : Governing and Annual. Upon the first named class, numbering at present 104, devolves the general management of the affairs of the institute. They pay an initiation fee of $100 and annual dues of $10. The annual members, numbering over 300, are entitled to all the privileges of the institute except the right to vote and to fill the office of trustee. The institute has a bonded debt of $60,000 amply secured by mortgage on real estate. Annual loan exhibitions of paintings, statuary, bric-a-brac, etc., are given, and the galleries, filled with loan objects of various kinds, are kept open throughout the year. In 1883 there were about 15,000 visitors to the exhibitions. The only acquisitions thus far made toward a permanent collection are two paintings — " The Beheading of John the Baptist," by Charles Sprague Pearce, and " Les Amateurs," by T. Alexander Harrison. A leading feature of the institute is the School of In-

229

ture and illustrated works. James B. Runnion has one of the finest collections of plays in the country, to which he is constantly adding. There are many other private libraries in the city, quite a number of which contain rare and valuable books. The collections here given represent a cash value of fully a half million of dollars.

Other Libraries, of both a general and special character, are numerous. Several of the public schools, and nearly all the private educational institutions (see chapter on "Educational Institutions") of importance, have good libraries—notably the University of Chicago, the Northwestern University, St. Ignatius College, Allen Academy, the medical colleges, the theological seminaries, and many Sunday schools, churches and church societies, and charitable institutions, as well as various scientific, social and religious organizations. Some of these, owing to their special character, are quite valuable. Among the leading libraries not already specially referred to in this chapter, are those of the Chicago Academy of Sciences, 1,000 volumes and 1,500 pamphlets; Dearborn Observatory, 1,000 volumes; Chicago Medical Press Association, 188 Clark Street; State Microscopical Society; American Electrical Society—library at Chicago Manual Training School; Svea Society (Swedish), 1,600 volumes; Plattsdeuchen Verein, Low Dutch; Chicago Turngemeinde, 3,000 volumes, mostly German; Irish-American Club; Dania Society. The Art Institute has recently begun the collection of works on art. The society for the Home Teaching of the Blind, No. 10 Arcade Court, has 300 volumes in raised letters. The Board of Trade has a library of 300 volumes; the Young Men's Hebrew Society, 3,000 volumes; the College of Pharmacy, 5,000 volumes.

𝔄𝔯𝔱𝔰 𝔞𝔫𝔡 𝔖𝔠𝔦𝔢𝔫𝔠𝔢𝔰.

THE ART AND SCIENTIFIC INSTITUTIONS, AND THE PRIVATE ART COLLECTIONS.

THE aspirations as well as the progress of Chicago in the higher walks of culture are well illustrated in the numerous organizations which may be considered schools of art and science. And the architectural splendor of many of her buildings, the scenery of her parks and boulevards, her high standard of musical effort, and her liberal patronage of all that is improving and elevating, are among the many tangible results of cultivation in these lines.

The Art Institute, formerly known as the Chicago Academy of Fine Arts, was incorporated May 29, 1879, and is now located in a handsome brick building at the corner of Michigan Avenue and Van Buren Street—the property of the association. Nearly all the art societies in the city occupy rooms in the building, or in some way make it their headquarters. It may, in fact, be termed the home of art in Chicago. The land, 54×170 feet, with the building originally upon it, cost $45,-000, but an addition was built to the Van Buren Street front at a cost of $22,000. The objects are to maintain schools of art and design, form art collections, and generally to promote art culture. The members are of two classes, viz: Governing and Annual. Upon the first named class, numbering at present 104, devolves the general management of the affairs of the institute. They pay an initiation fee of $100 and annual dues of $10. The annual members, numbering over 300, are entitled to all the privileges of the institute except the right to vote and to fill the office of trustee. The institute has a bonded debt of $60,000 amply secured by mortgage on real estate. Annual loan exhibitions of paintings, statuary, bric-a-brac, etc., are given, and the galleries, filled with loan objects of various kinds, are kept open throughout the year. In 1883 there were about 15,000 visitors to the exhibitions. The only acquisitions thus far made toward a permanent collection are two paintings — "The Beheading of John the Baptist," by Charles Sprague Pearce, and "Les Amateurs," by T. Alexander Harrison. A leading feature of the institute is the School of In-

229

struction, which has now been in operation for five years and which will compare favorably with any similar school in the country. It has been self-supporting for two years. The receipts for the year 1883 were $6,588; expenditures, $6,539. The classes are divided into Cos-

ART INSTITUTE, MICHIGAN AVENUE AND VAN BUREN STREET.

tume Model, Nude Life, Painting from Still Life, Water Color, Drawing from the Flat and Cast, Composition, Perspective, Artistic Anatomy, Saturday Sketching, Evening Life, Evening Antique. The fall term includes the time between October 1 and December 22; the winter term from January 2 to March 22; and the spring term from March 31 to June 21. A matriculation fee of $2 is required, which is applied to the purchase of books for the library open to all students. For a full term, every day each week, the fee is $25. Evening Life Class, $10 per term, or $4 per month ; Evening Antique Class, $6 per term, or $3 per month ; Children's Class, $10 per term of two days a week, or $6 for one day. At the close of each term an exhibition of students' work is held, and prizes are awarded at the close of the school year. C. L. Hutchinson, president ; Edson Keith, vice-president ; L. J. Gage, treasurer ; N. H. Carpenter, secretary.

The **Chicago Society of Decorative Art** occupies rooms in the Art Institute. In its sales·rooms are displayed collections of works of art appropriate for decorative purposes. The working department of the society is in rooms especially arranged for the purpose. The society was organized May 24, 1877, its objects being to create a desire for artistic decoration and for the best methods of ornamentation ; to provide training in artistic industries and enable decorative artists to render their labors remunerative. Any person may become a member by the annual payment of $5. There are now about 200 members. The society maintains classes, and gives private lessons in embroidery. Pupils are admitted free for two months, when there is a demand for additional assistance to do the work. Exhibitions are held annually. The society also receives consignments from abroad, which are displayed for sale in the sales-rooms. Mrs. John N. Jewitt is president ; Mrs. Clinton Locke is recording secretary ; Mrs. McGuire, corresponding secretary ; Mrs. John A. Yale, treasurer.

The **Chicago Art League** occupies rooms in the building of the Art Institute. It was organized in March, 1879, its objects being to benefit the artists of Chicago, and to furnish a meeting place for the general discussion of art by its members. There are now twenty members, all young professional artists. Candidates for membership must submit a study in color, from nature. The initiation fee is $5, and the monthly dues fifty cents. Annual exhibitions are given in the galleries of the Art Institute. J. H. Vanderpoel is president ; S. Wilder, secretary ; J. L. Schlanders, treasurer.

The **Bohemian Art Club** was organized in 1880, and occupies rooms in the building of the Art Institute. It aims to promote mutual improvement and good feeling among local artists. Its members consist of ladies only. Candidates for membership are required to submit an original drawing or sketch from nature. The initiation fee is $3. At present there are twenty-three active and three honorary members. Annual exhibitions are held in the galleries of the Art Institute. Mrs. Theo. Shaw is president ; Miss Emma L. Trip, treasurer ; Miss Eva Webster, secretary.

The Chicago Pottery Club consists of twenty ladies interested in ceramic art. It was organized Feb. 27, 1883, and incorporated with a capital stock of $2,000. A cottage at No. 795 West Congress Street was leased, two kilns were erected and an efficient potter was employed. Recently the club sold the kilns and rented the property to Mr. Joseph Bailey, who now executes the work of the members. There is also a studio at the pottery, conducted by Mrs. V. B. Jenkins, where pupils are received and given instruction. Annual receptions of the club are held at the Art Institute. Mrs. Philo King is president; Mrs. V. B. Jenkins, treasurer; Mrs. John B. Jeffrey, secretary.

The Illinois Art Association was incorporated Sept. 15, 1882, for the purpose of collecting, exhibiting and distributing works of art. It has about 100 members, and a capital stock of $25,000. It holds annual exhibitions in November, and has also held one black-and-white exhibition. The association owns about twenty fine paintings by local and foreign artists, valued at about $12,000. The principal pictures are two hunting scenes by Philip Wormermann; a portrait by Gilbert Stuart; a large painting by A. Achilles Glesenti, said to be his most important work; and "Disputed Property," by L. C. Earle. It occupies rooms in the Illinois Club building at No. 154 South Ashland Avenue. The exhibitions and collections are open only to members of the association and invited guests. Jos. M. Rogers is president, and S. P. McConnell, secretary.

Art Collections of considerable interest and value are owned by a number of citizens, some of them consisting only of pictures, while others include statuary. Among the fortunate possessors of such collections are: L. Z. Leiter, N. Q. Pope, Henry Field, J. Russell Jones, Marshall Field, Samuel Nickerson, Geo. M. Pullman, Charles M. Henderson, Mrs. W. H. Stickney, E. B. Washburn, McGregor Adams, Geo. A. Armour, Phil. Armour, E. G. Asay.

The Chicago Academy of Sciences occupies a five-story brick building in the rear of buildings at 263 and 265 Wabash Avenue, the entrance to its rooms being through a long hallway opening on the avenue. It has a library of over 2,000 volumes, reading rooms, and a museum exhibiting a cramped display of about 30,000 specimens of living and extinct species, minerals, etc., besides a large variety of interesting and valuable material that cannot be shown for want of room. The institution was founded in 1857, and incorporated in 1859. Its first important collection was a large number of specimens gathered by Mr.

Robert Kennicott, in an expedition to the Arctic regions. Mr. Kennicott was made the first director of the museum, but died on an expedition to Alaska, and Dr. Stimson, of the Smithsonian Institute, was appointed to his place, bringing with him a fine collection of invertebrates taken by himself in Japanese waters. These and many other valuable collections were destroyed by the fire of 1871, including the Smithsonian collection of crustacea, said to have been the finest in the world. Dr. Edmund Andrews, M. D., LL. D., is president.

Dearborn Observatory originated in a movement inaugurated in the winter of 1862, by gentlemen connected with the Chicago University, to establish an astronomical observatory in this city. Subscriptions were secured and a telescope, at that time the largest refractor in the world, was purchased in January, 1863, from Alvin Clark, the noted lens manufacturer of Cambridge, Mass., for $11,187 for the glass and $7,000 for the mounting. The instrument has an aperture of 18⅝ inches and a focal length of twenty-three feet. The subscribers to the fund organized in November, 1863, as the Chicago Astronomical Society, with Hon. J. Y. Scammon as president. The telescope was mounted and ready for use in April, 1866. The tower is ninety feet high, and the center of the telescope about 685 feet above sea level, in 40° 50′ 1″ north latitude, and 10° 33′ 40.4″ west longitude from the Washington meridian. There is also a transit telescope near the tower, the axis of which is 612¾ feet above sea level. The tower is located on the west side of the Chicago University buildings. Prof. Truman H. Safford, of Harvard Observatory, was the first director of Dearborn Observatory. In 1868 a meridian circle was purchased at a cost of $5,000. In 1874 Elias Colbert was chosen director. In June, 1875, the Astronomical Society was reorganized, and in May, 1879, the present director, Prof. G. W. Hough, of Dudley University, N. Y., was appointed. The equipment and work of this observatory has caused it to rank among the leading observatories of the world. In the spring of 1882, Mr. Scammon resigned his presidency of the astronomical society, after occupying that position for nearly twenty years. Dr. Hosmer A. Johnson was elected to the vacancy. C. H. S. Mixer is secretary.

The Philosophical Society was organized Oct. 12, 1873, and owes its existence largely to the efforts of Rev. H. W. Thomas, D. D. The object is to foster a love of philosophy and the discussion of its principles. There are about 200 members, of both sexes. Regular meetings are held at Apollo Hall every Saturday evening. At these meetings papers are read and discussed, the subjects being limited to Natural

Science, Speculative Philosophy, Current History, Moral Philosophy and Social Science. Sidney Thomas is president; E. T. Cahill, secretary. The **Illinois Social Science Association** occupies Room 35, No. 99 Washington Street. It was organized in October, 1877, for the discussion and treatment of all questions pertaining to social science, including philanthropy, domestic economy, woman suffrage and the improvement of the condition of humanity. The active membership is composed entirely of women, men being admitted only as associate members. Regular meetings are held monthly, from September to May, at the club rooms of the Sherman House. The annual meeting partakes of the character of a convention, and generally continues for several days. Mrs. Helen E. Starrett, is president.

The **State Microscopical Society** meets at the rooms of the Academy of Sciences. It was organized in 1868 under the name of "The Chicago Microscopical Society." In March of the following year the name was changed to its present form, and the society incorporated. Its purpose is to encourage and assist microscopical investigation. A valuable library and an excellent instrument are owned by the association.

The **Chicago Electrical Society** was formerly a branch of the Academy of Sciences, but became an independent society in 1875. Its aim is to keep pace with the improvements and discoveries made in electricity and electrical science. There are about 125 members. Meetings are held monthly at the Grand Pacific Hotel. W. R. Patterson, 10 Winchester Avenue, is secretary.

The **American Electrical Association** was organized in 1877 as a national society for the encouragement of electrical improvements and discoveries. No meeting has been held for several years, but the organization is still alive. It has a small library of scientific books. C. H. Wilson, Pullman Building, is librarian.

The **Western Society of Engineers** was organized May 1, 1869. The object is the advancement of the members in the science of engineering, and the promotion of the interests of the profession generally. There are semi-monthly meetings in Room 20, American Express Company's building, for the reading of scientific papers, and discussions.

The **Chicago Numismatic and Archæological Society** was formed for the promotion of antiquarian research through the coinage and other historical vestiges of the past. It was organized in 1879, and now has thirty-five members. It has a nicely furnished room at No. 91 Dearborn Street, where regular monthly meetings are held. S. H. Kerfoot is president.

Places of Amusement.

THE THEATRES, PUBLIC HALLS, MUSEUMS AND OTHER PLACES OF AMUSEMENT.

CHICAGO occupies a position as a patron of dramatic and musical art, second to no city on the continent. The first artists of the world regard Chicago as a center which is sure to reward true art lavishly, and no great artist who visits this continent ever dreams of leaving this city out of the line of engagements. Irving found it worth his while to alter his original plans, and give the city a second visit. Patti, Gerster, Hauck, Materna, Lucca, Rubenstein, Gottschalk, Ole Bull, Nilsson, Bernhardt, Rossi, Sembrich, Albani, Salvini, Rachel, Janauschek, Brignoli, and scores of other great operatic and dramatic stars have shone in the firmament of the Garden City, and have never found their rays dimmed in the quality of its atmosphere. The first attempt at anything like permanent theatrical entertainment was in 1846. The well-known John B. Rice, who came to Chicago about that period, established the first regular theater in a small building which he erected on Randolph, between Dearborn and State Streets for the purpose. The first opera given in Chicago was in 1860, in McVicker's Theater, by Strakosch, who brought out Brignoli and Patti. The next year J. Grau brought out an opera company, which filled a three week's successful engagement in this city. From that time to the present, Chicago has been an operatic center. In the winter of 1883–84, two of the greatest opera combinations in the world were here at the same time, and both received most liberal patronage.

McVicker's was the second theater erected in Chicago, but really marks the beginning of the permanent drama in this city. McVicker, who had already become a star in two continents as a comedian when he made his venture as a manager in Chicago. erected his first theater on the site of the present one. at a cost of $83,000. It was known for a time as "McVicker's New Chicago Theater," but soon assumed the name which it now bears. It was opened on the night of Nov. 5, 1857, with the "Honeymoon" as the leading piece, and the farce of the "Rough Diamond" in conclusion. In 1864 it was reconstructed at an

235

additional cost of $25,000. The season of 1871 closed May 27, when it was again reconstructed at a cost of $93,000, and was opened on the night of August 20th, with the comedy of "Extremes." Within less than two months it was destroyed in the great fire, but nine months later the present building stood on the ruins of the old one. It was at that time the largest building which had been erected after the fire, and was opened with Douglas Jerrold's play bearing the significant title, "Time Works Wonders." McVicker's was remodeled in 1886 at a cost of $145,-000, making the total cost of the theatre $538,000. It covers 82 × 190 feet of ground and is surrounded on both sides and in the rear with wide alleys, and iron stairways lead to the ground from every part of the auditorium, thus securing the best possible means of exit. The theatre is lighted throughout with incandescent electric lights, and the interior decorations are unique and beautiful. The auditorium seats 800, the balcony 461, and the gallery 500. There are twelve private boxes. "McVicker's" has always been a first-class theatre, and nearly all the great lights of the profession who have appeared on the American stage have played to appreciative throngs in its spacious auditorium. Mr. J. H. McVicker has been the proprietor and manager from the foundation of the enterprise, in the fall of 1857. McVicker's is on Madison Street, between State and Dearborn.

The **Academy of Music** is a popular West Side theatre, located on Halsted, near Madison Street. It was built by Wm. B. Clapp, in 1871, and has survived a series of mishaps that threatened to summarily end its career—having once been burned to the ground. It was for a considerable time simply a variety theatre, but since 1880 it has presented a higher grade of performances and maintained a higher standing among the people. Many of the best combinations presenting light comedy attractions now include the Academy in their routes. Extensive interior improvements to the building were made during the summer of 1884, and it is now one of the best furnished theatres in the city. The parquet and balcony have a seating capacity of 1,800. There are four private boxes. The stage is 34 feet wide and 38 feet deep. Wm. Emmett was succeeded by Daniel Shelby, the present lessee and manager, in 1881.

The **Standard**, Halsted and Jackson streets, was built in 1883, and opened December 31 by the Fay Templeton Opera Company. It is a first-class play-house in every respect and is remarkable for the elegance and taste with which the interior is finished. It has a double balcony, parquet circle, orchestra and proscenium chairs and ten private boxes. The stage opening is 36 feet, and its depth 36. Sixteen exits provide for the speedy exit of the audience.

The **Columbia** (formerly Haverly's Theatre), 108 East Monroe Street, was opened on the evening of June 12, just ninety days from the time ground was broken for its construction. The opening piece was Shak-spere's "Twelfth Night," by Robson and Crane, who played respectively Sir Andrew Aguecheek and Sir Toby Belch. It has always been a first-class play-house, only the higher grade of performances being permitted, and its stage has been occupied by many leading stars of both sexes. Henry Irving and his English troupe filled a three-weeks' engagement here while on their American tour. It is the largest theater in Chicago, and the extensive improvements made during the summer of 1884 make it one of the most attractive places of amusement in the country. Its seating capacity is over 2,500. The parquet and dress circle are furnished with 683 opera chairs; the balcony has 614 seats, and the gallery will seat 1,200 persons. There are twenty-one private boxes, each of which will accommodate four persons. The

HAVERLY THEATRE, MONROE STREET.

walls of the auditorium present some exquisite specimens of the painter's art. The entrance is through a spacious and elegantly decorated hallway, twenty-three feet in width, leading to the foyer and art galleries. The walls and ceiling of the hallway are covered with bronzed papier-mache of a unique and original design, with wainscot of tile and mosaic work, and panels of tiling on walls and wainscot illustrate scenes from Shak-spere. The fine-art gallery and reception rooms are elaborately finished and furnished. The walls and ceiling are finished in papier-mache similar to the main entrance. They contain over thirty oil paintings of the modern school, and other works of art including several pieces of statuary. The theater is well provided with exits and fire escapes, and is lighted throughout by the Edison incandescent electric light. Haverly Theater (formerly Haverly's Theater) had a predecessor located within the walls of the old post-offi. e which were left standing after the fire of 1871. The interior was rebuilt and the structure transformed into the Adelphi Theater, by W. W. Cole. In 1877 it fell into the hands of the well-known manager J. H. Haverly. who changed the name to Haverly's Theater. The building was·torn down in 1881 and the name was transferred to the new theater, of which Mr. Haverly was also proprietor and manager Jan. 1, 1884, when C. H. McConnell leased the theater and took charge. The Columbia Theater Co. succeeded in Feb., 1885; J. M. Hill is president, and manager of the theater; J. S. McConnell is treasurer and acting manager.

Hooley's Theater, on Randolph Street opposite the new City Hall, was built immediately after the great fire, and was opened to the public Oct. 9, 1872, just one year from the date of that event. The opening play was Kiralfy Brothers' spectacular burlesque, entitled "Enchantment." The theater ran four seasons with an excellent stock company, but it has since been managed on the combination system, which has held almost undisputed possession of the American stage for more than a decade. The entrance is through a hallway eighteen feet wide and seventy feet long. The box office is situated on the west side of the hall, and further in, on the same side, is the stairway leading to the balcony and gallery. The house will comfortably seat 1,412 people. The stage is 65×42 feet, the opening between the proscenium boxes being thirty-two feet and extending back to a depth of thirty feet. The proscenium is almost entirely of cast iron, and consequently fire-proof. There are twelve private boxes. The exits are spacious and easy, the interior arrangements comfortable and convenient, and the decorations handsome and appropriate. From the first Hooley's took high rank in

HOOLEY'S THEATER.

popular favor as a place of amusement, and has since steadily maintained its standing. Originally intended for a first-class comedy theater, it has always been more or less devoted to that line, from which it early became popularly known as "Hooley's Parlor Home of Comedy." But the heavier comedies, melodramas, and the best productions of the tragic muse have been presented on its stage by such brilliant stars of the theatrical firmament as Salvini, Neilson, Barrett, McCullough, and others. Its habitues have also heard Kellogg and other leading

representatives of the English and Italian schools of opera. From the first it has been under the management of its present proprietor, Richard M. Hooley, the veteran theatrical manager.

The Grand Opera House, 87 and 89 Clark Street, can trace its descent through a series of calamities and vicissitudes of unusual severity and most uncommon occurrence. About 1860 the site was occupied by Bryan Hall, which for many years was of public service as a place for lectures, fairs, concerts, and similar uses. Then it was transformed into Hooley's Opera House, which was destroyed by the fire of 1871. The Hamlin Brothers erected on the site of the old hall a

GRAND OPERA HOUSE, 89 CLARK STREET.

great billiard palace, which became world-renowned under the management of Tom Foley. In 1874, its owner turned it into what was called the "Coliseum," in which there was a garden, fountains, resplendent galleries, and a band of music, with the famous violinist, Le Clerque, at its head. As the work of development went on, a stage was added, and performances were given to great audiences. Then the senior partner, Mr. John A. Hamlin, took the matter in hand, remodeled the building and changed the Coliseum into "Hamlin's Theatre." It so remained until 1880, when it developed into the present structure, known as "The Grand Opera House," by which term it is now popularly known. It was opened under its new title September 6, 1880, with the "Child of the State," by the Hoey & Hardy combination, and has since been a first-class play-house in every respect, affording the public some of the most delightful entertainments given in modern Chicago. It has presented Salvini, that charming French actress; Rhea, Modjeska, the Boston Ideal Company, and many other attractions in which the finest class of light operas have been a conspicuous feature. It is artistically furnished and decorated, and is well ventilated, heated and lighted, and the exits are numerous and ample. Its seating capacity is as follows: Parquet, 600; balcony, 400; gallery, 600. John A. Hamlin continues in successful management of this interesting place of amusement.

The Chicago Opera House is the newest and the largest theatre in the city. It has a seating capacity of 2,300. It was constructed during the early part of 1885, and was opened in August of that year. It is situated on the corner of Washington and Clark Streets, the most central portion of the city, and the starting point of nearly all the street car lines, and is said to be the only theatre in the United States, except the Metropolitan Opera House in New York, that is absolutely fireproof. Every improvement known to modern theatrical architecture has been utilized to the fullest effect. The house is lighted by the Edison incandescent light throughout, over 1,000 lights being used in the theatre and upon the stage. The decoration is in gold, bronzes, crimsons, buffs and blues, so artistically blended as to produce the most striking effect. The stage is one of the most complete in the country. It has a depth of 52 feet and a height of 70 feet; this enables the management to produce almost any kind of entertainment. The working machinery of the stage is us elaborate and perfect as are the provisions for the comfort of the audience. The large, comfortable and finely furnished dressing-rooms, constructed in accordance with the auditorium, are entirely fire-proof. Within one year this theatre has taken a leading place among the places of amusement in the Northwest. Among the attractions that have given it this prestige are: Mary Anderson, Edwin Booth, Mme. Modjeska, Mapleson's Italian Opera Company, Lawrence Barrett, Keene, the McCaull Opera Companies, Duff Opera Company, Helen Dauvray's Comedy Company, Clara Morris, Kiralfy, Robson & Crane, and other leading attractions. The lease of the theatre is held by the firm of John W. Norton & Co. for ten years, and the active manager is Mr. David Henderson.

Weber Music Hall, corner of Wabash Avenue and Jackson Street, has a seating capacity of 400, and is a favorite place for readings and musical exercises, etc.

Central Music Hall, corner of State and Randolph Streets, is the

CENTRAL MUSIC HALL, STATE AND RANDOLPH STS. ADLER & SULLIVAN, ARCHITECTS

finest hall in Chicago. The building is seven stories in height, and covers 125×151 feet of ground. It is of stone from the Lamont quarries, and the portico over the entrance is supported by massive pillars of polished red granite. It cost $215,000. It was designed by Messrs. Adler & Sullivan, architects, who supervised its erection, introducing

16

into the construction a new scientific system of heating and ventilation that has proven eminently successful. There are twelve establishments devoted to trade on the State and Randolph Street fronts,
and the building also contains seventy rooms for offices and a small
hall known as Apollo Hall. Central Music Hall was designed for the
higher and more intellectual class of entertainments, such as classical
concerts and lectures. It has no facilities for theatrical or operatic pre-
sentations. The main entrance is on State Street, through a lofty hall
eighteen feet wide by sixty-five feet long. The auditorium is 83×125
feet in dimensions; is arranged with parquet, dress circle, and upper balcony, all richly furnished, and has twenty-five private boxes,
being capable of seating about 2,000 persons. It is also supplied with
a fine double organ, erected at a cost of $14,000. The stage, which is
without scenery or curtain, is 33×50 feet. There are numerous easy
exits. The hall was opened on the evening of December 5, 1879,
the entertainment being a colossal concert by the Apollo Musical
Club.

Apollo Hall is a small hall in Central Music Hall Building. It is
specially adapted to chamber concerts, rehearsals, etc., and contains
400 seats. Nicely fitted up parlors and reception rooms are attached.

The Exposition Building was constructed by the Inter-State Exposition Company. It is located on the lake front at the foot of Adams
Street, is 240 feet wide, nearly 800 feet long, and 110 feet high,
surmounted by three towers with ornamental domes, and has a
broad gallery entirely around the interior of the building. It has an
arched roof of glass in a frame-work of iron, which is the largest clear-
span roof in the world. It was opened in the fall of 1877, with the first
of a series of exhibitions that have annually attracted thousands of visitors to the city. It has since been the scene of many great assemblages,
such as gathered at the May Festivals, and the grand instrumental concerts given by Theodore Thomas; at the nomination of Garfield and
Arthur by the Republican national convention in 1880; at the nomination of Blaine and Logan by the same party in June, 1884; and
two weeks later at the nomination of Cleveland and Hendricks by the
Democratic national convention.

Farwell Hall, on the second floor of the Young Men's Christian Association Building, is one of the principal halls of the city. It was
formerly used for concerts and lectures, but it is now devoted mainly
to exercises of a religious character. The main floor and gallery
have seating capacity for about 1,800 persons.

The **Windsor Theatre** is a new venture on the North side, located on North Clark, near Division Street, and was opened September 15, 1886. Its seating capacity is about 1,500, the orchestra containing 150 seats; parquet, 170; orchestra circle, 400; balcony, 200; gallery, 600. There are six boxes for four persons each on the first floor, two in the balcony, and twelve large boxes with a seating capacity of three each. The house is newly fitted up, and presents an attractive appearance. Only first-class attractions are played. P. H. Lehnan is the proprietor, and Bruno Kennicott is manager of the theatre.

The **National Theatre** is a small frame building located at Nos. 26 and 28 Clybourn Avenue. Seating capacity, 1,000.

Weber Music Hall, corner of Wabash Avenue and Jackson Street, has a seating capacity of 400, and is a favorite place for readings and musical exercises, etc.

The **Lyceum Theatre,** Desplaines, near Madison Street, has recently been rebuilt. It has a seating capacity for 1,100 persons. Variety performances.

The **People's,** formerly a variety theatre, is now devoted to legitimate dramas. It is located on State Street, near Harrison. It has a main floor and two galleries, seats about 2,000, and was opened Sept. 27, 1884.

The **Olympic,** Clark Street, between Randolph and Lake, is a popular variety theatre, and one of the oldest places of amusement in the city. It has experienced numerous changes in name and management. Seats 1,100.

The **Criterion Theatre** was first opened in September, 1880. It is situated on the corner of Sedgwick and Division Streets, has a seating capacity of 1,600, and is a pleasant place of amusement, presenting only the legitimate drama.

Kohl and Middleton's Museum at No. 150 South Clark Street and No. 150 West Madison Street, respectively, are places of cheap entertainment, ten cents being the popular price of admission to each. Each contains a small stage for variety performances. The upper floors are devoted to museums of natural curiosities and works of ingenious mechanism.

The **Halsted Street Opera House,** is a small frame building on the corner of Halsted and Harrison Streets, on the West Side, It seats about 800 persons. Miscellaneous plays and variety performances are given at intervals.

Madison Street Theater, occupies the premises at 85 E. Madison

Street, formerly known as Hershey Music Hall. A good class of attractions are presented.

The Casino Theater occupies McCormick Hall, on the corner of North Clark and Kinzie Streets. It is encircled by a gallery and seats about 2,500.

Washington Driving Park has been noted in connection with Washington Park Club in the chapter on "The Clubs and Societies," on page 146.

The Chicago Driving Park lies just south of Madison Street and west of Garfield Park. It was until recently the only race course in the city. The grounds consist of eighty acres, held under lease, on which are a mile track, a grand stand with a seating capacity of 15,000, public and pool stands, club house, stables, grooms, cottages, etc. The association was organized in 1881, and has a capital stock of $100,000. There are 400 members, and the property and franchises are valued at $200,000. The meetings are for trotting and pacing only, and the most famous trotting stock of the country appears on this track, which is regarded as very favorable for speed. The stakes and purses for the season of 1884 were the largest ever offered in America, aggregating $280,000. The office of the association is at 116 East Monroe Street.

Central Driving Park occupies, as tenant-at-will, an unused portion of Garfield Park grounds lying south of Madison Street. The association was formed in January, 1876, for social driving and the pleasure of the members in speeding and practicing their horses. There is a mile track and suitable buildings on the grounds. Regular "matinees" are held every Saturday during seasonable weather, but no racing for stakes or purses is allowed. There are about 300 members, and non-members are allowed to purchase season tickets admitting them to the privileges of the grounds. W. H. Kane, 173 LaSalle Street, is secretary.

The Newspaper Press.

THE NEWSPAPERS OF THE PAST AND PRESENT, THEIR FOUNDERS AND EDITORS.

THE history of the newspaper press of Chicago, although comparatively brief, affords interesting and instructive study to any one who wishes to trace the development of journalistic enterprise into great and powerful interests. The first newspaper published in Chicago was The Chicago Democrat, and its first edition was issued Nov. 26, 1833. The village had become an incorporated town, and the location attracted a printer named John Calhoun, who set up his press at the corner of Lake and South Water Streets. The paper was an ardent advocate of Jacksonian democracy, and was what was then known as "imperial" in size—four pages of six columns each. It had 134 subscribers, and the paying advertisements occupied a column and a half. The difference between this business exhibit and that of one of the great daily issues of to-day, is a fair measure of the difference between the Chicago of 1833 and that of 1884. Just three years from its commencement the Democrat passed into the hands of John Wentworth, under whose direction it grew in influence until 1840, when a daily issue was commenced. The second newspaper was the Chicago American, commenced May 8, 1835, by T. O. Davis. It was a weekly six-column paper, Whig in politics. In April, 1839, under the proprietorship of William Stewart, a daily edition was started—the first daily paper published in Illinois—but the publication ceased in October, 1842. The Chicago Commercial Advertiser was started in October, 1836, and ran one year. The weekly Tribune made its first appearance in 1840, with Edward G. Ryan, afterward chief justice of Wisconsin, as editor. but it was removed to Milwaukee about a year later and became the Milwaukee Journal. In July, 1842, the Quid Nunc, the first penny paper in the west. began an existence which lasted through thirty-seven issues. In the fall of the same year the Chicago Express appeared as a daily afternoon paper, and the successor of the American, but lived only two years, when it was purchased by a stock company and the name changed to the Evening Journal. This and

245

the next twelve years witnessed the inauguration of many newspaper enterprises of more or less promise, most of which "died and left no sign," except the one over the office door. In that period no less than fifty-six of these unfortunate ventures were born, and after a brief struggle for existence, were quietly laid away in the journalistic cemetery. During the same time, however, the most extensive of the great newspaper establishments of this day were founded.

The Evening Journal is the veteran among Chicago newspapers. It is the successor of the American, the first daily paper published in the city, by purchase of its successor, the Express, the second Chicago daily, in 1844, when the present title was assumed. It is distinctly a family and business-man's paper, and has always enjoyed great confidence and liberal support of the best class of readers. It was started as a Whig newspaper, and was an ardent supporter of Henry Clay for president, but early affiliated with the Republican party, to whose principles it has ever since remained faithful. The paper gained largely in patronage during the war and became a very valuable property. It is issued every evening, except Sunday, at 3 and 5 o'clock, and has a weekly edition. The paper has eight pages with six and often seven

EVENING JOURNAL BUILDING, DEARBORN STREET.

columns to the page, and Saturdays twelve and sixteen pages. It sells for two cents per copy, or $6.00 per annum. The weekly is issued Wednesday for $1.00 a year. Since the change in form and reduction in price, the circulation has increased rapidly. It is printed on two of the fastest Bullock perfecting presses and is issued from the Journal Building, Nos. 159 and 161 Dearborn Street. The Journal was originally owned by a stock company, but was sold to Richard L. Wilson, one of the editors, at the close of the campaign of 1844. In 1849 the publishers were Richard L. and Charles L. Wilson. Upon the death of the former in 1856, Charles L. Wilson became the sole owner, and continued to be until his death, in 1878. His estate continued its publication until 1881, when Andrew Shuman, its editor since 1861, and John R. Wilson leased the office. The establishment was destroyed in the great fire of Oct. 9, 1871, but the paper appeared the same afternoon, although somewhat diminished in size. A year later it occupied the present handsome and commodious building. Here it was again visited by fire in December, 1883, but, as before, brought out its regular issue without a day's interruption, from another office. The ownership was organized as a stock company in 1883. Mr. Shuman is its editor. Mr. Wilson, the business manager, has been connected with the paper since Oct. 9, 1871. W. K. Sullivan has been its city editor since 1874. The Journal has always maintained its reputation as a careful, conservative newspaper, clean and trustworthy, and keeps on " in the even tenor of its way" staidly, and yet keeping up with the spirit and progress of the times.

The **Times** was started in 1854 as a Democratic paper, with the special purpose of serving the personal and political fortunes of Senator Douglas. It maintained its party allegiance until 1868, when it took an independent stand, and has since ranked as one of the foremost expositors of independent thought in the northwest—with a tender recollection of its previous Democratic associations. It was a war Democratic paper until the issuance of the emancipation proclamation, which it opposed vigorously, and passed through some very exciting experiences during that heated period. Its publication was once suspended by order of Gen. Burnside, but the suspension lasted for two days only. It occupies an elegant fire-proof building at the corner of Washington Street and Fifth Avenue, built of Michigan sandstone, at a cost of over $600,000. It is 80×183 feet, five stories, and is one of the most thoroughly equipped newspaper establishments in the country. It has six Bullock perfecting presses, each of which has a capacity for

printing and folding, with cut leaves, 10,000 sheets per hour, or an
aggregate of 60,000 per hour. A handsome business office occupies
the corner room of the first floor. The editorial rooms and the composing rooms are on the fifth floor. Pneumatic tubes connect the office
with the telegraph office, and pneumatic and speaking tubes connect
the different departments of the paper. The force of compositors
averages about 115; the immediate editorial, reportorial and clerical
staff about fifty; and there are some 500 special contributors and correspondents throughout the old and new worlds. The Times is an
eight page daily, eight columns to the page, but frequently appears
with a supplement of two, four, eight or sixteen pages. It also has a
weekly edition of eight pages. The leading feature of the paper is the
fullness and freshness of its news department, and it is fearless in its
publication of everything that comes under the head of news. It was
this policy, inaugurated by Mr. Wilbur F. Storey immediately upon the
purchase of the paper in 1861, that transformed The Times from a
losing concern threatened with bankruptcy, to one of the most valuable
newspaper properties in the country. The original purchase was made
by Mr. Storey. A. Worden became a partner in the concern in 1862,
was succeeded in 1865 by Henry B. Chandler, who retired in 1870,
leaving Mr. Storey the sole owner. The office was on Dearborn Street
between Washington and Madison in 1871, and was destroyed by the
great fire. A temporary wooden structure was occupied during the
erection of the present building. Mr. Storey's health finally gave way
under his labors, and for several years he was unable to give the paper
any attention, and in August, 1884, Austin L. Patterson, for many
years business manager of the Times, was appointed conservator of Mr.
Storey's large estate, and on Oct. 27th following, Mr. Storey died.
Chas. R. Dennett is managing editor of The Times, and Guy Magee is
the city editor.

The Chicago Tribune is the leading Republican paper of the northwest, and is not only a power in its party, but also a prominent factor
of the commercial and industrial interests of the country. It owns and
occupies a handsome five-story fire-proof building, of Lake Superior
red sandstone, at the corner of Dearborn and Madison Streets, which
was built at a cost of $200,000. The establishment is complete in all
its appointments. In the basement are employed five Bullock and
Kahler perfecting presses, with Kahler folding and cutting machines
attached, having a capacity of 60,000 sheets per hour. The business
office, one of the handsomest in the city, is on the first floor; the edi-

torial rooms on the fourth, and the spacious composing room occupies all of the fifth. An average force of 100 compositors is employed ; the editorial and reportorial staff usually numbers forty men, and the paid

TRIBUNE BUILDING, MADISON AND DEARBORN STREETS.

contributors and correspondents located at all important points are several hundred in number. It pays nearly $100,000 per annum for special telegraphic reports. The paper is a daily seven-column quarto, but the usual issue consists of twelve pages, the Saturday edition of sixteen, and the Sunday of twenty-four pages. The Sunday issue, which averages over 60,000, is resorted to voluminously by advertisers, especially in its "wants" department, a fact which is at least partially responsible for the immense size of the Sunday paper. It also publishes a weekly edition of, at present, 90,000 copies. It was started in July, 1847, as a Whig paper with free-soil tendencies, and in a few years, after passing through several changes of firm and editorial management, it came under the direction of Mr. Joseph Medill, when it entered upon a career of prosperity that has steadily carried it up to its present eminent position in the ranks of the American press. July 1, 1858, it was consolidated with the Democratic Press, that paper having come to the position of the Tribune on the Kansas-Nebraska question. For a year or two it carried the title of the Press prefixed to the Tribune, when the prefix was dropped, and the ownership was organized as a stock company, with a capital of $200,000 which has not been changed. During the war it was a staunch, radical, and influential supporter of Lincoln's administration, and no agency rendered more effective service in that behalf among the people of the northwest. In 1871 its fine building, erected in 1868 at a cost of $175,000, was ruined by the great fire, and the present structure was erected on its site. The Tribune is the wealthiest paper in the city, and felt strong enough with its constituency in 1880 to make a powerful and effective fight against the candidacy of Gen. Grant for a third term in the Presidency. It has had a number of prominent men connected with it, notably Gen. Wm. Duane Wilson, Gen. J. D. Webster, Dr. C. H. Ray, Horace White, Lieut. Gov. Wm. Bross, Alfred Cowles and the Messrs. Joseph and S. J. Medill. Mr. Joseph Medill. and Messrs. Cowles and Bross have been with the paper for nearly thirty years. Joseph Medill is editor-in-chief; R. W. Patterson, managing editor ; Alfred Cowles, business manager ; Fred. Hall, city editor; E. Colbert, commercial editor.

The Inter Ocean is the stalwart Republican newspaper of the northwest, and ranks among the leading and most influential journals of the country. The paper was started March 25, 1872, by Hon. J. Y. Scammon, avowing itself in the first issue, "Independent in nothing—Republican in everything." Its efficient service in the second Grant campaign of that year gave it a standing and circulation in its party that constituted a strong foothold from which to achieve public favor. Hon. F. W. Palmer purchased an interest and became editor-in-chief in the spring of 1873; but the great panic, and the depression which followed, financially embarrassed Mr. Scammon, the principal owner, and in 1875 the paper was sold to a new corporation, of which Wm. Penn Nixon was the principal member. Mr. Nixon had been business manager of the paper since the spring of 1872; he now became general manager as well as responsible editor, controlling every department. The Inter Ocean has probably gone back on Mr. Scammon's famous motto about independence, but it has kept in good standing with the party and improved as a newspaper. Since its change of proprietors it has had an increasingly prosperous career. It has a daily edition of eight seven-column pages, with frequent supplements of four, eight or sixteen pages, and issues a musical supplement of several pages every Wednesday. The weekly edition has eight seven-column pages, and enjoys probably the largest circulation of any similar publication in the west, ranging from 100,000 to 120,000. The Inter Ocean occupies a handsome five-story stone front building at 85 Madison Street. It is supplied with one Scott and two Bullock perfecting presses, with machines attached to fold, paste and cut the paper, which it was the first to use, and which are the invention of Walter Scott, former superintendent of its machinery department. The business office and editorial and composing rooms are all conveniently arranged and connected. A force of 105 is employed in the composing room, the immediate staff —clerical, editorial, reportorial and others employed in the office, numbers about 110 persons, and the corps of special correspondents about 350. The immediate predecessor of the Inter Ocean was the Republican, which was started shortly after the war. Charles A. Dana, the well-known editor of the New York Sun, was engaged as editor and manager. He brought a numerous staff, and the publication was commenced with all the advantages of money, brains and journalistic experience. It failed, however, and after the return of Mr. Dana to the east the paper was made a two-cent sheet, and placed in the hands of J. B. McCullogh, now of the St. Louis Globe-Democrat. In 1871 the great fire obliterated the establishment, and the owners refused to proceed further with it. Mr. Scammon then purchased the Associated Press franchise, and in order to hold it continued the publication until everything was ready for the inauguration of the Inter Ocean. Wm. Penn Nixon continues general manager, and Wm. H. Busby, managing editor; J. R. Dunlop, city editor.

The **Chicago Daily News** commenced originally as a penny evening paper without the associated press franchise, and has made a conspicuous success. It was started in Dec. 20, 1875, by Melville E. Stone, Wm. E. Dougherty and Percy Meggy; but within a year the last two sold out to Mr. Stone, leaving him sole proprietor. During the same year Victor F. Lawson became a partner, and the firm became Victor

CHICAGO DAILY NEWS, FIFTH AVENUE.

F. Lawson & Co. Jan. 1, 1883, the partnership expired by limitation, and the ownership was reorganized as a stock company, the entire stock being and remaining the property of Messrs. Lawson and Stone. The circulation increased with great rapidity; from 15,000 in 1876 it grew to nearly 40,000 within the two years which followed. In 1881 a two-cent morning edition was started, but it progressed very slowly until it was admitted into the Western Press Association. There are now four editions of the News; one in the morning, at two cents per copy; one at twelve o'clock, another at three o'clock, and the regular evening issue at five o'clock—the last three being penny papers. In November, 1884, the combined circulation of the editions reached over 200,000 copies daily. In politics the paper is independent. It is very enterprising, especially in the direction of exceptional and unexpected efforts. It is liable at any moment to astonish the community with the publication of a fac-simile telegram from the premier of England on some international question, or a letter from Bismarck giving his opinion on some matter of similar importance. There is no Sunday edition. The morning issue is a seven-column folio except on Saturdays, when it is a quarto. The later issues are eight-column folios. Five Hoe perfecting presses are employed to print the various editions. It owns the building it occupies at 123 Fifth Avenue. A force of about sixty compositors is employed, a clerical and editorial staff of about seventy-five, and an active corps of special telegraphic correspondents. Victor F. Lawson is business manager; Melville E. Stone, editor. The Weekly News was founded in 1876. It average circulation is about 45,000.

The **Illinois Staats-Zeitung** is printed in the German language, and is independent in politics, and the principal organ of the German-Americans in the northwest. It was founded in the spring of 1848, by Robert Hœffgen, whose entire capital amounted to $200. From this small beginning grew an enterprise which probably is second only to the Staats-Zeitung of New York. At the start the paper was a weekly, and the publisher was able to carry on the business by himself. He set the type, did the press work, acted as solicitor, collector, carrier, cashier, and editor. When money was scarce, he would take his pay in rags which he sold to the paper dealer, and in this way received really a higher price than if he had taken in only cash. Dr. Hellmuth was editor in the autumn of the year in which the enterprise was started, and again in 1850, during which year. it was issued twice a week. In 1851 George Schneider became connected with it. and a daily edition was commenced with seventy subscribers, the weekly list being then a little over 200. Two years later the daily subscription had reached 300. and in 1854 the paper had 800 subscribers. The circulation steadily increased, and the paper exerted a powerful influence on the attitudes of the German-Americans toward its party. In 1861 Wm. Rapp became the editor, and in the same year Lorenz Brentano bought

out Mr. Hœffgen's interest and a year later that of George Schneider.
Soon thereafter A. C. Hesing bought a third interest, and in 1867 he
became the sole owner, paying to Mr. Brentano $80,000 in cash for his
remaining two-thirds. A stock company was subsequently organized,
with a capital of $200,000, the stock being all owned by six persons,
each of whom is actively connected with the paper. During the great
fire the office was totally destroyed, but the paper was reissued within
forty-eight hours after, and in due season was located in its present
quarters at the corner of Fifth Avenue and Washington Street. It
occupies a fine five-story stone front building, which cost, with the
outfit of machinery and type, about $300,000. It publishes a daily
edition of four pages, nine columns to the page, a weekly edition of eight
pages and a Sunday literary edition called the Westen. The press-room
is in the basement, an elegant business office on the first floor, and the
editorial and composing rooms above, all conveniently connected by
speaking tubes and dumb waiters. The paper is printed on two Clause
perfecting presses, employs an average of fifty compositors, a clerical,
editorial and reportorial staff numbering forty, and a large corps of correspondents. Herman Raster is editor-in-chief, having held the position
since 1867. William Rapp is assistant editor. A. C. Hesing is president of the company ; Washington Hesing is vice-president, and C. F.
Putsch, secretary and treasurer. Emil Mannhardt is editor of the Westen.

The Neue Freie Presse is printed in German, and was established
in 1871 as the Freie Presse, by the German-American Publishing Company. It issues a morning and evening edition daily, and has a weekly
and Sunday edition. It is independent in politics, with a leaning to
Republicanism. It has a substantial circulation and business patronage.
It is located at 92 Fifth Avenue. The daily issues are in quarto form,
and the Sunday and weekly in octavo. Richard Michael, the editor,
has held that position from the start. Carl Lotz is business manager.

The Saturday Evening Herald, established in 1876, is the leading
society, dramatic, musical and literary weekly. It is published at 89
Clark Street. The editors are Lyman B. Glover and John M. Dandy.

There are at present 274 regularly issued papers and periodicals
in Chicago, including the fifteen dailies. There are six semi-weeklies,
134 weeklies (including Sunday papers), twenty-two semi-monthlies,
eighty-eight monthlies and nine quarterlies.

The Chicago Herald, 120 Fifth Avenue, is a two-cent morning
paper, and was established in May, 1881, by Hon. Frank W. Palmer,
postmaster, as editor-in-chief, W. D. Eaton, musical and dramatic

writer of The Times, as managing editor, and Jas. W. Scott, of the Daily National Hotel Reporter, as business manager. In 1882 Messrs. Palmer and Eaton withdrew, and John F. Ballantyne became managing editor till August, 1883, when John R. Walsh, president of the Western News Company, acquired a controlling interest, and Martin J. Russell, late editorial writer on 'The Times, became editor in-chief, Jas. W. Scott retaining the business management. The stock is owned by the three persons mentioned, and A. F. Hatch. In politics the Herald claims to be entirely independent, although until it came under its present management it was the organ

THE CHICAGO HERALD BUILDING, FIFTH AVENUE.

of Stalwart Republicanism. In style it is modeled after the New York Sun, and typographically it is the handsomest daily in the city. It is a seven-column folio, except on Sundays when it is an eight-column quarto. It has had a severe struggle to achieve its present position as a fixed institution with a very promising future. H. W. Seymour, late one of the editors of The Times, is managing editor; and Wm. A. Taylor, city e litor.

The Newspapers sketched in the foregoing pages include the leading dailies of the city. The other dailies are as follows : The Evening Telegram, a penny paper, Democratic in politics, started in 1879 ; the Chicago Demokrat, German, established in 1883 (weekly in 1856), published every morning, and Democratic in politics ; the Arbeiter-Zeitung. German evening, started in 1872 as a weekly, added a daily issue in 1876, and is devoted to the interests of socialism , the Scandinaven is a morning paper, Republican in politics, wielding considerable influence among the Scandinavian people ; the weekly issue was started in 1865, and the daily in 1866; the Daily National Hotel Reporter is published every morning in the interest of hotels, and kindred interests, has a wide circulation and was established in 1871; the Drovers' Journal, in the interest of the live stock trade, was founded in 1873, and has a weekly, semi-weekly and daily issue; the Sun, established in 1868, is published every evening at the Union Stockyards; the Svornost is an independent Bohemian paper, published every morning, and weekly, and was started in 1875. Altogether there are fifteen daily newspapers.

The Chicago Mail is the successor of the Evening Mail established in 1884, and of the Chicago Press established in 1883. It passed under the management of the Hatton-Snowden Company on June 16, 1885, and over $100,000 has been expended since then in improving the plant of the paper, and making it one of the most popular and enterprising dailies of the country. It has four daily issues: 11 A. M., noon, 3 and 5 P. M,, besides frequent extras as the exigencies of the news department require. Its daily circulation averages over 50,000. Six months ago, the St. James Hotel, on Fifth Avenue, was transformed for its use into a model newspaper printing office, and it is now known as "the Mail Building." Ex-Postmaster General Frank Hatton, and Clinton A. Snowden, late of the Chicago Times, are its editors, assisted by C. McAuliff, E. R. Dillingham, and A. G. McCoy. Mr. John J. Flinn, formerly of the Daily News, the assistant manager, has the charge of the advertising business. It has gained immensely in circulation and influence during the past year, and has taken a front rank among it ; contemporaries.

The Current, published from 123 and 125 La Salle Street, is a thirty-two page weekly journal, devoted to first-class current literature, comments, discussions, essays and criticisms, regarding social and political movements, events of the day, and all timely topics and matters of general and important interest. Among Western publications of its character it is without a rival, and it is to the West and Wetsern literature what the best monthly magazine of the East is to that section. Its circulation extends to every reading community on the continent, and embraces a considerable list of European readers. It is filled every week with bright, charming stories, timely essays, poetry, comments, reviews, critiques, literary notes, and its contributors embrace some of the best writers of the country. It receives praise from the severest critics, and commendation from the best writers of this and other countries. It was started Dec. 22, 1883. A. H. Harryman is editor, and A. E. Davis is president and manager.

The Musical Societies.

THE MUSICAL ORGANIZATIONS, THE DATES OF THEIR FORMATION AND THEIR LEADERS.

THE musical societies of Chicago have contributed much toward the promotion and cultivation of the musical taste of the people. The "Apollo" and "Mozart" Clubs are the leading (English) musical organizations, the Beethoven Society having recently disbanded.

The **Apollo Musical Club** is the oldest existing English musical society in Chicago, and its work in advancing the standard of musical culture in this locality can hardly be over-estimated. It was organized in 1872, with S. G. Pratt as musical director. Mr. Pratt was succeeded by A. W. Dohn, who occupied the position for nearly three years, and it was under his directorship that the first public concert of the club was given. Carl Bergstein conducted the chorus during the season of 1874-5. W. L. Tomlins was appointed director in the spring of the latter year, and continues to act in that capacity. As originally constituted the club was exclusively a male chorus, but under Mr. Tomlin's leadership an auxiliary ladies' chorus was formed, and has since been merged into the club proper, making it a mixed chorus, numbering at present about 150 voices. In addition to the 150 active members, there are nearly 500 associate members. Three regular subscription concerts are given each season, tickets of admission being issued to members only. The public are admitted to the annual Christmas performance of the Messiah. The membership includes some of the best vocalists in the city. The club has convenient clubrooms, and meets for rehearsals in Apollo Hall.

The **Mozart Club** was organized in 1880. It was first known as the Mozart Society, but the name was changed to Mozart Club in 1883. During its first year the society had about ninety active singing members, but the number has been reduced from time to time until it is now about forty. The club gives three concerts annually in Central Music Hall. Tickets of admission are issued only to the associate members. The chorus consists wholly of male voices. It is devoted to the performance of oratorio and other choral music of a high order.

17

Hans Balatka was the first musical director. He was succeeded, after one or two seasons, by Marro L. Bartlett, who still directs the chorus. The club occupies rooms at 24 Adams Street.

The St. Cecilia Choir, led by Wm. L. Tomlins, was organized Feb. 11, 1883, to afford some of the lady singers of the May Festival chorus practice during the time between the festivals. The organization was not intended to be permanent.

The Musical Festival Association was formed to meet a demand for the rendition of the great works of the most famous masters, that had grown out of the advance of musical culture. It was organized in 1882, and gives a grand musical festival every two years. The festival occurs in May, and lasts five days, with concerts every evening, and matinee concerts on Thursday and Saturday. The association is supported by the receipts from the festivals, and is secured from loss by subscriptions to a guarantee fund sufficient to cover the bulk of the expense. Fifty-nine prominent citizens subscribed for $1,000 to the fund for the festival of 1884. On this occasion there was an orchestra of 175 pieces and a chorus of 900 voices. The works of Wagner, Beethoven, Schubert, Haydn, Handel, Mozart, Gounod and others were represented in the programme, and the leading parts were executed by Nilsson, Materna, Winkelman, Scaria and others. The high perfecti n reached by the chorus is due to the able and untiring efforts of Prof. W. L. Tomlins, whose skillful training produced an artistic success that was a grand feature of the concerts. There have been two festivals, the first in 1882, and the last in 1884, both given in the Exposition Building under the direction of Theodore Thomas. The loss on the first was $9,210, and on the last $5,817. The latter loss would have been much greater but for the sum of $9,000 received from the two national political conventions, which used the seats and other property of the festival association. N. K. Fairbank is president; Millard Adams, secretary; George Sturgis, treasurer.

The Quartettes.—There are numerous quartettes in the city, among which the following are the most noted: The Chicago Quartette, male voices, organized in 1877, and reorganized and incorporated in March, 1884; the Schubert Quartette, male voices, organized in the summer of 1883; and the Oriental Quartette, also male voices. The Schumann Quartette, organized in the fall of 1882, the St. Cecilia Quartette, organized in 1878, the Chicago Lady Quartette, and the Weber Lady Quartette, are all composed of female voices. The Harmonia Quartette, male and female voices, was first organized about ten years ago,

German Singing Societies are numerous. They all partake largely of a social character and are, without exception, composed of gentlemen only.

The **Germania Mænnerchor** is the oldest German musical society in Chicago, having been organized in 1865. Soon after its organization the society was divided, some of the members forming themselves into a society under the name "Concordia." Soon after the great fire they were reunited under the original name. The first musical director was Otto Lob. At the time of the split Mr. Lob became director of the Concordia society, and Hans Balatka of the Germania. The society has rendered many operas of the highest order. The chorus consists of about thirty members. They meet for rehearsal in private rooms in Brand's Hall. There are about 250 associate members. The excellence of the music rendered by the society, and the delightful sociability that has characterized its entertainments have given it wide popularity among German people of refinement and culture. The concerts of the society are generally private.

The **Orpheus Mænnerchor** is the second oldest German musical society in the city. It was organized in 1867. The first musical director was Otto Lob. It gives public concerts occasionally and was formerly a mixed chorus. The music is of a "popular" character. Meetings are held every Wednesday evening for rehearsal at the society's hall on West Lake Street. Gustav Ehrhorn is the director.

The **Chicago Musical Club** is one of the latest German musical organizations. It was organized October 14, 1882, with Hans Balatka as director, and he still retains that position. It gives concerts on a larger scale than any of the other German singing societies, and renders only works of the higher order. The plan is to give five concerts every season. The concerts given the first year were all public, an admission fee being charged. Latterly the rule has been to admit only members of the club, except that each member is allowed to introduce friends once during the season. Rehearsals are held every Monday evening in Room 24, American Express Building. The associate membership numbers about seventy and the active membership numbers thirty-six.

The **Schweizer Mænnerchor** was originally a singing section of the Schweizer Bund, but organized as a separate society in May, 1869. It cultivates the music of popular German authors, and gives three or four concerts every season. It has 115 members, mostly Swiss, and a chorus of thirty-five voices. It has taken prominent part in all the great saengerfests from 1870, and in the national festivals and parades of the Swiss societies, some of the latter being remarkably interesting representations of the history, costumes, customs, and pursuits of the Swiss people. H. von Oppen, leader.

The **Eintracht Liederkranz** cultivates sentimental and comic choral music for male voices, by popular German composers. It was organized June 27, 1876, and has thirty members in the chorus, all Germans. It is noted for its concerts, balls, masquerades, and picnics. Meetings are held every Friday evening, at 378 West Twelfth Street. The first leader was Edward Roos; the present leader is Emil Zott.

The **Teutonia Mænnerchor** has fifty-two active and about 175 associate members, and meets every Tuesday evening in Aurora Turner Hall. The society sings popular music, holds monthly entertainments for members only, and gives three grand public concerts every season. Its excursions during the summer are largely attended. The musical director, Gustav Ehrhorn, has held the position from the organization.

The **Fidalia** singing society was organized in December, 1872. Like the other musical clubs, it is composed of professional and associate members. There are about thirty-five of the former and the same number of the latter. The annual membership fee is $6.00. It is strictly a German society, having only German members and singing only popular German music. A limited number of public concerts is given each season, tickets of admission being disposed of by the members to such persons as they may select. The Fidalia meets in North Side Turner Hall on Thursday evenings. The director is H. von Oppen.

The **Turner Mænnerchor** consists of members of the Chicago Turngemeinde. It numbers about twenty-four voices, and meets in the North Side Turner Hall on Tuesday evenings. Its public singing is principally at entertainments given by the Turngemeinde. The director is Julian Heinze.

The Exchanges.

THE EXCHANGES AND OTHER TRADE ASSOCIATIONS, AND THE UNION STOCKYARDS.

THE number of exchanges and other trade associations in Chicago indicate the opinion of her business men as to the value of combinations for the advancement of related interests. There are few important lines of trade, or few groups of kindred lines, that are not represented by some organization of the kind.

The **Board of Trade** is a great commercial exchange in which the transactions are confined to grain and provisions, and it is the largest and most powerful institution of the kind in the world. It was organized in 1848, incorporated under the general statutes in 1850, and in 1859 secured a special act of incorporation from the legislature. The building in which it has been located since 1872, is a large and substantial stone structure, at the corner of LaSalle and Washington Streets, known as the Chamber of Commerce. It was built on the site of the structure occupied by the board from 1864 until it was destroyed by the fire of 1871, and was opened Oct. 9, 1872, just one year from the burning of its predecessor. Pending the construction of the new building, the board occupied rooms on Franklin Street. The exchange hall is eighty-seven feet wide, 142 feet long, and forty-five feet high. Within this space have been fought some of the greatest commercial battles in the history of trade. Here fortunes have alternately multiplied and melted, the hand that records the fluctuations of the market registering the defeat of one and the triumph of another, as inexorably as if it were the hand of fate. But the historic arena has grown too small for the contests of the gladiators of trade. It was held under a lease for ninety-nine years, which has been canceled, and a larger and more elegant structure is now approaching completion. The new building has a front of 173¾ feet on Jackson Street, at the south end of LaSalle, and extends back 225 feet. The rear portion, which is occupied by about 100 offices, is 160 feet in height, and the front part, which contains the exchange hall, is 140 feet high, and surmounted by a stately tower, the tallest in the city, rising 304 feet above the ground.

The tower is thirty-two feet square at the base, and built of masonry to the height of 225 feet, where each face is supplied with a clock dial. From the masonry to the pinnacle, seventy-eight feet, the construction is of iron. The entrances are large doorways supported by polished columns of gray granite, and the entire edifice is built of Fox Island

CHICAGO BOARD OF TRADE BUILDING, JACKSON, PACIFIC AND SHERMAN STREETS.

granite, at a cost of $1,500,000. Near the top of the east and west elevations are very striking and appropriate allegorical figures in granite. The committee and directors' rooms are on the third floor. The president's office connects with the secretary's office, both being on the second floor. They are very elegantly finished in mahogany, with artistic wood mantels, and are exquisitely frescoed. Four powerful elevators give easy access to all parts of the building. Two flights of polished vari-colored granite stairways lead from the Jackson Street entrance to the "exchange hall," which is 152×161 feet, and eighty feet high. The skylight of stained glass overhead is 72×75 feet, and there are seventeen windows, each eight feet and two inches wide and thirty-two feet high, arranged in pairs, with a 10×18 feet transom over each pair, the stained glass of the transoms bearing representations in heroic figures of Commerce, Agriculture, Order, Fortune. At the north end of the hall is a private gallery, with the president's rostrum, and ante-rooms in connection. The public gallery is on the west side of the hall. Smoking, cloak and private rooms for the members are conveniently located adjoining the hall. It is supplied with tables systematically arranged for the display of samples ; the grain and provision trades each has its separate "pit ;" the bulletins are conveniently placed ; the telegraphic service is complete and thorough. The building and hall are undoubtedly the grandest of the kind in the world. The membership of the board numbers about 2,000, which is intended to be substantially the limit. The membership fee is $10,000, but the places of retiring members can usually be purchased for $3,500 to $4,500. No transaction is allowed on the board involving less than 5,000 bushels of grain or 250 packages of pork or lard. The sessions of the board are from 9:30 A. M. to 1 P. M., and from 2 to 2:30 P. M.

The Produce Exchange was incorporated June 11, 1874, and has nearly 500 members engaged or interested in the trade in butter, cheese, eggs, potatoes, flour, fruits, vegetables, etc., in which lines the transactions are conducted. The exchange rooms and hall are at the corner of Lake and Clark Streets. The rooms are kept open for private transactions from 8 A. M. to 5 P. M., daily. 'Change hours are from 2 to 3 P. M.

The Chicago Mining Exchange started out in 1882, with a fair prospect of success, but there has been a great falling off in interest and attendance. There are over 100 members, and meetings are held daily, between 11 A. M. and 2 P. M., at Room 24 Portland Block. Calls are made at 11:30 each day, but very little business transacted.

The Lumberman's Exchange is one of the strongest trade organizations in the city. It collects and distributes statistics of the lumber trade, maintains a judicious system of classification by careful inspection, and generally takes an active part in everything calculated to advance the lumber interests. Its rooms, at 252 South Water Street, are much visited by men interested in the lumber business, from all parts of this country, and many from abroad.

The **Chicago Open Board of Trade** is similar in its purpose and methods to the Board of Trade, commonly called the "Big Board." Its operations are confined to the same commodities, though they may be handled in smaller amounts, the minimum limit of deals being 1,000 bushels of grain or twenty-five packages of lard or meats. The quotations of the "Big Board" are the guide in all trades in the Open Board, and are promptly received and bulletined. The Open Board was organized Dec. 15, 1877, and incorporated May 12, 1880, and was first located in Calhoun Place, near the Chamber of Commerce. June 2, 1884, with a membership of about 400, it moved into new and spacious quarters on Pacific Avenue. The building is a fine six-story edifice of red pressed brick. The exchange hall, on the ground floor, is eighty feet wide, 100 feet long, and thirty feet in height to the sky-light, which measures 45×50 feet. The membership fee is $500, and the annual dues $50. The daily sessions are open to spectators, from which fact it derived the name "Open Board." The sessions are held daily from 9:30 A. M. to 1 P. M., and from 2 to 2:30 P. M.

OPEN BOARD OF TRADE, PACIFIC AVENUE.

The **Chicago Drug, Paint and Oil Exchange** was organized in 1877, and is located at No. 51 Wabash Avenue. It has about twenty-five members, including the leading jobbers, wholesale dealers and manufacturers in the lines to which it is devoted. 'Change hours are from 11:30 A. M. to 12 M.

The **Commercial Exchange** has 150 members, and meets daily between the hours of 11:30 and 12:30, in its hall on the corner of Dearborn and Randolph Streets. It was incorporated Nov. 25, 1882. Its membership is limited to residents of Chicago, engaged in the wholesale grocery business and kindred branches. The transactions are, as a rule, not speculative, but involve the actual transfer of goods. Telegraphic reports of concurrent transactions in the New England fish markets, the New York and Boston sugar markets, and the New

York Coffee Exchange, are received and posted during the sessions, and all trades in those lines are based on those quotations.

The **Chicago Stock Exchange** is situated at 126 Washington Street. The membership includes the leading bankers and brokers in the city, and many prominent merchants. Many members of the New York and Philadelphia stock boards are also members of the Chicago Stock Exchange, there being at present 750 on the rolls. Two "calls" are held daily, one for the sale of bonds and one for stocks. The exchange was established in May, 1882.

The **Chicago Real Estate Board**, Rooms 5 and 5½ National Life Building, 157 to 163 LaSalle Street, is an exchange, incorporated in 1883 as The Chicago Renting Agents' Association, but filed new articles of incorporation under the present name, June 4, 1884. It was formed for purely business purposes. The daily call-board sessions are held from 12 M. to 1 P. M. The membership emb aces about eighty of the leading real estate agencies.

The **Builders' and Traders' Exchange** was organized Jan. 21, 1884, and now has nearly 500 members, composed of mechanics, manufacturers, and traders whose avocations connect them with the building trades or industries. The exchange rooms, at No. 159 LaSalle Street, are open daily.

The **Union Stock Yards**, Halsted and Fortieth Streets, are the center of the greatest live stock trade in the world. They occupy a large portion of a tract of 375 acres, the pens taking up 240 acres and having a capacity for 180,000 head of hogs, 45,000 head of cattle and 15,000 head of sheep, or a total of 240,000 head of stock of all kinds. There are 100 acres under cover, and 180 acres of open pens. The stables afford accommodation for 1,500 horses. All important railroads entering at Chicago connect with the yards, and the company has 100 miles of railroad track, including switches, to facilitate the receipt and shipment of stock. Telegraph, mail, and banking facilities are provided on the grounds. The exchange hall is in a building covering 60×240 feet, in which are the offices of the company, and of numerous firms engaged in the live stock trade. There are thirty-two extensive packing houses in the immediate vicinity of the yards. The yards were first opened Dec. 25, 1865, and have since been greatly enlarged and improved. The receipts at the stockyards during the year 1883 were : Live hogs, 5,640,625; dressed hogs, 55,538; cattle, 1,878,944; sheep, 749,917. The yards are owned by the Union Stock Yards and Transit Company.

Trade Associations:—The principal trade associations, other than exchanges, are shown in the following table:

NAME.	Organized.	No. of mem's.	NAME.	Organized.	No. of mem's.
Anthracite Coal Association..	1882		Chicago Retail Coal Dealers'		
Board of Marine Underwriters.		15	Association............	1883	125
Boss Horse Shoers' Protective			Chicago Vessel Owners' Ass'n.	1881	
Union............	1875	50	Chicago Cigar Manuf'rs' and		
Boss Horse Shoers' Protective			Dealers' Association.........	1877	180
Association............	1884	25	Custom Cutters' Association..		25
Chicago Board of Underwrit'rs		25	Lumber Manufac'rs' Associa-		
Chicago Boot, Shoe and Leath-			tion of the North West ...	1873	100
er Association....	1878	25	National Association of Lum-		
Chicago Brickmakers' Asso'n.	1883		ber Dealers............	1877	1000
Chicago Drapers' and Tailors'			Pork Packers' Association....	1872	30
Exchange....	1878		Railway Exchange............	1884	30
Chicago Jewelers' Association.	1876		State Protective Association		
Chicago Liveryman's Associ'n.	1882	65	(liquor dealers)...............	18	750
Chicago Master Masons' and			Underwriters' Exchange......	80	25
Builders' Association........	1880	75	Watchmakers' and Jewelers'		
Chicago Master Plumbers' As-			Association..................	1880	
sociation...........	1882	145	Western Railroad Association.	1867	82

The **Lumber Manufacturers' Association of the Northwest** was organized March 18, 1873. It aims to further the interests of its members, by united action among them, in everything that pertains to operations in lumber in Chicago and the Northwest. It collects and publishes, annually, statistics touching the prices, sales, production and consumption of lumber and other matters of general interest. E. S. Hotchkiss, 252 South Water Street, is secretary.

The **Chicago Clearing House Association** was organized in 1865, and incorporated in 1882. The object was to substitute a safer and more convenient method of settlements and collections between banks than the old-time system of messengers. Nineteen banks send their messengers at eleven o'clock every morning to the Clearing House at No. 80 LaSalle Street, and there in a few minutes transact the whole business that previously required several hours' time. The "losing banks," as those are called which bring in a smaller amount of checks on other banks than the latter bring in on them, are required to settle the balance before 12:30 o'clock, and the "gaining banks" come in after that time for balances due them. Many private bankers make their clearings through members of the Clearing House Association. About $1,400,000 change hands through the Clearing House every day.

The Hotels.

THE EARLY TAVERNS AND THE LEADING HOTELS OF TO-DAY AND THEIR RATES.

THE first tavern in Chicago was built in 1828 by James Kinzie, and was opened in 1829, by Archibald Caldwell, as Caldwell's Tavern. It was located on Wolf Point, and was afterward known as Wolf Tavern. An illustration on page 11 shows the building as it appeared in 1830. Samuel Miller opened a tavern on the east side of the "North Branch" in 1830, which he called the "Miller House." The building, a small log cabin, which afterward became the famous Sauganash Hotel, was improved, by a frame addition, in 1831, by Mark Beaubien, and was the first frame house in the city, and is generally spoken of as the first hotel in Chicago. It stood on the south side of Lake Street at the corner of Market. The Green Tree Tavern, corner of Lake and Canal Streets, was built in 1833. The first Tremont House was also built in 1833. From this date hotel enterprises increased rapidly with the growth of the village and city. The Green Tree, afterward the Chicago Hotel, and later the Lake Street House, ceased its existence as a hotel in 1859. In 1880, the building, a quaint frame structure, was removed to No. 35 Milwaukee Avenue, where it still stands. In 1835 the Western Hotel, a two-story frame building which still stands at the southeast corner of Canal and Randolph Streets, was erected. The Lake House was also built in 1835, at the corner of Kinzie and Rush Streets. It was a brick structure and the first really costly hotel in the city, the cost of building and furniture being about $100,000. But it is with the hotels of the present that we have to do. The hotel facilities of Chicago to-day are equal to, if not superior to any city in the country, if not in the world.

The Palmer House, corner State and Monroe Streets, is one of the largest and grandest hotels in the world. It occupies the site of the old Palmer House which was destroyed by the great fire. It was opened for the reception of guests Nov. 1, 1873. The cost of the building, which is fire proof, was $2,000,000, and over $500,000 were expended in furnishing it. It is six stories in height above the basement, and has a frontage on State Street of 281 feet, and on Monroe Street of 253 feet, and an L extending through to Wabash Avenue 131 feet in width. The fronts are of stone. An additional story was added in 1884 and the hotel now contains 815 rooms. The grand hall through which the rotunda is reached is 28 feet wide and 70 feet long. Its wainscoting is of thirty-four different kinds and colors of marble. The rotunda is 64×106 feet, and the floor, office counters and staircase are all of Italian marble. The grand reception room and the Egyptian parlor, are furnished in the most artistic and luxuriant manner. The bridal chambers of the Palmer are celebrated; the furniture is unique and costly, and in the frescoes are cupids and doves, wreaths of flowers and filmy veils of lace. The ball room is 40×140 feet, and through its center is a row of fluted columns finished in artistically blended colors. The grand dining hall is 64 feet wide and 76 feet long; the architectural decorations are in old Corinthian order, treated in modern French style. The club room is 60×30 feet, the floor is of marble tiling, and the sides are laid in colored tiling to the height of four feet. The ladies' and gentlemen's cafe is in the rear of the rotunda, and the lunch room is situated on the State Street front, just south of the main entrance. The Palmer is conducted on both the American and European plan. The charges range from $3.00 to $6.00 per day for room and board, and from $1.00 to $2.00 for room without board. It is one of the great institutions of Chicago; and at times of popular excitement the focus of interest is here; and it is here that the prominent political leaders of the Democratic party congregate to exchange views and discuss topics of political moment. The hotel was built by Potter Palmer, and is now owned by the Palmer House Company. Willis Howe is manager.

The Grand Pacific Hotel fronts on Clark, Jackson, LaSalle and Quincy Streets, and covers an entire half-square of ground. It stands on the site of the Pacific Hotel which had just been completed at the time of the great fire. Like its predecessor, it was built by the Pacific Hotel Company, but is much larger and costlier than the original structure. It is just across the street from the postoffice on the east, and the new Board of Trade Building on the south. Its erection was commenced soon after the great fire of 1871, and it was completed and opened June 3, 1873. The hotel is conducted on the American plan, the terms being from $3 to $5 per day. The building is of a mixed style of architecture, the three main fronts being of stone. It is six stories high above the basement, massive and solid, and one of the

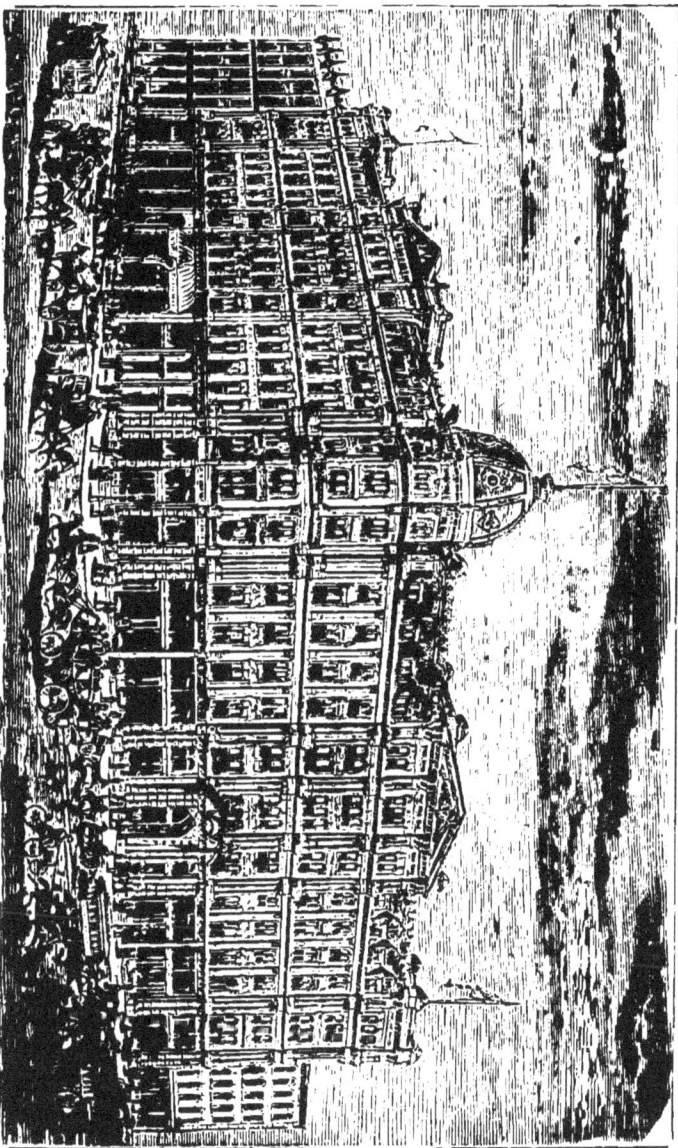

THE PALMER HOUSE, STATE AND MONROE STREETS.

ornaments and attractions of the city. Near the main entrance on
Clark Street is a grand court 70×70 feet, in which is the office, commanding a view of each entrance. Near the LaSalle Street entrance,
and also connected with the grand court, is an "exchange" 100×60
feet. The parlors, dining halls and kitchen and culinary department are on the second floor. The grand parlor fronts on Jackson
Street, and is 100×24 feet. The dining room is 130×60 feet. A grand
promenade from the parlors to the dining room is 30×130 feet, and the
corridors are twelve feet wide. In all there are over 500 rooms in the
house. The annual game dinner given at the Grand Pacific has become
famous, and the cuisine on all occasions is noted for its excellence.
The Grand Pacific is the meeting place of many clubs and societies, not
only local but also state and national in character. It is also the principal
headquarters in the west of the Republican party, and has been the
scene of many exciting political events. The cost of the building was
$1,300,000, and the furniture $360,000. The present proprietors,
John B. Drake & Co., took charge Dec. 25, 1874.

The Tremont House, on the corner of Dearborn and Lake Streets,
is one of the oldest, best and most attractive hotels in the city. It was
first erected in 1833, on the opposite corner of the street, rebuilt in
1839-40 on the present site, and again in 1850. It was remodeled
and greatly improved in 1861, the entire structure being raised about
seven feet, and new foundations placed under it; and in 1871 it was
destroyed by the great fire. The present structure was completed in
1874 at a cost of about $700.000, including the furniture. The Tremont was founded by Hanson Sweet, and passed into the hands of Ira
and James Couch in 1836, and is still owned by the Couch estate. The
building far surpasses its predecessors in size and architectural beauty,
and it is one of the most luxuriantly furnished hotels in the country.
It covers 50.000 square feet of ground. It is six stories high above the
basement, crowned with five towers of two stories each. The fronts
are of Amherst (Ohio) sandstone. carved and otherwise ornamented.
The office is in the rotunda. 50×100 feet, on the ground floor, and is
a model of architectural art. It is surmounted by lighted domes and
the woodwork of black walnut is very elaborate. The parlors, drawing
and reception rooms are on the second floor. as is also the culinary
department. The grand dining hall is 64×100 feet. There are about
300 private rooms for guests. The Tremont is conducted on the American plan. the rates ranging from $3.00 to $4.00 per day. It is popular as a family and business men's hotel. It is farther north than any

other first-class hotel in the city, and in the midst of a busy wholesale district. John A. Rice & Co., the present proprietors, took charge in 1879.

The Leland is one of the best conducted hotels in the United States. It is situated on the southwest corner of Michigan Boulevard and Jackson Street, overlooking Lake Park and the broad expanse of Lake Michigan, the view being one of great beauty and grandeur. The great Exposition Building is just across the street on the northeast;

THE LELAND HOTEL, MICHIGAN BOULEVARD, CORNER JACKSON STREET.

the new Pullman Building—which is said to be the finest business block in the world—stands just one square north; the Chicago Art Institute is removed one square to the south, while the Postoffice and Custom House are only three squares away on the west; and the new Board of Trade Building and many other places of interest and note are in the neighborhood. The building is an imposing brick structure. It is six stories high above the basement and is massive and solid, and essentially fire proof. Each of the main fronts is provided with numerous iron balconies, and iron fire-escapes, accessible from hallways on each floor, furnish easy means of escape in case of fire. The hotel contains 216 rooms, and is sumptuously furnished throughout. It is more

exclusive than any other hotel in Chicago, being the stopping place of
the very best class of people and the permanent home of many wealthy
and aristocratic citizens. It is conducted on the American plan, the
rates ranging from $3.00 to $5.00 per day. Warren F. Leland has
been proprietor and manager since April, 1881.

McCoy's European Hotel is the best appointed and most elegant
hotel west of New York, conducted exclusively on the European plan ;
and it is the only strictly first-class European hotel in Chicago. Its
site was well chosen, being easily accessible from all parts of the city.
It is just across the street from the Rock Island and Lake Shore Depot,
and only one square away from the postoffice ; and it is adjacent to the
New Board of Trade and convenient to the large wholesale and retail
stores and principal places of amusement and interest. The locality
is improving with greater rapidity than any other portion of the city,
and many massive and handsome business blocks have recently been
erected in the neighborhood. The building is seven stories in height
above the basement, and is crowned with three ornamental towers. It
was designed by the well-known architect, Greg. Vigeant, is essentially
fire proof, and is one of the best constructed and most substantial
hotels in the world. The walls are of red pressed brick, and the columns, girders, towers, mansard, gables and stairways are all of iron.
There is a large double fire escape on each front of the building, immediately accessible from hallways on each floor, and each contiguous
window is provided with a spacious iron balcony. And a complete iron
stairway in the court in the rear, extending the entire height of the building, also affords easy means of escape in case of fire. The building
has a frontage of 95½ feet on Clark Street and 110 on Van Buren, and a
court in the rear separates it from all other buildings. There are 200
rooms for guests, and each apartment is luxuriously furnished, and provided with all modern conveniences. The finish of the first two stories
is of hard wood—oak. The rotunda, in which is situated the office
commanding a view of each entrance, is located on the second floor.
It is reached by wide stairways from both streets, and by a superb
hydraulic elevator near the Van Buren Street entrances. The three
main parlors and the reception and club rooms are on the same floor,
and all the rooms on the entire floor are so arranged that they can be
thrown into one grand *salon*, at pleasure. The restaurant is on the
first floor, and adjoining the grand dining-hall are convenient private
dining and toilet-rooms. The five upper stories are divided into suites
and single rooms, each with natural light and perfect ventilation, and

McCOY'S NEW EUROPEAN HOTEL, CLARK AND VAN BUREN STREETS.

a new and original system of alarms by which every guest may be immediately awakened, this being the only hotel in the world having this device. Everything seems to have been done to make the house homelike, comfortable and attractive. The rates range from $1 a day upwards. The cost of the hotel was about $500,000. It was completed and opened June 1, 1884, and has rapidly grown in popular favor. Wm. McCoy is the sole owner and proprietor. The first McCoy's Hotel was located at 140 and 142 Madison Street, and was originally called Burk's Hotel. Mr. McCoy bought it in 1879, and afterward changed the name to McCoy's Hotel.

The **Sherman House** is on the corner of Clark and Randolph Streets, opposite to the new City Hall. The present building was opened to guests in the spring of 1873. It is seven stories high above the basement and has a tower on each front rising two stories higher. The fronts are of Kankakee stone, light brown in color, and the entire building is solid and substantial. It fronts 181½ feet on Clark Street and 161 feet on Randolph. There are about 300 rooms for guests. The dining room is 115×144 feet. The Sherman was furnished at a cost of $360,000. The building cost $600,000. As a family hotel it is unexcelled, and it is a popular resort for the best class of commercial travelers. It is the headquarters of the State Board of Agriculture and the meeting place of numerous societies. The first hotel on the site was built in 1836 and was called the City Hotel. This was supplanted in 1861 by a better building which was destroyed by the great fire, 1871. The Sherman took its name from F. C. Sherman, formerly mayor of the city, by whom it was built. The rates are from $3.00 to $5.00 per day. J. Irving Pearce has been the proprietor since July, 1882.

Other Hotels.—The following are among the better class of hotels not heretofore mentioned : Clifton House, corner Wabash Avenue and Monroe Street, 165 rooms, rates $2.50 to $3.00 per day. Commercial Hotel, Lake and Dearborn Streets, the great $2.00 per day house of the city ; 300 rooms. Matteson House, Wabash Avenue and Jackson Street, 200 rooms, $2.50 to $3.00 per day. Briggs House, Randolph Street, corner Fifth Avenue, 150 rooms, $2.00 to $2.50 per day. Atlantic Hotel, corner Van Buren and LaSalle Streets, 160 rooms, $2.00 per day. Gault House, Madison and Clinton Streets (West Side), 125 rooms, $2.00 to $2.50 per day. Brevoort House (European plan), 145 Madison Street. 125 rooms, $1.00 to $1.50 per day. Windsor European Hotel, 147 Dearborn Street, 75 cents to $2.00 per day.

Real Estate Interests.

REAL ESTATE SALES, PROMINENT REAL ESTATE DEALERS, AGENTS AND LOAN BROKERS.

THE real estate interests of Chicago are naturally of immensely greater magnitude than any other line of investment, and are growing rapidly and constantly with the growth of the city. This class of property is far less subject to violent fluctuation than any other, and although there have been several reactions in the history of Chicago, resulting from speculative " booms" that placed prices far in advance of the time, the market was never long in recovering and carrying up the ruling rates more firmly than before, thus proving the highest figures to have been merely anticipative. The story of these fluctuations, with notes of the rise of realty in value, the improvement in building operations, the movements of the bonded debt, and other matters bearing upon the real estate interests of the city, appear in the opening chapter of this work.

The aggregates of real estate sales during the last decade will convey some idea of the extent of these interests. They are shown in the following table :

1874, total sales	$67,871,653	1879, total sales	$38,123,591
1875,	"	53,119,852	1880,	"	43,692,922
1876,	"	42,153,596	1881,	"	54,859,186
1877,	"	38,153,291	1882,	"	65,735,185
1878,	"	42,126,821	1883,	"	44,164,243

Grand total for ten years, $489,990,623. The sales for the two years immediately following the great fire of 1871 were: for 1872, $78,183,458; for 1873, $78,427,931.

Nearly all of this immense business is transacted by the real estate agents, and a large part of it for extensive owners who reside in the various money centers of the world. Hence there is great and widespread interest in the subject, and a general desire to know something about those who handle this large volume of investments. With the view of supplying such information, we present herewith brief sketches of a few of the firms and individuals engaged in this line of business, together with special mention of prominent loan brokers and others whose operations are an important factor in the handling and develop-

275

ment of real property. There are nearly one thousand of these agencies in Chicago, buying, selling and managing for themselves and others, many of them on the most extensive scale, and those noted below may be taken as fairly representative of all branches of the business.

S. H. Kerfoot & Co., No. 91 Dearborn Street. This firm, composed of Samuel H. Kerfoot, Sr., and Samuel H. Kerfoot, Jr., is the oldest real estate firm in Chicago, having, in 1852, succeeded the firm of Rees & Kerfoot. S. H. Kerfoot, Sr., came to the city from Maryland, in 1848, and, by his continuous operations in real estate has contributed very largely to the gigantic growth and success of the city. The mile and a quarter of territory on the south branch of the Chicago River, in which is now transacted the bulk of the enormous lumber business of Chicago, was brought into the market through the efforts of Mr. Kerfoot, at a time when it was a beautiful farm, outlying the city. The effect upon the lumber trade alone, by the addition of this land to the city's territory, has been of inestimable value. After the great fire (Oct. 8-9, 1871), this firm opened its new office for business on the day following, October the 10th.

In 1875, having completed his studies, S. H. Kerfoot, Jr., returned from Europe and entered his father's office, and, on the first of January, 1880, he was admitted to partnership in the firm. Their operations have been particularly heavy in bulk property, they having been the resident agents of some of the largest estates sold in the city. One estate, of about sixty acres, which originally cost less than $40,000, was sold, in lots, to the amount of $1,500,000, by them, and another of less acreage—taken by the owners, twenty-five years ago, in payment of a hopeless debt—has, during the last four years, sold for more than $400,000, under their management. They act largely for non-resident owners, but their transactions are almost entirely confined to Chicago property. No rentals receive attention, the business being solely that of purchase and sale on firm account, or on commission, and placing loans on realty. Their maps, atlases and records are at all times open to their clients and the public generally.

The long experience of this firm has given great weight to their knowledge and opinions of not only the present values of real estate, but of such values at different periods within the past thirty years. Consequently, such knowledge and opinions are constantly sought and given, both orally and in depositions, in litigations as well as in amicable adjustments of claims and differences.

Francis B. Peabody & Co., No. 115 Dearborn Street, succeeded about nine years ago to the firm of Gallop & Peabody, which was established in 1866. For about ten years prior to 1866 Mr. Peabody was engaged in the practice of law in this city, but since that date he has devoted himself exclusively to the business of investing money upon mortage loans in Chicago and vicinity. During that period he has placed many millions of dollars for Eastern capitalists and corporations, seeking safe investment for their surplus funds; and, during his long experience, he has found mortgages on Chicago realty to be as safe and reliable investments as government bonds—and at the same time much more productive. Mr. Peabody's legal training, his long experience in his present business, and his thorough familiarity with Chicago real estate and its values, have obtained for him the fullest confidence of investors. The junior partners in the firm are James L. Houghteling and Francis S. Peabody, both men of high character and standing in the community, and thoroughly posted in the business. The house affords to borrowers a convenient and reliable source of obtaining such funds as they require and to capitalists a safe medium of investment.

Baird & Bradley, No. 90 LaSalle Street, are successors to L. D. Olmsted & Co., established in 1857 by L. D. Olmsted, Lyman Baird becoming a partner in 1860. At Mr. Olmsted's death in 1862 Francis Bradley was admitted, and in 1864 the name of the firm was changed to Baird & Bradley. The transactions of the firm have always been largely devoted to placing loans on real estate for Eastern corporations and capitalists, and formerly an extensive life and fire insurance business was also done. Some years ago a real estate and renting department was added, which, together with the loan department, has grown to very large proportions.

James B.Goodman & Co., 68 Washington Street, stand in the front rank of the real estate houses of the city. The firm consists of Jas. B. Goodman and Marvin A. Farr, both gentleman of long experience and thoroughly posted in real estate matters. They do a general real estate business. One of their specialties has been the handling of property desirable for packing house purposes. They have been very successful in this line, having sold to most of the great packing establishments at the stockyards, the sites of which are advantageously and satisfactorily located. An important feature of their business is the handling of valuable tracts of timber, mining and farming lands, of which they control a quarter of a million of acres in Michigan and Wisconsin alone.

Malcom McNeill & Bros., 92 East Washington Street, constitute one of the most enterprising and promising real estate firms in the city. The members of the firm are Malcom, B. F. and A. C. McNeill, all ranking high as active and successful business men, and thoroughly posted in their line. Their acknowledged integrity, thorough experience and reliable judgment offer advantages which practical investors, especially n realty and real estate securities appreciate, and hence the house, established no longer ago than March, 1886, already commands an extensive and still increasing clientage, and holds a long list of desirable city, suburban and country properties for sale or exchange. They also collect rents and negotiate loans on favorable terms, and transact a considerable business as private bankers. They are conversant with all the best opportunities for sale or purchase, keep constantly posted on the growth and prospects of localities, and hence are resorted to with entire confidence by all parties seeking reliable information and advice in regard to real estate matters. This house is perfectly responsible and trustworthy, and conducts every transaction with a careful regard for the interest of the patrons in whose behalf it was undertaken.

Bernard F. Weber, real estate and loans, Rooms 15 and 16, 84 LaSalle Street. Mr. Weber began in the real estate business in 1870. He was afterward a member of the firm of Miller, Weber & Blumenthal for about two years, then B. F. Weber & Co., then in partnership with Godfrey Schmid. As Weber & Schmid the firm was dissolved in 1883, since which time Mr. Weber has conducted business alone. He is one of the most prominent among the dealers in suburban property, making a specialty of subdivisions for residence settlements. He has in charge at the present time a large subdivision in the north end of Lake View, which is to be named High Ridge, and makes a specialty of Lake View and Evanston property. He also has in charge other subdivisions in Ravenswood, and other desirable suburban localities. He buys and sells real estate on his own account as well as upon commission, and loans money upon real estate and mortgage security. He does a purely real estate business, and undertakes no collecting. He enjoys a large patronage, always having a fine list of desirable suburban properties on hand. His facilities for the transaction of a legitimate real estate business are not excelled by those of any firm in the city.

Barnard & Calkins, real estate dealers, etc., 109 LaSalle Street. This representative business house, the principals of which are M. R.

Barnard and C. R. Calkins, occupies commodious, convenient and centrally located offices, specially fitted up for their business, at 109 LaSalle Street, in the old Chamber of Commerce, This firm takes charge of every description of real property, securing good tenants, collecting rents, paying taxes, and having the sole charge of property when desired; it buys and sells on commission, city and suburban real estate improved and unimproved, negotiates loans, and effects mortgages in large or small sums in Cook County when the security offered is beyond question. It assumes the care and management of commercial and residence property, paying the same attention to all business intrusted to them that they do to their own property. The members of this house are connected with the Chicago real estate board, and take an active interest in everything that pertains to the welfare of the great metropolitan commercial center of the West. This firm has enjoyed a ·prosperous career, its business having increased from year to year, and its affairs are conducted with enterprise and good judgment. It enjoys the confidence and patronage, to a large extent, of capitalists and landed proprietors.

John N. Young, real estate and loans, 204 Chicago Opera House Block. Mr. Young established this business in 1868, coming here from Peoria. He possesses superior facilities for the transaction of business, and owns large tracts of Chicago realty. He handles much city and suburban property in almost every locality for others, and can offer it on terms to suit customers. He gives special and faithful attention to the management of rental properties, making them as remunerative as possible. He is a recognized authority on values, and many fortunes have been made in consequence of taking his advice relative to speculative purchases. Mr. Young effects loans on bonds and mortgages at low interest and on satisfactory terms. He is held in high estimation by the business community.

. Charles P. Silva, real estate and loans, 133 LaSalle Street. This gentleman, formerly of the firm of Hopkinson & Silva, has transacted a general real estate and loan business since 1865. His offices are centrally located, and he buys and sells realty personally and upon commission, and manages several valuable estates, including the Rhodes estate, of Cleveland, Ohio, and the estates of H. J. Ward, of Wisconsin, and William Hopkinson, He is also agent for the Morgan Park property, unexcelled for residence purposes. Long experience and an intimate knowledge of values give Mr. Silva unsurpassed advantages, and he has made many large and satisfactory deals for his clients. By industry and fidelity he has attained the confidence of owners and investors, and an unexcelled business standing.

Byron A. Baldwin & Co., real estate and mortgage loans, 154 Washington Street. This firm is composed of Messrs. Byron A. Baldwin, member of the Chicago real estate board; Jas. W. D. Kelley, secretary of the Bookkeepers' Building and Loan Association, and Walter S. Baldwin, notary public. Mr. Byron A. Baldwin owns a considerable amount of city and suburban property, and the firm does a large business in selling real estate on commission, negotiating mortgage loans, collecting rents, managing estates, paying taxes and protecting the interests of non-resident and local owners. They are now placing on the market 155 choice lots in Maplewood, known as "Byron A. Baldwin's Subdivision," which fronts south on Humboldt Boulevard about 500 feet west of California Avenue. The close proximity of Maplewood to the business center of Chicago makes it a desirable residence section for those who wish to reach the city quickly and secure homes at a moderate price. The rapid growth of this attractive suburb is unprecedented; present population over 20,000 and rapidly increasing. Mr. Baldwin also owns two blocks of city property, consisting of seventy-four lots fronting on Central Park Boulevard, Kedzie Avenue, Tray Street and Albany Avenue, located east of and near Garfield Park. This first-class city residence property is just being put on the market at such prices as will insure its rapid sale and improvement. The business of Byron A. Baldwin & Co. is large and steadily increasing, their promptness and reliability being such that they give satisfaction to their clients in all their dealings.

Schraeder Brothers, real estate brokers, No. 80 East Washington Street. The business of this widely-known and enterprising house was established in 1865, and has steadily increased ever since. The firm deal both in city and suburban realty. Their long practical experience in the business has given them a comprehensive knowledge of the value both present and prospective, of all kinds of business and residence property, and they have on their books full descriptions of desirable property offered for sale, and freely advise those contemplating making purchases. They effect leases on bond and mortgage securities to the safety and profit of the investor, and at the same time to the advantage of the purchaser. The Schraeder Brothers make a specialty of taking the entire charge and business management of property, securing reliable and prompt paying tenants, collecting rents, making necessary repairs, placing insurance, paying taxes, etc., and insuring the greatest possible net income of the property. Their commercial connections are of a superior character, and they have won a high reputation for sterling business methods, and fair and liberal treatment of their patrons.

Greenebaum Sons, mortgage bankers, 116 and 118 LaSalle Street This business, established in 1855 by Elias Greenebaum, is conducted by him and his sons, Messrs. H. E. and M. E. Greenebaum. They negotiate loans on real estate and place investments. This firm stands high among the financial institutions of Chicago, and has placed millions of dollars for clients safely and profitably. Long experience gives them unsurpasse⁴: facilities for placing loans and their accurate knowledge of values makes their house a safe and reliable medium for advantageous investments, while their established reputation for fair dealing affords borrowers a reliable source of supply for needed funds. The firm has the fullest confidence of investors and does a large business in first mortgages on Chicago and suburban real estate.

J. A. Bartlett, real estate and loans, 152 La Salle Street. Mr. Bartlett is one of the most enterprising and public-spirited men in real estate circles in Chicago, having been a resident of the city for more than thirty years, and been identified with the real estate interests for seventeen years. He has been zealous and active, and has secured a large clientage among the leading landed proprietors and owners of commercial blocks and residence property. He is a resident of Englewood, and has the charge of extensive properties both in Englewood and Normal Park. He negotiates loans, collects rents, both of residence property and commercial blocks, and pays special attention to the property of non-residents, or persons who are unable to attend personally to their own affairs. His office at room 15, 152 La Salle Street, conveniently located, is fitted up with perfect adaptation for his business. Mr. Bartlett has enjoyed a prosperous business career, and his affairs are conducted with enterprise and rare judgment.

J. F. Lyon, real estate, 177 LaSalle Street, established this business in 1875. He handles all descriptions of city and suburban realty, embracing commercial blocks, residence property and tenement houses, both on his own account and on commission. His chief business is on the West side, and, aided by his appointment as notary public, he does a large business in conveyancing, examining and perfecting titles, executing deeds, and attends to every detail of purchasing or transferring real estate. He has superior facilities for effecting loans on bonds and mortgages at favorable rates, and is enabled to place money on the very best real estate security. He gives particular attention to the care of property, renting and making collections, looking after insurance, taxes, special assessments, water rates, etc., making the property as remunerative as possible, and exercising the same care that would be given it by the owner.

Carne & Coombs, successors to Carne & Drury, tax abstracts and real estate, 78 LaSalle Street. To supply the need, generally felt by property owners, of a reliable agent to look after tax matters, this business was established in 1874 by Mr. John Carne and Mr. Edwin Drury. Recently the latter retired, and was succeeded by Mr. Hiram Coombs, who was with the firm of Carne & Drury from its inception, and is thoroughly familiar with all the details of the business. The experience and intimate knowledge possessed by this firm of all matters connected with the assessment and collection of taxes give assurance to those who place tax matters in their hands that they will be attended to promptly and correctly. The care and fidelity with which every item of business is transacted by this house is attested by the steady growth of its patronage since its inception.

Haddock, Vallette & Rickeords, abstract makers, 85-87 Dearborn Street, constitute a thoroughly representative firm in the important branch of the real estate interest to which they are devoted. Their facilities for accuracy and despatch in the work of giving the history of Cook County realty are the very best; and their long acquaintance with the importance and responsibility of the business has given the public a confidence in their work that can only be obtained by years of careful and painstaking labor.

Barnes & Parish, consisting of F. A. Barnes and S. M. Parish, are located at No. 157 LaSalle Street. The house was founded in 1874. Messrs. Barnes & Parish are widely known as leading real estate and renting agents; conducting all transactions pertaining to a legitimate real estate business. They negotiate loans on the most favorable terms, employ the best opportunities for making safe and profitable investments, and buy and sell property for non-residents and others. Their facilities and standing are such that they are frequently given *carte blanche* for extensive purchases, their clients often not seeing the property until after it is paid for, but trusting entirely to the judgment of their agents, which has in all cases proven satisfactory. They manage property for non-residents and others, taking full charge and attending to all the details as carefully as the owners could do it, and more satisfactorily, their superior experience and knowledge in such matters enabling them to secure desirable tenants, collect and remit promptly, pay taxes, insurance, repairs, etc., all to greater advantage than is possible for any one less thoroughly informed. Their specialty is renting, and in this department they do a very extensive business, having now over seventeen hundred tenants occupying residence houses, stores and other business property.

Wm. Garnett & Co. are located at No. 180 Dearborn Street. The business was established in 1868 by William Garnett, the senior member of the present firm. John L. Garnett was admitted in 1880. They buy and sell all kinds of improved and unimproved real estate in the city and county. They manage estates and give special attention to management of property for non-residents, and solicit correspondence with all persons having real estate to be looked after, either in the city or the county. They negotiate loans, pay taxes, collect rents, in fact conduct a general real estate and renting business. Sixteen years of uninterrupted experience in real estate transactions give the firm all the advantages known to the business. Reference: L. J. Gage, First National Bank.

Henry H. Walker, 116 Monroe Street, has been prominently identified with real estate interests in Chicago since 1869. At that time he became associated with his brother, Samuel J. Walker, who commenced dealing in real estate in this city in 1853. The latter was one of the most extensive real estate dealers and owners in Chicago. To him is largely due the development of property in the southwestern part of the city, where he located many of the most extensive manufacturing establishments, such as the McCormick Reaper Works, the Chicago Malleable Iron Works, the Chicago Stove Works, etc. In fact, he contributed more to the development of West Side property than any other person. Mr. S. J. Walker died April 15, 1884, and since that time the business has been continued by Henry H. Walker alone, whose practical experience in the real estate business is of incalculable value in making investments and in the purchase, subdivision, sale and general management of property, which are the leading features of his business.

Bogue & Hoyt, Room 1, 182 Dearborn St., composed of Geo. M. Bogue, Henry W. Hoyt and Hamilton B. Bogue, were organized in 1873, as successors to the senior partner who established the business in 1867. They have at all times on their books a large line of improved and unimproved property for sale, in the most desirable locations for investment, and do an extensive business in mortgage loans on first-class real estate security. They buy and sell on commission, and give special attention to the care and management of property for non-residents, rent property, collect rents and pay taxes. They have also been very successful in buying acre property suitable for subdivision and sale in lots, their transactions in this line proving profitable to all concerned. They handled a very large amount of residence property during the past few years, especially on the South Side, having extensive and desirable property along Drexel and Grand Boulevards, and in the attractive Kenwood section, in Hyde Park and along the lake shore, and along the route of the suburban trains of the Illinois Central Railroad, in all of which their list embraces many of the handsomest and most favorable building sites to be found anywhere around the city. The firm brings a large experience to bear in all its transactions, and occupies a leading position in the business.

Nelson Thomasson, Room 3, northwest corner of Washington and Dearborn Streets, is both agent and dealer, giving his attention to buying and selling for himself and others. He makes a specialty of business property (stores) and boulevard and acre property, and has conducted some extensive transactions, especially in acre property, from which his clients have realized large profits. In one case he made $40,000 for a client by an investment in Pitner's subdivision. He is also very successful in favorably locating manufactories, and has secured many advantageous sites, especially along the Belt Railway. He established the present business in 1870, and his long experience enables him to avail himself of all desirable opportunities, which advantage he employs freely for the advancement of the interest of his extensive list of patrons. He always has a list of desirable property to offer investors at great bargains. As to personal standing he refers to all Chicago banks.

F. A. Bragg & Co., 95 Washington Street, do an extensive business in buying and selling real estate, negotiating loans, renting and collecting and generally managing property for non-residents and others. Mr. Bragg, who has been a resident of Chicago for a third of a century, established his business in 1867, and has been remarkably successful in it. For about nine years he was City Superintendent of Assessments, in which position he acquired information of great advantage in his present pursuit; and at the outbreak of the late war he was First Assistant Engineer of the Fire Department. Few men are as well posted in Chicago property, or command as implicitly the confidence of owners and investors.

The Financial Institutions.

THE NATIONAL, STATE AND SAVINGS BANKS, BANKERS AND CLEARING HOUSE STATISTICS.

THERE are seventeen National banks in Chicago, with a combined cash capital of $14,700,000, and a total surplus of more than $2,000,000. There are thirteen state banks (including three savings banks) with a combined capital of $5,536,700, and a total surplus of $3,112,000. There are also twenty-four private banking houses, and two branch Canadian banks, employing a large capital. Thus it will be seen that the total banking capital of the city is not less than $26,-000,000. According to the statements returned to the Clearing House* in Dec. 31, 1886, the twenty banks belonging to the association had on deposit $97,635,979, and their loans at the same date amounted . $79,112,291.46.

The National Bank of Illinois is one of the strongest monetary institutions in the west. It was organized Sept. 1, 1871, and although not as old as some of the other city banks, it long ago attained a reputation for financial worth and integrity, and acquired ·a business patronage of such extensive proportions as to place it in the very front rank of the leading banking organizations of the country. Its management from the outset embraced a most substantial array of experience and success in financial lines, including some of the leading and most prominent business men and financiers in Chicago, and at once commanded the fullest confidence of the public. Founded just before the great fire of 1871, its funds had not been loaned out to any great extent when that memorable conflagration swept so much of the city to destruction. Hence, it escaped the losses—if not the utter ruin— that bore so heavily upon some of its contemporaries at that time. Its first location was at No. 95 Washington Street, and its initial capital was $500,000. The latter has since been increased to $1,000,000, and there· is an accumulated surplus fund of $300,000. Its average deposits amount to over $5,000,000, and its stock is quoted at $1.45

---

* See Clearing House Association, page 266.

on the dollar. There has not been a year in the history of the bank that it has not made substantial progress, having gone steadily forward from the very first. It transacts all business pertaining to legitimate banking operations. Receives deposits, discounts commercial paper, makes collections, deals in U. S. and home securities and foreign exchange, issues letters of credit, etc. Its correspondents at the principal monetary centers are of the highest standing, and it has responsible connections at all desirable collection points. Unlike many of the banks in Chicago, its transactions are not limited to any particular line of trade or manufacture, but embrace every branch of commercial enterprise, and are therefore of the most diversified character. On the 20th of Feb., 1885, Grannis Block, in which the bank had its home, was burned to the ground, but before the part of the structure in which it was situated was fairly afire, steps had been taken to procure another office, and on the following morning it opened within five minutes of the usual time, and made its appearance at the clearing house with accustomed regularity. Mr. Geo. Schneider, the president of the bank, and Mr. Wm. H. Bradley, vice-president, have occupied these positions from the date of its organization. Mr. W. A. Hammond, cashier, and Mr. Geo. A. McKay, assistant cashier, both entered the bank within six months after it was opened, and each has successively filled every position from the lowest up to the responsible place he now occupies. The Grannis Block, Nos. 109 to 115 Dearborn Street, will be immediately rebuilt and will hereafter be called the Illinois Bank Building. It will be an elegant and thoroughly fire proof structure, and will be re-occupied as the permanent home of the National Bank of Illinois.

Charles Henrotin, 115 Dearborn Street, dealer in bonds, stocks and commercial paper, conducts a business that is in the aggregate an important factor in the financial and commercial prosperity of Chicago. He deals specially in investment securities, of the highest order, and the large amount of securities handled by him annually is a significant indication of the preference of the capital of the country for investments in this section. Mr. Henrotin established his business in 1878. Prior to that time he had been connected continuously from 1860 with one of the strongest financial institutions in the city, for twelve years of the time as its cashier. He makes a specialty of the purchase and sale of first mortgage bonds, especially of the Chicago, Milwaukee & St. Paul, the Chicago & Northwestern, the Chicago & Alton, and the Chicago, Burlington & Quincy Railroads. He also handles a large amount of local and railroad stocks and first-class commercial paper, and always has an extensive and desirable line of securities for the inspection and selection of investors. His long experience gives him special qualifications for the judicious investment of funds for capitalists, trustees of estates, etc. Mr. Henrotin has been President of the Stock Exchange for two consecutive years, is Consul at this port for Belgium and Turkey, and holds a high rank as a business man and financier.

The First National Bank is one of the great institutions of Chicago ; and for nearly a quarter of a century it has been a prominent landmark in the monetary system of the city, and, in fact, of the country. It was

THE FIRST NATIONAL BANK, CORNER DEARBORN AND MONROE STS.

founded in 1863, with a capital of $300,000, and with E. Aiken as president, Samuel Nickerson as vice-president, and E. E. Braisted, cashier, and at once entered on a career of prosperity that has never been broken. It has steadily grown in strength and influence from the date of its organization, increasing its capital from time to time, until it is now the largest of any national bank west of New York City. The first president held his office until his death, in 1867, when he was succeeded by Mr. Samuel Nickerson, the present incumbent Mr. Lyman J. Gage became cashier in 1868, and continued in that position until his election to the vice-presidency in 1882. H. R. Symonds succeeded

Mr. Gage in the cashiership, H. M. Kingman and R. J. Street becoming first and second assistants respectively. The " First National Bank" was re-chartered in 1882, with a capital of $3,000,000; it has a surplus capital of $500,000; its average deposits amount to about $16,-000,000, and its stock is quoted at $2.00 to $2.25 on the dollar. The bank transacts all business pertaining to legitimate banking operations, both domestic and foreign. It receives deposits, discounts commercial paper, makes collections, deals in United States and home securities and sterling exchange, issues letters of credit, etc. It has established correspondents in London, Paris and other European capitals to assist, through the purchase and sale of foreign exchange, in that great interchange of industrial products by which the value of human labor is everywhere made more effective. The bank is also prepared to invest moneys for estates and trusts, under order of court or otherwise, in designated securities, which it will hold separately for such trusts, etc., and will collect the interest and coupons upon same for reinvestment or otherwise, upon moderate charges. The home of the bank is a magnificent structure on the corner of Dearborn and Monroe Streets, and the banking office proper is one of the largest and finest in the world. It is 95×195 feet; the floor is laid in mosaic of black and white marble, and the counters of vari-colored marble are finished in cherry and plate glass.

N. W. Harris & Co., the well-known investment bankers, removed to the finely appointed offices now occupied by them in Montauk Block, Nos 115 and 117 East Monroe Street, on the 1st of May, 1885. Established in 1882, the business was not long in assuming large proportions. It has grown steadily and rapidly, and the transactions now aggregate several millions of dollars annually. The Messrs. Harris confine their transactions mainly to that branch of the banking business popularly known as investment banking, making a specialty of the purchase and sale of county, city, town and school bonds.

S. A. Kean & Co. (S. A. Kean and John Farson), successors to Preston, Kean & Co., one of the leading banking houses of Chicago, are located at No. 100 East Washington Street, where they have been for twelve years. The old house was founded by S. A. Kean, who began business in 1860. In 1861 Mr. D. Preston became connected with the house, and in 1872 the firm became Preston, Kean & Co., and so remained until February, 1885, when the present firm was organized. Through all this time, more than a quarter of a century, Mr. Kean had been the active manager of the business, and it was to his energy and ability that the house owed its remarkable success, growing from a small beginning to the highest eminence in financial circles. The operations of the bank increased rapidly after the fire of 1871, and it acquired the largest private banking and investment business west of New York. Messrs. Kean & Co. transact all departments of the banking business, receiving the accounts of merchants, bankers and others, advancing money on good collaterals, discounting approved paper, buying and selling exchange on the principal European cities, etc. They also deal largely in government, state and municipal bonds and local securities, and during the year just ended they have effected sales of bonds amounting to millions of dollars. A special feature of their business is the negotiation of county, city, town and school district securities, frequently buying the entire issues of such bonds and negotiating them to the advantage alike of the municipality, the purchaser and themselves. They also deal largely in government land warrants and scrip, available in payment for govern-

S. A, KEAN & CO,, BANKERS, 100 WASHINGTON ST.

ment lands. The rapid growth of the operations of the bank has necessitated the establishment of a New York office, which has been recently opened at the corner of Broadway and Wall Street for the facilitation of their investment business in the East. Messrs. Kean & Co. are also publishers of a valuable digest of laws governing the issue of securities which, in consequence of their extended experience in such matters, is regarded as the highest authority.

Bank clearings through the Chicago Clearing House† (from 1866 to 1886, inclusive):

1866.....................$	453,798,648.11	1877.....................	$1,044,678,475.70
1867.....................	580,727,331.43	1878.....................	967,184,093.07
1868.....................	723,293,144.91	1879.....................	1,257,756,124.31
1869.....................	734,664,949.91	1880.....................	1,725,684,894.85
1870.....................	810,676,036.28	1881.....................	2,229,097,450.60
1871.....................	868,936,754.20	1882.....................	2,366,536,855.00
1872.....................	993,660,503.47	1883.....................	2,525,622,944.00
1873.....................	1,047,027,828.33	1884.....................	2,259,680,391.74
1874.....................	1,101,347,948.41	1885.....................	2,318,579,003.07
1875.....................	1,212,817,207.54	1886.....................	2,604,762,912.35
1876.....................	1,010,092,624.37		

The following is a complete list of the National banks:

NAME.	CAPITAL.	SURPLUS.
*American Exchange	$1,000,000	
*Atlas	700,000	
*Chicago	300,000	$ 100,000
*Commercial	1,000,000	200,000
*Continental	2,000,000	133,000
Drovers'	250,000	38,000
*First	3,000,000	750,000
*Hide and Leather	300,000	80,000
Home	250,000	100,000
*Merchants'	500,000	1,000,000
*Metropolitan	500,000	100,000
*National Bank of America	1,000,000	140,000
*National Bank of Illinois	1,000,000	350,000
*Northwestern National Bank	200,000	50,000
Park	200,000	9,500
*Union	2,000,000	300,000
Union Stock Yards	500,000	171,000
	$14,700,000	$2,335,500

†See Chicago Clearing House Association, page 266.

*Banks marked thus belong to the Clearing House Association.

The following is a complete list of the state and savings banks, with their capital:

NAME.	CAPITAL.	SURPLUS.
Chicago Trust and Savings Bank	$ 500,000	
*Corn Exchange	1,000,000	$ 500,000
Dime Savings	50,000	
*Hibernian Banking Association	111,000	
*Home Savings		
Illinois Trust and Savings	500,000	286,000
*International	500,000	
Merchants' Loan and Trust Company	2,000,000	1,000,000
*Prairie State, Loan and Trust Company	100,000	51,000
*Rock Savings	100,000	
*Traders	200,000	
†Twenty-Second Street		
*Union Trust Company	125,000	389,000
United States Bank	300,000	
	$5,536,000	$3,412,000

*Banks marked thus belong to the Clearing House Association.

†Capital not reported.

Business Houses.

PROMINENT AND INTERESTING MERCANTILE AND MANUFACTUR-
ING ESTABLISHMENTS.

A MONG the most interesting features of Chicago are her great factories, salesrooms and counting-houses, many of which have had
such prominent part in the rise and progress of the business interests
of the city that their history would be, in fact, a business history of
Chicago. A work of this kind would, therefore, be incomplete unless
this important element had some representation in it; but of the large
number of representative firms whose establishments and business
methods fairly illustrate the spirit of enterprise that has built up the
great commercial interests of the city, and that is still reaching out for
new fields to conquer, we have space to note only the few which follow.

Among the many topics discussed in the political economies, none is
of so absorbing interest or pre-eminent importance as that of trade,
the great mainspring actuating the wheels of industry and influencing
the prosperity of persons, communities and nations.

As in all other spheres of life, so in trade leaders spring up in the
various branches, who, by their enterprise, make famous the town or
city favored by its presence, and to whom redounds the credit of good
works. The requirements of modern commerce elevate each branch
of trade to the rank of a science to be carefully studied and progres-
sively followed, and the law of the survival of the fittest is absolute.
This must refer in large proportion to the dealer in art manufactures,
who must have a strong infusion of art knowledge and appreciation,
not unmixed with mercantile vim—the mainspring evolving science—
the foundation of all the higher occupations of life. In no field
of industry has progress been so remarkable as that of wall paper.
In 1860 the entire manufacture in this line in America amounted
to barely $2,000,000, and to meet the requirements as much
more had to be imported. The production has now grown to $12,-
000,000 annually, while the imports have fallen to $150,000.
One-third of the grand total of this trade is handled through Chicago,

although not a single piece of paper-hangings has been manufactured west of the Alleghenies. This astonishing fact leads us to seek some cogent reason for its existence. A brief sketch of the history of the trade will furnish an answer. In 1854 a young, active mechanic, just out of his apprenticeship and full of ambition and vigor, came to the city with a few hundred dollars and keen business ability. His enterprise found friends and enemies. The former encouraged him to greater ambition, while the latter spurred his enterprise to increased effort. The foundation of future success was laid deeply while quietly working at his business; the value of a day was learned and time became to him a very sacred thing. Thrift followed, and the largest wall paper house in the world was thus founded in Chicago by John J. McGrath. His refined appreciation of the art involved in his business induced him to constantly send able artists to Europe for the sole purpose of getting the most advanced ideas and the best works of designers of the highest celebrity, such as Christopher Dresser, William Morris, Welby Pugin, Moyer Smith and B. J. Talbot. The European manufacturers, not slow to perceive his approaching success, solicited his aid in distributing their products in the American markets, and he became the sole agent for

JOHN J. McGRATH, 106-112 WABASH AVENUE.

one German, two French and four English houses whose works are the foremost of their countries. The handsome building now occupied by Mr. McGrath contains 80,000 square feet of floor space, devoted exclusively to the jobbing and retailing of wall papers, and this great establishment has a frontage equal to four ordinary stores, on the east side of Wabash Avenue, between Madison and Washington Streets. The special importations of this house are sent to New York, Boston, Philadelphia, and all the great Eastern cities, and westward as far as San Francisco. Stuffs from India and Japan are to be found piled side by side with French, English and German goods, both woven and printed, and of rare beauty and value, and these with much more may be seen in a visit to this great establishment of the West.

Jansen, McClurg & Co.—It is a frequent remark among visitors from the east that Chicago possesses the best and most complete book-store in the United States; and traveled visitors sometimes add, "Yes, the best book-store in the world." This may at first seem extravagant, but after one has thoroughly explored the great establishment of A. C. McClurg & Co., at the corner of Wabash Avenue and Madison Street, the seeming extravagance is pretty sure to fade away. It is not merely that the firm occupy the entire six stories of a beautiful build-

ing 150×72 feet in size, but that here are found, in most surprising profusion, the finest and rarest books of all countries and times. In no one store in London can the purchaser of a well selected library find so varied a representation of the best editions of the classic English writers. This seems like strong language, but let the test be made, and see if it be not found true. Not only are all the best authors, English and American, found here in every variety of edition and binding, from the cheapest to the most sumptuous, but also the finest art productions of the European presses. The rarest masterpieces of book illustration

A. C. McClurg & Co., Wabash Ave. and Madison St.

from the pencils of Turner, of Stothard, of Blake, of Cruikshank and of Leech, as well as the later work of Gibson and of Vedder, are quite as likely to be found, in their earliest and best states, in this rich collection as the newest French novel or Mr. Howells' last fiction.

The vast realm of current literature is represented by every worthy English or American book. Medicine and surgery, science and political economy, form departments by themselves; and school-books, from the primer and spelling-book to the calculus and lexicon, are piled in the basement more like cordwood than literature. But when it is remembered that the multitudinous schools dotting the country, from Indiana to the Rocky Mountains and from the Ohio River to the northern borders of Montana, draw a large part of their supplies from this one source, the school-book mountains seem none too large. All parts of the great Northwest look to this house for their literary supplies, and libraries, book clubs and private buyers, as well as the local book-sellers in all parts of the western states and territories, are in daily communication with the firm, which has long maintained a very high reputation for fair dealing and courtesy. Although mainly book-sellers, their own publications are already getting a high character in the east as well as in the west. Should the visitor ascend beyond the second floor, which contains the general offices and counting rooms, he will find the upper parts of the building largely occupied with every variety of blank books and stationery, in which branch of trade their dealings are very extensive.

The merchant who comes to buy, the traveler who wants to pick up a new book, and the visitor to Chicago who desires to study its various phases, should none of them miss a visit to this really remarkable book-store.

J. M. W. Jones Stationery and Printing Company, stationery and printing, 167, 169 and 171 Dearborn Street. This is the oldest-established house in its line in Chicago, having been founded in 1835 by Stephen F. Gale. The firm afterward became A. H. & C. Burley, and in 1857 the business passed into the hands of Jones, Perdue & Small, in 1862 becoming Jones & Small, in 1866 J. M. W. Jones, and in 1876 being incorporated under its present style. The officers of the company are J. M. W. Jones, president and treasurer, and J. H. Swart, vice-president and secretary. They occupy a five-story and basement building, 63x120 feet, and two floors of the adjoining building, 40x120 feet, the premises being fitted up with modern improved machinery and appliances suitable to the requirements of the business. They employ 450 skilled and experienced workmen, and do a general printing, lithographing and stationery business, making a specialty of railroad printing and lithographing and railroad ticket printing. They also do general commercial printing and electrotyping in the finest style of the art, and keep on hand a large and thoroughly diversified stock of everything pertaining to the stationery line, including blank books, inks, ink-stands, hand-bags, fancy stationery, etc. The business is one of the largest in the country in its line, and the company has achieved an unexcelled reputation for the superiority of its work, promptness in filling orders, and correct methods in the transaction of business, enjoying the patronage of leading railway and other corporations, and the most prominent business firms of the West. Mr. Jones, the head of the firm, has had a long and valuable experience in the business. He was engaged in it at Troy, N. Y., his native place, prior to his removal to Chicago, and embarking in the firm of Jones, Perdue & Small in 1857. By close attention to all the details of the business he has built up the prosperous trade now enjoyed by the company and directed it to the achievement of a great and merited success.

The James Cunningham, Son & Co., builders of fine carriages and hearses, 390 to 396 Wabash Avenue, was established by Mr. James Cunningham in 1838, and was incorporated in 1884 with a capital stock of $803,000. The factories of the company, at Rochester, N. Y., are among the largest and best equipped in the world, and the vehicles manufactured are unsurpassed in every requisite of design, quality of materials and durability of service. The leading specialties of manufacture are landaus, coaches, broughams and victorias, and their trade extends to all parts of the United States. A large stock is kept in the repository in this city—390 to 396 Wabash Avenue—and the prices are always the very lowest. The Chicago house is under the personal management of J. W. Phillips, long experienced in the business. Branch houses have also been established in New York City, St. Louis and San Francisco.

S. Hyman & Co., diamond merchants and jewelers, State and Madison Streets. This house maintains an enviable position in this trade. It is located corner of State and Madison Streets. Founded in 1859 by one of those pioneers whom instinct led to this spot, the house has passed through wondrous mutations to be known in 1877 by its present name, when, on moving into its spacious and elegant quarters, Mr. M. H. Berg was added to the partnership. The firm ranks high in the character and quality of goods handled. The long lines of show cases, under a perfect system of lighting, dazzle the spectator with brilliant gems of exquisite cut and polish. The specialties of this house are pure water brilliants, their choice white stones being unsurpassed in loveliness. A visit to their rooms can scarcely fail to give one a considerable addition to their diamond lore. Thirteen salesmen are employed and the house does an extensive trade throughout the West. Mr. Hyman goes to Europe annually purchasing goods, making a personal selection and procuring the finest stock of diamonds and precious stones. Messrs. Hyman and Berg are both well and honorably known, and are thoroughly identified with the attributes of good citizenship.

John V. Farwell & Co., wholesale dry-goods; Monroe and Market Streets. This great house was established in 1855 by Mr. John V. Farwell, on Wells Street. The steady growth of his trade led to an early removal to more commodious and central quarters on Wabash Avenue, where the establishment stood at the head of the dry-goods enterprises of the West, when the business was wiped out and the stock reduced to ashes in the great fire of '71. But Messrs. Farwell & Co. bravely resolved to make the best of the situation, and soon opened in a new and large building which they put up on Monroe Street, and remained there until the completion of their present palatial block, which covers the largest superficial space devoted exclusively to dry-goods, staples and specialties of any house in the world. The building is majestic and imposing in appearance, and is a monumental edifice eight stories high, covers an entire block, is conveniently arranged and handsomely and substantially finished. Each of the eight floors embraces 52,000 feet of space, all of which is found necessary to adequately accommodate the enormous stock of goods herein stored, and representing the manufactures and products of all the leading commercial and manufacturing centers of the world. A thorough system of perfect organization characterizes every department of the colossal business, which employs 600 persons. The house of John V. Farwell & Co. has personal representatives in all the leading markets of Europe and America. The immense and varied stock of this house is adapted to the wants of purchasers in all parts of the country, and selected with special reference to the assortment required in each of the various departments of the business. It embraces foreign and domestic silks, satins, velvets, dress fabrics in all textures, white goods, linens, domestic cottons, laces, ribbons, embroideries, shawls, wraps, etc., with furnishing and upholstering goods, blankets, flannels, hosiery, gloves, underwear, carpets, Yankee notions, fancy goods, etc. The members of the firm are John V. Farwell, Charles B. Farwell, John K. Harmon, John T. Chumasero, and John V. Farwell, Jr. The senior member of the firm, Mr. John V. Farwell, stands high in the esteem of Chicago as one of the most public-spirited of her citizens, prominent in every charitable, philanthropic, moral and religious movement and in all humanitarian enterprises. The house includes among its customers all the leading dry-goods houses of the Middle, Southern, Southwestern, Western and Northwestern country, and the annual sales aggregate many millions of dollars. Strict commercial integrity and correct business methods have combined to place this among the leading dry-goods houses in the United States.

J. V. FARWELL & CO., WHOLESALE DRY GOODS, CORNER MONROE AND MARKET STREETS.

The Campbell Printing Press and Manufacturing Co., lithographic and printing machinery, 298-306 Dearborn Street, and 43-47 Fourth Avenue. The first Campbell press was built in 1858 by Andrew Campbell, of New York, and from that time on the Campbell press has been growing in favor with every class of printers and publishers. No company, in the cylinder printing press line, has probably made such strides in public favor as has the one of which we now write. Without doubt, one reason why the Campbell Company has so successfully appealed to American printers, is that its machines are not only American in every sense of the word, but *sui generis* in their mechanical movements. We believe every other cylinder printing press manufacturer has, in the main, copied and adhered to the leading features of the old Napier press; though, naturally, the form of these features has been changed from time to time backward and forward, in order to make them appear new or different; but, notwithstanding this, every cylinder printing press built during this century, except those built by the Campbell Company as also "Stop Cylinders," has been practically the same old Napier press which was not even American in its original conception. In short, during the last quarter of a century, the Campbell press has stood alone; and has therefore been the target of the more or less bitter denunciations of the older companies who were (and are) all tarred with the same stick, *i. e.*, manufacturing the same Napier movement presses, hardly varying them even in outward appearance sufficiently to enable the average business man to tell the one from the other. No one, however, has even seen a Campbell press who will not immediately recognize another on sight. The fact is, the Campbell press is like an American locomotive or an American bridge or American machinery generally, in that its builders cut loose from every foreign prototype and tradition, and being thus unhandicapped struck out for themselves and built a handsomer, lighter, faster and more durable machine, which does its work cheaper and better than any other similar machine ever did. Therefore, it probably is not to be wondered at that the Campbell Company should become possessed of such an immense and valuable business as theirs is now, and that this was done in the very teeth of all their competitors.

The home office of the Campbell Company is at 160 William Street, New York, and its Western office is at the address given at the beginning of this article. The factory is located at Taunton, Mass., where some 500 men are employed in manufacturing the sixty odd styles and sizes of machines comprised in its catalogue. At Brooklyn, N. Y., a very large repair shop is run in most commodious quarters, where some seventy-five expert machinists are constantly at work repairing second-hand machinery. Indeed, this concern deals so largely in second-hand printing presses that a spacious repair shop in this city (Chicago) has been run for years, in which in the neighborhood of twenty-five expert machinists do the repairing on the second-hand machines taken in trade in the Western States.

The officers of this company are: Mr. John T. Hawkins, president; Mr. John L. Brower, vice-president and secretary; Mr. Ogden Brower, treasurer and general manager; Mr. A. T. H. Brower, Western manager.

The Western business alone, of this company, counts up into the hundreds of thousands of dollars annually. It is not surprising, therefore, that the Western department of this concern being located in Chicago, is regarded with pride by all Chicagoans, and is esteemed as, in the best sense, a *home* institution.

The Gage-Downs Corset Co., corset manufacturers, 172 and 174 Market Street. This firm commenced business in 1884, under the management of L. A. Downs, president; and F. N. Gage, secretary and treasurer, and with a capital stock of $40,000. They do an annual business of $300,000; employ from fifty to sixty persons in their factory, and keep from six to ten commercial salesmen on the road. Their business is extensive, and principally in the Western and North-western country. They manufacture fifty dozen corsets per day, and occupy two floors, each 45×160 feet, at 174 Market Street. Their line of goods embraces corsets, hoop skirts, bustles, etc., while their specialty is the improved Downs patent self-adjusting corset. Their main office is at 172 and 174 Market Street, Chicago, but the house has several other agencies. This house is agent also for the Dr. Schilling Coiled Spring Elastic Section Health Preserving corset, the celebrated P. D. imported corset, imported French woven corsets, improved Madame Foy corset, the Duplex supporter, Thompson's Patent Glove-fitting corset, Madame Mora's Aldine corset, Dr. Strong's Tampico corset, the Honest Full-boned all whalebone corset. The materials from which the corsets are manufactured are the brightest and best, the machinery of the latest improved patterns, and their facilities for showing, handling and filling orders for corsets, entirely unexcelled. Its proprietors are men of sterling ability and marked honesty, and by their generous and cordial business manners they have won the confidence, respect and good will of the community, and the firm friendship of all with whom they have commercial relations.

Brown, Pettibone & Co., printers, stationers, and blank book manufacturers, 194 and 196 Dearborn Street; manufacturing departments, 194 to 214. This is a representative house in its specific line of industries. It was established nearly six years since, by Brown, Pettibone & Kelly. Subsequently, Mr. Kelly retired from the firm, and a little later Mr. Brown deceased, when the firm was reorganized, the present members being Mr. P..F. Pettibone and Mrs. A. C. Brown, widow of the former partner. From ninety to one hundred persons are constantly em loyed at the printing works and bindery, which are among the most extensive, and fitted up with all the latest and most approved styles of machinery and mechanical appliances. This house does all kinds of commercial, mercantile and general printing, book, job and catalogue work, and makes a specialty of county printing and blank book and card work, and has specially prepared itself for doing the legal printing and publishing of the several counties in Illinois and Dakota. Their convenient salesroom is stocked with every variety of stationery goods, and enjoys a liberal patronage, many of the largest firms in the city uniformly purchasing their entire supplies of this firm. In the line of blank books, Brown, Pettibone & Co. take the lead, their work being regarded as of very superior quality, only the best material being used in their manufacture, and only the most skilled workmen being employed. The manufacturing department comprises the entire basement floor of the Dearborn Street front of the Honore Building, reaching from the alley to Adams Street. The firm have a high commercial standing, and their business reputation is second to that of no other house of its kind in Chicago, while all who have ever had dealings with this house, unite in a general testimony of honest and fair dealing, and liberal treatment. We unhesitatingly recommend this house to such of our readers as have occasion to purchase stationery, or who have work to be done in either the printing or binding line.

Schweitzer & Beer, wholesale and retail dealers in toys and fancy goods, 111 South State Street, constitute one of the oldest and best known firms in their line in Chicago. The house was established by John D. Weber, in 1842, and the present proprietors succeeded to the business in 1868, since which time it has grown with steady and rapid strides. The salesrooms present at all times a busy and attractive scene, and the six capacious floors are stocked with a line of goods of the most diversified and comprehensive character, embracing everything known to the toy and fancy goods trade, including the products of the most noted American and foreign manufacturers. Mr. Carl

Beer, the junior member of the firm, crosses the ocean every year to make purchases and still further augment the wide acquaintance he has so long maintained with the trade in the old world. Mr. Edmund Schweitzer, the senior member, gives his entire attention to the management of the home business.

The Elgin National Watch Company, manufacturers of watch movements, American Express building. This representative Western in-

dustry was established in 1864. The present corporation, reorganized in 1865, has a capital stock of $2,000,000, and its officers are: T. M. Avery, president; J. W. Scoville, vice-president; William G. Prall, secretary; George Hunter, superintendent of works. The celebrated trade mark goods of this company are the "B. W. Raymond," "H. H. Taylor," and the "G. M. Wheeler" movements. All other movements bear the name of the "Elgin National Watch Company." The Chicago general agency occupies an elegant suite of rooms, where President Avery and Mr. John M. Cutter, the general agent, make their headquarters. The company started out on a capital stock of $100,000, and the business has grown so rapidly as to distance all competitors. They sell only to the wholesale trade, and do an annual business of

Davis & Morse Co., retail dry goods, furniture, etc. This is the largest general emporium of dry goods, fancy goods, millinery, china and general merchandise, in Chicago. This hive of busy industry, the Davis & Morse Company, is centrally and prominently located at the corner of State and Van Buren Streets. The establishment has a frontage of 260 feet on State Street, and extends 150 feet in depth, on Van Buren Street, covering an area of more than two acres. The bazars herein contained are devoted respectively to the sale of general dry goods, carpets, millinery, fancy goods, crockery, housekeeping goods, etc., and represent a stock of merchandise sufficient to fill a number of ordinary stores. The stores or different bazars in this grand system of salesrooms are systematically arranged, in the most uniform and complete manner, and in accordance with the ideas of convenience and economy in the expenditure of time and trouble. The counters divide the stores into rectangles, and pneumatic tubes radiate from each counter to the cashier's desk, so that there is no delay in making change, the customer's money being literally shot at the cashier by the force of a 60-horse-power engine, and the change instantly fired back at the clerk, while the goods are wrapped up before the customer. Nearly four hundred salespeople are employed in this unique village of retail stores, all under one management, and so perfect are things systematized that everything moves as smoothly as clock work. This grand central bazar was established in 1884, by Davis & Morse, but is now under the exclusive management of Mr. H. A. Morse, president of the company, Mr. Davis having withdrawn from the enterprise. This colossal retail house does a magnificent business, and in accordance with the original plan of selling all articles at retail at very nearly wholesale prices.

S. S. Barry & Son, house, sign and decorative painting, 258 and 260 Wabash Avenue. This is one of the largest and best known business houses in its line in Chicago, and was established by Barry & Cushing, in 1840. It employs from 50 to 150 sign, ornamental and decorative artists, and prosecutes every description of work in its line. Its office, workshop and salesroom, at 258 and 260 Wabash Avenue, occupy a floor 40×175 feet. The house carries a large stock of paints and oils, varnishes, putty and painters' and artists' material generally, and transacts both a wholesale and retail business. Their treatment of customers secures success, and they command the respect and admiration of the purchasing public for the spirit of generous liberality which characterizes all of their dealings.

Tompkins & Mandeville, manufacturers of harness, saddlery and turf goods, 180 Wabash Avenue. This representative house was established some thirty years since, by Benjamin Lane, who was succeeded by the present firm, consisting of W. L. Tompkins and D. V. Mandeville, in 1877. Their factory is located at Newark, N. J., where they employ between fifty and one hundred skilled workmen, and turn out annually several hundred thousand dollars' worth of goods. The Chicago branch of this extensive house is under the management of Mr. C. A. Meeker, who was, previous to coming to Chicago, in the employ of the firm at their factory, and who is well posted in all branches of the business. Their store at 180 Wabash Avenue is a large and commodious building, and their stock comprises a complete assortment of harness, robes, whips and turf goods generally. The Chicago branch does a retail business principally and makes a specialty of fine goods.

The Blakely Printing Company, 184 and 186 Monroe Street, have one of the best equipped and most complete printing establishments in the country, comprising twenty steam presses and all the other "ingredients" of a first-class printing office, in proportion. The enterprise was started in 1871, by C. F. Blakely, and the firm subsequently became Blakely & Brown, then Blakely, Brown & Marsh, and, in 1883, was incorporated as the Blakely-Marsh Printing Co., changing to its present title in 1885. D. Blakely is president, C. F. Blakely, vice-president and treasurer, and J. A. Bockius, secretary. The capital stock is $50,000, and the company do an annual business of over $200,000, with 132 employes and a pay-roll of over $7,000 per month. They occupy two floors, each 45×90 feet, giving them over 17,000 feet of floor space. They do all kinds of printing, including a great deal of newspaper work, but make a specialty of fine book and catalogue work.

·S. J. Surdam & Co., general hardware and stoves, 178 East Lake Street. This business was begun by Mr. S. J. Surdam, in 1839. The existing firm was established in 1852, the members being S. J. Surdam and A. Stelle. The building they occupy is owned by Mr. Surdam and embraces four stories and basement, each 20×160 feet. They carry a large and diversified stock of shelf and heavy hardware, cutlery, stoves, etc. This firm have enjoyed a prosperous career, their business having steadily grown from the first. They have cultivated favorable relations with producers, enabling them to offer superior inducements to buyers. Their affairs are conducted with enterprise and judgment, and the firm have the confidence and patronage of the trade to whose needs they minister.

George B. Carpenter & Co., and their immediate predecessors in the house they now represent, have been prominently identified with every step of the commercial development of Chicago for more than a third of a century. The business was established in 1840 by Geo. A. Robb, only three years after Chicago had been incorporated as a city. Five years later, in 1845, a partner was admitted under the name and style of Payson & Robb. In 1850 Payson retired and Gilbert

GEO. B. CARPENTER & CO., COR. SOUTH WATER ST, AND FIFTH AVE.

Hubbard entered the firm, the name changing to Hubbard & Robb. Upon the death of Mr. Robb in 1857. Gilbert Hubbard & Co. succeeded, and during the twenty years following advanced the house to a leading position in the trade, and the name of Gilbert Hubbard & Co. became a household word throughout the whole western country. Gilbert Hubbard died in May, 1881, and on the first day of the following year the vast business of the old concern passed into the hands of Geo. B. Carpenter & Co., who have since managed it with the same far-reaching enterprise and unswerving integrity that characterized the old establishment

OCCUPIED FROM 1859 TO 1871.

through so many years of eventful history. To-day Geo. B. Carpenter & Co. constitute the oldest and most favorably known ship chandlery house in the west. From 1859 until the great fire of 1871 reduced the city to ashes, the concern occupied a large iron front building at Nos. 205 and 207 South Water Street. An accompanying illustration presents the building as it then appeared. It was burned to the ground on the night of October 9th of that memorable year; but before the ruins were yet cold a tent was erected above the smoldering embers, and Gilbert Hubbard & Co. announced that they were ready to proceed with business. The tent answered the purposes of more ap-

AFTER THE FIRE OF OCTOBER 9, 1871.

propriate quarters until the ruins of an old grain warehouse at 14 and 16 Market Street were boarded up and put into order for the reception of a stock of ship chandlery goods. The new establishment was occupied in November following the fire, and was considered a great curiosity in its way at that time. Fully half of the rude structure was below the level of the sidewalks, as will be seen by the illustration on this page. In April, 1872, the business was removed to a capacious three story building—one of the largest and best that had been erected after the fire—located at 226 to 232 South Water Street. In 1874 the

14 AND 16 MARKET STREET, 1871.

erection of the present building was begun, and a year later it was completed and occupied. It is situated on the northeast corner of South Water Street and Fifth Avenue, is five stories in height, and is one of the best business structures in that locality. The upper story is used as a general storage room. The sail loft is on the fourth floor, and is the best equipped apartment of the kind in the country. The third floor is devoted chiefly to manufacturing purposes, and presents at all times a busy scene. On the second floor is stored a large variety of the lighter class of goods, such as cotton duck, in all widths, and twines and cordage of all weights. The offices and general salesrooms are on the first floor. In the cellar—a light, airy and perfectly dry apartment—are stored large quantities of heavy goods, including wire-rope, large sizes of manilla rope, heavy hardware and supplies for saw-mills, flour-mills, rolling-mills, mining companies and railroads. As manufacturers of tents, of every description, awnings, rain-proof covers, and, in fact, everything belonging to this branch of business, Messrs. Carpenter & Co. stand without a peer.

OCCUPIED FROM 1872 TO 1874.

Albert Dickinson is the leading seed merchant of the west, if not of the country, and his house is one of the oldest in the business. It was established in 1854, in a very modest way, by A. F. Dickins n, father of the present proprietor, as a South Water Street general commission and seed house. Albert Dickinson succeeded to the business in 1872, since which time the transactions of the house have been confined exclusively to the trade in field seeds of every variety. The busin ss has grown very rapidly, especially during the last ten years, and the trade of the house now extends to all parts of the United States ; also to Canada, Europe and other foreign countries. The buildings occupied comprise three spacious warehouses located, respectively, at 115 to 119 Kinzie Street ; 104 to 110 Michigan Street, and 198 to 204 Market Street. The stock carried embraces every variety of field seeds—clover, timothy, millet, flax, orchard grass, blue gra s, red top, etc., also bird seeds and pop corn—and is always sufficient to meet any demand. The office and salesrooms are at 115 Kinzie Street.

The **Diebold Safe and Lock Company** is represented in Chicago by its vice-president and western manager, John W. Norris. Although the manufactory of the company is located at Canton, Ohio, it may justly be classed as a Chicago institution. The vice-president of the company resides here, and its principal ware and sales-rooms are located in this city, which is the leading distributing point for the enormous product of the Canton factory. The business was established in 1860, and has steadily grown to the present immense proportions. The works now constitute one of the largest safe manufactories in the world. They give employment to nearly 1,000 operatives, and have capacity for turning out about fifty safes every twenty-four hours. The equipment of machinery and tools is the most complete that has been devised for the manufacture of fire and burglar-proof safes. Much of the machinery and other appliances were made expressly for the manufacture of special portions of the Diebold safes and locks, and are used exclusively by this concern. The use of the very best materials and the employment of these facilities in the hands of thoroughly skilled workmen in every department of the manufacture, secure a production as nearly perfect as it is possible to be, and the quality of the Diebold safe is unequaled by that of any other makers. Branch offices are established in all the principal cities of the country, and over 100,000 of these safes are now in use. This Chicago house has supplied all the leading banks, railroad companies, express companies, hotels, newspaper offices and corporations in Chicago and throughout the northwest with fire and burglar-proof protection of their valuables. Among such concerns in this city are: The First National Bank, the Commercial National Bank, the Merchants' National Bank, the Northwestern National Bank, and the National Bank of Illinois. The new City Hall has fifty vault doors and much other work of the Diebold Company's, and over $40,-000 worth of its work has been placed in the new county court-house. The Diebold safe is the standard and accepted champion throughout the great northwest, and this popularity is well deserved, as is shown by the thousands of voluntary testimonials sent to Mr. Norris by patrons whose safes have been tested by burglars or by fire. The sales of the Chicago house now aggregate nearly $1.000.000 annually. It is located at 57 State Street, the leading business thoroughfare, and in the very business center of the city. The stock of safes displayed here is always large and interesting. Visitors in Chicago should not fail to go through these salesrooms and inspect the wonderful safes, and time and combination locks, the mysterious workings of which are at all times cheerfully explained by an expert in the employ of the company.

Edward Ely & Co., the famous tailors, occupy rooms at the southwest corner of Wabash Avenue and Monroe Street. These apartments are located on the second floor of the building, and are fitted up in complete harmony with the purposes for which they are used. Messrs. Ely & Co. have long held the leading position of their vocation in Chicago, and they have, without doubt, done more to promote a high standard of elegance in gentlemen's dress than any other house in the entire west. Their fame is not confined to local or narrow boundaries, and the name of Edward Ely & Co. is familiar to people of refinement and culture in all parts of the country; and from this class is largely drawn their extensive patronage. The line of goods kept in stock by them represents the products of the most celebrated looms of the world. And possessing rare judgment and taste and the high artistic talent requisite for clothing a man of refinement and character with true fitness and expression, coupled with ample capital, extensive patronage, and a long, varied and successful experience, they are enabled to meet every demand of an exacting and appreciative public.

Sargent, Greenleaf & Brooks, automatic sprinklers, Gray's Patent Dry Pipe system, 43 and 45 Franklin Street. This representative Chicago house, established in 1872, is represented by Mr. S. N. Brooks. resident partner, and has for its correspondent the house of Sargent & Greenleaf, of Rochester, N. Y. Its specialty is the manufacture and sale of the celebrated Gray's Automatic Sprinkler, a patent dry pipe system, which automatically and unfailingly extinguishes a fire originating in any building where the pipes have been placed. The pipes are attached to the ceiling of the buildings, and the automatic sprinklers to the pipes; a generation of 160 degrees of heat melts the solder in the sprinkler head, releases the water gate, and the flames are quickly drowned out. A very small fire almost immediately sets the device in operation, and the flames are speedily extinguished. This fire-extinguishing device is approved by insurance companies, and a much lower rate of insurance is exacted from buildings protected by the Gray Automatic Sprinkler. Hundreds of testimonials are on file from property holders whose buildings have been saved by this device, and also from associations of fire underwriters, etc. This house deals in adjustable sheet metal elbows, Sargent & Greenleaf's unpickable key locks, time and combination bank and safe locks, spiral riveted pipe for compressed air, exhaust steam, city water works, hydraulic mining, etc. This company, at their Chicago house, 43 and 45 Franklin Street, employ some twenty persons. A specialty is made of an adjustable sheet metal elbow for stoves and other pipes, from one and one-half inch to ten inches in diameter, which in tin, galvanized, Russia, planished or charcoal iron is sold to jobbers in every large city from the Atlantic Coast to the Missouri River.

Abram Cox Stove Co., stoves, ranges and furnaces, 76 Wabash Avenue. This is one of the oldest, largest and most important houses in its line in the United States. It was established in 1847, and ever since has maintained the supremacy for the extent of its manufacture, excellence of workmanship and the superior quality of its goods. The company was incorporated, with Abram C. Mott, as president; George E. Hopkins, secretary, and R. Kahmar, treasurer. The Chicago branch was established in 1885, and Edward P. Mott, a brother of the head of the house, was instituted general Western agent. The works are at Philadelphia, and employ 275 men. The Western agency has attained to high importance, having an extensive trade in Minnesota, Wisconsin, Iowa, Missouri, Kansas and Nebraska.

U. S. Desk and Office Fitting Co., store and office furniture and fixtures, 194 LaSalle Street. This business was established in 1868, by Mr. William Lumley. In the great fire of 1871, he was burned out, but soon after reopened business at Monroe and LaSalle Streets, where he remained for nine years, removing later to 128 Fifth Avenue, since which he has remained in the immediate neighborhood of his present offices and salesrooms, 194 LaSalle Street. The business was incorporated in 1886. The factories are in Calhoun Place, between LaSalle Street and Fifth Avenue, and at Nos. 18 and 20 Sloan Street. The firm makes a specialty of fine office and store furniture and fittings, and keep a constant supply of the best kiln-dried lumber. They employ only the most efficient workmen and are always prepared to undertake any work in their line. Their trade is with the best business firms of Chicago and neighboring towns, and surrounding country.

R. W. Tansill is a name as familiar as any household word all over the western hemisphere and the Southern Pacific. His cigars are the best known of any proprietory brand in the world. In many Southern countries the name of Tansill is almost talismanic in its significance.

The business is solely the manufacture of cigars, in which such special and well known excellences are reached, that it is the largest cigar manufacturing house in the world. Especial efforts have been put forth in the manufacture and exploiting of the justly celebrated "Tansill's Punch" cigar, and the returns are gladdening to the projector's soul. The sales of this one brand from their Chicago house alone have exceeded 12,000,000 per year.

The history of this business is the history of Mr. Tansill's life. It most signally illustrates the value of brains and ideas in the well worn fields of advertising. The start of the new, young and untried enterprise was necessarily laborious and painful, but when the merits of the system and the value of uniformly reliable goods once became known, the public was more than generous in its recognition of merit.

At present the house has every facility to supply its immense trade, but it could be indefinitely increased if needed. As they aim to only keep up with the retailers all over the United States, Canadas, South America, Australia and New South Wales, there is no pretense of carrying a stock beyond these needs, and there is absolutely no old stock to carry at a loss or work off at a sacrifice. With from 1,200 to 1,500 employes engaged in the manufacture of cigars, under the most central and economical system possible, with the unique system of selling through local agents, and without a single drummer in their employ, the force of genius compelling the printing press and the government mail service to do what must otherwise, under the old systems, cost, the keeping of an army of salesmen, the whole of which is saved to the dealer (their agents) and the consumer. Taking these into consideration, and the secret of success of this immense concern is not hard to apprehend. Mr. Tansill has grown up in the pursuit of his business; his life has entered into it. Born in Virginia, yet he is the most typical of Chicagoans, and his qualities as a citizen are not the least lustrous in his career.

Giles Brothers & Company, jewelers, 99–101 State Street. This is the largest and oldest established jewelry house in the Northwest, and the only house which has ever engaged in diamond and precious stone cutting. The brothers, W. A. and C. K. Giles, established the jewelry business in Chicago a quarter of a century ago, and have prosecuted it ever since. The senior brother retired from the firm, but the junior partner remains, and is president of the incorporated company, associated with E. Morris, vice-president, and J. V. Ridgway, secretary and treasurer. The manufactory and salesroom occupy two spacious floors, at 99 and 101 State Street. In the workshop, on the second floor, upward of one hundred skilled men are employed, in the manufacture of new and original designs of jewelry, principally for the wholesale trade. The superiority of the goods manufactured by

Giles Brothers & Company is known and recognized throughout the country, and their manufacture stamp is sufficient to popularize all goods. The Giles Brothers are the sole manufacturers of the patent anti-magnetic shield for the protection of fine watches from electrical influences. This house imports largely from Europe, new designs in jewelry, statuettes, *bric-a-brac*, clocks, and articles of *virtu*.

Clement, Bane & Co., manufacturers of clothing, 202 to 210 Franklin Street, is another of those old and solid concerns, whose immense trade, wide reputation and substantial financial and commercial character, are the foundation of Chicago's mercantile empire. The house was founded in 1867, by H. C. Clement and others, as Clement, Ottman & Co. Subsequently the firm was changed to Clement, Morton & Co., and the latter were burned out at Nos. 27 and 29 Randolph Street during the

CLEMENT, BANE & CO., COR ADAMS AND FRANKLIN STREETS.

great fire. They continued business for the year after the fire in a frame building on Michigan Avenue, and for the next three years found better quarters at the corner of State and Madison, removing thence for greater room and convenience to the corner of Madison Street and Wabash Avenue, where they remained five years, when they removed, in 1880, to their present spacious and central premises at the northwest corner of Adams and Franklin Streets. They occupy an elegant five-story block, with basement, fronting 100 feet on Franklin Street and 160 feet on Adams, and giving them 96,000 square feet of floor space in which to store, display and handle the enormous stock necessary to enable them to meet all demands of their extensive trade promptly and satisfactorily. They keep thirty to forty cutters constantly employed, each keeping thirty to forty hands occupied in making up after him, so that the number of their employes, including twenty travelers, exceeds 1,000. Their trade extends eastward into Michigan and Ohio, and throughout the West and Northwest, and their annual business is about $1,200,000, while their yearly pay-roll requires one-fourth that sum. The firm was incorporated as a stock company in 1885, with Austin Clement as president and Levi B. Bane as treasurer. The capital stock is nominally $300,000, but abundant additional funds are furnished by the stockholders, and the average capital actively employed in the business is more than a half million of dollars. Before the incorporation the trade aggregated over two millions per annum, but the company has since pursued a conservative policy that has cut down its output more nearly within reach of its capacity, which is still close pressed to supply the demand.

The Erie Express, Wm. W. Chandler, Jr., general agent, Nos. 140 and 142 Monroe Street, illustrates the wisdom of extensive railroad systems undertaking their own express business. It must be said, however, that the express inaugurated in May, 1886, by the Erie system, has been under exceptionally judicious and energetic management. The Chicago office was opened July 15th, the U. S. Express Company withdrawing their equipment and service, and the new enterprise started auspiciously over all the lines of the New York, Lake Erie and Western railway branches and connections. It commenced with reduced rates, but has shown a remarkable increase of business, and the Erie Express now takes rank with the first-class express accommodations of the country. Mr. W. M. Clements, the general manager, was for a long time general manager of the B. & O. R'y main lines, and afterwards of the N. Y. P. & O., and is thoroughly experienced and competent. His enterprising management has been admirably supported and advanced by able lieutenants. Mr. Chandler was for two and a half years agent here for the Adams, but was induced to take charge of the Erie's interests at this point. Under such experienced control the Erie is doing most excellent and prompt public service, and handling its business to the satisfaction of its patrons. The main office at the numbers given is commodious and central, and supplied with every needed facility. Twelve wagons are constantly traversing the city, and forty-six men are employed. The stables are in the rear of 396 Wabash Avenue, and the depot office on 3d Avenue near Taylor Street.

Haines Bros., piano manufacturers, 366 Wabash Avenue. The Haines Brothers (Napoleon J. Haines and Francis W. Haines) are one of the oldest houses in the United States engaged in the manufacture of pianofortes, having been established in New York City in 1851, and continued the trade with marked success for the past thirty-five years. Their two immense factories are located on the east side of Second Avenue, occupying both corners of Twenty-first Street. Over 200 skilled workmen are constantly employed in the various departments turning out some 1,400 instruments yearly. The claim that this house manufactures the best upright piano in the market is generally acknowledged. They use the best seasoned wood in making their cases, felt for hammers, glue, varnish, and every other article required, price being no object. The Haines Bros. pianos are sold all over the United States and Canada, and many of them are exported to Europe and South America. Their merit has been recognized by the greatest musical artists. The prima donna, Adelina Patti, ordered one to be made for her which she now has in her castle at Swansea, South Wales, and she has many times expressed her great delight with it. Etelka Gerster also ordered one, which she has at her villa at Bologna, and says: "Neither in Europe nor America have I seen an upright that equaled yours in pure singing quality and great volume of tone or elasticity and evenness of action." Alwina Valleria and Emma Abbott are also the happy possessors of one of these remarkable upright pianos. Christine Nilsson, Clara Louise Kellogg, Scalchi, Marie Roze, Carl Formes, Ole Bull, Brignoli, used and commended them in the highest terms. The Haines Bros. have but one branch house, which is located in Chicago, at 366 Wabash Avenue. Same being established for the convenience of their Western trade, so that their numerous dealers can be supplied direct from headquarters at factory prices. It is under the management of Mr. Thos. Floyd-Jones, who has been connected with them for the past sixteen years. Their warerooms are filled with beautifully designed styles. Cases being made of rosewood, figured mahogany, French walnut, and ebonized finish on cherry. They are grand in appearance, and in tone, power, responsiveness of touch, evenness of register, singing capacity, and clear and sustaining articulation; they are truly a superb instrument. Manager Floyd-Jones has won a high reputation for his superior business qualifications in conducting the branch house, and the firm could not be better or more fittingly represented in the Empire City of the West.

The **Henry Dibblee Co.**, mantels, grates and tiles, 266 and 268 Wabash Avenue. This house was established in 1873, by Henry Dibblee. It was incorporated in 1886 with a capital stock of $75,000, and Henry Dibblee was chosen president, E. D. Redington, secretary and treasurer, and Anson S. Hopkins, vice-president and general manager. The trade of this house extends over every section of Illinois, and also into Wisconsin, Nebraska, Missouri, Kansas and Indiana. The house is one of the largest in its line of goods in the country, and in the specialty of mantels, tiles and grates, leads all other houses. They manufacture both wood and slate mantels, and control the sale of the celebrated Low's art tiles. The liberal and honorable dealings which have characterized this popular house, have had the result to favorably extend their reputation. The individual members of the firm are held in the highest esteem, both commercially and socially.

The **Barbour Brothers Co.**, manufacturers of linen thread, 108 and 110 Franklin Street. This is the largest thread manufacturing establishment in the world, and was started originally at Lisburn, Ireland, by William Barbour, 104 years ago, where the colossal thread manufacturing house of the world employed 4,000 operatives in their mills. The business was extended to the United States some twenty-three years ago, and the house now has works established at Paterson, N. J., which employ 2,000 operatives. The firm manufactures shoe and tailor thread, wax and sewing machine threads, carpet, saddlers', glove, bookbinders', seine and gilling threads, sail twines and macreme lace threads in all sizes. Robert and William Barbour conduct the business in this country, the former making his regular headquarters at the mill in Paterson, and the latter at the sales warehouse and general business office in New York City, while John D. manages the original business in Ireland. They are grandsons of the original founder, William Barbour, of a century ago. The Chicago branch of this patriarchal house was begun some eight months since, in order to supply the Western trade, which has grown to be enormous. The Western agency is in charge of General Manager Ben. Bartlett, who has a commodious and pleasant office, centrally located at 108 and 110 Franklin Street. Mr. Bartlett is a thoroughly practical man, and has been with this house the past twenty years, most of the time as their traveling Western agent. He has several commercial men on the road in all parts of the South, West and Northwest. The house which Mr. Bartlett represents has branch agencies in Boston, Philadelphia, San Francisco, Manchester, Glasgow, Dublin, Paris, Hamburg, Montreal, Melbourne, Sydney, Brussels, Amsterdam, Madrid, Milan and Naples.

J. Dunfee & Co., wood carpet or American parquetrie, 102 East Washington Street. The business of this house was established, in 1872, by Jonathan Dunfee. From 1880 to 1883, the firm was composed of Jonathan Dunfee and Goram F. Baker, but since 1883, Mr. Dunfee has conducted the business alone. In addition to the business of manufacturing wood carpet and inlaid floors, the firm makes a specialty of moldings and weather strips, and have a celebrated line of weather strips called the "Champion" of which they manufacture 40,000 feet per day. Their factory is located at 201 to 212 South Clinton Street, occupying the whole of the second floors, while their office is at 102 East Wash ington Street. Their trade extends all over the Union, and into Canada, and amounts to $100,-000 annually. Their wood carpeting, or ornamental hard-wood floor laid on top of the original floor, is growing in popularity and coming into general use, and combines beauty and utility. The work of this firm has been pronounced to be equal in durability, beauty and finish, to the best in Europe. A vast variety of designs in centre-pieces, borders, etc., is kept constantly in stock.

J. DUNFEE & CO., 102 EAST WASHINGTON STREET.

Murphy & Company, varnishes, 262 Wabash Avenue. This house is a branch of an extensive Eastern incorporation, having directors and resident managers in New York, Cleveland, St. Louis and Chicago. Franklin Murphy, of Newark, N. J., is the president; Charles D. Ettinger, of Chicago, is the secretary, and F. H. Taylor, the resident manager. The factories are located at Newark and Cleveland. Their business was begun in 1864, and has now reached an extent of half a million gallons annually. The Chicago warehouse and office, 262 Wabash Avenue, is adapted to a business requiring most watchful care and exercise of judgment in meeting the necessities of the many trades in which varnish is an important factor. In the warehouse is carried a stock of from 35,000 to 40,000 gallons of all the different qualities, kinds and grades of railway, carriage, cabinet, piano and house painters' varnishes and japans. "The Story of the Murphy Varnishes" is an elegant pamphlet of twenty-four pages, published by them for gratuitous distribution and describes in colloquial style the process of manufacture of varnish, the detail and extent of their business, and is elegantly illustrated with interior and exterior views of their factories and departments. This house stands unquestionably as the largest and most important in the business, whether considered as regards quality of their product or amount of sales.

E. S. & W. S. Fowler, manufacturing opticians and optical goods, 103 to 107 State Street. That the Fowler Bros., still young men, should locate in Chicago is no more a tribute to their business sagacity than it is proof of the cosmopolitan character of the Great Western metropolis. In the manufacture of optical goods a nicety and precision is required. The business of E S. & W. S. Fowler in five years' time has become firmly established. This firm makes a specialty of grinding lenses for all kinds of of optical instruments, and is the only firm in Chicago which utilizes steam power for this purpose. They manufacture exclusively spectacle frames, and in their test cases for oculists and opticians, in which a graduated scale determines the proper selection of lenses for the customer, they have conferred a decided boon upon suffering humanity. This house is introducing a new order of industry west of the lakes, and though only five years in operation, it is one of the most successful enterprises of the city. At their store and factory 103 to 107 State Street, all kinds of optical instruments, materials and findings for the trade can be found. This house deals in telescopes, microscopes, thermometers, lenses of every kind and description, opera glasses, optical instruments of all kinds, spectacles and eyeglasses, scientific instruments, etc.; while their factory possesses facilities and their workmen the skill, which enables them to undertake successfully the grinding any kind of lens and executing to order any optical work. The whole South and West pays willing tribute to the excellence of their goods.

Union Steam Boiler Works, McGarry & Leonard, proprietors, 36 to 42 East Indiana Street. This business was established in 1881, by Messrs. P. McGarry, J. Leonard, B. McCarron, Nic. Schneider and Wm. Becker. In 1884, Messrs. McCarron, Schneider and Becker retired from the firm Mr. E. Krueger taking Mr. Schneider's place, which he held until August 1, 1886, when he also retired. The firm occupies the one-story and basement building, 86×100 feet, at 36 to 42 East Indiana Street, which is specially adapted to the business of boiler-making, and is fitted up with all the machinery necessary to the efficient prosecution of the business. The firm manufactures every size and description of marine, stationary and locomotive boilers, lard tanks, coolers, sheet iron work of all kinds and everything in the iron plate line. As only the most skilled labor is employed and the best materials used in the work turned out by this firm, it has established a reputation for superiority of workmanship which has extended the trade of the firm to every section of the country, and they have even shipped work to the West Indies. In addition to the manufacturing branch of their business, the firm pays special attention to repair-work of all kinds, which they do in good, workmanlike manner, giving prompt attention to all orders and guaranteeing satisfaction in every instance. The twenty-five experienced workmen in the employ of this firm are kept constantly at work to supply the demands of their trade, which shows a steady increase every year and indicates a successful career for the firm.

Orr & Lockett, dealers in hardware, cutlery and tools, 184 and 186 Clark Street, make a specialty of fine building hardware for public and private houses, but carry a heavy stock in all lines. The firm is composed of Frank B. Orr and Oswald Lockett, both experienced hardware men, having been in the business for over twenty years. Their operations have figured largely in the re-building of the city, and their business has had a marked and rapid growth, due to their energy and enterprise, their thorough acquaintance with all the details of the trade, and their strict integrity in the fulfilment of contracts. This is the leading retail hardware house of the city.

Chicago Stained Glass Works, Max Suess & Co., proprietors, 216 East Lake Street. This house manufactures artistic, domestic, ecclesiastical and ornamental stained glass, furnishing designs and estimates on all orders on receipt of size of windows. The business has steadily increased since its inception, and the house has an extensive trade in the East, West, North and South. The firm occupy the third floor at 216 East Lake Street, 25×120 feet, and succeed Reimer, Flannigan & Vogt. That the reader may form an idea of the standing of the house and the esteem it is held in in local circles, it may be mentioned that they were awarded the contract by the city for furnishing glass signs for 12,000 street lamps. Their factory is equipped with all the modern machinery and appliances for the successful prosecution of their business. They carry a large stock of imported articles, embracing everything in their line, and have established most favorable relations with producers enabling them to offer unsurpassed inducements to customers.

P. Ringer & Co., book-binders, Nos. 52 and 54 Wabash Avenue. In this establishment one gets an earnest of the peculiar excellence of some of Chicago's enterprises. Some twenty years ago, when Mr. Ringer began the establishment in a humble way, there were book-binders here, but it was supposed that if any one wanted anything of peculiar excellence, or artistic design and execution, or of costly and novel character, done in this line of work, it would of necessity be done across the ocean, barely possible in New York or Philadelphia.

This is all changed now in Mr. Ringer's establishment; everything known to the book-binders' art in the use or manipulation of any kind of materials, all mechanical devices, and where known and approved, skill and ingenuity in design, experience in application, besides novel and peculiar features of their own, can be found in this house. It has grown because of its many excellences, and is a survival of those fittest to survive.

It is appreciated and honored by doing the sole work for many of our wealthiest, most literary and artistic citizens and eleemosynary corporations. It employs through the year some thirty skilled employes and saves to the country in general and Chicago in particular a large sum that erstwhile was spent abroad. People only consult their own benefit and inclination when patronage is bestowed on this firm.

Mr. P. Ringer is an old and well known citizen, who has conceived and carefully worked out, his idea; the value of his contribution to Chicago's enterprises can scarcely be over-estimated. Mr. H. Veit, the co-partner in the enterprise came, in later years, when the growth of the concern had made a division of labor necessary. Mr. V. is a practical workman and the details are in his hands, every item of which undergoes his constant scrutiny.

Coffin, Devoe & Co., leading manufacturers and importers of paints, white lead, colors, varnishes, brushes and artists' materials, occupy a spacious four-story and basement building, 190 feet in depth, at No. 176 Randolph Street. It is thoroughly equipped for handling the large and increasing business of the firm. The parent house—F. W. Devoe & Co., New York—was established in 1853, and has the largest works of the kind in the world. The Chicago house dates from Jan. 1, 1883. It is composed of Frederick W. Devoe, president; Gorham B. Coffin, vice-president; J. Seymour Currey, secretary and treasurer.

Mr. Devoe was formerly of the firm of Raynolds, Devoe & Pratt, the oldest paint house in the United States. Thus, with unsurpassed facilities, commanding the highest order of skill and experience in the preparation of their goods, using only the purest materials and employing the most convenient and prompt methods for supplying the trade, the remarkable success of this house is clearly the natural result of the conditions mentioned. They are masters of their business, and have made the best interests of the trade their study and aim. A heavy stock is kep in every line. The specialties of their own manufacture include

COFFIN, DEVOE & CO., 176 RANDOLPH ST.

chemically pure dry colors, coach and car colors, prepared paints, varnishes, brushes, tube colors, and artists' materials. These goods are prepared with extreme care at the extensive works of F. W. Devoe & Co., in New York, under the direction of Mr. James F. Drummond, member of the firm, who has superintended this department for thirty years. This fact is a sufficient guarantee of the excellence of their manufactures. Messrs. Coffin, Devoe &

Co. are pleased at all times to receive visits from all merchants and manufacturers who are interested in their line of goods, and an examination of their entire st.ck and premises is most cordially invited.

The Chicago Furniture Storage Co., Nos. 350 and 352 Wabash Avenue. Prominent among the leading and most reliable storage warehouses in Chicago is that of the Chicago Furniture Storage Company, at Nos. 350 and 352 Wabash Avenue. The building occupied is spacious and substantially constructed, the interior arrangements being perfect and affording every facility for the safe and secure storage of furniture, pianos, mirrors, works of art, and personal property of every description. The floors are large, well ventilated, and free from moist ure or dampness. There is also a number of private compartments with lock, key, etc. The premises are guarded night and day by watchmen, and only the most experienced men are employed to handle goods. This company was organized in 1875 and since its inception has enjoyed a most successful career. They have occupied their present handsome building since February, 1885. Mr. D. C. VanCott, president, is an energetic, clear-headed business man, honorable and fair in all transactions, and deservedly popular with all classes of the community. Mr. F. G. Sutton, the secretary and treasurer, is a gentleman of marked ability and sterling integrity. Under the judicious and liberal management of these gentlemen the affairs of the company are prospering, and its patronage steadily increasing.

The Chicago Rawhide Manufacturing Co., rawhide belting, lace leather, etc., 75 and 77 East Ohio Street. The officers of this company, which was established in 1877 and incorporated in 1878, are A. B. Spurling, president; A. C. Krueger, superintendent, and W. H. Preble, secretary and treasurer. The business was started at 38 and 40 West Monroe Street, and removed to its present location in 1882. The company manufactures rawhide belting, lace leather, rope, lariats, fly nets, picker leather. stock and farm whips, washers, hame straps, hame strings, halters and other rawhide goods of all kinds, by Krueger's patent. They have a patent on their hide curing process, two patents on hide working machines, five on stuffing, one on belt trimming machine and one on stretching machine, all of which are very valuable. The belt trimming machine will do the work of twenty-five men, and trims both edges at once. The company makes everything in the line of belting, round, square and flat rope and twist styles, that is used, from the smallest to the largest diameter. The rawhide twist and rope belting is made in sizes from one-sixteenth of an inch to three inches or larger, and this is the only house in the country that makes it. The premises occupied are a four-story and basement building 50×100 feet, and the largest in the Union in this line of business. Forty men are constantly employed in the factory, which is fitted up with the special machinery covered by the patents owned by the company. The trade of the house, which amounts to fully $100,000 annually, extends all over the Union, besides which the company has a very large and rapidly increasing trade with Australia and Canada. The success achieved by the company is demonstrated by the fact that the capital stock of the original par value of $150,000 is now worth $375,000, net. Their processes of manufacture exclude the use of either lime or acid, and as the life and strength of the hide is preserved and only the very best native hides are used, the belt and lace leather manufactured by the company is the most pliable and durable ever used for these purposes. At the "National Exposition of Railway Appliances" held in Chicago, in 1883, the first prize for rawhide belting and lace leather was awarded to this company.

Blake, Shaw & Co., Dake bakery, corner Clinton and Adams Streets. This representative and pioneer Western industry was begun twenty-five years ago by Joseph M. Dake, and has been conducted the past seventeen years by E. Nelson Blake, William W. Shaw and C. H. Marshall, under the firm name of Blake, Shaw & Co. The company occupy the entire building, four stories and basement, each floor 65×200 feet, at the corner of Adams and Clinton Streets. The firm consume in their baking operations 1,000 barrels of flour weekly. They employ upward of 150 persons in their extensive business, and their weekly pay-roll is about $1,200, paid to help in said building. Their city trade is enormous, and they ship hundreds of barrels and boxes of crackers, biscuits, etc., daily to all important points in the North, South and West. Their specialty is crackers and cakes, absolutely the finest goods in the country. This house has experienced a steady growth in its business from the first. Its bakery is equipped with every modern improvement for successful operation, and the company maintains the most favorable relations with millers and producers for the purchase of all its supplies, and is enabled to offer its patrons unsurpassed inducements. The business is conducted with ability, enterprise and judgment, and the company have an enviable reputation and command the confidence of the trade to whose requirements their efforts have been so earnestly and successfully directed.

Billings, Sheldon & Co., dealers in iron mines and mining stocks. This firm, composed of H. F. Billings, E. P. Sheldon, J. M. Lyon and Moore, Benjamin & Co., was established in 1886. Its offices and Gogebic Mining Exchange, are at 84 Washington Street. In addition to their business in iron mines and iron mining stocks, they also deal in mining properties of every description, in timber lands, ranches and land grants. The specialty of the firm is iron mines in the Gogebic range, and iron mining stocks. The Gogebic range, lying in Ashland County, Wisconsin, and Ontonagon County, Michigan, has recently attracted interested attention because of the wonderful developments and discoveries of immense bodies of iron ore in that district. Many valuable mines have been developed, and many more only await the hand of enterprise to yield up their wealth to those who will invest in them and utilize their resources. The soft and workable nature of the ore, and its close proximity to the surface, makes the mining much cheaper than in competing districts. Messrs. Billings, Sheldon & Co. are in a position to offer valuable mining property and stock in producing mines on advantageous terms, and they will make quotations to any person who may feel interested in the rich iron deposits of the wonderful Gogebic region.

C. Jurgens & Bro., 14 and 16 Calhoun Place, are practical and skillful electrotypers and stereotypers, and conduct one of the best equipped establishments in their line in the West. The house was established in May, 1884, by C. R. Perry & Co., the firm being composed of C. R. Perry and A. P. Sandberg. Mr. Perry retired, in October of the same year, when Mr. Sandberg and Mr. C. Jurgens succeeded to the business, under the name of Sandberg & Jurgens. On the death of Mr. Sandberg, in February, 1885, Mr. Jurgens took charge, and was joined by his brother Frederick the following June. The concern has an extensive city trade, and does a large business with all parts of Illinois and Michigan. The firm have all the latest and most approved machinery, including two of the most powerful batteries ever in use. Only the most skillful workmen are employed, and only the best material used, as the rule is to make the business satisfactory in every respect through the superior excellence of their work, their promptness in its execution, and their reasonable charges. They keep in stock leads, slugs, metal furniture and tint plates, and handle all kinds of type, cuts, borders, etc., and also fill all orders for engravers' wood, and for wood, photo and wax engraving, in all of which lines they do a large and steadily increasing business.

Fuller & Warren Company, No. 56 Lake Street, proprietors of the Clinton Stove Works, Troy, N. Y., are the recognized leaders in the wholesale stove trade not only in Chicago and the west, but of the entire country. The Clinton Stove Works were established in Troy in 1831, over a half-century ago, and since that time they have manufactured a greater variety and a larger annual production of first-class goods than any other establishment of a kindred nature. From a small beginning the concern has steadily grown to its present vast proportions, and to-day its goods are in demand in all the markets of the civilized world. The works at Troy are of mammoth proportions; they cover an area of nearly six acres of ground. The principal stores of the company are at Troy, Chicago, Cleveland and New York City. The Chicago house was opened in 1862, and the first building occupied, with all its contents, was burned in the great fire of 1871. But it was not long till the present commodious store at 56 Lake Street was erected. The building has five stories and a basement. The iron front, with its spacious plate-glass windows, is thirty-two feet in width, and the store extends through to the next street, a distance of 170 feet. It was built expressly for the purpose, and is provided with every possible convenience for the rapid handling of the extensive business.

FULLER & WARREN COMPANY, NO. 56 LAKE STREET.

The managers', book-keepers', and general offices are located on the main floor, at the right of the center, the remainder of the floor and the entire floors above being used exclusively for the display of samples. The basement, third, fourth and rear half of the fifth floors, are used for the storage of manufactured goods. The front half of the fifth story contains a tin shop, where a large force of workmen are employed in the construction of furnace casings, hot-air pipes, etc., used by the local furnace department. In addition to the Lake Street establishment a large warehouse is also required for storing the extensive variety which it is necessary to carry to meet the demands of the trade. This warehouse is situated on the north pier. It is five stories in height, 75×200 feet, and thoroughly equipped for the purpose. The stock carried embraces a complete assortment of the various styles of stoves, ranges and hot-air furnaces manufactured by the Clinton Stove Works, which includes everything in these lines that is demanded by the western trade. The transactions of the Chicago house are confined exclusively to the wholesale trade.

C. K. Luce & Co., manufacturers' agents, 152 and 154 Lake Street. This firm was established two years ago, Mr. Luce having been connected with another leading house for thirteen years previous to embarking in this business. They are agents for the Backus fire-place steam heater, the Backus patent improved bit brace, the Globe horsenails, etc., and add constantly to their line new and staple articles in hardware. They make a specialty of the Backus steam heater, a device of great merit which can be used in any room without stovepipe or chimney connection and can be moved at pleasure, using either oil or gas. The oil burner is peculiarly adapted to heating offices, parlors, dining rooms and sleeping apartments, and a great convenience for sick-rooms, the temperature of which can be regulated more surely by them than any other means. But very little time is consumed in keeping them in order, and ashes, smoke, smell and dirt are avoided by their use. The trade in these heaters is constantly increasing, attesting their growth in public favor.

Ira H. Tubbs Mfg. Co., carriages, harness, etc., 356 Wabash Avenue. This representative Chicago industry was established in 1871, and was this year incorporated with a capital stock of $30,000. Ira H. Tubbs is president and treasurer, and W. H. Tubbs, secretary. From thirty to forty men are regularly employed at the works, 356 Wabash Avenue, where 10,000 sets of harness are turned out yearly. The firm deal, at wholesale and retail, in carriages, landaus, victories, robes, harness, road carts, cutters, blankets, halters, whips, etc., but their specialty is the wholesale harness trade. They manufacture harness very largely, and exchange with carriage makers in all sections of the country. They make a specialty of selling complete outfits of horse furnishing goods, carriage and harness at low prices, and are always open to a trade for horses and ponies. Their harness manufactory is at 62 North Canal Street, and is a scene of busy industry. Mr. George Gale is salesman and business manager of the company. He is a practical, experienced man, and knows just how to handle their extensive affairs successfully, and the good results the business is experiencing are due largely to his well-directed efforts.

Fitz Simons & Connell, contractors for public works, dealers in lumber, etc., 1 and 2 Sibley Building, 2 and 4 North Clark Street. The business prosecuted by this enterprising and widely-known firm was begun in 1868 by Gen. Charles Fitz Simons, who has associated with him C. J. Connell. The firm contract for dredging, foundations, docking, canals, railroads, piers, etc., and for public works specially, and deal in pine and oak timber. The company own five dredges, which are constantly in operation on the pier and in the harbor, and at various points on the lake. Three of these dredges were built at a cost of $25,000 each. The firm put in the foundation of every double bridge in Chicago. They have lumber yards and saw mill on the north pier, with 800 feet dock front, over 200 feet in depth. This company built the Fullerton Avenue conduit, connecting the north branch of the Chicago River with the lake, and constructed many other important public works. The firm is entirely responsible, and have every facility for the successful prosecution of great public works, and undoubted ability to fulfill all contracts promptly in a satisfactory manner, and on reasonable terms.

The Mutual Trust Society, No. 95 Washington Street, was organized in March, 1867, with $300,000 capital. It is managed by a Board of Trustees, with Thos. B. Bryan, president; John D. Jennings, vice-president; Samuel D. Ward, treasurer; Franklin Hatheway, cashier. The objects of the organization are to execute trusts, manage and settle estates, make safe and profitable investments, arrange annuities, make collections, etc., in all of which it has many advantages over individual trustees, and gives every desirable guarantee. The charter being perpetual, the corporation can continue in charge of a trust for any length

of time. Mr. Bryan was the founder of the first safe depository in
Chicago. Mr. Ward is highly esteemed for his able and faithful execution of many public and private trusts.

The E. Howard Watch and Clock Co., manufacturers of fine watches
and clocks; Chicago office, 170 State Street. This well-known Boston
house established their Chicago branch in January, 1886. It is under
the efficient and energetic management of Mr. H. E. Howard. The
company is the pioneer in the business of manufacturing watches by
machinery, having preceded all others in this great industry. They
manufacture exclusively fine watches
and clocks in all styles, and in their
clock department making a specialty
of tower clocks, striking clocks, electric dials and electric watchman's
clocks. The company does a large
business, the superiority of their
goods and the solid reputation
achieved by them having caused their
trade to extend to all parts of the
world. A staff of energetic and experienced traveling men is employed
to represent the company on the
road. The Chicago branch has greatly increased and extended the trade
of the company in the West and
Northwest, and the commodious
salesrooms in this city, which are
conveniently and centrally located

THE E. HOWARD WATCH AND CLOCK CO.,
170 STATE STREET.

are completely stocked with the fine watches and clocks of the company's manufacture, attracting the patronage of the trade, by whom
these goods are regarded with the just appreciation due to their great
merit.

Field, Benedict & Co., importers of woolens and tailors' trimmings,
Franklin and Quincy Streets. This business was established in 1849
by Messrs. Field & Benedict. The present members of the firm are
Messrs. Amzi Benedict, Richard I. and Peter W. Field and Lewis S.
Perry. They carry an immense and well-assorted stock of all kinds of
woolen cloth, including broadcloths, cassimeres, tweeds and other
suitings, which they import direct from Great Britain, France and Germany. They buy direct from the manufacturers, with whom they have

established the most favorable relations, and by reason of their large trade and as a result of their judgment in buying, they are enabled to offer great inducements, both in quality and price, to the clothing manufacturers, jobbers and dealers who are their customers. The large and convenient premises occupied by the firm are favorably located in the heart of the wholesale business center, and are stocked from top to bottom with goods. The firm carries on an extensive business, not only with the dealers of this city, but also with those of Kansas City, St. Louis, Omaha, St. Paul, Minneapolis and the entire Northwest. All the partners, except Mr. Peter W. Field, who has charge of the New York branch of this great house, reside in Chicago, and the affairs of the house are managed upon progressive and honorable business principles which, together with the superiority of the goods handled by the firm, account for the continued growth experienced by the business since its inception and the present success of this old and thoroughly reliable house.

C. J. L. Meyer & Sons Co., manufacturers of sash, doors, blinds and interior woodwork, 133 and 135 Wabash Avenue. This business was established in 1860 by Mr. Charles J. L. Meyer, the present company being incorporated in 1883, with a capital stock of $300,000. The officers are: C. J. L. Meyer, president; H. P. Meyer, vice-president, and J. P. Meyer, secretary and treasurer. The company manufacture sash, doors, blinds and every description of interior woodwork and fine wooden mantels. Their large factories and warehouses at the north pier, foot of Michigan street, consisting of buildings five and six stories high, cover about two acres and are completely equipped with all machinery and appliances suitable to the requirements of the business. They are conveniently located, with every facility for the shipment of goods by rail or water. Their salesrooms and warehouse premises, at 133 and 135 Wabash avenue, are 50×160 feet, and five stories high. The business of the company is very large, giving constant employment to four hundred skilled workmen, and, in busy seasons, to a still larger number; and in addition to a large city patronage, their trade extends to all parts of the Union, and is especially large in Texas and all the Southern States. Mr. C. J. L. Meyer resides at Fond du Lac, Wisconsin, where he has the Fond du Lac Sash and Door factory. Mr. J. P. Meyer, the secretary and treasurer, has the general management of the business here, and Mr. H. P. Meyer has charge of the outside business of the company. The retail branch at Wabash Avenue is under the efficient management of Mr. G. W. Harrison, who has been with the company for four years. Five efficient traveling men represent the interests of the company on the road. The high reputation and great success of the company are the result of the uniform excellence of their work and the correctness of their business methods.

Simpson, Hall, Miller & Co., manufacturers of silverware, 145 and 147 Wabash Avenue. This business was established fifty-two years ago by Samuel Simpson, who is the president of the present company, which was incorporated in 1867, with a capital stock and surplus of $700,000. The other officers are: Gindon W. Hall, general manager; A. Andrews, secretary, and Charles D. Yale, treasurer. The factory is at Wallingford, Conn., and employs four hundred skilled workmen. The main stores of the company are at New York, Philadelphia and Chicago, and their business amounts to $1,200,000 annually. Their goods are of standard and acknowledged excellence, and their trade extends all over the world. Twelve experienced traveling men are employed by the company. The Chicago branch, which is under the careful and efficient management of Mr. N. M. Burchard, has steadily increased the local and Western trade and materially aided in the success of the company.

Rhoads & Ramsey Co., miners and shippers of coal and coke, and manufacturers and dealers in sewer-pipe, fire-brick, fire-clay and foundry supplies; general office, 107 LaSalle Street, Chicago. This company, of which Theo. Rhoads is president, C. H. Vehmeyer, vice-president, W.W. Ramsey, treasurer, and W. B. Mather, secretary, receive large quantities of best quality of Indiana block coal from mines at Brazil, Indiana, and Pittsburg coal from mines near Pittsburg. They also receive large quantities of anthracite, Hocking, Brier Hill and Piedmont smithing coal. Their Connellsville coke is acknowledged to be the best for rolling-mill and foundry use. They have three yards for the benefit of their trade, from which they will deliver any of the above coals in any quantity at desire of the trade. Their extensive yards are located at 89 North Elizabeth Street, 35th and Clark Streets, and at Englewood. At all these yards they carry a full stock of sewer-pipe, fire-brick, fire-clay, etc., and the yards are connected with the general office by telephone, enabling the filling of all orders promptly. All the yards are connected directly with the railroads, and coal of all kinds is received fresh from mines daily. The business of the firm is very large, and supplies with coal the leading industrial establishments of the city, and also ship largely to points west of Chicago.

STUDEBAKER BROS.' NEW CARRIAGE FACTORY AND REPOSITORY, 203, 204, 205 AND 206
MICHIGAN AVENUE BOULEVARD.

The four upper floors and basement of this building are devoted to manufacturing purposes, and the four lower floors are used as a repository, filled with all the leading styles of carriages and buggies, and a complete line of novelties. The manufacturing department is under the personal direction of Mr. J. F. Studebaker, who has made the building of fine carriages a life study, and who possesses the combined tastes of the best manufacturers in Europe and America. The Messrs. Studebaker also carry a full line of harness, robes, whips and turf goods.

Sweet, Wallach & Co., photographers' supplies, 229 and 231 State Street. This business was established in 1865, by Charles W. Stevens, who was succeeded by Douglas, Thompson & Co., he remaining a partner in that firm until January 1, 1886, when they were succeeded by Dexter B. Sweet and John F. Wallach, under the firm name of Sweet, Wallach & Co. This firm are importers, manufacturers and jobbers in every description of photographers' supplies, including cameras, lenses, backgrounds, frames, mats and all the standard and most recent publications on the art of photography and kindred subjects. Their premises are commodious and conveniently located in the heart of the business center, and their stock is large and diversified, embracing everything in their line. They have a large force employed in their warehouse, salesroom, manufacturing and shipping departments, to fill the numerous orders which they daily receive from all sections of the country, and have a number of commercial men on the road, who are practical photographers, extending their field of operations, and securing for Chicago a large and valuable line of trade which formerly went to the East. The business of the house, which had reached large proportions under the management of their predecessors, has greatly augmented, as a consequence of the energetic and enterprising methods of the present firm, the members of which are practical and experienced and attentive to every detail of the business. Their facilities are of the best character, and their promptness in filling orders, the superiority of their goods, and the liberal inducements offered to their customers have combined to achieve for them an assured and merited success.

B. D. Baldwin & Co., manufacturers of perfumes, 177 Wabash Avenue. This firm is an old-established one, and the goods produced by them are well and favorably known to the trade by reason of their superior quality. Their manufactory and store are completely fitted to suit the requirements of their business, which extends to every part of the Union, seven experienced traveling men being employed to represent them on the road, and their trade is constantly increasing as a result of the merit of their goods and the correctness of their business methods. The affairs of the house are supervised by Mr. B. D. Baldwin, to whose judicious management may be attributed the success achieved by the firm.

B. O. Van Bokkelen, manufacturers' agent and commission merchant, 46 and 48 Michigan Avenue. This business was established in 1878 by Mr. Van Bokkelen, who represents some of the leading houses in the United States, including among others C. Gilbert, manufactures of starch; the R. W. Bell Manufacturing Co., soap and sal-soda; the Dunham Manufacturing Co., St. Louis, cocoanut; the Quaker Mill Co., Ravenna, O., oatmeal and rolled oats; Winters & Prophet, Mt. Morris, N. Y., canned corn; Littlefield, Allison & Co., San Francisco, California, fruits, etc.; Southern California Packing Co., Los Angeles, Cal., canned fruits, etc. Mr. Van Bokkelen makes a specialty of California raisins. He employs fourteen salesmen, packers and clerks, and does an extensive trade throughout the West and Northwest. He is a practical and experienced business man, and has achieved success as the result of his industry and enterprise.

W. W. Boyington, architect, room 107, No. 157 LaSalle Street. Established in Chicago about thirty years ago, and continuously engaged in the practice of his profession ever since, Mr. Boyington has achieved a reputation as an architect not surpassed by any in this country. That great triumph of the architectural art, the new Board of Trade building, was built from his designs after competition with all the leading architects. This immense structure, built at an expense of $1,500,000, is the pride of Chicago. Many others of the most prominent buildings in this city attest the skill of Mr. Boyington, among them the Rock Island and Northwestern depots, the Royal insurance building, the Grand Pacific hotel, the Sherman house. In the general rebuilding of the city after the great fire of 1871, Mr. Boyington bore a prominent part, having in charge three miles of continuous street front of buildings. His extensive patronage by the wealthiest and most enterprising of our citizens has been achieved by proficiency and his careful supervision of every detail of his business.

Dahinten, Feulner & Scott, art glass-stainers, 16 and 18 Third Avenue. This firm is composed of F. X. Dahinten, Sr., John Feulner, and John Scott. The business was established some two years since, at 16 and 18 Third Avenue, and has built up a large trade, extending all over the country. The members of the firm are practical men, with a long experience in this special line of business. This house does first-class work, which has attracted a deal of attention, and in consequence of their superior quality of stained wares has built up a large business. The house furnishes church work, stained memorial and chancel windows, and work for public buildings and private residences. Their factory and storerooms at 16 and 18 Third Avenue are commodious and convenient, and well calculated for the successful prosecution of their business, each room being 30×60 feet.

Monrad, Pushman & Co., importers and commission merchants in Turkish goods, 215 Wabash Avenue. This, the only establishment in its special line in the city, is under the management of G. M. Monrad and H. T. Pushman, both of whom have had a large experience in this branch of trade, being Turkish Armenians and acquainted with the goods they handle, which includes Turkish rugs, Oriental carpets, embroideries and art treasures. They have been established here three years and had a similar store in New York for two years before coming here. Their trade has grown since its inception and extends to all parts of the country, the great merit of their goods securing them the success they have achieved.

L. B. Mantonya & Co., wholesale commission boots and shoes, 227, 229 and 231 Adams Street, Chicago, Ill. This house was established in 1865 by Lucius B. Mantonya, and is the oldest and largest exclusive commission boot and shoe house in the city. They sell bankrupt stocks and job lots of boots and shoes from manufacturers, jobbers and retailers, and also have a large line of boots, shoes and slippers from manufacturers who must find an outlet for their over-productions. They are also sole agents for the production of many makes, such as the Rochester Seminary and the Queen Anne shoes for ladies and misses, the Pilgrim for men, the Nabob for boys and youths, the College Philadelphia grain for children's and misses' school shoe, the genuine Sucker boots in Chicago kip, real kip and calf, and the Boston Ideal Rubber Co. Country merchants should call upon them when visiting Chicago, or send for their beautiful illustrated price list.

Palmer House Livery, Leroy Payne, proprietor, 169 to 173 Michigan Avenue. This business was established by Mr. Payne in 1875, after an extensive experience in the same line in other cities, at 145 Michigan Avenue. The rapid increase in his patronage caused him to remove, in 1880, to the commodious buildings which he now occupies, and which are not surpassed in extent or equipments by any establishment of its kind in the West. His stable is stocked with fine roadsters and carriage horses, and his carriages are of the best makes and include coaches, coupes, buggies, victorias, T-carts, road-wagons, etc., in great variety. A large force of skillful assistants are employed in each department of the business, and the excellence of the service and the superiority of the animals and vehicles provided by this livery have earned it an immense patronage among the prominent citizens of and visitors to the city. The guests of the Palmer, Leland and other first-class hotels patronize this livery extensively. A valuable adjunct to this business is the "Horse's Home," at Chebanse, Ill., fitted up at a great expense as a resort where animals can rest, recuperate or go into comfortable winter quarters, with nearly half a mile of stalls, large paddocks, a half-mile track and ample accommodations for 500 horses. A large oval-shaped building, one-eighth of a mile in circumference, has recently been added at an expense of $20,000, enclosing a track for exercising horses in extremely cold or other inclement weather. A 40-horse power engine is used for grinding grain and cutting hay for the horses, and with careful grooming and constant attention this great equine resort justifies the name it bears. The farm rates are low, considering the service, and transportation is furnished free both ways for horses sent for two months or more.

American Waltham Watch Company, Robbins & Appleton, selling agents, 104 State Street, Chicago, Ill.; also represented at New York, Boston, Sydney, N. S. W., London, England, and Geneva, Switzerland. The nucleus of this corporation was established at Waltham, Mass., in 1852, since which time its growth has been phenomenal. Their present daily production exceeds 1,500 movements, and an equal quantity of watch cases, employing in all the departments of manufacture upwards of 3,500 skilled workmen. It may interest the reader to know that the average Waltham movement undergoes 3,746 operations in the process of making, requiring an average of twelve months to complete. No American industry has made such substantial progress as the science of watch-making, and its success can be attributed solely to the untiring vim and enterprise common to our people. It is unnecessary to laud the time-keeping qualities of the Waltham watch. Over 3,000,000 of them are now being carried in the pockets of consumers, who will, no doubt, attest to their merits.

Chandler-Brown Co., commission merchants, by close application to the interests of their customers and honorable dealing for the past twenty years and upwards, have earned for themselves a reputation second to none in the business. Their specialties are grain, seeds and provisions. Their Chicago office is in the Board of Trade, and Milwaukee office, Chamber of Commerce. They are also receivers of live stock, with offices at the Stock Yards in both cities. They are strong financially, their acquaintance is extensive, and by their correct business methods have earned and maintain a leading position with the trade here and elsewhere. The officers of the company are: E. H. Chandler, president; G. W. Chandler, treasurer, Milwaukee; and J. Austin Brown, secretary, Chicago.

Oscar Cobb, theatrical constructor, architect and superintendent, Major block. Mr. Cobb has for years devoted his attention to the architectural designing and construction of theatres, etc. He has made a special study of the subject, and is believed to be the safest authority upon it in the country. He is the inventor and proprietor of most that is valuable in the way of new discoveries in regard to the safety, comfort and adornment of theatres, such as fire-proof proscenium screens, side graduating or drop boxes, undercurrent system of heat and ventilation, fire-proof asbestos drop-curtain, upper front proscenium head-light, stage smoke escape and ventilation, all of which have met with remarkable success and a complete recognition of their practical utility. Among other theatres built or remodeled in accordance with his plans and designs are: Wieting Opera House, Syracuse, N. Y.; Grand Opera House, Minneapolis, Minn.; the Columbia Theatre, Chicago, Ill.; Grand Opera House, St. Louis, Mo.; Schultz & Co.'s Opera House, Zanesville, O.; Coates' Opera House, Kansas City, Mo.; Academy of Music, Chicago, Ill.; Keokuk Opera House, Keokuk, Ia.; Standard Theatre, Chicago, Ill.; Heuck's New Opera House, Cincinnati, O.; Louisville Opera House, Louisville, Ky.; New Grand Opera House, St. Louis, Mo. Mr. Cobb's business flourishes because of the peculiar and exceptional ability and zeal which he brings to every commission entrusted to his hands.

George H. Edbrooke, architect, 110 Dearborn Street, has been engaged in the active practice of his profession in Chicago for about twenty-three years, and has achieved a reputation as a leader among the architects of Chicago, and has aided by his skill and taste in the great architectural improvement in the city since the fire of 1871. He attends to all the details of his art and the business connected with it, gives estimates, furnishes plans and supervises the construction of buildings from his designs. Among the buildings erected upon the plans and under the direction of Mr. Edbrooke may be mentioned the Otis Block, Old Republic Life Insurance building, J. M. W. Jones building, Adams Express, Hiram Sibley's fire-proof warehouses, Chicago College of Physicians and Surgeons, Chicago Homeopathic College, the South Congregational Church, and many other important business and public edifices, as well as a large number of the finest residence buildings in Chicago. He is also the architect of many public and private buildings at the East and throughout the West, and has now in course of erection a ten-story block, for commercial purposes, both in St. Louis and Detroit, that will be, for the uses designed, far superior to any structure in either city. Mr. Edbrooke is master of his art, and the buildings planned by him are much admired for their happy combination of the practical with the artistic, and the careful attention given to every minute detail of construction. Among the many elegant private residences designed by him, his own dwelling, at No. 3316 Calumet Avenue, called the "Amoy Cottage," is a beautiful example of the Queen Anne style, and is a model of convenience and exquisite taste. His success in his profession has been very great and has been fully deserved, as being the result of a conscientious performance of everything he has undertaken and the great skill with which he has executed every commission.

S. J. Stebbins, builders' hardware, 231 State Street. This business was established in 1860 by Jones & Reardon, the firm afterward becoming Jones & Stebbins, and now being conducted by Mr. Stebbins as successor. The salesrooms and offices are centrally located, and the stock embraces a full line of builders' and general hardware, is well assorted and the product of the best manufactories. The house does a large trade with builders and contractors in this city and all parts of the West, and also sells largely to jobbers and dealers. By careful supervision of every detail of business, promptness in filling orders, and the application of correct methods to all his transactions, Mr. Stebbins has maintained the high reputation established by this house and achieved a merited success and the confidence of the trade.

William C. Stevens & Co., foreign and American works of art, 24 and 26 Adams Street. Mr. Stevens is the leading representative of art in the West. He commenced business in Chicago nine years since, and is associated with Mr. Charles F. Haseltine, of Philadelphia, the largest importer of works of art in the United States, who, several times a year, exhibits and places on sale at the Stevens' gallery fresh European importations. Last year this house sold one picture alone for $55,000—Meissonier's "Vidette,"—the purchaser being Mr. Albert A. Munger. The Stevens galleries are large, well lighted and usually hung with many thousands of dollars' worth of paintings by eminent artists. Mr. Stevens manufactures artistic frames to order, the framing and carving being hand work. In his extensive storerooms are displayed proof engravings, etchings, etc. Mr. Stevens' patronage embraces wealthy art connoisseurs, and he issues special invitations and gives art receptions two or three times a year—whenever he has an exhibition or new importation of famous paintings—which are society events of considerable importance.

A. Zinn & Sons, machine and hand-sewed shoes, 24 State Street. This firm, established two years ago, are wholesale manufacturers of fine shoes for women's, misses', children's and infants' wear exclusively. Mr. A. Zinn was formerly a prominent retailer in the same line, and his sons and partners, Messrs. Frank, Henry and John Zinn, were trained to the business. The premises occupied by the firm are commodious and central, and the stock is large and diversified. Their trade has grown since its inception and extends all over the West and North-west. Mr. A. Zinn gives his personal attention to the manufacturing operations, while Mr. Frank Zinn attends to the office business, and Messrs. Henry and John Zinn travel in the interest of the firm. The great merit of the goods manufactured and the correct business methods employed have earned for the house a good reputation and substantial success.

C. C. Holton, parlor furniture, lounges, etc., 224–228 Wabash Avenue. This is one of the most extensive furniture houses in Chicago. It occupies five stories, 60x160 feet, and employs 100 men, and does an annual business of $300,000. Mr. Holton established the business in 1869, which he has successfully prosecuted the past seventeen years. His trade reaches every section of the country. His business is confined to the upholstering of parlor furniture. The richness and excellence of his work is unexcelled. Mr. Holton came to Chicago from California eighteen years ago, and has identified himself with its interests, is a prominent and honored member of society, and holds several important positions of honor and trust.

D. Webster King & Co., one of the most pushing and energetic houses in the country, have recently located here, and it speaks well for Chicago that she can draw within her borders such representative firms. In addition to their large and commodious store, Nos. 52 and 54 Wabash Avenue, they have stores in Boston, New York, St. Louis, and a resident agent in Cincinnati. Their business is immense, and in their stock of glue can be found the largest variety of domestic and foreign carried by any house in this country. In addition to their own standard grades, so favorably known throughout the country, they carry the entire stock made by several New England glue factories, and one must be hard to please who cannot make a selection from their large variety. They have for many years sold the New England flint paper, and still continue to handle it in all of their stores. An important addition to their business is the sale of Wellington mills London emery, for which they are the sole United States agents.

Patton & Fisher, architects, 115 E. Monroe Street. The Scoville Institute is the pride of the beautiful suburb of Oak Park, and is prob-

THE SCOVILLE INSTITUTE, OAK PARK.

ably the finest library building in the West. It is the gift of Mr. James W. Scoville, who has spared neither pains nor money in carrying out the designs of the architects, Messrs. Patton & Fisher. The exterior walls are constructed of rock-faced ashlar of a handsome, bluish limestone, with trimmings of buff Bedford limestone. The interior is thoroughly fire-proof. The broad stairway and the wainscoting of the halls are of marble, and the various rooms are finished in oak and mahogany. On the first floor is a book room, to contain 30,000 volumes, a reading room,reference library and reception room. The second story contains a lecture hall and committee rooms, and an elegantly furnished suite of rooms for the use of the trustees. The spacious attic is used as a gymnasium. The ventilation has been most carefully planned by the architects, and nothing left undone to make the building a model of its class and a monument to the generosity of the donor.

The Pope Manufacturing Co., 115 Wabash Avenue, manufacturers, of the Columbia bicyles and tricycles. This company was established and incorporated in 1878, under the joint stock laws of Massachusetts, with a capital of $100,000. The principal office is in Boston; Albert A. Pope, president, and Edward W. Pope, secretary. Their factory at Hartford, Ct., which is the largest of its kind in the world, employs 400 men and has a capacity of fifty machines per day. This company was the pioneer in the bicycle business of America, and to-day there is not a State in the Union in which the "Columbia" is not a household word. The popularity of the Columbia is proved by the fact that there are more of them sold every year than the product of all other manufacturers and importers combined. In connection with their bicycles and tricycles, they are Western agents for the Shipman automatic steam engine, the greatest invention of the age, and also for R. J. Douglas & Co.'s pleasure and hunting boats and steam yachts. R. D. Garden, formerly with the Boston office, has full charge of the Chicago branch, and under his intelligent management the business is increasing from month to month.

E. H. Sargent & Co., importers and dealers in drugs, chemicals, etc., 125 State Street. In 1851 Mr. Sargent became a partner in the house of F. Scammon & Co., one of the pioneer drug houses of Chicago, which, in a few years, became Sargent & Ilsley, and in 1860 adopted the present style. This is the only drug house in the city that makes a specialty of all kinds of chemicals and chemical apparatus, including assayers' materials, assayers' furnaces and mining chemicals, and a full line of glass, platina and porcelain ware of their own importation, and every known drug and chemical is kept in stock. The firm are agents for the Battersea Crucible Co., of London; Fletcher's laboratory apparatus; Troemner's, Becker's and the best German analytical and assay balances; Beck's microscopes and Brown's assay furnace. They are also publishers of Brown's Manual of Assaying, and carry surgical instruments of every conceivable kind, many of their own manufacture. The business is very large, the firm sustaining a high reputation throughout the country. Mr. E. H. Sargent, the head of this firm has, at different times been honored with the presidency of the Chicago College of Pharmacy, the American Pharmaceutical Association, and more recently of the Illinois College of Pharmacy, a department of the Northwestern University.

L. Manasse, optician, wholesale and retail dealer in optical, mathematical and surveying instruments, 88 Madison Street. Manasse's name is as a household word and is familiar to every man, woman and child within a radus of one hundred miles of Chicago. Manasse is the leading optician of the Northwest, and meteorologists invariably swear by his weather reports and his incomparable thermometers. He established the business of optician in this city in 1868, and ever since has taken the lead in the manufacture and sale of spectacles and eyeglasses, opera and field glasses, telescopes, microscopes, barometers, thermometers, medical batteries, artificial human eyes, and in the importation of drawing materials for engineers, architects, surveyors and draughtsmen. Mr. Manasse is a practical optician, and in the department of scientific knowledge of the eye is an acknowledged expert. He has made the manufacture of optical instruments a scientific study, which he has put to practical application all his life, both in Germany and in America. His business occupies three floors of the immense building, 88 Madison Street. His trade extends all over the Eastern and Western country, orders by mail and express being received daily. A large force of men are constantly employed both in his manufacturing establishment and in the store. Mr. Manasse's meteorological reports, which have been regularly kept up for a number of years and daily furnished to the public, are standard authority, and rank with the records of the government weather bureau. Mr. Manasse stands high commercially, and is honored and esteemed socially by all who know him.

Baldwin & Durham, wholesale and retail dealers in furniture, 280 and 282 Wabash Avenue. This firm, composed of Messrs. L. Baldwin and James Durham, was established four years ago. They carry a full stock of furniture, embracing parlor and bed-room sets and a general line of folding beds, all of the finest and most select quality, which they sell at the lowest prices. They maintain pleasant relations with the purchasing public, and have a large trade, extending through the East, West and South. Mr. Baldwin attends to the office and financial transactions, while Mr. Durham supervises the buying and selling. Their correct business methods and fairness of dealing have popularized this house with the public.

M. W. Kerwin & Co., Kentucky whiskies, 10 and 12 Wabash Avenue. The members of this representative house are M. W. Kerwin and M. W. Murphy. The business was begun in 1871 by Messrs. Keely & Kerwin, who were subsequently succeeded by the present proprietors. They are wholesale dealers in hand-made sour mash whisky and in wines and liquors generally. They have a large city trade, and their goods are shipped in enormous quantities to all parts of the Western and Northwestern country. They import in large quantities wines, brandies, gins, whiskies, etc., and deal extensively in wines of native product and the most approved California vintages. The house carries a large stock of the best goods, selling nothing which has not an age of three years, and having in store hundreds of barrels and thousands of bottles of liquors and wines from four to eight years of age.

Charles A. Allen, gold, silver and nickel plating, 182 State Street. Mr. Allen established himself in the business of gold, silver and nickel plating, and repairing and repolishing, in Chicago fourteen years since, and his works have grown in extent and increased in the magnitude of their operations every year since that time. His plating shop is fitted up with all the machinery, apparatus and appliances necessary or convenient for the prosecution of the business, and the quality and finish of his work stands high with the trade. Goods which are worn are replated and refinished and made as good as new. Mr. Allen has always paid assiduous attention to his avocation, and his faithfulness to the interests of his business, and his systematic and efficient management have proven the prime factors of a pronounced success. His business reputation is an honorable one, and his close attention to all the details of his business has attracted a large and constantly increasing patronage.

E. B. Millar & Co., importers of teas, coffees and spices, 41 to 43 Wabash Avenue. This business was established about ten years ago, and was formed into an incorporation in 1881, with a capital stock of $100,000. The officers of the company are S. O. Blair, president; H. W. Dudley, vice-president; G. E. Fuller, secretary, and G. H. Clark, treasurer. They are direct importers of teas from Japan, and they make a specialty of first pickings of the new crop Uji leaf purchased for them specially and protected under their trade-mark brand of "The Mikado Tea," which is an absolutely pure uncolored tea of the choicest quality. They also import and roast coffees of all grades, and their mill is one of the largest in the city. They are also importers and grinders of spices, in the selection of which they take special care to get nothing but the best and purest, protecting them with their trade-mark of "Penang Spices." Another specialty of the firm is Millar's Genuine Cream Tartar Baking Powder, a perfect, practical and hygienic article of the highest merit. The firm are manufacturers of mustard, flavoring extracts and other articles in their line. Seventy-five skilled employes are kept busy in the operations of the firm, and their trade is a very large one, extending to all parts of the West, North-west and Southwest. Mr. E. B. Millar, who established this business, was an old importer of teas. He now resides in California and takes no active part in the business.

E. L. Hedstrom & Co., shippers of coal, 115 Dearborn Street. This business was founded in 1857 by Mr. A. B. Meeker, and the present firm was founded July 1, 1885, by Messrs. E. L. Hedstrom and G. W. Meeker, Mr. A. B. Meeker then retiring from the firm. Mr. J. N. Brown was admitted into the firm January 1, 1886. The docks of the firm are at Erie and Roberts Streets on the North side, and they have extensive yards at 2348 Archer Avenue, and at the corner of Twenty-fourth and Clark Streets. About one hundred men are employed at these establishments, which are provided with every facility for the convenient and expeditious handling of the coal. The firm deal in bituminous and anthracite coal, and are the Chicago agents for the products of the coal mines of the Delaware, Lackawanna & Western Railroad Company. Their trade is very large, extending to all parts of the West, and they are at all times prepared to supply coal in any quantity in the promptest manner and at the lowest market rates.

Chicago Dredging and Dock Company, contractors for public works, 210 South Water Street. The officers of this company, which was organized in 1877, are: C. S. Crane, president; Daniel Booth, vice-president; Frank R. Crane, secretary; William H. Woodbury, treasurer; and Fred Davis, superintendent. The company contracts for public work of every description, including canals, railroads, bridges, harbors, foundations, breakwaters, etc., dock and pier building and dredging. It is fully equipped with the plant necessary to the requirements of its business, and owns seven superior dredges, five pile-drivers, twenty hopper and deck barges, and four tugs, one of which is the largest in this harbor. The company give employment to three hundred men, and possess all the necessary facilities for the execution of any contract in their line of business. A large number of valuable contracts have been filled by the company in a manner which has gained for it a reputation for good work and reliability in all its operations, and achieved for it a successful career.

Western Moxie Nerve Food Co., Moxie Nerve Food, 33 North State Street. This company was incorporated in 1886, at Portland, Maine, and at Chicago, with a capital stock of $2,000,000, and officered as follows: George P. Walker, president and manager; J. F. Chute, Portland, Me., secretary; L. T. Trall, Lowell, Mass., treasurer. The capacity of the laboratory in Chicago is 500 cases of nerve food per day. From May to October $40,000 worth of this nerve food was sold in Chicago alone. The manufactory in Chicago is splendidly equipped, and employs a large force of assistants. The original company, established in 1885, at Lowell, Mass., by Dr. A. Thompson, sold upward of 5,000,-000 bottles of Moxie the first fifteen months, and wholesalers predict that its sale next year will reach fifteen million bottles. The united companies have factories at Montreal, Canada, Lowell, Mass., Rochester, Baltimore, Norfolk, Va., Chicago, Atlanta, Ga., Galveston, Tex., Denver, Col., Little Rock, Ark., San Francisco, and local agencies in most principal cities. Their goods are handled by wholesale druggists, and are sold everywhere in all parts of the world.

W. S. Thurber, importer and dealer in fine arts, 210 Wabash Avenue. This house, established in 1860, does a large business in Chicago, the West and Northwest. Mr. Thurber's specialty is fine artistic framing, and he deals only in first-class goods, including pictures, engravings, water-colors and etchings by the best American and European artists. His salesroom and art gallery, covering 25×130 feet, form a popular resort for art patrons, artists and connoisseurs, both professional and amateur, and are arranged with surroundings which appeal to the artistic eye. Mr. Thurber, who came to this city from Ogdensburg, N. Y., has earned popular recognition and success, stands high commercially, and has gained an enviable reputation and esteem in business and social circles.

H. W. French, manufacturer of carriage lamps, 84 and 86 Market Street. This house was established twenty-two years since by Mr. A. H. Heyner, upon whose decease, two years ago, Mr. H. W. French, the present proprietor, succeeded to the ownership. He is a practical man, and with an adequate working and factory force, is extensively engaged in the manufacture of every style of carriage, hearse, hook-and-ladder truck, hose cart, fire engine, signal, bicycle and side lamps, etc., in fine or cheap grades. Mr. French sells principally to the carriage trade and to jobbing houses, but has a good private patronage. He is enterprising and progressive, and his trade is yearly attaining to vaster and more marked commercial importance.

Blauer Watch Case Co., gold and silver watch cases, 149 and 151 State Street. This company was established in 1867 by Fred Blauer, since deceased, and was incorporated in 1883. The following are the officers: Mr. William Dickinson, president; Mr. William C. Taft, vice-president and general manager; Mr. Robert W. Patton, secretary and treasurer. Its capital stock is $80,000. The company, at its factory, 123 and 125 LaSalle Avenue, manufactures a large line of gold and silver watch cases, making a specialty of the invisible joint watch case. It controls several valuable patents, which are utilized in the manufact-ure of their watch cases, thus rendering their goods superior to those manufactured by other firms. This firm sell only to jobbers, and have several traveling men representing their interests the country over. Mr. Taft has charge of the manufactory, and Mr. Patton attends to the office and financial affairs. The president, Mr. Dickinson, is a member of the Board of Trade and a director of the National Bank of America. The strict integrity which marks the company's successful career has secured it the confidence of the trade and the public.

N. A. Williams, dealer in Akron sewer pipe, fire-brick, etc., 219 Washington Street. This business was established by Mr. Williams in 1869. The premises occupied by him consist of a commodious three-story building, well stocked with every species of articles in his line, including chimney tops, fire flue-linings, plaster, fire-sand, drain tiles, fire brick, etc. In his extensive yards he carries a large stock of fire brick, cement, fire-clay, etc. Mr. Williams is the sole agent for the cele-brated Akron vitrified sewer-pipe, and does a very extensive trade in these goods, which he carries in all varieties and large stock, including socket-pipe, ring-pipe, curves, elbows, Y's, T's, etc. All the goods handled by him are of the best manufacture and finish, and his trade is very large, aggregating fully $300,000 per year and extending to every part of the West and Northwest. He employs fifteen hands with teams, and is prepared to fill the most extensive orders on short notice. With an experience of twenty-seven years in the business, and keeping a close supervision of all its details, he has achieved a leading position among the dealers in his line.

Andrew Bolter & Sons, Illinois Iron-works, 172 and 174 East Van Buren Street. This business was established by its present proprietor in 1856. The works are carried on in a commodious building 50×125 feet, and employ from thirty to fifty skilled mechanics. The line of goods manufactured consists principally of iron building work, such as iron doors, shutters, railings and ornamental designs in iron. In this latter specialty Mr. Bolter has no superior. Hé is himself an expert draughtsman and supplies the designs. The works are fitted up with all the machinery and appliances adapted to the requirements of the business, and all the operations of the works are under the personal supervision of himself and his two sons, Joseph C. and Edward Bolter. The long and honorable career of Mr. Bolter has always been prosperous, except when he, in common with so many thousands of others, was burned out in the great fire of 1871. But since he rebuilt after the fire his business has been more extensive than ever, the improved character of the buildings since erected causing an enhanced demand for the goods of Mr. Bolter's manufacture.

G. A. Crosby & Co., manufacturers of presses and dies, and special machinery for sheet-metal workers, 259 to 263 Randolph Street. This business was established in 1866 by Mr. G. A. Crosby. The factory is commodious and completely equipped with all the machinery and necessary appliances for the business, and gives employment to a large force of competent mechanics. They manufacture presses and dies suitable for every description of work, and special machinery of all kinds for the use of sheet-metal workers. All the machines produced by this factory are of the latest and most approved design, embacing every principle calculated to enhance their usefulness, and made in the most complete and substantial manner. The firm does a very large business among the leading metal workers of the United States and Canada, and supply machinery to meat-canning establishments, not only in this country, but also in New Zealand, Australia and South America. They are prepared to fill orders on short notice and in the most satisfactory manner, and have built up their high reputation and great success by the superior merit of their work.

Hughes & Johnson, general lithographers and steam press printers, 253 and 255 East Kinzie Street. This firm, composed of Thomas Hughes and Peter C. Johnson, was established in 1879, removing to their present building in 1884. They occupy ten floors, each 50×100 feet, equipped with all modern machinery, and employ from fifty to sixty skilled workmen. They have a large and growing patronage in Chicago, the West and Northwest, and receive large orders from New Zealand, Canada, and other foreign countries. Their specialty is designing and printing fine colored show cards, and their stock of goods and material is very large. They conduct their business with enterprise and judgment, and enjoy the confidence and patronage of the trade.

J. Leland Fogg, dealer in garden seeds, 31 Michigan Avenue. 'In 1843 James P. Fogg, father of the present proprietor, started the business of this house at Rochester, N. Y. He established the Chicago house in 1863, as the Western Seed Co., which afterward became J. P. Fogg, Son & Bro. In 1886 the present proprietor purchased the entire business, which has attained mammoth proportions, employing forty persons in its packing and shipping department. The seeds are purchased in all parts of America and Europe, and are raised by contracts, conditioned that they must germinate at a very high percentage, otherwise they are not received. The goods are placed with merchants throughout the country for sale on commission. If any remain at the end of the season they are returned, and at the opening of the ensuing season a fresh stock is supplied. This is the only establishment in Chicago dealing exclusively in garden seeds.

Charles L. Tate, manufacturer of artificial limbs, was born in Orange County, N. Y., in 1846, and left there with his parents, Henry W. and Mary Tate, at the age of twelve years, moving to the present town-side of Hinsdale, Ill., where they rented a farm. He was educated in the country schools, completing his studies at the academy built at Hinsdale several years after taking up his residence there. He went to Philadelphia, Penn.,·in 1865, but returned to the West and located at West Lyons, on the Chicago, Burlington & Quincy Railroad, and was appointed agent of the company. He also opened a store, and was appointed postmaster, afterward giving this up to take a position on a passenger train on the railroad. He came to Chicago, and was foreman of the Howe Sewing Machine Shop after the fire, and subsequently was employed by the Singer Manufacturing Company, and the Wilson Sewing Machine Company, also the Wheeler & Wilson Sewing Machine Company, soon becoming expert in the sewing machine business. His mechanical genius attracted the attention of the manufacturer of artificial limbs for Sharp & Smith, and he was induced to enter the employ of that firm, remaining with them most of the time from 1875 to 1883, when he concluded to open business for himself, and occupied for one year, a portion of a store with S. S. Bliss, on Randolph Street. He is at present located in the Bryant Block, No. 89 Randolph Street. His superior mechanical abilities have rendered him good service, enabling him to already build up a satisfactory business and his customers are well pleased with the limbs furnished. He speaks of one customer who has for some time worn an artificial leg of his manufacture, who entered a contest for a prize given to the

best waltzer and who captured the prize. Mr. Tate manufactures appliances pertaining to physical deformities, and has had remarkable
success in fulfilling his promises of satisfactory results. His persistent
efforts to attain superiority, and his pride in his profession will undoubt-
edly accomplish a noteworthy success.

The **Chicago Window Shade Works**, Kaumeier & Anderson, proprietors, Nos. 75 and 77 Market Street, are convenient and capacious,
being thoroughly equipped for the purposes to which they are devoted;
they employ a large force of skilled workmen in the manufacture of
every style of window shades and carry a full line and complete stock
of shade cloth, fixtures, and trimmings. Mr. Kaumeier is an experienced designer and has every facility for making fancy dadoes and
borders and decorating window
shades, his experience and skill enabling him to compete with any of
the Eastern houses. The firm have
an extensive local trade, and daily
receive orders for their goods from
all parts of the country. Their place
is also headquarters for the Tripp adjustable shade bar, which is a new
and convenient trimming for the
bottom end of window shades. The
accompanying cut shows the bar attached to the shade. For a neat and
durable trimming this bar is highly
recommended, and all orders for the
same receive the promptest attention
of Messrs. Kaumeier & Anderson, and
all work done by them is guaranteed to be entirely satisfactory. The
large and prosperous business which the firm control is the fullest
possible proof of the popular esteem in which their house is held in
commercial circles. They are gentlemen of high social abilities, as
well as the best business qualifications, and are deserving of the prosperity which has always crowned their efforts.

CHICAGO WINDOW SHADE WORKS, 75 AND
77 MARKET STREET.

The **Chicago Forge and Bolt Co.** was organized and incorporated
in 1880, and at once became an important factor in Chicago's industrial enterprise. Its operations have steadily increased from the
start, and its trade now extends to every part of the West, Northwest, and
South. The works of the company, located at Fortieth Street and

Stewart Avenue, and corner Michigan and Franklin Streets, respectively, are among the largest and best equipped manufacturing establishments in the city. They are wanting in no requisite necessary to
the rapid and economical prosecution of the industry to which they are
devoted, and they contain much valuable and powerful machinery to
be found in no similar works. The iron testing machine in use here
is the largest and most powerful in this country, excepting only those
owned by the national government. The range of manufacture
embraces car axles, iron and steel shafting, shape work, dock rods,
forgings, blacksmith work, rods and bolts of all kinds, iron bridges,
viaducts, iron roofs, engine turn-tables, iron and wooden cranes, der-
ricks, etc., and, in fact, everything pertaining to forging, iron bridge
building and miscellaneous railroad supplies. A large force of skilled
workmen are employed, the best materials only are admitted into the
manufacture, and the output of the works is recognized by the trade as
of the very highest quality to be obtained. The general office of the
company is at No. 234 S. Clark Street, and the officers are: A. E. Adams,
Pres., Fred M. Steele, Sec., Francis King, Treas., and C. Weatherson,
Supt.

The G. M. Jarvis Co., wine growers and dealers, office and salesrooms, 39 North State Street. This business was begun in 1860 by Mr.
G. M. Jarvis, and was incorporated into a stock company in 1885, with
a capital stock of $50,000, and officered as follows: G. M. Jarvis,
president, and J. F. Jarvis, secretary. The vineyards are in Santa
Cruz County, California, where they were planted by Mr. Jarvis in
1860, and during a quarter of a century the wines and brandies manufactured from them have become famous, and the name of "The G. M.
Jarvis Co." is known all over the country. They were awarded the first
prize for the best wines and brandies at the World's Fair, New Orleans;
at the Illinois State Fair, held at Springfield, in 1872, and several other
first prizes on other occasions, thus attesting the superiority of the
goods over all others. The Messrs. Jarvis also hold unqualified testimonials as to the absolute purity of their wines and brandies from the
most eminent analytical and assaying chemists and physicians in the
United States. The capacity of the vintages and distilleries is 150,000
gallons of wine and 25,000 gallons of brandy yearly, and the trade of the
house extends to nearly all parts of the United States, and is rapidly
increasing in volume. A very large demand comes from the wholesale
drug trade (the goods being recommended by physicians), and the
wines and brandies are in wide demand for family use. The G. M. Jar-

vis Co. are also agents for Arpad, Haraszth & Co.'s Famous Eclipse Champagne.

Geo. Daniels' composing and printing rooms were originally established at No. 69 Dearborn Street, in 1878; but his growing business soon demanded more room and increased facilities, and in 1881 the present commodious quarters at Nos. 79 and 81 Randolph Street were occupied. The office affords excellent conveniences for conducting the printing · business. It is equipped with typographic appliances, which, for extent and variety, are surpassed by few of the most extensive printing establishments. Mr. Daniels has always given special attention to the composition of books, pamphlets, catalogues and periodical literature, and many works requiring special accuracy in typographical preparation and the most perfect proof-reading, have been "set up" in his establishment. The composition for "Marquis' Hand-Book of Chicago" was done in this office; as has also been that of many other important historical works, and theological, scientific and literary publications. Among the periodicals regularly issued from this office are the following: "The Universalist," "American Artisan," "Stationer and Printer," "Picture and Art Trade," "Mining Review," "Song Friend," "Record and Appeal," "Watchmaker and Metalworker." The house is also prepared to execute all kinds of commercial job printing.

O. A. Thorp & Co., exporters and importers, 218 LaSalle Street, Insurance Exchange Building, constitute a leading and representative house in their line of business. The business was founded in 1880, and has grown steadily in volume and magnitude, the transactions embracing the purchase and sale of provisions, grain, seeds, etc., on commission, and the exporting of grain and provisions, etc., to Europe, and in turn importing European goods to this country, a special feature of the latter being the importation of herring and other cured fish. A member of the Board of Trade, and formerly a resident of Christiana, the principal seaport of Norway, where his established business relations are of the most advantageous character, Mr. Thorp possesses every facility for successfully and satisfactorily conducting his rapidly growing trade.

INDEX TO ILLUSTRATIONS.

FULL PAGES.

SMALLER ILLUSTRATIONS.

INDEX TO TEXT.

www.ingramcontent.com/pod-product-compliance
Lightning Source LLC
Chambersburg PA
CBHW021107270326
41929CB00009B/770